Fender

THE SOUND HEARD
'ROUND THE WORLD

Fender

THE SOUND HEARD
'ROUND THE WORLD

Richard R. Smith

Edited by William Koon and Tom Wheeler
Book Design by Robert Perine

Garfish Publishing Company
Fullerton, California

PHOTO CREDITS
Leo Fender: 4, 5, 6, 7, 8, 11, 28, 30, 31, 34, 35, 41, 50, 51, 53, 56, 57 (top right), 58, 62, 66, 68 (b&w), 69, 71 (top), 72, 75, 81 (b&w), 82, 84, 90, 91, 103, 104, 105, 107, 108, 111, 112 (factory), 113 (factory), 114 (factory), 116, 117, 118, 120, 123, 124, 125 (b&w), 126, 127, 128, 129 (top), 132, 133, 135 (top), 139 (left), 140 (b&w), 142, 143, 146, 148 (middle), 151, 154 (bottom), 157 (middle and bottom), 168 (top), 172 (right); **Dean Hesketh:** 192 (right), 194, 203 (catalog), 205; **Allen A. Hodges**/Buck Owens Productions: 188 (bottom); **John Peden:** cover (color), 15, 18, 19, 33, 54–55, 63, 67, 68 (color), 76, 83, 92 (bottom), 93, 99, 100, 105 (color), 140 (color), 141 (color), 144, 149 (bottom), 161, 190, 191 (left), 210 (bottom), 240, 284; **Robert Perine:** cover (b&w), 59, 125 (color), 160 (right), 168 (bottom), 169 (top, middle), 170 (bottom), 173, 176, 182 (factory), 183 (factory), 184 (building), 187 (bottom), 188 (top), 189, 196 (bottom, 198 (teen fair), 199, 202, 204 (left), 206, 209 (teen fair), 212, 213, 214 (left), 215, 220, 221, 222, 223, 225, 227, 229, 233, 234 (top), 236, 238 (right), 239, 242 (top), 244 (bottom), 247, 250 (middle, bottom), 251, 252 (top), 253 (top), 254 (top, bottom), 255, 256 (color), 257, 258; **Jon Sievert:** 64, 95, 266, 269; **John Sprung:** 49; **Forrest White:** 96, 97 (right).

Additional photos are courtesy of these sources: Nolan Beauchamp: 14; Jody Carver: 187 (top); City of Fullerton: 8–9; Robert J. Dalley: 240 (top); Fender Custom Shop 261, 262, 263, 264, 265; Fender Musical Instruments: 259 (right); Al Frost: 78; G&L Musical Products: 259 (left), 283; Dale Hyatt: 271, 273 (top), 275, 276, 277, 279, 280; Doc Kauffman: 17, 21; J. Fred McCord: 43, 45, 71 (right), 148 (top); Raymond Massie: 28; Tiny Moore: 46, 47, 48; Donald D. Randall: 10, 27, 148 (bottom), 184 (portrait), 186, 216 (bottom), 231; John Hall/Rickenbacker International Corporation: 26; Eldon Shamblin: 164; Maxine Smith: 12, 13, 22; Steve Soest: 160 (top left), 171, 172 (guitars), 191 (right), 192 (left), 195, 197, 198 (top), 203 (b&w), 204 (top), 208 (top), 211, 217 (right), 218, 219, 228, 230, 241 (top), 252 (left), 253 (product), 254 (top left, right).

Every effort has been made to identify and locate the copyright holders of photographs in this book. Anyone with additional information in this regard is requested to contact the publisher so that all credits may be included in future editions.

Garfish Publishing Co.
P.O. Box 5872
Fullerton, CA 92635

© 1995 by Richard R. Smith

ISBN 0-9648612-7-5

Library of Congress Catalog Number 95-094998
Library of Congress Cataloging-in-Publication is available.

Exclusive Distributors for the World:

Music Sales Corporation
257 Park Avenue South, New York, NY 10010 USA

Music Sales Limited
8/9 Frith Street, London W1V 5TZ, England

Music Sales Pty. Limited
120 Rothschild Avenue, Rosebery, NSW 2018, Australia

Book design: **Robert Perine**
Color separations and typography: **ColorType**, San Diego
Printed in Hong Kong by **Global Interprint**

1st printing 1996
2nd printing 1996

Acrylic painting by Robert Perine, 1961, courtesy Donald D. Randall.

Table of Contents

To Ray and Eileen Smith,
my parents. Thanks for my
first electric guitar.

Foreword by Tom Wheeler   ix

Introduction   xii

Chapter 1   "Progress Is Progress"   5
Leo's Early Years; Radio Repair for Fun; Radio Repair for Profit; Donald D. Randall

Chapter 2   Old Friends   13
Doc Kauffman; The First Fender Guitar; The K&F Manufacturing Corporation; K&F Steels and Amps; Francis Cary Hall and Radio-Tel

Chapter 3   Take It Away, Leo   29
The Fender Electric Instrument Company; Early Fender Steels; Manufacturing Problems and Early Amps; The Direct String Pickup

Chapter 4   Fender in the Spotlight   41
Salesmen; Charles R. Hayes; David K. Driver; Western Swing and the Rise of Guitars; More Fender Steels; TV-Front Amplifiers

Chapter 5   Towards an Improved Electric Guitar   57
Traditional Notions; Early Electric Guitars; Enter Leo Fender; George Fullerton; Prototypes

Chapter 6   Guitars for Everyman   71
The Esquire; The Broadcaster; Classic Telecasters; The Travis-Bigsby-Fender Connection

Chapter 7   Leo Goes Uptown   99
Pre-Precision Basses; Introducing the Precision Bass and Bassman Amp

Chapter 8   Often Copied but Never Equalled   107
Wide Panel Amplifiers; Fender Sales, Inc.; Bill Carson and Freddie Tavares; The Stringmasters; Outdoing the Telecaster

Chapter 9   Contours and Cutaways   125
The Stratocaster; More Advanced Features; Introducing the Stratocaster; Forrest White; Revising the Precision Bass

Chapter 10   Fender Fine Electric Instruments   145
Narrow Panel Amps; Transitions at Fender Sales; New Student Standard and Steel Guitars; At the Factory in the Late 1950s; The Electric Mandolin; The Pedal Steel; Classic Late-1950s Amps and Basses; Custom Colors

Chapter 11   You Won't Part with Yours Either   165
Fender Advertising; The Jazzmaster; The Electric Violin

Chapter 12   More Firsts from Fender   183
Service with a Smile; The Telecaster and Esquire Customs and Rosewood Fingerboards; Behind the Amplifier Designs; Tolex-Covered Amplifiers; Corporate Logos; The Jazz Bass

Chapter 13   The Surf Is Always Up   205
The Bass VI; The Jaguar; The Vibroverb, Twin Reverb, and Blackface Amps; Fender Acoustics; The Mustang; The Electric XII; The Fender-Rhodes Pianos; The End of an Era Draws Near

Chapter 14   The Sound of Success   241
Fender for Sale; CBS-Fender; CBS-Fender in the 1970s and 1980s; A New Fender Emerges after CBS; Today's Custom Shop

Chapter 15   Leo after Fender   265
Music Man; G&L Musical Products; Accolades from the City; Full Circle with the Real Ones

Epilogue   Faded Love   284

Appendices   285

Index   295

Acknowledgements

I would like to thank everyone who helped make this book possible. William Koon, my former college professor, guided me through the early drafts and pushed me at our weekly meetings—where we discussed everything from guitar switches to comma splices—until I had a manuscript in hand. Tom Wheeler, my former editor at *Guitar Player* and one of the world's foremost experts on the guitar, further organized, culled, and focused the material. My art director, Robert Perine, who also helped edit the manuscript, designed the book and led me through the publishing process. John Peden contributed his wonderful photographs. (I'll be forever grateful that he never gave up saying, "Richard, where's the book?") John Sprung, and Steve Soest provided photos and valuable details. Bob Mytkowicz critiqued the manuscript. Tom Hassett's proofreading was invaluable.

Thanks also go to Leo Fender and Don Randall and to past and present Fender employees and their relatives who provided interviews, source material, and photos: Phyllis Fender, Forrest White, Dale Hyatt, George and Geoff Fullerton, Doc Kauffman, Maxine Smith, Jody Carver, Freddie and Tamar Tavares, Dave Driver, Bud Driver, Bill Sterle, Elizabeth and Gordon Hayzlett, Jerrie Massie, Speedy West, Charlie Clark, Bill Carson, Dan Smith, John Page, Alan Hamel, Fred Stuart, and Yasuhiko Iwanade. Many others made important contributions: Michael Lee Allen, Cliff Archer, Bill Blackburn, John Blair, Cash Calloway, Evelyn Cadman, Gary Cooper, Dave Crocker, Dick Dale, Robert J. Dalley, Ken Donnell, A.R. Duchossoir, Joe Felz, Al Frost, Greg Gagliano, Noë Goldwasser, George Gruhn, F.C. Hall, John C. Hall, Alan Hardtke, Norman Harris, Gordon Keane, Rich Kienzle, J. Fred McCord, John McLaren, Steve Melkethesian, Tiny Moore, Karl Olmsted, Buck Owens, Jerry and Joan Patterson, John Quarterman, Alvino Rey, Jeff Ridolfi, Laura Lee Roe, Alan Rogan, Sharon Seal, Eldon Shamblin, Jim Shaw, Jon Sievert, Diane Smith, Eileen Smith, Sharon Smith, Michael Stevens, Gary and Sharon Sunda, Kim Turtenwald, Jim Washburn, Phlange Welder, and James Werner.

Finally, special thanks to my wife Mary and to my daughters Sarah and Amy for the their patience throughout this fun ordeal.

Foreword

by Tom Wheeler

There's no doubt about it. Leo Fender was a high-voltage pro-peller-head genius, the kind of independent screwdriver brainiac we don't see much anymore. The raw electric power of his mind (and periodic massive jolts of good luck) made him a millionaire decades ago, but he never graduated into the cushy country clubs or rose-wood-paneled boardrooms. The only rosewood he was interested in got sawed up for fingerboards. Leo Fender puttered and tinkered and tweaked in his modest shop till the day before he died, closing a 50-year saga of industrial brilliance, personal eccentricity, and musical revolution. We won't see his like again.

Much has been written about Leo and how he restructured the way we think of guitars—how they sound, what they do, even what they mean. Some articles and books have adequately covered rel-atively small pieces of an intricate puzzle, and a few have sketched the big picture. But until now no account has managed to weave the threads of information about the man and his cre-ations into the fabric of the larger cultural, economic, and musical tapestry. It's a riveting yet convoluted tale. No previous effort has been up to the task.

Fender, The Sound Heard 'round the World is the first book to do justice to this vast and thorny topic, and Richard Smith is the only person I know who could have written it. We were introduced by Mr. Fender, who at the time was having trouble recalling some details about the origin of the Broadcaster. He passed along Richard's number, and in the 45-minute conversation that followed I encoun-tered a researcher with attributes all too rare among guitar histori-ans. (Before long he was contributing to *Guitar Player*, setting records straight.)

For one thing, while Smith saw Leo Fender up close over a period of years, admired him deeply, and grasped the significance of his designs as only a working guitarist could, he resisted the kind of hero worship that fogs objectivity. The author looked at his subject and saw talent, vision, and unwavering dedication to quality (Leo's compulsive perfectionism was "the engine that powered Fender"). But he also saw anomalies that contradicted the familiar, romanti-cized histories, and detected that among some of his sources there were personal agendas, axes to grind, perhaps even scores to settle.

A researcher with less stamina might have taken the easy way out or given up, but Richard Smith went back again and again to Mr. Fender; to key execs, factory workers, salesmen, distributors, retailers, cowboy musicians, and collectors; to personal letters, patents, inventories, shipping ledgers, old magazines, court documents, and municipal records. Digging hard for details, he filled many ancient gaps. (Along the way he even tried to poke holes in his own theories to test their durability.) While other books have logged changes in instrument construction details—someone coined the term "screwology" for such efforts—and dutifully repeated the company history as told by its principals, this book evidences unprecedented guitar research and scholarship.

Apart from its historical significance, *Fender* is a terrific read, thanks in part to Richard's precise but colorful style ("He enjoyed taking new guitars to a local country bar where waitresses carried change in their bras and truckers slept off their beers in the parking lot before the final leg to Carson"). In these pages familiar names come alive in the pre-freeway, clear-skied southern California where dreamers, misfits, and risk-takers worked and lived amid the orange groves, oil derricks, farms, rail depots, and honky tonks. Here's F. C. Hall, spending his boyhood summers picking lima beans in what is now Irvine, and the young Doc Kauffman, getting paid for his Depression-era parking-lot gigs with mason jars full of vegetables. Here's George Fullerton, drawing freehand the profile of a guitar soon to be christened Esquire, then Broadcaster, then Telecaster. Here's the shy, introverted inventor himself, a "rather square young entrepreneur," lugging a freshly wired amp and an unpainted prototype steel into a glitzy nightclub to see if the musicians might try them out; and here's a strapping, beefy-fisted Dale Hyatt, selling the newfangled solidbodies out of a truck in dance hall parking lots.

Previously unpublished correspondence provides not only authoritative documentation but also narrative power, capturing the heady chaos of the Fender experiment. We're in on the excitement. We're there in 1950, sweating it out in Chicago with Don Randall. We're worried that the unstable neck on the electric Spanish prototype might be a fatal flaw, but even more worried that Gibson or Valco or Gretsch will beat us to the punch and all will be lost. We can feel the pressure of Randall's pen on paper as he fires off a communiqué from his outpost at the NAMM show, imploring F. C. Hall to squeeze Leo harder to *finish the guitars in time*: "I wouldn't let Leo sleep until this is done. *Immediately Immediately Immediately.*" And: "Nothing has . . . created the excitement and speculation among dealers, players and even our competitors as has this instrument. . . . If Leo misses the boat now I will never forgive him."

Richard Smith not only clears up common misconceptions but explains how they arose—with a catalog picturing the prototype instead of the production model, or with Leo altering an amplifier circuit right in the middle of a production run. Some of the anecdotes disclose aspects of Leo's character that would show up in his durable products, such as his demanding that a second roof be installed over his cinder block factory to eliminate even the possibility of leaks (a demolition crew would one day have a hell of a time tearing it down). Other tales reveal that this stubborn, proud, sometimes withdrawn and insecure man also had an affectionate side. When Doc's wife died, Leo knew that his old friend was lonely. Taping Doc's number by the phone in the lab, he called him often to boost his spirits.

Those of us who never tire of Fender tidbits will find much to nibble on. Random samples: Leo guzzled so much carrot juice that it yellowed his skin. There was a Fullerton resident who collected discarded Fender necks for firewood at the Temple Baptist Church at Christmas time, and an early salesman who tried placing steel guitars for sale at gas stations. Leo or one of his helpers simply snipped the model names off the Broadcaster decals, giving rise to the "No-caster" nickname.

Although the reminiscences and historical details are fascinating, Richard's greatest contributions are his big-picture insights, which explain how Leo's steel guitar design philosophy was extended into the Telecaster, and how genius, unintended consequences, and shifting tastes all converged to make history. An example of particular interest to vintage buffs: "Leo rarely sequenced and categorized the evolution of the Fender guitars as others did. He saw his body of work as one continuous stream of ideas, trials, and experiments. In his recollections, the specific guitar models usually blurred together into the generic 'Fender guitar,' a dynamic, unfolding concept and process—a child growing up."

There are other talents at work here as well. Bob Perine's Fender catalogs and ads of the late 1950s and 1960s are among American guitar's most distinctive commercial literature, and his collaborating with Richard Smith makes this project even more exciting and worthwhile. John Peden is a fashion photographer who, lucky for us, likes instruments, and his guitar images are more interesting than those of any other photographer; several are included here.

Leo Fender was hard to please. To meet his standards, a product had to be intelligently designed, functional, durable, and appealing. So I think he would have admired this book. As I finish this foreword, my old Tele sits at my side. It left the factory in January 1960 and undoubtedly changed hands many times before it fell into mine. Staring at the computer screen, I pick up the guitar and absentmindedly twang around a bit, no amp. Man, it rings like a bell. My pal Jas says it's the best electric guitar he ever played. I think about how lucky I am to have it. I think about the man who brought it into the world, and how much we owe him.

The author of *American Guitars: An Illustrated History* and *The Guitar Book* and former editor of *Guitar Player* magazine, Tom Wheeler is an associate professor at the University of Oregon's School of Journalism and Communication.

Introduction

In September 1945, on what merchants called Hospitality Night, a musical performance shook listeners' senses in otherwise serene downtown Fullerton, California. As shopkeepers up and down Spadra Road served cookies and punch to faithful customers, a little-known group called Buzz Bazzell and his Cowboys played requests from the audience at Fender's Radio Service. The melodious yet hard-hitting sound of electric guitars bounced out the shop's open door, off the sidewalk, and into the street. Inside, Leo Fender labored as hard as the musicians. His own biggest critic, he wanted everything with his name on it up to date and perfect, so he scurried around making sure the PA system and instruments worked properly. As the band hit the downbeat on its next number, he smiled and thought to himself: "Yeah, that's the way it oughta sound. It's a shower of brilliance!"

That night people within a block-long earshot of Fender's radio shop heard music history in the making—Buzz and his crew showcased Leo Fender's first electric instruments and amplifiers. Fender would go on to become the most prolific instrument inventor of his generation. In a lifetime full of achievement, he brought a shower of brilliance and a whole lot more to electric guitars: both the old-style steel guitars played by western swing and Hawaiian musicians and the modern electric standard guitars played today in all styles of popular music. The *Los Angeles Times* reported that when the Rolling Stones' Keith Richards accepted his induction into the Rock and Roll Hall of Fame, he said, "Thank God for Leo Fender, who makes these instruments for us to play." His contribution to making music compares to what Henry Ford did for driving and Levi Strauss did for dressing.

Leo Fender armed a music revolution's foot soldiers with affordable guitars and amplifiers designed and manufactured to exacting standards of durability, tone, and performance. He invented and refined the electric bass guitar—an instrument that made playing lower frequencies a higher art form. Fender also worked on Harold Rhodes' electric pianos, facilitating their development and adding a new sound to keyboards. Almost lost and forgotten are Leo's electric mandolin and electric violin, as well as the steel guitars that laid the foundation for modern pedal steels commonly played in country-western music. Of lesser significance, but rounding out Fender's career in instrument design, was a line of acoustic gui-

Newspaper ad from September 26, 1945.

tars. On the business side of music, Leo founded or helped found several companies, including K&F (Kauffman and Fender) Manufacturing, the Fender Electric Instrument Company, Fender Sales, Inc., CLF (Clarence Leo Fender) Research, Music Man, Inc., and G&L (George Fullerton and Leo Fender and later, Guitars by Leo) Musical Products.

Most players remember Leo for his guitars. When people say the word *guitar*, they usually mean *standard guitar*, also called *Spanish guitar*. A player frets the notes on the standard or Spanish guitar. In contrast, the steel or Hawaiian guitar, which sits horizontally on a stand or in one's lap, is played with a metal bar, using a technique born in the late-nineteenth-century Hawaiian Islands. The strings never touch frets, so steel guitar technique can be used on any standard guitar with high string action. However, many manufacturers like Fender designed instruments specifically for Hawaiian playing. So over the years the terms *Hawaiian guitar* and *steel guitar* have come to mean both a style of playing and a type of guitar.

Any story about Fender guitars must also distinguish between acoustic, acoustic-electric, and solidbody electric guitars like the Telecaster and Stratocaster, Leo's two most famous instruments. On acoustics, the strings, bridges, and tops vibrate while the backs and sides help project the sound through the soundholes. Acoustic-electrics are just what the name says: acoustic guitars equipped with pickups that translate vibrations into an electrical signal. The first guitar pickups sensed vibrations on the bridge or top, while later, more efficient units sensed the strings' vibrations. Solidbody electric guitars have pickups but no acoustic chambers, and to perform as designed they require amplifiers.

Guitar amplifiers, once described by writer Jim Washburn as boxes with knobs that make everything real loud, consist of cabinets and chassis. Their electronic circuits boost signals created by guitar pickups, and loudspeakers convert this electrical energy into sound energy. Most of the audible sound from a solidbody electric guitar emanates from its amplifier, which usually sits on the stage behind the guitarist. Turn off the amp and a solidbody electric makes about as much sound as a rubber band stretched between two fingers. With the amp on, electric guitars can whisper, shout, or cause permanent hearing loss.

The first electric models appeared in the 1930s and have since helped make the guitar in its many forms the most popular musical instrument in the world. Leo's first steel guitars came out in 1945; his widely accepted solidbody standard guitars were introduced in 1950. Since those days virtually everyone has heard the guitars Leo Fender designed. Their piercing yet pleasing jet-age tone has peppered records from Johnny Cash's "Folsom Prison Blues" to Bonnie Raitt's "Thing Called Love." For nearly fifty years the sound of Fender has electrified the world's popular music, from James Burton's solo on Ricky Nelson's "Hello Mary Lou" to Jimmy Page's solo on Led Zeppelin's "Stairway to Heaven," from the twin Stratocasters of the Beatles' "Nowhere Man" to the weird sound effects in the classic film *War of the Worlds*. Fender instruments have been seen on stage with virtually all the stars: Elvis, the Rolling Stones, Bob Dylan, Bruce Springsteen. Timeless classics, the instruments endure. The Stratocaster Buddy Holly played in the 1950s and the one Jimi Hendrix played at Woodstock are just as appropriate on MTV or the *Grand Ole Opry*.

No other instrument designer has had a greater influence than Leo Fender on the way musicians compose, play, and hear music or on the way instruments are made. By creating a manufacturing revolution that provided musicians with new types of instruments, Leo Fender fueled a musical revolution with global implications. Today musicians play Fender-designed instruments in every country on every continent, as the current company leads the world in electric guitar sales. (The Fender Musical Instruments Corporation, headquartered in Scottsdale, Arizona, makes guitars and amplifiers at several factories. G&L Musical Products, owned by BBE Sound Inc. in Huntington Beach, California, makes many of Leo's 1980s G&L designs in a factory Leo built on Fender Avenue in Fullerton.) Many other companies manufacture Fender-like designs and shameless copies.

Although Leo died in 1991, his immeasurable impact on nearly every area of music still reverberates everywhere. His guitars, basses, and amplifiers defined the music of at least two generations born after World War II and will continue influencing musicians from virtual unknowns like Buzz Bazzell to the Rolling Stones for years to come. This book is about those instruments and the men who made them. This book is Leo Fender's story.

Contrary to published stories and the impressions of some close associates, Leo Fender received no formal training in electrical engineering.

Leo Fender at age 14. He played saxophone during grammar school and loved music, but radios interested him more.

Leo and his sister Wilda
on the beach in La Jolla,
California, 1921.

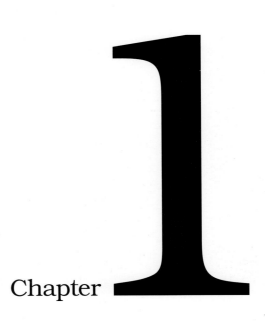

Chapter 1

"Progress Is Progress"

Leo's Early Years

In the late 1980s a Fender fan saw Leo Fender overwhelmed by the volume listening to the Desert Rose Band at the Crazy Horse Saloon in Santa Ana, California. Sitting at eye level in front of the amplifiers, he was holding his hands over his ears as John Jorgenson cranked his G&L ASAT to ear-splitting volume. The scene seemed ironic because more than any man Leo Fender had made the dynamics and intensity of Jorgenson's guitar possible. The tone and volume of the electric guitar was to be Fender's legacy. Still, in 1991 his widow Phyllis told the *Los Angeles Times*: "Leo never felt he deserved any glory of any kind. He just felt he was put on earth to make things better for musicians." Better indeed: Leo Fender's instruments and those he inspired laid down the soundtrack for the post-World War II, Cold War era.

Leo's life and the sound heard around the world began humbly in California's once sleepy Orange County amid acres of citrus groves and oil derricks under clear blue skies. The story began only ten miles but eighty years and a hundred decibels away from that electrified concert in Santa Ana. Leo Fender was born in a barn on August 10, 1909, on his parents' ranch. As he described it, "There were horses on the east side, a hay mound in the center, and we lived on the west side." A year later a house was built. Although the property straddled the border between Fullerton and Anaheim, on what is now La Palma Avenue in Anaheim, Leo and his sister went to Fullerton schools. He considered Fullerton, a typical California small town with an agricultural economic base, his home town as he grew up. In addition to Americans from the Midwest and South, German, Basque, Irish, and Mexican immigrants had settled there. With his heritage lost in the melting pot, Leo always thought that his given name—Clarence Leonidas Fender—sounded German, but he was not sure.

Leo, second from left, poses with some dead ducks after a hunting trip.

Fender's love of automobiles—and the way they were engineered—started at an early age. Almost the only sign of his wealth in the later years was a Lincoln.

Leo, as he always called himself, attended elementary school at the original three-room Orangethorpe School. Sometimes he wore knickers. Many kids in rural Fullerton were poor and came to school barefoot, but Leo and his family were better off. His dad, who had started farming with vegetables and melons that he sold once a week off a wagon in Long Beach, soon switched to oranges, the area's most viable cash crop. Leo's parents took him on camping trips to Yosemite and the Sierra Nevada. They picnicked on the then pristine beach at La Jolla and owned a cabin at Big Bear Lake in the San Bernardino Mountains.

One real tragedy, with echoes lasting a lifetime, marked Leo's early years. Wilda Gray, Leo's younger sister, remembers their mother saying that he suffered from a glioma-like tumor. Tragically, the growth progressed too far before getting a doctor's attention, and he removed the whole eye. Much later Leo unhappily learned that his loss had been preventable. One has to speculate on how the misfortune shaped his life. Perhaps he made up for his limited vision by perfecting his sense of hearing. Never making much of his disability, he took wonderful photographs and learned technical drawing. A photo in the Fenders' picture album shows Leo, his dad, and a friend, rifles in hand, with a string of dead ducks—the trophies of good shooting for a boy with just one eye.

The impact of losing an eye manifested itself more in psychological ways than physical limitations or compensations. Leo's missing eye made him self-conscious and insecure. Most people who met him as an adult realized that he had an artificial eye, but few outsiders knew. He preferred to keep it that way by shying away from photographers at work and by taking the pictures himself at family gatherings. He closely examined images used in advertising and always chose the one that best portrayed the appearance of his sometimes droopy glass eye. His reticence rubbed off; Leo's closest friends rarely talked about it. However, his lab assistant at the Fender company, Freddie Tavares, remembered in the 1980s that Leo once claimed he lost his eye to a BB gun. Freddie always took the story seriously, having no reason to believe that Leo needed to cast himself in a more favorable light. But Leo, insecure as he was, did. He undoubtedly thought that losing the eye in an accident was preferable to losing it to a mother's neglect. Perhaps an accident seemed more manly.

Radio Repair for Fun

At 13, Leo took up electronics as a hobby. He told a group of former classmates at a high school reunion: "I had an uncle [John West, husband of Leo's Aunt Sally] who ran an auto-electric shop in Santa Maria. On Christmas of 1921 he sent me a package containing a storage battery and a lot of discarded automobile electric parts." Leo visited Santa Maria in 1922 and saw a homemade radio West had put on display in front of the shop. The radio's large speaker horn pointed towards downtown Santa Maria, and Leo's uncle turned up the system for everyone in the neighborhood to hear. By the decree of fate, this loud music made a lasting impression on the kid from Fullerton.

Leo also developed an interest in music during eighth grade and his first years at Fullerton Union High School. He took piano lessons but soon switched to the saxophone. He explained, "Saxophone was coming on a little stronger than the piano then." He practiced his horn while his classmate Laura Johnson accompanied him on the piano. She thought that the experience was frustrating from a musical standpoint. Later she said, "He couldn't keep the beat." Apparently, Leo also nurtured an early interest in guitars, building a crude acoustic in the 1920s. He learned to build better guitars, but never learned to play them.

Aside from the basic guitar, Leo started building and repairing radios and audio amplifiers. He set up shop at home and did repair jobs for fellow high school students like Waldo Johnson, whose radio had stopped working. In the 1980s, Johnson said that Leo not only fixed the set but eagerly explained in detail what went wrong and how he had made it right. Even as a teenager, Fender was already an authority.

And so Leo graduated from high school in June 1928. Graduating seniors in jest bequeathed items or thoughts to underclassmen. In the Senior Class Will of 1928 Leo wrote, "I, Leo Fender, realizing that aviation is taking the interest of the public away from radios, will my own interest to (my younger friend) John McElheny. Progress is progress." Leo entered Fullerton Junior College that fall and majored in accounting. He took other courses that interested him, but contrary to published stories and the impressions of some close associates, he received no formal training in electrical engineering. He mastered the subject on his own while studying to become an accountant.

Out of junior college Fender worked as a delivery man for the Consolidated Ice and Cold Storage Company in Anaheim, but had difficulty wrestling ice blocks out of the truck. He was never athletic, so his boss wisely moved

"The beginning of the Fender guitar traces back to grammar school days of about 1921. I had an uncle who ran an auto-electric shop in Santa Maria. Christmas of 1921 he sent me a package containing a storage battery and a lot of discarded automobile electric parts. This was my introduction to electronics. About 1922 he had built some radio equipment and had a large wooden trumpet speaker in front of his shop, pointed downtown to handle radio programs. This acquainted me with radio and led to my building amplifiers for musicians. Amplifiers led to electric guitars and their repair and design and to the Fender Guitar and G&L guitars. All of our instruments result from musicians' suggestions and much field testing. Also, from an understanding of musicians' needs."

—Text from a speech Leo Fender made at his high school reunion in 1983.

Fender in front of Orangethorpe School in Fullerton, 1924.

Esther Fender outside what she would later jokingly call "that damned fiddle factory," 1952.

him into a bookkeeping position. He held other part-time jobs, and continued doing radio repair work at home. In 1932 he became acquainted with an orchestra leader sponsoring dances in Hollywood. (When asked in the 1980s, Leo had long forgotten the man's name.) This man contracted Leo to build the first of several public address systems he assembled in the 1930s, each using two large horn speakers with a separate amplifier chassis. No one knows how many sound systems he built in those days, although Leo remembered several groups using his equipment at these Hollywood dances. Wilda, eight years younger than her brother, remembers him also providing a sound system at her Fullerton high school dances. Meanwhile, the young accountant-cum-radio tech met a girl named Esther Klosky.

Radio Repair for Profit

Leo and Esther married in 1934. (She died of cancer in 1979; Leo remarried in 1980.) He landed a job as an accountant for the State of California Highway Department in San Luis Obispo where they lived until 1938. In a convoluted management switch, Leo found himself working for a privately owned tire company. Six months later, in a shakeup of that company's accounting department, Leo lost his job. He returned to Fullerton and borrowed $600 using his Ford Model A as collateral. He then set up a full-scale radio repair shop in a shared space at a Golden Eagle automobile service station. Repairing radios still interested him. After all, he possessed the skills and natural aptitude for it.

Some people have insisted that Leo was not a good businessman. Yet in 1940 the repair shop outgrew its first location, and Leo moved to a larger rented building across the street at 112 South Spadra. He did warranty repair work for all products manufactured by Crosley, Admiral, Bendix, and Motorola, and for all electronic products sold by a large retail chain, the McMahan furniture stores. Customers came from as far south as El Centro, near the border with Mexico, and as far north as Santa Barbara. At one time he employed eight people, including students who worked after school. Eventually, he got into tax trouble for not withholding enough wages for these part-timers. Leo loathed anything to do with taxes, believing they only interfered with his ability to employ people.

The Fender Radio Service quickly became a retail outlet, an all-purpose electronics general store, as his newspaper ads said, "specializing in every branch of sound." Leo sold almost every electrical device available in that day: radios, appliances, phonographs, guitars, and

Leo often manned one of his portable PA systems at functions such as this dedication of Fullerton City Hall in 1941.

public address systems. Later the store carried sheet music, records, and hearing aids as well.

As if these products were not enough, Leo drove a mobile sound truck with *Fender Radio Service* emblazoned on the side. He rented it to political candidates and others who wanted to drive around town and blast out their message. The shop performed another lucrative service—installing car radios. A classified ad for Leo's shop in April 1941 advised, "Change your radio to push button to your favorite station." Leo also sold wire recorders. He rented one such machine, the Wilcox Recordio, to people having parties. (Apparently, having a good time was simpler in those days before World War II.)

Leo always learned the strong and weak points of the products he sold. His natural curiosity led him to examine everything in the store. Away from the shop, odd, seemingly unrelated mechanical equipment caught his attention: hoists, boat anchors, and plumbing. Without warning he would crawl underneath new cars to examine suspension systems. His mind processed all this information for future use, making connections others missed. Sure enough, years later he applied his knowledge or used it in riddle-like explanations of how his products worked. (For instance, he once pointed out that a truss rod binding inside a guitar neck was like a fishhook caught on a sock.) He concluded that he could choose any product in his store and devise a more economical and improved design. One of Leo's first projects was upgrading a Philco Cobra automatic record changer. Customers liked its photocell switch, a feature that made it the shop's hottest seller. Yet the Philco had a major flaw: a wobbly die-cast turntable. Leo figured out the problem—the cast was uneven—and bought a lathe to true up turntables returned to the shop.

Leo's ad in the North Orange County Directory, 1945.

Donald D. Randall, 1943.

Donald D. Randall

Sometime shortly before World War II began, Leo met Donald D. Randall at the radio shop. Most of the men walking into the Fender story, including Randall, sought the California dream. By the 1930s and early 1940s California was more than just a place out west. It was a magnet for those wanting better-paying jobs and a more exciting life. Hollywood promised beautiful girls movie careers. Handbills offered agriculture jobs to displaced Oklahoma farmers. Before World War II, the state attracted the adventuresome, the creative, the risk takers. After the Japanese attack on Pearl Harbor, California became a sure bet for a job in the expanding government-funded defense industry. Thousands came to build planes, bombs, and artillery.

Don Randall came to California with his parents when he was 10 years old. Of Scottish stock, he was born in Kendrick, Idaho, in 1917. Like Fender and F.C. Hall, who would figure prominently in Fender's early career, Randall became absorbed in radios and audio amplifiers as early as high school. He earned a ham radio operator's license in 1934 (his call letters were W6KQD). In the throes of the Big Band Era, Randall made a portable amplifier with a big speaker system that he took to parties and dances. He remembers: "You'd play for high school dances in the gym or wherever you'd want to have a party. And you'd take equipment out there like DJs do today." In contrast to Fender, Randall had interests besides radios, notably athletics. He was captain of the basketball team in high school and later became an avid and accomplished golfer, playing in tournaments with Bob Hope and other celebrities. When Randall attended Santa Ana College, he majored in life sciences: "I thought I was going to be a doctor originally. I intended to be a surgeon, but I didn't follow through with it." He did realize one early dream, flying, receiving his pilot's license in the early 1950s and logging over five thousand hours in his own planes.

The 1939 Orange County Business Directory listed Don as a warehouseman for the Smart and Final grocery chain. He held this job while attending Santa Ana High School and Santa Ana Junior College. When not working or going to school, he spent hours hanging around Howard Taylor's Santa Ana Radio Supply, the source of his radio parts. Eventually Don picked up a part-time job as a salesman calling on various radio shops in southern California for Taylor's. In the course of these duties, he met Leo Fender and learned about his unfocused ambitions.

The Fender clan in the early 1950s.

Randall says, "Even before the war, I used to call Leo when I had the radio store, and I'd accuse him of having a book of a thousand formulas. . . ." Don knew Leo had a self-help book with many ideas for entrepreneurs who wanted to start manufacturing businesses.

Leo would tell Don, "We gotta make something. We gotta make something!"

Don says, "He'd stir up a scratch remover/polish or some darn thing he'd find in this book. And he'd say, 'Look, we can sell this stuff.'" Determined, Leo wanted to be more than a shopkeeper. He wanted to be a manufacturer and searched for ideas; a problem solver at heart, he wanted a challenge. In those days, Fender's unfocused creativity and dreams did not necessarily include musical instruments. He could have gone in several directions: he was capable of inventing stereo record players or electric typewriters.

Because Fender's store sold all manner of musical equipment and records and because Leo owned a professional-quality direct-to-disc recording device, he met many musicians. He saw electric guitars and amplifiers that came in for repairs and modifications; he learned what worked and, more important, what failed. In the 1930s, Electro String, Gibson, National, and a host of others made amplifiers. Nevertheless, at the time the amp was the sound chain's weakest link, prompting Leo to make his own. He pieced together the first one for a guitar player working at a Silverado Canyon, Orange County, roadhouse. (Poor at remembering names, Leo once explained, "You can't always keep them in the top drawer like your socks.") Fender said many times that his interest in amplifiers led to electric guitars. At the request of a musician from San Diego, he converted an acoustic guitar into an electric with a homemade pickup that resembled the well-known DeArmond pickup, a unit that fit into the soundhole of a flat-top acoustic.

By coincidence, on the same day the customer picked up this guitar, another musician visited Leo. His name was Clayton Orr "Doc" Kauffman, and his Rickenbacker amplifier needed repairing. Before Doc brought up that topic, he talked with Leo about pickups. Leo immediately liked Doc. Virtually everyone did. Kauffman already owned a couple of guitar-related patents and had experience as a musician. Leo would learn much from him. As Fender would later acknowledge, this meeting accelerated his interest in musical instruments. Kauffman, more to the point about his early days with Leo, quipped in the 1980s, "Yeah, I helped Leo start a $13 million business!"

These musical instruments were new and different. And as Don Randall said in the 1980s, "Electric guitars were something you could sell that every Tom, Dick, and Harry wasn't selling."

Leo Fender and Doc Kauffman in the early 1970s.

Kauffman in the early 1920s.

Chapter **2**

Old Friends

Doc Kauffman

Doc Kauffman grew up in Pratt County, Kansas. He studied violin and learned to tune pianos at Bethany College in Lindsbourg. In the winter of 1920, he came to California and landed a job accompanying silent films on his violin at a Selma movie theater. In addition, he took a daytime job tuning pianos. When spring came, he returned to the wheat fields of Kansas, married, and worked on the family farm. He moved permanently to southern California in 1922, tuning pianos and repairing instruments at the B.J. Chandler Music Company in Santa Ana. Doc played violin at night, but this time in a dance band that worked all over Orange, Los Angeles, and Riverside Counties.

Many musicians considered Kauffman one of the best violinists in the area. Nevertheless, he earned the nickname Doc tuning pianos. One day he had a difficult time locating a client's house, but came upon an address that looked familiar. He went to the door and a woman quickly

and quietly ushered him into the back room. Kauffman removed his coat, put down his little bag, and asked to see the piano. The woman gasped, "Piano? Why . . . why . . . aren't you the doctor? Aren't you here to deliver the baby?" The tale leaked to Kauffman's friends, and a nickname was born.

By the late 1920s Kauffman moved his young family to Fullerton and solidified his career as a dance band musician by learning to double on saxophone. He also bought a cheap flat-top, 4-string tenor guitar, teaching himself how to play it. Almost immediately Doc decided his new instrument lacked something, but he could not pinpoint what it was. This kind of vague perception sets tinkerers into action. He had become an amateur inventor growing up in Kansas, working on farm tools, combines, even tractor seats. Now, with the challenge of this incomplete tenor guitar, he went to work developing a new tailpiece for it

13

George D. Beauchamp (left) with vaudeville partner Slim Hopper, circa 1924. Beauchamp was co-founder of both National and Electro String (which made Rickenbacker guitars). His 1930s electric innovations in large part set the stage for Leo Fender's rise in the 1940s and 1950s.

with a lever that allowed him to subtly change the pitch of the strings as he played. Later he named the new device the Vibrola and had the Adams-Camel machine shop in Los Angeles manufacture it. Doc began playing his tenor guitar in the dance band, although in his mind the instrument remained wanting.

Then one night Kauffman discovered a new world as he listened to a music program on his homemade kit radio. The show originated at the Los Angeles Biltmore Hotel and featured the Earl Burknet Orchestra. During the orchestra's intermission, the Biltmore Trio—featuring a steel guitar, a standard 6-string guitar, and a ukulele—played popular tunes in a style Kauffman called "high-grade Hawaiian." No matter the song, the trio's guitarist captured Doc's attention with the full, dynamic sound of 6-string chords. With both ears glued to the little crystal radio, he made a decision: in addition to a Vibrola, a guitar needed six strings to sound complete.

Kauffman bought a flat-top, 6-string Gibson, and installed another homemade vibrato on it. He reasoned that learning thirteen chords would give him a good start playing the new guitar in the dance band. Confident he could learn these fingerings from an expert, Kauffman drove to the Biltmore one evening and offered the trio's guitarist a vibrato tailpiece in exchange for chord diagrams. The guitarist agreed and drew thirteen squiggles on a piece of paper. Doc then created his own reference chart and in six weeks started taking his new guitar to gigs with his dance band. He expanded his repertoire on the Gibson but was still unhappy with it, so he bought a carbon microphone and made an amplifier. His newly amplified guitar sounded better than ever, and he played it full-time, providing a rich back-up sound for the band. Kauffman had found a somewhat radical formula for the time—a 6-string guitar plus an amplifier. Nonetheless, this combination made him (and many players to come) the hit of the party.

Work was interesting but still hard to find. In the Depression's earliest days, promoters bartered with musicians, paying them with Mason jars filled with home-grown fruits or vegetables. These goods were the admission tickets to many dances where Doc's group performed. Kauffman also worked at a market coupling his homemade amplifier to a phonograph. Between records, he announced weekend specials, a 1930s precursor to "Attention K-Mart shoppers . . ." His wages were $10 a day in groceries, high pay for the Depression and more than enough to feed his two daughters and son. At another job in

nearby Brea, someone asked Doc if a little girl named Frances Gumm could come onstage to sing a song. After some pestering from the audience, Kauffman reluctantly agreed. The unknown youngster did an excellent rendition of an old standard. Several years later Doc learned that she had changed her name to Judy Garland.

Behind his house in Fullerton Doc set up a small shop where he came up with a variety of imaginative inventions, including a portable dishwasher. He unsuccessfully presented it to both the Philco and Norge manufacturing companies. He also invented a floating seat for tractors and what he called an automatic hot water bottle. During the mid-1930s, he became increasingly involved in improving musical instruments.

Kauffman had met George Beauchamp, one of Los Angeles' most inspired musician/inventors, in 1929 when Beauchamp was the National String Instrument Corporation's general manager. Doc soon befriended George's associates, Adolph Rickenbacher and Paul Barth. In the early 1930s Beauchamp and Rickenbacher formed the Electro String Instrument Corporation, makers of the Rickenbacher electric guitars, now commonly spelled *Rickenbacker*. (Adolph's cousin was war hero Eddie Rickenbacker. After years of indecision, the company settled on the Americanized spelling of *Rickenbacker* Eddie used rather than Adolph's original Swiss-German spelling ending in *-her*.) In free-spirited discussions on fishing trips and over drinks, the four shared ideas about electric guitars and manufacturing techniques. Doc even sought a permanent job at Electro String in 1936, but the company, just barely making a profit, had no openings. Electro String did become the sole manufacturer of Doc's Vibrola tailpiece. Originally designed for acoustic guitars and banjos, the device became standard on Rickenbacker's electrics in May 1936. Rickenbacker also sold the

Vibrola separately to players and to other manufacturers such as Gibson. In the 1930s and 1940s professionals such as Les Paul and many amateurs mounted Vibrolas on their instruments.

Kauffman, taking the vibrating tailpiece a step further, had another invention up his sleeve. Electro String had introduced its Bakelite Spanish guitar in 1935, and Doc had built a variation with an extra-thick body holding a motor and pulleys attached to the tailpiece. (Bakelite was a molded plastic used to make everything from jewelry to bowling balls in the 1930s. Adolph Rickenbacher used it to make toothbrush handles.) The motor changed the pitch of the strings as the player strummed. Doc built five prototypes, initially called Vibratone Guitars, at his Fullerton workshop. Three of them featured handmade walnut bodies and Bakelite necks, while the other two were all Bakelite. Doc created the pickup coils—an essential part of pickup designs—on a winder Paul Barth showed him

Doc Kauffman's Vibrola Spanish Guitar—Rube Goldberg, eat your heart out!

how to make with rubber bands and a sewing machine motor. At a demonstration at his house in July 1936, Doc convinced Adolph and George of the guitar's possibilities and negotiated an agreement for Electro String to manufacture it.

Electro String named Doc's new instrument the Vibrola Spanish Guitar, introduced it in December 1937, and manufactured it on a regular basis until October 1941. The company produced ninety complete units before World War II. Inventory sheets from 1942 listed two Vibrola Spanish bodies, probably the last ones made. (There were no advertisements for the instrument after the war.) Some of the most prominent guitarists in 1930s show business played the Vibrola guitar at one time or another: Pinky Tomlin, a popular Hollywood comedian; Georgie Smith, of Paramount Studios; Perry Botkin, of the Kraft Music Hall and Bing Crosby Show; Hugh Pendergraft; and Les Paul. Doc was definitely in the mainstream of electric guitar playing, having met all of these players, but his inventions never produced much income.

For a short time, starting in September 1938, Doc ran a business called the Kauffman Fix-It Shop in a shared space at 111 East Commonwealth in Fullerton. He made repairs, tuned pianos, and taught guitar. He also sold new and used musical instruments and accessories. However, before economic conditions could improve in the late 1930s, Doc's downtown store failed. He went to work in the jig-building department at Douglas Aircraft in Long Beach and on Saturday nights played in a band at Camp Pendleton, more than sixty miles from Fullerton. About this time, he took his guitar amp into Leo Fender's radio repair shop.

In the early days of the war, the War Production Board halted the manufacture of many consumer goods, making new products like radios, phonographs, and guitars hard to find. Leo's service-based business picked up as a result, and he fell behind making repairs. Leo phoned Doc and asked if he wanted to work at the shop. The offer sounded good to Kauffman, who started repairing changers in the evenings, keeping his day job at Douglas. After several months, Doc became frustrated with a Philco record changer that a customer had returned several times. Calling Leo into the repair booth, Kauffman asked for permission to make the changer simpler and more reliable by eliminating several parts. Essentially, Leo told Doc that if he was sure he could do the job, do it. Doc would later say, "Our minds first came together at that moment." When the modification was complete, the owner reported that the machine worked better than ever. Doc claimed the incident touched off the short but significant partnership that soon turned to guitars.

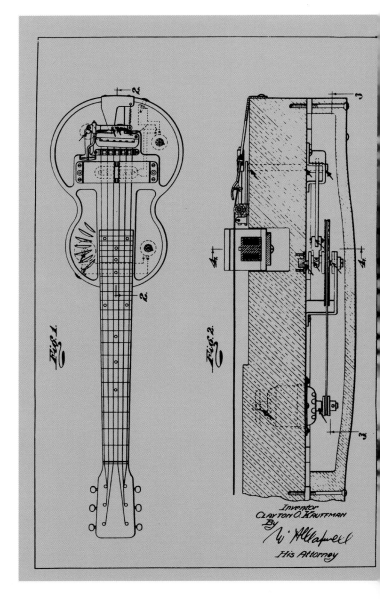

Leo knew that Doc had made electric steel guitars in his backyard shop and that Electro String had made his Vibrola Spanish guitar. Kauffman had sold several of his steel guitars in Fullerton and Santa Ana before he met Fender. But when Rickenbacker, Doc's parts supplier, converted to the war effort, components became scarce, and Doc started using whatever materials he could find. Magnets were an essential pickup ingredient that Doc found on salvaged twenty-five-cent Model T flywheels. He ground the magnets flat, making them suitable for his pickups.

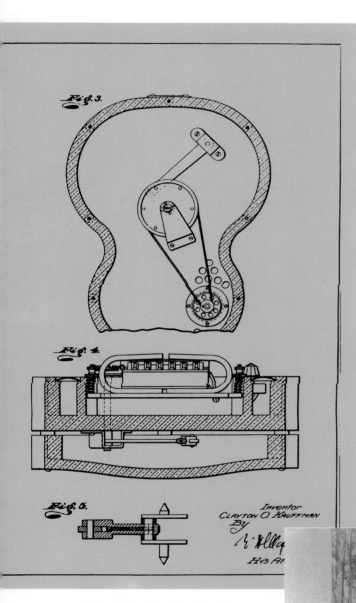

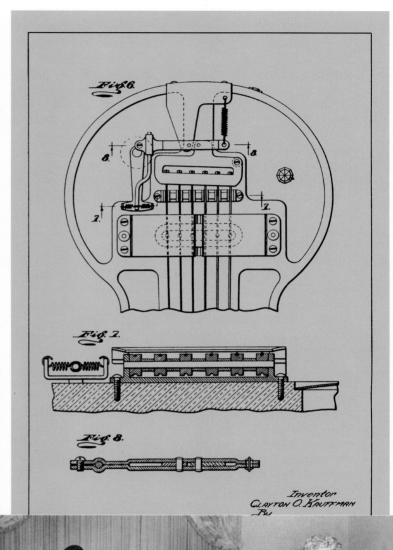

Patent drawings for Kauffman's ingenious but impractical invention. Note the pulley system (Fig. 3) for changing the strings' pitch as the player knocked off a melody such as "Tiptoe Through the Tulips."

Doc playing with the Buck Brawner Orchestra in 1948.

The First Fender Guitar

One evening at the radio shop Leo asked Doc if a pickup with the strings suspended through the coil would work well on a guitar. (For more information on this design, see *The Direct String Pickup* in chapter 3.) On most pickups the coil sat under the strings. Doc thought Leo's new pickup would work, so the two made one and installed it on a board strung with a guitar string. Indeed, the unit did the job. Leo coined the name Direct String Pickup to describe it, and the two made a 6-string test guitar using the same concept. Logically, it had a round neck and frets for the Spanish playing Doc had mastered; he could barely handle Hawaiian guitar techniques at the time. Shortages of materials during the war dictated the instrument's size. According to Leo, the two inventors fashioned it from the only wood in the shop, a piece of oak, and a prefabricated fingerboard bought from a mail-order house. Both remembered finishing the guitar about 1943.

Often mistaken for a lap steel (a steel guitar played on the lap) because of its small size and irregular shape, the radio shop guitar proved that its inventors could innovate, albeit with dubious craftsmanship—their work looked extremely amateurish. Leo and Doc unabashedly bypassed what tradition said guitars should look like; they did not pretend their guitar was traditional. It followed the new path cut by George Beauchamp and other electric guitar makers. Like 1930s Rickenbackers, the first Kauffman and Fender had a virtually non-resonant body with a pickup designed to translate the strings' vibrations to an amplifier, rather than a pickup made to translate the body's or bridge's vibrations. The concept would be the cornerstone of Leo's designs for decades to come.

Leo claimed that musicians often rented the little black radio shop guitar during the war years. Doc agreed that some guitarists did, but not too many. The guitar's awkward shape and size made it difficult to hold sitting down, and it had no strap pins. No one played this guitar standing. The intonation at the twelfth fret was off by at least a quarter-tone, and the pickup's obtrusive boxcar-like shape made dampening the strings a nearly impossible task.

But it was a good test guitar and had an earthy, full-bodied resonance with distinct treble tones. (In 1965 Leo gave it to country music legend Roy Acuff. It can be seen at the Acuff Museum at Opryland U.S.A. in Nashville, Tennessee.) Leo soon discovered that the pickup worked better for Hawaiian than Spanish guitar. The steel player's annoying pick-click—the sound metal guitar picks make on the strings—was virtually eliminated with the design. It resisted, however, the percussive attack desirable in Spanish guitar styles. While the pickup acted like a hand rest in the bridge position, Leo did not even try to put another

The radio shop guitar had a neck-through-body design, one piece from head to toe. No one chorded it standing up without trouble, and it played ridiculously out of tune. A close-up view of the peghead shows that the strings pulled across the nut at an angle, just one fault in conventional designs that Leo would soon remedy. The strings traveled through the pickup, which followed the design of a phonograph pickup with its needle suspended through a coil. The recessed roller knobs seen here would be used on a few K&F lap steels and Fender's Jazzmaster guitar.

(Opposite) One of the first six K&F lap steel and amp sets. Notice the steel's roller knobs, bone nut, and headstock shape—features that Leo would subsequently change. Rear view of the amp shows hanging tubes, characteristic of Fender-designed amps to follow.

Ad from 1945 that described Doc and Leo's record changer. The inventors lost a small fortune when they let its patent applications drop—Leo was convinced that guitars held a brighter future than records. The patent application for the radio shop guitar was filed on September 6, 1944.

one in the neck position, where most Spanish electrics had pickups. There Leo's unit interfered with strumming.

On September 26, 1944, Kauffman and Fender applied for a patent on the new pickup, but temporarily delayed manufacturing it (or guitars). The radio shop was still in a rented building at 112 South Spadra and had no extra space; the radio business took too much of Leo's time. But more important, Leo, Doc, and a man named Clifton T. Abbott, who probably worked for Leo, had already started another project—a newly designed record changer. In October 1944 Fender bought a building across from the old store and moved. For a short period he did business at 109 South Spadra while he remodeled 107 for the radio business. After the move, the shop's business continued to improve as the Allied victory seemed certain.

By February 1945, Fender, Kauffman, and Abbott finished the new changer design and prepared two patent applications for it, the first filed on May 25 and the second filed on August 28. Leo put the device on display in the radio shop window on April 2. The changer ran flawlessly around the clock all spring and summer, an accomplishment in which the men took pride for years.

The K&F Manufacturing Corporation

Leo and Doc had formed a company called the K&F Manufacturing Corporation to make steel guitars, amplifiers, and perhaps record changers. (Abbott was not involved in the guitar venture. In fact, it seems that his name was added to an early agreement about the record changer almost as an afterthought.) No one remembered the exact nature of the K&F agreement or the date it was struck, but it was unconventional. Doc worked for a wage, and Leo considered himself the owner. In April 1945, when

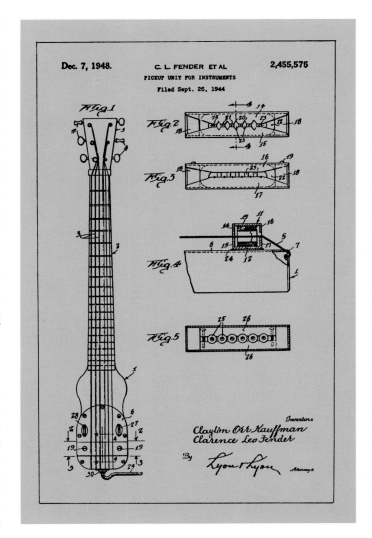

Leo first demonstrated the changer, he also ran an ad in the Fullerton *Daily News Tribune* announcing that the steel guitars were on display.

Kauffman remembered making six steel and amp sets about this time, probably the only ones made before the end of the war. The photos of an early set show how the steel differed from later K&F instruments. It had a stenciled logo and fingerboard markers on a hardwood finish. The pickup had a long baseplate with the roller knob volume and tone controls recessed like the controls on the standard guitar (the so-called radio shop guitar) built to test Leo's Direct String Pickup. The first six K&Fs used conventional bone nuts, and the pegheads were wider at the top than most later K&Fs. Another ad the following summer solicited custom orders for steel guitars and amps.

Despite the war, the steel guitar was at the height of its popularity. Its history went back at least fifty years before dovetailing into Leo Fender's guitar revolution. Nineteenth-century Hawaiian musicians had blended the guitar styles of Mexico, Portugal, and America into a simmering stew spiced with Polynesian, Asian, African, and Indian influences. In the middle of the Pacific's busy shipping lanes, East met West to produce the Hawaiian guitar, perhaps the first non-European instrument after the banjo to change the course of America's popular music. The steel's unique, seductive sounds whispered of a faraway mythical paradise with swaying palm trees, hula girls, and rumbling volcanoes. It produced more than a singer's accompanying rhythm: a Hawaiian guitar melody imitated and even rivaled the human voice.

Around 1900, Hawaiian musicians playing in tent shows, vaudeville theaters, and expositions introduced the romantic, ethereal, yet exotic Hawaiian steel guitar style to an eager American public. The instrument sounded foreign for good reason. Hawaiian guitarists could play all the in-between notes outside the standard Western diatonic major and minor scales, an impossible feat on the standard guitar without bending the strings. Sounding vastly new and capturing America's imagination, the steel guitar held another promise. Unlike the standard guitar, which required relatively complicated fingering, the steel used so-called open tunings that produced a chord without fingering. Sliding the steel bar up the strings raised the pitch of the chord. Wiggle the bar, and palm trees of the mind dropped their coconuts. With a little ingenuity, these simple movements became a song of the Islands most beginners could learn in one lesson. Impressed by the quick results teachers achieved, many parents signed up their children for a music education, steel guitar style. Mail-order catalogs and traveling salesmen in the guise of music professors made buying a steel guitar easier and more fun than slopping pigs or planting corn.

By the late 1920s and early 1930s, the steel guitar fad had swept across rural America. Adapting the instrument to new styles, players went beyond Hawaiian music into popular music. Jimmie Rodgers used Hawaiian musicians and steel guitar on landmark country recordings. After the introduction of electric guitars, several big bands featured steel players. Bob Dunn, who played with Bob Wills' former singer Milton Brown, first used an amplified steel guitar to play jazz horn lines in the mid-1930s. The Hawaiian guitar became an adopted voice of western swing and country music, one of the main melody instruments. By 1941, Leon McAuliffe and Noel Boggs combined the diverse influences of jazz, country,

Fender and Kauffman remained friends, even after parting ways in the guitar business.

The colorful K&F logo plate on a crinkle finish.

swing, and Hawaiian into an advanced art form. Steel guitar technology evolved parallel to the techniques these players developed.

At first, any standard guitar with high string action and steel strings would do. Companies sold new guitars with a metal extension nut for raising the strings. As the style became more sophisticated, companies designed instruments specifically for Hawaiian playing. Ironically, most of the important innovations took place in California rather than Hawaii. (As mentioned in the introduction, *Hawaiian guitar* and *steel guitar* came to mean both a style of playing and a type of guitar.) Except for their thick, square necks, the first Hawaiian guitars looked like standard guitars. Then designs from Weissenborn and Hilo appeared; their bodies and necks seamlessly flowed together. National and Dobro inventor John Dopyera added resonators. Electric pickups made a standard hollow body superfluous, even a detriment: a cheaply made solid body of wood, metal, or plastic improved the tone produced by pickups. By the mid-1930s, at least a dozen companies made electric lap steel guitars. The steel guitar's maturation continued almost unabated, interrupted only by World War II.

When the war was over, Leo and Doc saw their chance to jump ahead of guitar companies put out of the music business by the War Production Board. (These companies would wait many months before getting permission to return to peacetime pursuits.) Leo and Doc deemed standard guitar production too complicated for them at this point, but the parking area behind the new shop provided space to erect a metal building suitable for a small production line of simple steel guitars and amplifiers. The financing came from the record changer invention.

Fender, Kauffman, and Abbott sold the rights for their turntable design to Voice of Music (V.M.) in Benton Harbor, Michigan, on October 9, 1945. The partners received $5,000 in advance royalties. (Later one of Leo's advisors, perhaps his barber or a customer, wrongly predicted that the record business' future looked dim. When a thirty-dollar invoice from the Patent Office arrived, Leo ignored it and let the patent applications drop. In the 1950s RCA used elements of the Kauffman-Fender-Abbott design in a highly successful 45 rpm changer, in which the partners held no claim. They lost more than $1 million in royalties by Leo's count, and he never forgave himself.) The V.M. Corporation's payment on October 9, 1945, for the record changer went to buy the tools necessary to begin making instruments on a larger scale.

In the early months Doc and Leo typically worked until midnight building benches and tools. Moving equipment from his home, Doc used his own band saw and drill press to make jigs. The partners made steel cutters for an all-at-once lock joint cutting machine, ideal for fabricating amplifier cabinets. Doc described this machine's operation, cutting four pieces of wood all at once, as particularly savage because of the merciless power of the blades. On the less ferocious side, the neophyte guitar makers used a drill press as a belt sander to smooth the edges of steel guitar bodies. Kauffman found the setup so handy that he took it to his home shop when he left K&F. Doc and Leo also engineered a wider belt sander for sanding the tops and backs of steel guitars and amp cabinets.

Leo bought a welding outfit, although neither he nor Kauffman welded. However, Doc had watched the welders at Douglas, and the process looked easy. He started asking questions at the plant each day, pressing the welders for pointers. One night Leo and Doc began building sturdy work benches with angle iron and plywood. To get a feel for it, they practiced with the torch on scrap metal for a few minutes. Moving to the angle iron, they discovered that they could weld.

In Doc's opinion, Leo found clever ways to be successful with barely adequate manufacturing equipment. A good example was K&F's punch press operation. At the time, Leo used a Benchmaster 4-ton press capable of cutting a 2-inch hole in 16-gauge cold-rolled sheet metal. Yet he needed to make the K&F pickup baseplate from a piece of 20-gauge steel 16 inches in circumference. The press failed to cut through. So he decided to try cutting one half at a time, turning the plate over for the second half. On the first try the press failed to go through again. Determined, Leo ran the press faster and made his cut. The overworked machine's crankshaft would bend over time, but not before K&F had its baseplates.

Both men made dies, the special devices for stamping or cutting materials on punch presses, using a 12-inch Craftsman lathe with a milling attachment. The way each man worked reflected different personalities. Laid-back, Doc ran the milling operation slowly, and he wisely used coolant from an oil can. His method saved the milling cutters from overheating. Leo, showing little patience, sped up the lathe. In his enthusiasm for getting the job done, he either forgot the coolant or did not take the time to use it. According to Kauffman, Leo needlessly burned several milling cutters. Fortunately, each learned to do his own cutter sharpening so that production had only short interruptions.

Simple, sparse design marked Leo's own K&F amp. Musicians would use the cavity in back to pack cords, straps, and empty beer bottles. The grilles on most K&F amps were covered in flock, a finely powdered cloth also sprayed onto phonograph turntables, among many other products. Leo stopped using it when another local manufacturer contracted a lung ailment by breathing the material.

One night Doc startled himself trying to locate some screws in a box on a top shelf in the storeroom. He reached up and discovered several glass eyes instead. Puzzled at first, he then realized they were Leo's spares and gingerly returned them without a word.

Newspaper ad, May 8, 1945.
The end of World War II in August would open the door for Doc and Leo to begin full production, and Leo stocked up on surplus components.

K&F Steels and Amps

Leo bought supplies of war surplus wire, tubes, capacitors, and speakers. Leo recalled that K&F's full production began in November 1945 after a month's preparation. Repair invoices for K&F instruments returned to the factory referred to Deluxe, Student, and Standard models. The Students and Standards were probably the most common K&F guitars. They sported an expedient, baked-on gray crinkle (or crackle) paint like many earlier Rickenbacker steels. As Doc and Leo taught themselves manufacturing skills, they searched for shortcuts. Presumably they learned the problems lacquer finishes posed when they made the first six sets during the war. In contrast to lacquer finishes, the baked-on finishes were easy to do on pine bodies. The partners used Doc's kitchen oven at first. After Doc passed away in 1990, one of his daughters told the *Orange County Register*: "When I was a teenager, I would come home and smell this terrible smell. . . . My mother just hated that." Soon the inventors set up a small industrial gas oven in the building behind the radio shop.

Pine-bodied crinkle-paint K&F steels led to hardwood-bodied K&F steels finished with either light or dark natural colors. The hardwood models were probably the Deluxe steels mentioned on repair invoices. However, neither Leo nor Doc remembered this detail. Nearly all K&F 6-string single-neck steel guitars had similar Direct String Pickups. Most used a 22 1/4-inch scale, shorter than 22 1/2-inch scales used on later Fender lap steels. All K&F steels probably used the same controls: one volume and one tone. Leo Fender commissioned a foundry in Brea, California, to make an unspecified number of cast aluminum bodies for K&F steels. He quickly decided that they were unsatisfactory because aluminum expands with temperature changes, pulling the strings out of tune. Doc could not remember the aluminum bodies, and none have surfaced for examination.

Much has been written about Doc and Leo's early guitars, but little about the amplifiers made to go with them. Unfortunately, the first ones are lost. Nevertheless, they played an important role in the development of Leo's guitars. While modern players and designers generally view amp design and guitar design as separate fields, to Leo and other designers in the 1930s and 1940s the two went hand in hand; they saw the electric guitar and amplifier as a single instrument connected by a patch cord. In a way, the amp was like a saxophone's flared bell, the opening at the end where the sound came out, the final and critical link in the chain of expanding sound. No electric instrument sounded good through a poorly designed amplifier. In this regard, Fender carefully weighed musicians' opinions on the nuances of tone. Fender Radio Service repairman Ray Massie held a lasting interest in amplifiers and made significant contributions to Leo's first designs. (Years later Ray would own an amplifier company called Massie Electronics. He had already lost his memory to Alzheimer's disease when finally contacted for this book in the mid-1980s.)

Aside from the few made during World War II, K&F amps were made in late 1945 through mid-1946. Three known models existed: a small student model, a mid-sized model with a 9- or 10-inch speaker, and a large model with a 15-inch speaker. There were variations even among these. Most K&F amps had gray crinkle-paint finishes; at least a few had luggage linen coverings. (Amp collectors often call luggage linen "tweed," although the material came in many patterns.) The cabinets had lock joints.

Leo managed to place K&F amplifiers into some important bands like the Texas Playboys. However, today's collectors have had an exceedingly hard time locating the large professional K&Fs because most were custom orders. Usually Fender took old models as trade-ins from the traveling bands. Because he disregarded his old designs, the trade-ins probably ended up in a landfill. Production continued.

Kauffman assembled the steel guitars, strung them, and played a song such as "Coquette" or "Paradise Isle" to test the instruments for flaws in workmanship. (His steel technique improved with the practice.) For the next five decades, all Fender guitars would get a final quality test by a professional player. Leo kept mental tabs on production by counting Doc's performances, and by January 1946 K&F was making thirty to forty steel guitars per week. Leo distributed them to southern California music instruction studios. About once a week, Pacific Music Supply, a Los Angeles-based music wholesale house, sent a car to Fullerton to pick up a load.

It is unusual to find two K&F steels exactly alike. Note body shapes and finishes on these three examples. The industrial-gray crinkle-paint guitar was a student model, simple to make and practical to use. The more traditional natural light and dark finishes were options. A metal fingerboard was a Deluxe feature.

F. C. Hall (left) at a 1956 trade show. The man who financed the Fender operation in the 1940s and bought Electro String in 1953, Hall was forced out of Fender in 1955. The Beatles and many other rock bands would later play his Rickenbacker acoustic-electric guitars.

(Copyright 1994 Rickenbacker International Corporation. All Rights Reserved)

Francis Cary Hall and Radio-Tel

While Leo struggled in these early months of production, the instruments he made caught the attention of Don Randall and another Orange County businessman, F. C. Hall. On several occasions since the 1960s Paul McCartney has mistakenly called Francis Cary Hall "Mr. Rickenbacker." The misnomer was an honest mistake because the music world best knows Hall for modern Rickenbacker guitars, made by the company he bought in 1953 from Adolph Rickenbacher. The Beatles and the 12-string sounds of the 1960s burned the name Rickenbacker into the public's consciousness. Still, before those times, Hall had spent many years in the music and electronics business.

He was born in Iowa in 1909 and in 1919 moved to Santa Ana where his father opened a small general store on Oak Street. As a boy, F. C. spent summers picking lima beans in what is now Irvine. In high school he studied radio and electronics, a serious hobby that led to a part-time business recharging household batteries for local residents. By 1927 he manufactured batteries at home, selling them through his father's store and making home pickups and deliveries throughout Orange County.

The battery business evolved into a repair shop called Hall's Radio Service and then into a prosperous electronic parts distribution outfit called the Radio and Television Equipment Company (R.T.E.C. or Radio-Tel). In the 1940s, Radio-Tel installed public address systems in many southern California public buildings, schools, and churches. In addition, Hall's speaker re-coning service repaired all major brands of hi-fi speakers. In the early 1950s, Radio-Tel exclusively distributed Tele-King television sets. Although Hall knew Leo Fender's name during the war, the two had never met. Don Randall would soon change that.

Randall had bought Howard Taylor's radio parts store in 1941, but then the war came. The Army drafted Don, and he sold his inventory to Hall. The war created a here-and-now, life-and-death urgency that abruptly put Randall's plans on hold. In the Army he readied himself for any event, tried to prepare his family, and put his life in order should he not return. His experience symbolized the psychological plight of those called to serve, a personal drama and defining moment Leo Fender never experienced. (Leo's handicap made him ineligible for military service during World War II.) Don once observed, "Strange thing, when I was in the Army, it's about the closest thing to being born again you can experience." Although he planned for the worst, he spent most of the war years in Orange County, like Leo, although Don wore a uniform. He

Don Randall, circa 1948.

While working for Howard Taylor Wholesale Radio in Santa Ana, Don Randall met Leo Fender.

passed his basic training in the Army Corps of Engineers, transferred into the Signal Corps, and then into the Army Air Corps. He became the communication chief for the pre-flight school located near Santa Ana.

Once in this stateside niche, Randall saw his Army career providing him the time to make a fresh start. He thought: "I can really plan my future now. I know I'm going to do something; I'm going to do it right." He planned to take his time selecting a new career and hoped to pick something he would enjoy. So he decided to wait four months after leaving the Army before taking a job. He also felt that he would prefer a job closer to manufacturing than wholesale parts sales.

The war ended, and Randall left the Army in early 1946. A bigger, even more compelling California dream was born. He saw a chance to start his life anew. But F.C. Hall, who suffered from a mild form of diabetes and wanted help running his business, immediately asked Randall to become Radio-Tel's general manager. Despite his three-year plan to start something new, Randall went right back into the radio business: the Army discharged him on a Thursday, and he went to work for Hall on the following Monday. Don signed his Form W-4 for Radio-Tel on February 4, 1946, and threw his well-laid plan out the window.

Up to his knees in tubes and capacitors, Don renewed his growing contempt for the radio parts business. He says, "It's not that I didn't like the electronic end of it, but we were selling radio parts that were sold by every wagon jobber in the country." From his perspective, competitors were undercutting Radio-Tel. "You know, some guy would load his truck up with a bunch of parts and run around selling to the dealers, making special deals and everything." Randall tried to run a legitimate business with paid salesmen, but found little support from manufacturers: "You take on RCA tubes, and they tell you how you are going to be protected. They don't care if you take them up and dump them out of a balloon as long as you pay for them." Although he worked hard for Radio-Tel, Randall grew impatient with the radio business and thought of Leo.

While Randall served Uncle Sam, Doc Kauffman had come onto the scene and focused Leo's imagination onto guitars. When Don finally saw the K&F steels and amplifiers, he judged them more worthwhile than scratch remover or the other ideas Leo had found before the war in his book for beginning entrepreneurs. These musical instruments were new and different. And as Don said in the 1980s, "Electric guitars were something you could sell that every Tom, Dick, and Harry wasn't selling." A natural-born salesman with the mind of an engineer, Randall had

no particular fascination with music. He did not play an instrument, but eventually learned a few chords to demonstrate guitars. Ambitious and highly motivated to succeed, Don thought that musical instruments represented an opening and a beginning. He suggested that Hall consider distributing Leo's guitars and amps, and Hall agreed. Radio-Tel's almost natural transition from radio parts to electric instruments had begun.

Leo remembered that one day in early 1946 Randall drove up in an old Ford with a business proposition: Would Leo accept Radio-Tel as the exclusive distributor for K&F instruments? According to Leo, Randall and Hall guaranteed that Radio-Tel would purchase 5,000 guitars and amps if Fender accepted the offer. On that day selling steel guitars seemed promising to everyone concerned, especially Randall, the spark plug Leo needed. Eventually, Randall's involvement selling Fenders would eclipse Hall's, and Randall would become the most important person in the Fender story besides Leo himself.

Fender signed his first agreement with Hall on March 1, 1946, and immediately started purchasing the wood he needed to fill Randall's order. Leo now ordered components by the hundreds—some items by the thousands. Seeing a need for help, he hired additional workers. Dale Hyatt had started at K&F on the day after he married, January 16, 1946; Leo thoughtfully told him to come in at noon. At first Hyatt worked in manufacturing, quickly learning every aspect of the amp- and steel-guitar-making process. Ray Massie now helped full-time designing and assembling amplifier circuits.

But Doc Kauffman, with fresh memories of the Depression and the debt he had initially incurred making Vibrolas, did not share Leo's optimism. Doc's parents had passed away, and he was to receive a monthly royalty check for oil discovered on the family's Kansas farm. About the time Leo signed on with Radio-Tel, Doc became afraid that Leo wanted to borrow money for expanding the business. Knowing how hard it would be to turn down a friend, Kauffman quit before Leo could ask. With no bitterness, Fender understood and accepted Doc's decision. The two divided up the jointly owned equipment and shook hands. Doc left in early 1946, returning once in 1948 to help Leo with an electric piano design. Afterwards, Kauffman had little input.

Correspondence from dealers to Don Randall indicates that customers ordered the K&F steels as late as September 1946. Leo explained that he made K&F guitars until he used all the nameplates. To fill earlier orders, perhaps the factory made some K&Fs concurrently with early Fender steels. K&F made about a thousand steel guitars. Some of the earliest Fender steels, which usually have just the Fender logo stamped on the pickup, resemble K&Fs in almost all details except name; one ad on the back of sheet music from the Bronson music publishing company hailed a "K&F Fender" steel guitar.

Doc remained one of Leo's best friends for nearly fifty years, and one of the few who without envy embraced Leo's success. Doc kept a shop next to his garage, repairing guitars and pickups and tinkering with new ideas. In the early 1980s he designed a simple but effective way to string a headless guitar, giving Leo the idea and asking nothing in return. Fender liked the concept (although he later decided it had little commercial merit) and in gratitude hand-delivered a new G&L guitar and bass to Doc's one afternoon. When Doc's wife died, Leo knew his friend was lonely and taped his number by the phone in the G&L lab. Leo called him frequently just to say hello and to raise his spirits. The venerable Kauffman passed away of natural causes on June 26, 1990, in Fullerton. His good-natured, inventive spirit, which had inspired Leo Fender to make his first guitars, touched players all over the world.

Repair invoice for
returned instruments
and amps, July 14, 1947.

No. A 8983

7-14-47

Cheapest Way

Now

n/c

Fender Mfg. Company
107 South Spadra
Fullerton, California

2   Double Neck Guitars Serial Nos. D-107 and D-53   Bad switches

1   Standard Guitar # 1384   Restring

1 2   Organ Button Guitars Serial Nos. 1044 and 991
                           #1044 restring 0257
                           #991   organ button shorted

1   Deluxe Blonde Guitar Serial B-52   No tone control 0271

1   Deluxe Walnut Guitar Serial B-741   Shorted tone control

1   Deluxe Walnut Guitar B-740   Scratch on volume control 0271

1   Blonde Student Guitar # A-229   Restring

1   Dark Student Guitar   # A-118   Dead 0271

1   Student Guitar   # A-355 needs refinishing   # 0260

1   Deluxe Amplifier # 477   Oscillates when instrument volume is
                                           turned up. Tone control burns when
                                           instrument is plugged into jack ad-
                                           jacent to tone control.

1   Deluxe Amplifier # 662   Same as above 0260

1   Deluxe Amplifier # 388   Complete refinish 0276

1   Deluxe Amplifier # 877   Very noisy 0281

1   Deluxe Amplifier # 769   Bad hum 0276

1   Deluxe Amplifier # 530   All jacks shorted. No response to guitar 0260

1   Deluxe Amplifier # 658   Noisy, oscillates and motor boats 0260
                                           when 6SC7 is touched. Shorted tone
                                           control.

1   Deluxe Amplifier # 656   Dead 0280

1   Student Amplifier # 29426   Chipped handle. Uneven with top
                                           of amplifier. 0259

Please repair or replace these defective units and return them to us
on a no charge basis per guarantee.

We are returning these units to you, via Mr. Fender.

Take It Away, Leo

Chapter

3

**Many of the first Fender amplifiers and instruments were
delivered in these early years with design and manufacturing
defects, and many were returned for repairs or replacement.**

The Fender Electric Instrument Company

Living in Fullerton, Leo was never far from the tracks. The Santa Fe Railroad Company founded the city in 1887. For years, railroad tracks carried trainloads of Orange County's cash crop to the rest of America, and Fullerton became the busiest shipping point between San Diego and Los Angeles. In the early days, two train depots and eight packing houses beat like hearts pumping Minute Maid. As Fullerton grew and the economy changed, housing developments and industry swallowed the orange groves. But the railroad continued playing a central role. Small factories like Leo's and vegetable processing plants like Hunt's sprang up alongside the tracks in the 1930s and 1940s. Appropriately, for several decades Fullerton was best known for two products—electric guitars and ketchup.

The radio shop and shed in back served as Leo's first lab and assembly area until the spring of 1946. As Leo's tinkering expanded, he erected another metal building a block north of the radio shop on the alley between Commonwealth and Amerige Avenues. In May 1946 he made plans for a real factory on three vacant lots at the corner of Santa Fe and Pomona Avenues. The new location was just east of central Fullerton and across the street from the Santa Fe station. Leo now called his operation the Fender Manufacturing Company.

The first Fender factory consisted of two 30' X 60' fabricated steel buildings fronting Santa Fe Avenue. The California Steel Construction Company of Los Angeles assembled the buildings. Leo said that within a month he moved his equipment and started manufacturing. According to records at Fullerton City Hall, the buildings passed final inspection in December 1946. The plant was rather primitive and certainly illegal by current standards. Both buildings lacked gas outlets and heating. Furthermore, there were no rest rooms: all employees used the facilities across the street at the train station. The building to the west served as the metal shop and assembly area while the building to the east served as the wood shop. Here the company made amp cabinets and steel guitar bodies (standard guitar bodies would come later).

One day in 1946 a lumber man from Arkansas traveling through town told Leo about a grove of walnut trees cut down to make rifle stocks during the war. The loggers had taken the burled lower sections of the trees, leaving the upper portions as waste. The man offered to mill the leftover wood and ship it to California at a bargain price. Leo ordered a load that filled a boxcar. When the wood arrived, Dale Hyatt, still doing every imaginable job for Leo, stacked it in the vacant lot west of the factory. It was a big chore, but Hyatt was a big, strong young man.

(Opposite) The two steel buildings on Santa Fe Avenue in Fullerton, where Fender started full-scale production in 1946. Pictured here in 1950, the construction of a new building had just begun.

Leo's work area in 1950 had an array of simple tools and ever-present clutter. A circuit diagram drawn on cardboard leaned against the piece of wood supporting the shelf. A 45 rpm record changer sat on an unfinished speaker cabinet while a prototype amp chassis awaited more tinkering.

While Leo bought the walnut for full production, Randall and Hall struggled to sell even a few guitars and amplifiers. Radio-Tel, one of southern California's biggest wholesale radio and electronic parts distributors, had few accounts with music dealers. Dale Hyatt reported that one radio parts salesman tried placing steel guitars for sale at gas stations. To sell quantities of instruments, Randall had to reach beyond southern California and establish a nationwide sales network among music dealers. Meanwhile, Leo tried to use his walnut, much of which had already begun to rot. It needed a protected storage area, a fact he had not considered when he made the order.

Leo stored new yet unsold wooden-cabinet amplifiers in a dirt-floor garage where they sat unattended for several months. California has termites. Dry wood termites emerge from their nests during the warm Santa Ana winds and land on rafters, decks, or siding. There they drop their wings to make new homes. Subterranean termites do not fly, but wreak more havoc living like ants in colonies in the ground. When they find wood on or near the surface, they attack like an invading army, forming mud tubes that conceal the devastation. One day Leo visited his storage garage to pick up an amplifier and discovered the telltale mud tubes. Breaking them off, he saw termites infesting an amp.

Randall, questioning Leo's memory while acknowledging his storytelling skills, claims that the factory never stockpiled enough instruments long enough to attract bugs, even in the earliest days. Don doubts termites ever ate Fender amps. Typically, many of Leo's claims were unverifiable. All agree, however, that business was not going well. Before the end of 1946, Leo found himself in a financial crisis. Because of the unreliable distribution and unforeseen difficulties with materials, he fell behind with his creditors. He needed cash as they began to hound him. Leo also had a lien on his property for failing to pay worker's compensation taxes to the state. One close friend remembers Leo spending part of late 1946 working at night to avoid bankers and tax collectors searching him out in the daytime. It is hard to picture him wearing disguises when he went shopping, but maybe he did—he was in a predicament.

Leo attributed his credit problems to Radio-Tel's inability to sell merchandise fast enough, plus Hall's slow way of paying bills. Yet Randall says that Hall always paid on time. Fender operated solely on cash from Radio-Tel, his only paying account. Still, Leo maintained that Hall reneged on the original distribution agreement by not accepting the whole order of 5,000 units. But the problems getting salesmen on the road to promote national distrib-

ution, like the difficulties with rotten wood and termites, were understandable. Everyone at the Fender factory and Radio-Tel office had something to learn about making and selling guitars. The difficulties resulted from inexperience. Fortunately, the newcomers quickly learned how to operate in a crisis atmosphere.

To stay in business, Fender needed a large influx of capital. He borrowed money from Hall as early as July 1946 and on January 10, 1947, mortgaged his factory's entire contents to Hall for $14,266.43. The cash kept Leo afloat, and the mortgage gave Radio-Tel a bigger incentive to make Fender products successful. Hall took an enormous risk, yet Leo let the loan feed his growing disdain for him. Said Fender in the 1980s, "If I'd had a good lawyer, I would never have needed the loan."

With the short-term problems eased, Leo concentrated on the long-term task of building a viable manufacturing plant. Because of the financial problems, the factory experienced several stops and starts in the 1946–47 period, closing once for three months. Even after Leo received his loans, there were few orders to fill in the spring of 1947. During idle periods, he laid off most of the factory workers. Dale Hyatt was one of the few who continued working during these lean times, but even he found little to do at the factory and ended up managing Leo's radio shop.

Early Fender Single-Neck Steels

The first steels carrying the Fender name appeared in mid-to-late 1946 at the new factory on Santa Fe Avenue, which produced three single-6-string-neck models and a double-8-string-neck model (chapter 4). Leo's factory fashioned all early Fender models from kiln-dried hardwoods: maple, ash, walnut, and mahogany, with some in oak and kelobra wood. Kelobra eventually proved too hard; cutting it broke or burned too many saw blades. Oak also proved unsatisfactory since its acidity blistered finishes.

The Organ Button Model was the highest-priced 6-string produced in 1946 and 1947. It retained the original K&F body with the waist starting at the seventeenth fret. While the early Fender Deluxe and Princeton guitars used a shorter profile pickup, the Organ Button retained two 1-square-inch magnets. Leo probably designed this model to use leftover K&F-sized magnets from another one of his over zealous bargain buys. The little red button located on the baseplate created a wah-wah effect reminiscent of an electronic organ or muted trumpet. Leo later admitted it

The 1947 dealer catalog included a wholesale price sheet.

The wooden amps included the mid-size Model 26 (three versions with different color grilles shown here), the large Professional Model, and the small Princeton. The top-of-the-line single-neck Organ Button Model, right, had a push button that gave the strings a wah-wah sound. The Deluxe had volume and tone controls and the Princeton had volume only.

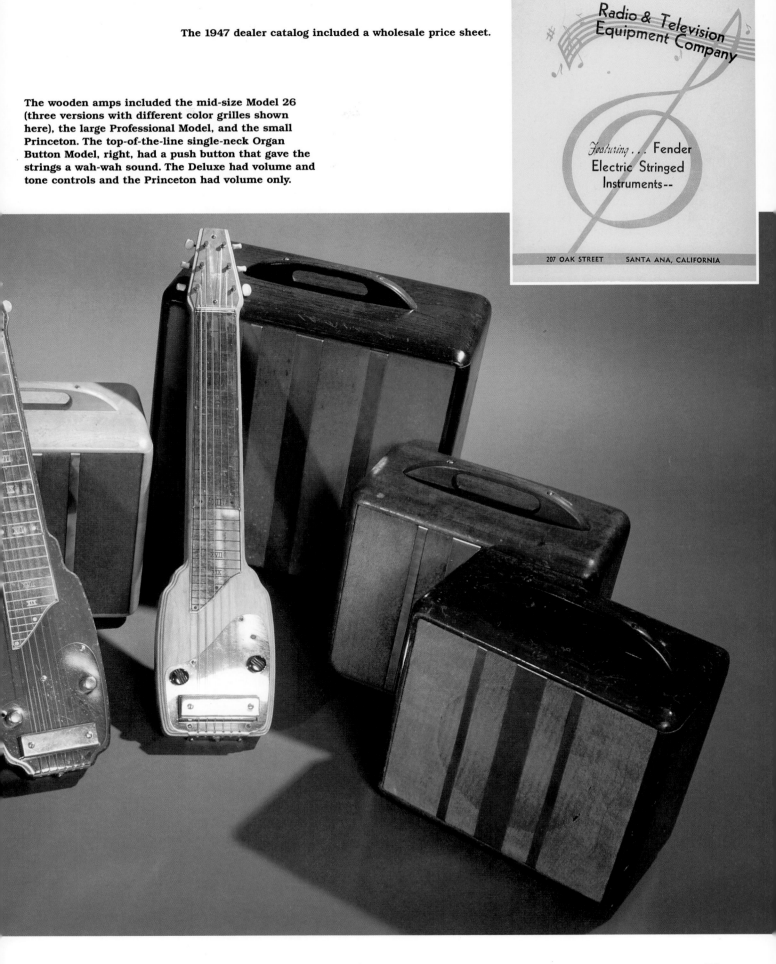

was a gimmick with little merit. Many professional steel players made similar sound effects with the regular tone control knob. The Organ Button's shortcut circuit required little playing technique, but it worked poorly and sometimes broke under heavy-handed fingers. It would be one of the few Fender guitar parts known to break.

From 1946 to 1948, Fender also produced an instrument called the Princeton or Student Steel. Radio-Tel sold it either by itself or with the wood-cabinet Princeton amplifier as the first Student Set. The Princeton guitar had a chrome-plated detachable fretboard, a volume control but no tone control, and usually came with an attached cord. The first Deluxe model, which shared the same body and fingerboard as the Princeton, came equipped with volume and tone controls.

Manufacturing Problems and Early Amps

Working for Fender was hardly glamorous, entirely safe, or lucrative. Workers did much of the metal work with punch presses that sounded like slow-motion jackhammers, only much louder. Catching a finger in a punch press meant no more barre chords. The painters, wearing no masks, worked in poorly vented spray booths filled with lacquer fumes. Leo used asbestos insulation in amplifiers until the 1960s. Workers handled this dangerous material, which is now virtually banned from all manufacturing, with no protective clothing or respirators. (Today, players should be concerned about the asbestos—the white material glued to amplifier back panels—if it crumbles or becomes airborne.) During several routine inspections, the fire marshal threatened to close the place. His biggest complaint was an electric flare heater used after 1948 to shrink-wrap steel guitar bodies in acetate. This plant never had a fire, but several accidents did happen there. A story Leo loved to repeat described perhaps the most infamous one.

Fender hired a fellow in 1947 and taught him how to cut walnut hardwood into steel-guitar-sized pieces using a table saw without safety guards. One day the employee, whose name was never revealed, cut an odd-shaped block into a rectangle, and a piece split into a stiletto-like splinter that nudged up against his groin. As he pulled the wood through, the saw yanked and whipped it out of his hands. One piece flew to the floor, but the splintered half thrust through the man's gabardine trousers. The man yelled and the factory room fell silent. He carefully unzipped his pants and pulled the splinter out of his private part. Relating this mishap as much as forty years later, Leo could hardly stop laughing.

Many of the first Fender amplifiers and instruments were delivered in these early years with design and manufacturing defects, and many were returned for repairs or replacement. Leo made a large batch of steel guitar bodies from unseasoned, green wood, and its tannic acid caused metal parts to tarnish, electronic components to corrode, and finishes to blister. He scrapped these defective bodies, losing at least $8,000. Throughout Fender's pre-CBS years, employees had an ample supply of free hardwood for their fireplaces. (Phlange Welder, a longtime Fullerton resident, remembered picking up discarded Fender guitar necks for firewood every year at Christmas time at the Temple Baptist Church in Fullerton.)

Other problems in manufacturing seemed to thwart sales efforts. The early steel pickups often failed because of a plastic sleeve that collapsed and shorted the coil. With the early amplifiers, tubes failed, filter capacitors literally exploded, and speakers rattled. If the wrong wires vibrated their way into a short circuit, the amps caught fire. A dealer from Montgomery, Alabama, summed up his dissatisfaction with the early Fender amps in a letter to Randall dated October 8, 1947: "Our radio tech tells us that the biggest reason for breakdowns in the Fender amp is poor work putting some of the jobs together."

Leo continued working up to sixteen hours a day on his research and on orders he needed to fill. Steel guitar great Speedy West remembered buying an amplifier directly from Leo in 1947. Leo told Speedy on the phone, "Come on down—the amp's ready!" When the musician arrived at 4:00 P.M., Leo told him to wait in the office. Meanwhile, Speedy heard Leo and Ray Massie working in the back room. Minutes turned to hours. Leo, oblivious to any inconvenience he had caused, finally emerged at 1:00 A.M. with the amp. Speedy said thanks and paid him cash. The solder joints on the new amp were still hot.

Amps needed more than strong cabinets and heavy-duty components. They had to make electric instruments sound good. Electric guitars sound quite natural to ears that grew up with them. Most of Leo's generation, coming of age with Benny Goodman and Glenn Miller, held a different opinion. Getting used to the electric guitar's new tone took some time and patience. It had few antecedents in nature or among classical instruments. Even the best electrics sounded unlike loud acoustics. In the early years nascent electric guitars sounded all too often more like musical buzz saws than bird calls or bugles. Leo had an impassioned vision of how electric guitars should sound. Although he would create modern sounds, his early days in radio and the music of that era shaped his attitudes and philosophy.

Leo toiled to make electric guitars sound as pure and natural as radio-age big band trumpets and trombones, that is, more acceptable to the average pre-rock listener and musician. He designed his first amplifiers with steel players like Noel Boggs in mind. Steel players stole many licks, especially jazz-flavored slurs and Dixieland flourishes, from respected horn players, and Boggs, who strove to make the steel an accepted instrument in serious jazz circles, wanted his instrument to sound like a horn. Leon McAuliffe made trombone-like slides with his Fender. Steel players in western swing bands played horn-like arrangements and took horn players' jobs in the process. Although Fender was not making his own standard Spanish guitars yet, he wanted the ones played through his amps to sound more like steels. But here he found a dilemma. Sitting in his lab in the 1980s, he said, "Well, I still haven't decided if a guitar should sound like a trumpet playing melody or a piano playing accompaniment." He believed that both steel and standard guitars were melody instruments, but since he worked with country singers, he recognized the standard guitar's additional role as an accompanying instrument.

Leo's early amps like the Pro and the Deluxe had both microphone inputs and instrument inputs. While the microphone input gets little attention today, Leo's design was there for a reason—a whole band could plug into one amplifier, and often did. The guitar amp doubled as a PA system. With a voice and an instrument coming through the same speaker, Leo wanted to avoid the mix sounding like mush. He felt that the guitar channel needed deep bass and high treble, notes above and below a voice's midrange. So the tone control was really a mush control on his first amps; it worked on both channels simultaneously to separate the voice frequencies from the guitar frequencies. Turning it up added highs to the instrument channel and cut highs in the microphone channel. Thus an amplifier's use prescribed the way Leo engineered it; he wanted to make instruments more than loud and considered the human voice in designing his tone circuits for guitar.

The first Fender amps employed basic, well-known circuits invented and patented by the Western Electric scientists at Bell Labs. To copy these circuits, Leo simply turned to the *Radiotron Designer's Handbook*, a thick reference volume he always kept nearby. Bell Labs designed vacuum

Test amplifier on Leo's bench. He spent hours, days, and weeks working out the best combinations of components and circuits to achieve the sound he wanted.

Back panel of a Model 26.
The tubes here are mounted
horizontally. On some versions they hang.

tube amplifiers to boost the faint sound of voices along long-distance telephone cables. Manufacturers such as RCA used vacuum tube circuits in audio amplifiers and radios. Later the same type of circuits were used in record players and televisions. Western Electric patents served as a starting point, but they failed to address the specific problems in amplifying electric guitars. Leo's musician friends complained that their prewar guitar amps delayed the sound coming out. Figuring out the problem, Leo rearranged the stages of the amplifier so that, in his words, "the sound came out almost before it went in." But he still faced another problem.

Most guitar-playing kids who plugged into their parents' hi-fi system discovered the loud and obnoxious sound of an electric guitar played through an amplifier designed for some other purpose. The hi-fi's flat response revealed the guitar pickup's natural harshness; all electric guitar pickups had what Fender called "performance deficiencies," peaks and valleys in the audio spectrum. Leo realized that a good guitar amplifier should compensate for these shortcomings and make the sound coming out of the amp better than the signal coming in from the pickup. Using empirical lab procedures, he spent hours, days, weeks, and years changing values in components, rewiring critical amplifier sections, testing, listening, and trying to improve the sound of Alnico magnet pickups. His first amps, like the Dual Professional, had little negative feed-back, a design that inherently boosted treble and bass in the power amp. Then Leo started breeding successive generations of preamp circuits that produced more and more treble and presence. Strong highs and strong bass—what

some amp technicians call a "midrange dip"—became Fender's sound signature.

As Leo fine-tuned his tone circuits to make up for pick-ups' intrinsic problems, he also confronted weaknesses in loudspeakers. In the 1940s, most speakers were designed for public address systems, record players, and radios rather than for musical instrument amplifiers. Guitar amps needed durable speakers that produced stronger highs. In the early years, Fender settled for whatever speakers he could buy and accordingly adjusted his circuits; he designed them around speaker foibles, again, usually by raising the treble.

Luckily, Leo found that raising the treble—his formula for good vocal accompaniment and his solution to speaker problems—also yielded the famous Fender take-off steel guitar tone that leaped across a stage on leads. Although he never decided whether a standard electric guitar was more a lead instrument than a backup one, he created amps that provided for both. Fender amps employed bass boosts and treble boosts in the circuits long after Leo dropped the microphone channels. The means for making guitars cut through the din of voices and for improving loudspeaker performance became an end in itself.

After Kauffman left K&F, the first Fender amplifiers appeared. Collectors call these rare beauties "wooden amps" because they have hardwood cabinets, the first from the leftover boxcar full of walnut Leo bought for steel guitars. He fastened these amps together with angle iron inside the cabinet—Doc had taken the lock joint cutter home—and finished them in a variety of natural wood grains. The decorative chrome strips on the grille gave the design some flair, but at the risk of rattles. Leo built three models in this mode: the Princeton with an 8-inch speaker, the Deluxe (Model 26) with a 10, and the Professional with a 15. Jimmy Bryant used a wooden Professional—the same one Leo and Ray Massie had assembled for Speedy West—long after Fender introduced newer versions. To Leo's chagrin, Merle Travis' wooden Professional carried a nameplate that reportedly said, "Custom- made by Ray Massie." (By the late 1940s, Ray had set up his own shop in Los Angeles County.) Rival guitar builder Paul Bigsby used a wooden Model 26 on his test bench for years. Bob Wills used a one-of-a-kind Professional Leo custom-built with two 15-inch speakers.

Leo produced the first Fender tweed amp, the Dual Professional, from 1946 to early 1947 at the same time he made

The enigmatic Dual Professional—which apparently never appeared on a price list or in a catalog— was the first so-called tweed or luggage-linen-covered amp. It was made in 1946. Leo designed the model to use up a large batch of 10-inch speakers he had bought at a bargain price. This example has a non-original extension speaker jack (seen in the rear view) and lacks several tubes.

Perhaps the first magazine ad for Fender instruments, 1947.

The Direct String Pickup

Leo studied many guitar pickup designs, including Rickenbacker's where the strings traveled over the coil and through two bulky horseshoe magnets. Yet his idea for the pickup used on the radio shop guitar, K&F steel guitars, and many Fender steels came from an early phonograph pickup that had a needle suspended through the center of a small coil. In Leo's unique design, the strings traveled through the middle of the coil rather than over it. Over the years Fender produced several versions of the design for steel guitars. He called it the Direct String High Fidelity Pickup Unit, or bridge pickup for short. (Collectors call early versions boxcar or streetcar pickups because of their shape.)

All versions of the Direct String Pickup had two Alnico V magnets mounted at opposite ends of a coil. Two chrome-plated steel shoes held

the wooden amps. A Costa Mesa luggage company covered the first ones for $8 per cabinet, until Dale Hyatt slyly learned the technique by looking over a worker's shoulder. Boasting to Leo how easy covering cabinets was after mastering a few simple tricks, Hyatt began doing the work at the Fender factory. The Dual Professional's twin-speaker design was a result of another buying binge. Leo had ordered a large number of 10-inch speakers and needed a quick way to liquidate them. The model's V-front, beveled cabinet was designed to disperse sound better. At times both Fender and Randall referred to the Dual Professional as the "twin" because of its two speakers. Leo gave one to Les Paul after lunch at the Brown Mug in Fullerton one day, and Les used it in the late 1940s and early 1950s.

Following the Dual Professional, the Super also had a beveled front from 1947 to 1952. Curiously, neither the Dual Professional nor the Super appeared in the earliest Fender literature. Professional players preferred the Pro and its 15-inch speaker, perhaps because it produced a better bass response.

While Fender kept busy making custom amps for pro-

fessionals like West, the nationwide effort to sell Fender products picked up speed. Hall and Randall's responsibility was to create a viable sales network for Fender. They placed the first, although meager, national advertising in a little magazine called Music that Harry G. Stanley published, and they recruited additional salesmen to work out of state. By the end of 1947, Randall decided to relinquish his responsibilities in the radio and TV business. He would concentrate on musical instruments, leaving the rest of the extensive Radio-Tel operation to Hall. Don's job included designing the magazine ads and catalogs for Fender, attending music industry trade shows, shipping merchandise, and handling correspondence. Hall's credit department still did the billing and the credit checks. After the setbacks of 1946 and early 1947, Don quickly set out to remake Radio-Tel's Musical Instrument Division into a serious distributor. In December 1947, Leo changed his business' name to the Fender Electric Instrument Company.

the unit together. The bottom shoe acted as a bridge for the strings, and there were no pole pieces. As a result, the unit produced its own characteristic tone and response and, as mentioned, virtually eliminated the first attack on the string, the so-called pick-click. No output was generated when the string moved back and forth in a lateral motion. Rather, the pickup generated a tone when the string began its natural periodic vibration in a circular motion.

The first production version of Leo's pickup had two 1-square-inch magnets, used on K&F steels and the first Fender steels. The front of the bottom shoe had six notched teeth concentrating the magnetic field under each string. In the earliest examples, the strings traveled through six individual holes in a wooden insert placed inside the coil. Few problems arose on these.

Leo used another version of the pickup on the Organ Button steel in 1946 and 1947. The shape of the baseplate differed, and the factory recessed the 1-square-inch magnets into the body of the guitar. This version had notched teeth on the lower shoe as seen on the earlier K&F pickups. Another version, which appeared from 1946 until mid-1949 on Princeton and Deluxe model steels, used smaller magnets and lacked the teeth notched into the bottom shoe. Leo intended the pickup with smaller magnets to have less overall mass and thus enhanced high-harmonic content. Small plastic tubes that replaced the K&F-style wooden inserts were glued into the coils on some early Fender steel pickups. The strings, which had to be insulated from the coils, went through the tubes. In still later examples, a plastic sleeve

separated the strings from the coil. This plastic often shrank, warped, or crumbled. Thus the strings often came into contact with the plastic and rattled. Sometimes the aged plastic opened the coil, causing the pickup to fail. Leo said that a more solid, molded plastic piece would have solved the problem, but at the time this part was too expensive.

With the final form of the Direct String Pickup, Leo tried to increase bass tones by making the pickup wider at the bass end. In the 1980s he expressed doubt that he had achieved much with the new design. Nevertheless, the asymmetrical design looked attractive and modern when compared with the early, rather clumsy-looking ones. Fender used the new design from 1949 to 1955 on the Deluxe, Dual Professional, and Custom Triple-Neck Steels.

In 1945 Leo advertised in the Daily News Tribune that he could adapt his pickup to all stringed instruments. Although the first Spanish guitar at the radio shop did have one, through trial and error Leo realized that he needed another type of pickup for the electric Spanish guitar and the electric bass. Eventually Fender phased out the Direct String Pickup even on steel guitars in favor of improved under-string units (made with the coil under the strings). However, many steel players loved the old pickup's tone. Jody Carver won the Arthur Godfrey Talent Scouts television show in 1955 playing his 1949 Custom Triple-Neck with Direct String Pickups. He says that the design had a versatile, full-bodied sound suitable for every style from Jerry Byrd's Hawaiian tunes to big band brass-like parts.

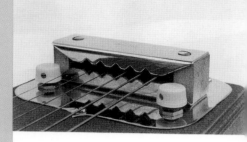

K&F lap steel.

Organ Button Model (1946–47).

Deluxe Model (1946–48), note shorter magnets.

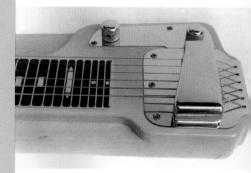

The most advanced version was used from 1949 through 1955.

When traveling western bands hit southern California, the Fender factory was usually the first stop. There Leo would either replace or refurbish all the equipment.

In the late 1940s, a steel guitar-style music education led to scenes like this: Darrell Lyons (sport coat, mustache, and Fender steel) pictured in an appearance on KGY radio with four unidentified students, who according to Lyons' press release had "skyrocketed to successful appearances in all facets of show business . . ." under his tutelage.

Kay Frances picks her Fender double-neck steel at an outdoor concert in Fullerton, circa 1950. Steel guitar—almost too easy to play badly— was fun for everyone.

Chapter 4

Fender in the Spotlight

Salesmen

Musical instrument distributors had served large territories with traveling salesmen for years. These representatives established the personal relationships with dealers necessary to make sales operations run smoothly. In the past, instrument salesmen also sold music lessons, like the dubious character Professor Harold Hill in *The Music Man*. When Leo established the Fender Electric Instrument Company, the industry still had its share of Professor Hills, but the successful traveling salesmen were for the most part honest and hardworking.

Two types of traveling salesmen worked in the business: independent jobbers and wholesale distributor representatives. Both types usually carried different lines of merchandise; before World War II, a salesman rarely represented a guitar line from just one factory. Independent jobbers bought instruments directly from the factories and sold on their own. For example, Jack Levy represented

both National and Rickenbacker guitars on the West Coast during the early 1930s. An early 1930s salesman for Chicago Musical Instruments (CMI), one of the biggest distribution companies, sold Harmony, Kay, National, Regal, and a variety of off-brands. In addition, CMI salesmen carried complete lines of banjos, violins, band instruments, and accordions. Eventually CMI owned and carried Fender's main rival, Gibson.

Radio-Tel salesmen sold only Fender guitars and amps, Shure microphones, Masco public address systems, and a variety of accessories. The emphasis on Fender meant that they walked into a music store expecting to take orders for one brand rather than orders for many. If they sold guitars, they sold Fenders. Whether by design or good fortune, Radio-Tel's arrangement with the Fender factory significantly simplified, enhanced, and focused Fender's distribution, creating another reason for its

A 1948 trade publication ad.

success. Whatever the initial problems, when Radio-Tel started to roll, Fender had the direct and effective distribution other factories like Gibson, Harmony, Kay, and National only imagined.

By and large, Radio-Tel had a highly capable and personable sales crew, notwithstanding a couple of losers. In late 1949 Jack Douglas, who had managed Tommy Dorsey's band, allegedly disappeared without accounting for $2,000 worth of merchandise. (Hall hired a credit agency to track him down.) Nevertheless, the core salesmen gathering under Fender banners at trade shows and traveling the highways of America soon gained the respect and friendship of the music industry.

Salesmen for Fender wore many hats. They maintained peace between retail dealers and the Santa Ana office, which sometimes made billing errors or sent orders late. Tempers flared when shipments arrived damaged, or COD instead of open account; salesmen took the heat. While they demonstrated instruments and took orders, they also collected unpaid bills for the credit department. From the Fullerton factory's viewpoint, salesmen acted as listening posts, determining the need for new products. They reported back new ideas, complaints, and suggestions from customers in the sales territories. Two words—patient and dedicated—describe these men. During Fender's early, lean years, they endured financial hardship and the inconvenience of constant travel while the company struggled to gain acceptance.

Charles R. Hayes

Although Hall's radio parts salesmen had tried to sell K&Fs in 1946, Radio-Tel had no full-time instrument salesman until Charles R. Hayes came on board. Leo had first hired Hayes to manage the Fender Radio Service. Previously, he had worked as a salesman and manager of the Santa Ana Montgomery Ward store. Sales managers like to think that if a man can move one product, he can move any product. Hayes, knowing little about steel guitars and amps, could still unload carloads of them. He was the quintessential salesman. Says Dale Hyatt, "Charlie Hayes could have sold snow-cones to the Eskimos."

Even with a salesman like Hayes, to move Fender steel guitars and amps in quantities large enough to keep the factory open Radio-Tel had to establish a nationwide dealer network. What better place to start than Texas, where Hayes had relatives, an area that would become Fender's first natural environment? Charlie also traveled through Arizona, Colorado, New Mexico, and Oklahoma. In the summer of 1946, he set up several Fender dealers in these states and opened accounts with many others.

Charlie Hayes, Fender's first full-time traveling salesman, 1953.

Fender's 1948 brochure was the first to show the new line of tweed amps.

When Charlie first visited Dallas, he met a music teacher named J. Fred McCord, who ran a successful instruction studio. Hayes, wanting to establish a dealer in the town, tried convincing a reluctant McCord to open a store. Other stores sent him students, however, so he told Hayes, "If I open a store, they'll stop sending me students." After several months of good-natured haggling, Hayes prevailed. McCord's Music in Dallas was established in 1947. But a problem arose—Fred had established credit only in Dallas, and he needed nationally recognized credit to buy instruments from Radio-Tel. Hayes called Harry Stanley, the owner of Oahu Publishing Company, and told him that McCord wanted to buy some Oahu merchandise (picks, sheet music, and accessories) on open account. Stanley's well-established company sold an amazing number of musical instruments and related items in the 1930s and 1940s and could absorb small losses by taking limited risks with new dealers. Because of Hayes' recommendation and Stanley's liberal attitude, the company shipped McCord the Oahu things he needed and established an open credit account.

Charlie then put Fred's Fender order—steels and amps—through to Radio-Tel, listing Oahu as a credit reference. Through this sleight-of-hand, Hayes faked out one of the Fender salesmen's biggest obstacles, F.C. Hall's unyielding credit department. (When interviewed for this book, Hall's 1940s credit manager spoke in clipped monosyllables, responding to questions as if the project were an FBI investigation. The interviewer was tempted to say, "Relax, this book is about guitars.") As a result, McCord's Music established credit and an open account with Radio-Tel. It became perhaps the most important Fender dealership in the Southwest. Many other dealers obtained the same kind of help from Charlie Hayes.

After McCord was established, Hayes offered him advice on managing the store. McCord's became a quasi-warehouse, a way station for Fender products shipped to the territory, even those bound for other stores. Moreover, McCord bought many early Fender instruments, some virtual prototypes sold to Dallas-area musicians. Understandably, McCord and Hayes became close friends. They often used Dallas as a launching pad for fishing trips and excursions to Mexico. On these trips, Charlie left his car at McCord's house and let Fred drive—Charlie hated dri-

ving and said so many times. Fred heard Charlie say, as if he could foretell future headlines, that someday he would die in an automobile.

David K. Driver

At age 50 in 1947, David K. Driver, who would soon join Charlie Hayes selling Fenders, was at a turning point: he felt too old to enter some attractive business arenas and too young to retire. Born in Missouri, he had sold life insurance and invested in real estate. He had also lived in Colorado, serving as a county clerk. When he moved to Ontario, California, searching for a new career, he had financial security and could wait to find the right job.

In early 1947, Driver answered a Radio-Tel classified ad offering a job as a traveling salesman. He had some sales experience, but none in the music business. When he drove to Santa Ana for an interview, he learned that nearly everyone involved in the Fender operation was green. During the interview, Hall invited Driver to visit the factory on the following Saturday and to meet Hayes. Driver

said yes. At the meeting, he realized that he would practically start from scratch building a clientele for Leo. Looking over the factory, he felt that Hall had exaggerated the size of the operation. However, the conversation with Hayes and the sight of Fender's humble factory did not deter Dave. He saw promise in the new instruments. Looking for a new life and perhaps an excuse for some adventure, Driver signed on and soon set out on his first road trip.

Since Radio-Tel had only two traveling salesmen in April 1947, Hall easily decided the states Driver would cover. One version of the story says that F.C., pointing to the Southwest, had told Hayes a year earlier, "You go that way." Now, pointing to the Northwest, F.C. told Driver, "You go that way." Although this colorful tale undoubtedly oversimplifies the assignment, since Hayes had already taken the Southwest from Arizona to Arkansas, Driver took the Northwest from northern California east to Minnesota. At first Randall handled the immediate southern California area.

Driver's first stop was Klamath Falls, Oregon. He continued north making his way to Washington State, every stop a new lesson in music sales. He quickly learned that dealers wanted to be asked what they needed, not told. They did not appreciate the hard-sell technique practiced by many of Fender's competitors. Deprived by Hall of catalogs or brochures, the only advertising material Dave carried was a mimeographed sheet that pictured Bob Wills and Spade Cooley using custom-built amps. When Driver took orders for an amp shown in the picture, he discovered to his chagrin that Leo's custom-built amps were not available to the public.

Driver soon learned the other side of the music business from the dealers, who according to Randall all liked Dave. He preferred doing business with dealers rather than hard-to-please, fickle studio operators who ran private music instruction programs aimed at school-age children. Driver learned that K&F instruments had a bad reputation with some of the teachers. So he avoided them and did not mention K&F to others. He quickly mastered the instrument salesman's agenda, but because of his twenty-year age difference with Randall never fully accepted Don's authority.

Salesmen for Radio-Tel and Fender Sales earned a 15 percent commission on the items they sold. They had to pay their traveling expenses except for gasoline, which they put on company credit cards. Salesmen nurtured some of their dealers, especially those in the little out-of-the-way towns with shaky economies. To keep some in business and merchandise, both Driver and Hayes on occasion paid overdue bills from Radio-Tel. Dave sprung for small repairs and for disputed shipping expenses. Sometimes an act as simple as replacing a condenser or a fuse in an amp kept a customer believing in the Fender product. Thus the salesmen built an image for Fender as a company that truly paid attention to its customers' complaints and needs.

Driver retired in 1965 soon after CBS bought Fender (chapter 14). Although he had lost money his first three years working for Radio-Tel, selling Fender guitars had ultimately made him a wealthy man, and he built a beautiful home among the redwoods in Los Gatos, California. A spacious deck overlooked the scenic Bay Area, a vista that proved that his patience had paid off.

Western Swing and the Rise of Guitars

Despite early setbacks for Hayes and Driver, Leo could not have asked for a better environment to found a business. In harder times, he probably would have failed. But the competition was still floundering because of World War II. Factory wages were low, and throughout his lifetime Leo's employees knew him as a fair employer but one who paid comparatively low wages. Everyone bought American because foreign competition did not exist. Until 1949, when a minor recession hit, the economy was booming, and consumers had disposable income.

But most important, Fender's success was tied to a trend in popular music—the historic rise of the guitar. Since the 1930s, guitars—steels and standards—had made many inroads into pop music and had a new expanded role made possible by the advent of amplification. When Leo started his radio shop in 1938, most bandleaders used standard guitar for rhythm accompaniment. Boosted by an amp, the standard guitar was coming into its own as a solo instrument. Charlie Christian is often credited as the this period's most important and influential electric guitar innovator. He played lead with Benny Goodman and borrowed from the styles of earlier jazz artists, notably reed players, to create a new voice for strings. Radio star Alvino Rey, who played both steel and standard guitars, was an early Rickenbacker and Gibson advocate. He led an orchestra heavy on guitar arrangements. His mainstream music celebrity status and endorsement of the electric guitar carried weight on both coasts.

Toward the end of World War II, the Big Band era peaked. Small independent record labels like Victory, Four Star, Atlas, and Bel-Tone, several located near Leo in Los Angeles, championed new styles of music, including incipient rock and roll. Roots-style bands, usually small combos, played dance music: boogie-woogie, rhythm and blues, western swing, and honky-tonk country. (Leo was well aware of the trend: he sold records at his radio shop.) Despite the need for better instruments, more of these groups adopted electric guitars after the war, and small dance combos grew in popularity. The guitar, still shunned and even scorned by many for its working-class, hillbilly connotations, became more acceptable. Les Paul's recordings and the Nat King Cole Trio, featuring Oscar Moore's electric guitar, inspired an army of imitators, all potential customers for new, innovative instruments. But the guitar's biggest promoters were out of pop's mainstream. They played the emerging styles such as western swing.

Believe In Yourself

There are thousands of people in the world, many of highest position and intelligence, who are not able to read a simple scale and play it on any instrument—they do not know a measure from a rest, or a leger line from a triplet.

BUT YOU DO!

You are doing things every day that others envy—and you are doing them because you have worked, studied and practiced—they are accomplishments you have worked for and no one can take them away from you.

If you do not believe in yourself, no one else will—there is a lot of truth in the idea that if you believe you can do a thing, it will be done.

Without confidence you are lost—but with confidence the world is yours!

DO YOU BELONG TO AN ORCHESTRA ?

Do you know the thrill of playing in an orchestra—of being an important part of a musical organization? It is something you don't want to miss!

GEORGE WEBSTER'S ORCHESTRA

Printed in U. S. A.
19

(Below) Charlie Hayes, left, socialized with Dallas dealer J. Fred McCord and his wife on many occasions.

(Above) One of countless ads extolling the virtues of "proper" music played on stringed instruments. This one appeared in the 1930s on the back of sheet music. Through such efforts (which countered the guitar's negative image) the guitar became more acceptable to middle-class parents who paid for music lessons.

Bob Wills and the Texas Playboys invented western swing, a countrified version of big band dance music with roots in traditional fiddle tunes, ragtime jazz, and the blues. The Playboys shaped pop to some degree with Wills classics like "San Antonio Rose," made famous by Bing Crosby, and Leo's favorite, "Faded Love." Western swing carried through to modern country-western with such artists as Merle Haggard, George Strait, and Asleep at the Wheel. Because of its hard-driving dance beat, it also helped shape rock and roll.

One critic in the 1940s called Wills' sophisticated band "cowboy-attired musicians that sounded like city-slickers." Most were trained musicians, and many played with other top swing bands of the era. The size and configuration of Bob's band changed over the years; he used horns, piano, drums, fiddles, and even plectrum banjo. After World War II, the guitarist and steel player sometimes joined an electric mandolinist, forming an electric string ensemble that could blast most horn sections off a bandstand. But most important, after the war, Wills usually featured an explosive lead guitar player. Many early rock guitar solos from

players like Scotty Moore, Elvis Presley's first guitarist, had their roots in the Playboys' style. Jimmy Wyble, Junior Barnard, and Eldon Shamblin, all heavily influenced by Charlie Christian, soloed with Bob Wills. Barnard used his hollowbody electric and early Fender amp to produce snarls, growls, and other stylistic distortions. If he had grown up a generation later in England, he would have been quite at home with the Yardbirds' Eric Clapton, Jeff Beck, and Jimmy Page.

Leo knew that Wills was probably the biggest regional star in the West and Southwest. Thousands of defense plant workers from Texas, Arkansas, and Oklahoma stayed in California after the war, as did many southern-born servicemen. The state's newest immigrants were Bob Wills' biggest audience. Bob Wills, with his Texas-Oklahoma origins, played the soundtrack for California's real-life *Grapes of Wrath*. The band had followed the displaced workers to the West Coast and filled the largest ballrooms in California. (Bob and his boys had also come to California to play roles in a few Hollywood Western movies.) In the postwar decade the Playboys set attendance records that stood for years.

At a time when a ticket to a Wills dance usually cost $1, Wills was out-grossing Tommy Dorsey and Benny Goodman. Bob's 1945 income was $340,000, mainly from sold-out dances. He recorded, but not nearly fast enough. From 1945 to 1950, virtually every side the Playboys cut became a hit. The demand was so great that in 1947 Columbia reissued seventy of the group's recordings from the 1930s. Furthermore, Bob was sought as a guest of honor and parade marshal at rodeos all over California. Leo wanted the Wills band to use Fender equipment.

Leo made a concerted effort to meet the top musicians and entertainers like Alvino Rey and Bob Wills where they worked. The rather square young entrepreneur had few reasons to frequent bars and dances before he chose musical instrument making as a career. Now he ventured into the dazzling world of entertainment, hanging out with celebrities and pretty waitresses and calling it work. Carrying an amp and a steel guitar fresh from the lab, he would stand in line outside dances. Sometimes the guitars were so newly designed they had no finish. Constantly changing circuits, he often finished a test amp in the afternoon and had it on a bandstand that night. He would buy his ticket and promptly rush towards the musicians. Sometimes Ray Massie or Dale Hyatt went with Leo. Other times they went on their own.

When the Fender men were not following one of the top bands, they drove to Los Angeles area clubs that featured guitarists. The 97th St. Corral in Los Angeles, with seating for 300 people, boasted "the biggest beer bar in the West." In 1946 bands booked there included Red Murrell and his Ozark Playboys, T. Texas Tyler and his Oklahoma Melody Boys, and Olie Rasmussen and his Nebraska Corn Huskers. During the same year, Deuce Spriggens and his band played at the Riverside Rancho in Los Angeles, and Hank Penny played at the Painted Post in North Hollywood. The Del Rio Club in San Pedro featured Jimmy La Fever and his Saddle Pals. Leo also listened to western bands with guitar players at the Hideout in Hawthorne and the Harmony Park Ballroom in Anaheim.

Before the music started, Leo or one of his men demonstrated products to the players. Many of these guitarists just barely survived with their old instruments and gladly tried the new ones for Leo. Players yearned for better equipment. Here was this short, knowledgeable man letting them try equipment that improved every week. Alvino Rey used a converted public address amplifier for his guitar until he met Fender at a job one night. Leo promptly gave him a Fender amp, and the PA was history. Soon Rey also retired his Gibson and Rickenbacker guitars to play Fenders exclusively.

(Top) **Bob Koefer (right), a well-known steel player of the early 1950s, worked with Pee Wee King, who wrote the classic "The Tennessee Waltz." Recorded by Patti Page, the song was one of the biggest hits in popular-music history and helped spur country music's early 1950s commercial surge.**

(Bottom) **The Texas Playboys circa 1947, complete with their regulation boots, hats, and Fender amps. This version of the band featured Herb Remington on steel, Tiny Moore on mandolin, and Eldon Shamblin on guitar.**

Bob Wills circa 1947 with his custom-built Fender amp, which according to Leo had two 15-inch speakers. The decorative chrome strips went horizontally, unlike those on production-model wooden amps.

Leo's efforts with Alvino Rey and many other musicians paid off. As early as 1945, some of the most important guitar players on the West Coast used Leo's amps. Noel Boggs played steel with the Texas Playboys in 1944 and 1946. He lived in Downey, a short hop from Fullerton. No one remembers how Leo met Noel—it was either at the radio shop or on a bandstand—but they became fast friends. Leo would eventually be godfather to Noel's daughter, Debbie.

The steel player's steel player, Boggs took the instrument into new pop and jazz realms with complex voicings and arrangements other players thought impossible. His ear and gift for music guided Leo in his quest for perfection. In return, he gave Noel new equipment, including one of the first K&F amps and the first double-neck steel made at the radio shop. Noel gladly tested every steel and amplifier model Leo made in the early days. He also played the role of matchmaker, bringing Leo and western bandleader Spade Cooley together.

Cooley, who much later murdered his wife in a crime that shook Los Angeles, led one of California's most popular western swing bands in the 1940s.

Boggs also introduced Leo to Bob Wills, for Leo a dream come true since Bob ordered amps for his whole band, including the special model with dual 15-inch speakers for himself. In less than a year, Fender products had become the *de rigueur* sound of western swing. They pleased Bob so much he established an unwritten rule: the band used nothing but Fenders. It was an unequivocal endorsement. In 1947 a picture of the band appeared on Leo's first known sales brochure. That Wills actually used Fenders gave Randall's sales effort enormous credibility.

The experience with Wills and the other traveling bands also helped Leo design better instruments. By sending his latest creations on tours, he put his progeny through fire and water. Road-tested Fenders knocked around in buses for thousands of miles, enduring countless nights in dance halls and bars. Leo saw the wear and tear working musicians gave to instruments. Tiny Moore, fiddle and electric mandolin player, remembered that when the Texas Playboys' tour bus hit southern California, the Fender factory was usually the first stop. There Leo would either replace or refurbish all the equipment. In doing so, he learned what happened to amps hastily moved on and off bandstands every night. He replaced speakers that broke rattling down the highway between gigs and discovered ways to make his equipment easier to service. Leo also padded his wallet. Moore said that Wills carried suitcases stuffed with ballroom proceeds, expected no favors from Fender, and always paid cash.

Working with professionals inspired Leo to make rugged equipment that could withstand all kinds of abuse, and he quickly learned to make amp cabinets as strong as stadium bleachers. Fender sought electrical components just as lasting. Kauffman had told Leo about Electro String's early quality control problems. According to the story, George Beauchamp had made his amps more reliable by using parts with 25 percent or more value than called for. If he needed a 20-watt speaker, he would use a 25-watt one. Leo saw the wisdom in overbuilding amplifiers in this manner. Thus the features he put into test-level professional equipment filtered down to products he designed and built for amateurs. Leo's factory made a student Champ Amp just as strong as Bob Wills' Pro. Likewise, professionals could buy mass-produced equipment just as good as the road-tested prototypes. An entire line of professional-quality steel guitars and amplifiers became one of Fender's lasting legacies.

Three variations of the Champion lap steel, Fender's best.

More Student Steels, Double- and Triple-Necks

In 1949 Fender dropped the Princeton steel and introduced a new Deluxe single-neck 6-string model with a totally redesigned body. It went through a revision before production. Don Randall described the first version in a 1949 letter to Charlie Hayes; the same instrument appeared in the 1949 catalog. The catalog picture showed that the ill-fated design had celluloid body binding and controls mounted through the body rather than on a control plate. The production model Deluxe had the improved, redesigned Direct String Pickup, but its tone and volume controls were mounted on a chrome control plate. The sculpted body on the production model had no binding. An 8-string single-neck Deluxe was available by 1950. Fender offered both 6- and 8-string Deluxe models in blonde and natural dark walnut finishes. (The last order for the Deluxe Eight was on May 18, 1955, while the last order for the Deluxe Six was on March 6, 1956.)

The Champion guitar made from 1949 to 1955, the quintessential Fender steel, has become the best-known Fender played on the lap. Don Randall thought that beginners would feel better about playing if their instruments were *champions* rather than mere *students*. Due to a request from the Grossman Music Corporation, which had registered *Champion* as a trademark in 1943, Fender changed the name to the Student Steel after April 16, 1951. The steel was available either by itself or in a set with a Champion 600 (later Champ 600) amplifier. When Leo designed the Champion, he atoned for the flaws in his earlier steels, missing few details with this new instrument. It had a detachable fingerboard, his notchless nut, and a new notchless bridge designed to eliminate string rattles. The new guitar employed tone and volume controls with chrome-plated brass knobs.

Workers painted the earliest Champion bodies blonde.

Worker hand-sanding a Deluxe steel body in the late 1940s.

Ad from 1949–50.

Soon the factory applied (in the particularly dangerous procedure that upset Fullerton's fire marshal so much) an acetate shrink-wrap sometimes called plastic mother-of-pearl. The same material covered many toilet seat lids, giving it the nickname "mother of toilet seat." Fender usually used a pearly yellow color and rarely a blue-gray that was not mentioned in company literature.

The Champion boasted an adjustable pickup almost identical to the standard guitar lead pickup Leo would introduce in 1950. However, the mounting screws on the Champion's were different, with no metal elevator plate underneath. The steels featured Kluson tuners, and the strings loaded through the body at the bridge end. Fred McCord, with his experience as a music instructor, remembers suggesting a hand rest for students: Leo's new chrome-plated pickup cover doubled as the hand rest.

While Leo made highly regarded student steels, he also made state-of-the-art double- and triple-neck steels for professionals. He had understood the tuning limitations of the single-neck 6-string steel guitars since befriending Noel Boggs during World War II. In early 1945 Boggs played a double-8-string-neck Epiphone. Most other professionals also used double- or triple-necks. Soon after the K&F lap steels went into production, Leo laid plans for his professional-level instruments.

Doc Kauffman remembered working on a double- or triple-neck steel in early 1946 before he left K&F. He also remembered leaving it unfinished and assumed that Leo scrapped it. Dale Hyatt says that he and Ray Massie started from scratch building what Dale believed to be the first Fender double-neck steel. The conflict in memories does suggest that two different instruments were made at K&F. Kauffman said that his guitar had aluminum binding on the edges. The one that Dale Hyatt described came close to the example illustrated in the 1947 Radio-Tel advertising literature. Leo took a photo of Noel Boggs playing what Leo remembered as the first double-neck, but it is obscured by a fancy Western shirt and glare from stage lights.

Steel player Herb Remington, who also worked with Bob Wills and the Texas Playboys just after World War II, told another confusing and conflicting story of the first professional Fender steel. Remington stated in a *Guitar Player* magazine interview that he took what he believed to be the first Fender double-neck on the road with the Playboys. He described a crude prototype instrument with threaded pipe legs. The necks were level rather than stair-stepped as on later multiple-neck Fender steels. No doubt Remington used one of the early Fender double-necks. However, Noel Boggs either had it first or had an earlier version. One photograph Leo took of Boggs shows that he played a double-neck with no legs. The bulky guitar sat on a table.

LEON McAULIFFE
Plays A
Fender ELECTRIC

Sincerely,
Leon McAuliffe

(Opposite) Noel Boggs plays the first Fender double-neck steel on July 3, 1946. The guitar was sitting on what looks like a table.

(Above) Leon McAuliffe was one of western swing's biggest stars and one of Leo's first advocates.

(Right) While worker Paul Dallmeir and a lady friend watch, Herb Remington tests a double-neck in one of the steel factory buildings, February 1950.

51

The earliest known catalog picture of a Fender double-neck, dubbed the Dual Eight Professional Steel, appeared in 1947. Curiously, Radio-Tel did not include it in an earlier sales folder. The 1947 guitar came in either a light wood (ash or maple) or dark wood (walnut or mahogany) natural finish. It used a boxcar-style Direct String Pickup on both 8-string necks, chrome-plated fingerboards with enameled Roman numeral fret markers, and a 2-position toggle for switching between necks. Customers could order it with detachable legs.

Leo updated the design in 1948 by replacing the old toggle with a 3-position lever switch. Players could then activate both necks simultaneously. Another improvement was painted fretboards that reduced glare and reflections. In 1948 Radio-Tel offered the painted blonde finish in place of the light, natural finish; walnut became the choice for dark finishes. Leo further updated the Dual Eight Professional Steel in 1949 with the final version of the Direct String Pickup. While retaining the 3-position switch, the guitar now had block-shaped fingerboard markers rather than Roman numerals. Fender dropped the double-neck with Direct String Pickups in the spring of 1955.

Steels with 8-string necks were the best professional-level instruments of the day, but some players wanted guitars with two 6-string necks. To meet this need and to enhance Fender's regular line with a less expensive double-neck, the company built the Dual Six Professional from 1950 to the spring of 1956.

Making a triple-neck steel guitar was a logical step to cover the professional market. Although no precise records of the first ones exist, Fender made some well before Radio-Tel advertised them in the 1949 catalog. Triple-necks appeared as early as 1947, and production records for 1948, although incomplete, show that Fender also made several in the first half of that year. By Leo's foresighted design, equipment for making the double-neck steels accommodated the construction of triple-necks, with the third neck easily bolting into place. Dave Driver remembered that Noel Boggs was upset when he learned that the first Fender triple-neck went to a friend of Charlie Hayes in Texas. Boggs still received one of the earliest ones, as did Leon McAuliffe.

The features on these early models corresponded to the features on the first advertised Fender double-necks. The triple-neck had a scale length of 22 1/2 inches, a volume control and a tone control, a 3-position lever switch, and a toggle switch. The earliest ones also used

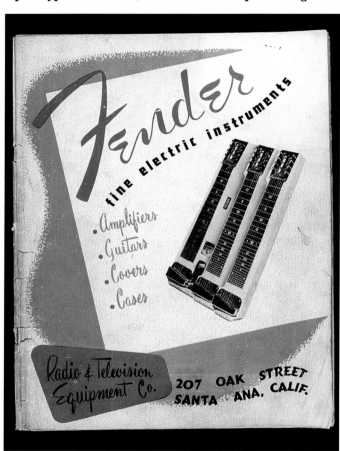

Catalog #1 from 1949, the first full-size over-the-counter Fender catalog for consumers, showed TV-front amps, the redesigned Dual Eight Professional, the Custom Triple-Neck, a prototype Deluxe steel, and the new Champion steel guitar.

chrome fretboards with Roman numerals and 8-string Direct String Pickups with symmetrical profiles—the boxcar pickups.

Don Randall officially introduced the Custom Triple-Neck as a redesigned version in early 1949 with a national ad campaign. The Custom was available through 1955; the last order to the factory dated March 23, 1955. It had a tone and volume control and two switches. With the toggle switch in one position, the player could use all three necks simultaneously. In the second position, which activated the 3-position lever switch, players could pick one neck and deaden the other two. This steel used the modern-looking asymmetrical Direct String Pickups, and the factory applied one of two finishes: blonde or natural dark walnut. This instrument topped all Fender steels until the Stringmasters of late 1953.

A worker pulls a nail that had helped elevate a newly painted steel body on the drying shelves. The same technique, which left some small holes under pickguards, was later used on standard guitars and basses.

Fred Fullerton, George's father and another longtime Fender employee, assembling a double-neck steel on a jig made by Leo. A girlie calendar on the wall was turned to December 1949, although Leo probably took the picture several months later (a template for cutting the Esquire standard guitar, which was introduced in 1950, hangs on a wall to the rear).

Two ads from 1948.

Left to right, Champion 800, Dual
Professional, 1948 Deluxe, Champion
600, and two early double-neck steels.
The Champion 800 was replaced by
the two-tone Champion 600 in 1949.

TV-Front Amplifiers

Fender introduced the so-called TV-front tweed Princeton, Deluxe, and Pro amps in the summer of 1948. Collectors coined the name *TV-front* to describe the picture-tube-shaped grille, which again illustrated television's postwar rise and influence on Leo. (He must have intentionally designed these cabinets to look like televisions.) He built the cabinets with ultra-strong, neatly cut lock joints that made lighter but even sturdier units. The standout from this period was the Pro, used extensively by Hank Thompson's, Spade Cooley's, and other western swing bands. The first Fender amplifier advertised in jazz music's *Down Beat* magazine introduced the Fender name to the national market. With an amazing bass response and high-fidelity sound for its time, the Pro opened many doors for Leo among professionals of all musical persuasions. The TV-front Deluxe quickly became the standard amp for small groups.

The first TV-front student amp, the short-lived, rare 1948 Champion 800, has become a Holy Grail to some serious collectors. It featured a new gray tweed, unlike the buff tweed used on other Fenders. The company replaced the 800 in 1949 with the popular Champion 600, covered in two-tone leatherette.

TV-front amps remained relatively unchanged during their years in production. However, the first versions used what collectors call straight tweed (as opposed to later diagonal tweed) and dyed wool fabric grilles also found on the Dual Professionals. Starting about 1949, Leo switched to brown monk's cloth for TV-front grilles. In the summer of 1951, he added a longer upper back plate to protect tubes in transit.

As the 1940s drew to a close, Leo Fender and Don Randall, with the help of salesmen and musicians, had established a name known throughout the Southwest. Listening closely to feedback from musicians, Leo had come a long way since Doc Kauffman first walked into the radio shop. Always creative, Fender learned to use others' ideas and solve problems—and he dealt with many problems in the early days. He watched what other companies made, and he learned the music business. Many players already considered Fender the leading innovator in steel guitar and amplifier design, and thus the company captured a major portion of the market from the older, established companies such as Rickenbacker, National, Gibson, and Epiphone.

1949 ad.

(Right top to bottom) Fender's first wood shop resembled a furniture maker's or cabinet shop more than a guitar builder's. Here a worker rounds off the corners and edges of a TV-front cabinet with a large disk sander, 1950.

A subsequent task was fine sanding the cabinet.

Another worker applied the tweed covering with glue and cut off the excess. Knots in the pine cabinets oozed pitch, which in time could cause yellow spots in the fabric.

However, Leo still struggled. He was in debt up to his magnifier glasses. His inefficient, chaotic factory lacked organization and strict quality control. If Leo needed to get something done, he usually taught himself how to do it. He wasted days, weeks, and months tinkering with ideas (such as an electric piano) he eventually discarded. The design of saleable products proceeded at a snail's pace. Furthermore, Fender remained a regional curiosity in some regards. Even so, Don and his salesmen attended the national trade shows and established dealers in many states by 1949.

Most revolutions take place in chaos. From the ashes of the old order, a new system based on different ideas arises. Leo Fender was not exactly George Washington, but amid the music industry's disarray after the war, Leo nurtured a revolution. In 1949 Fender envisioned a whole new family of electric stringed instruments in addition to the steels and amps he already made; he planned a piano, violin, tenor guitar, mandolin, standard guitar, and bass guitar. Amazingly, events had not overwhelmed him. By now Leo's business was more than just the sideline he and Doc created at the radio shop. Increasingly, Leo carried his future in a guitar case. Like most successful revolutionaries, he had little or nothing to fall back on if he failed. As Fender looked back over his shoulder for the creditors and tax collectors, he set the stage for his most significant contribution to music: the commercially successful solid-body electric guitar.

Covering Champion 600 amps with two-tone
leatherette, 1952.

A 1952 Princeton Amp.

A pre-1951 TV-front Deluxe
with the short back panel.

Fender said with an inventor's insight, "It isn't a radically different thing that becomes a success; it is the thing that offers an improvement on an already proven item."

Roy Watkins, wearing a white hat, field tested guitars for Leo in late 1949 and 1950. Here he backed up a show in Fullerton with the second prototype of the Fender Esquire standard guitar. The singer played an early Esquire, 1950. Leo's first mission was to build instruments for professionals.

Parents bought thousands of electric steel and standard guitars for their children in the late 1930s and 1940s from studio operators. Don Randall says, "Some of the kids even got a little musical training." Randall knew that an improved, more economical guitar would only boost these sales.

Chapter 5

Towards an Improved Electric Guitar

Traditional Notions

As the recording industry commercialized country, blues, and western swing, fretted instruments grew rapidly in popularity. Some well-placed but misguided people thought the industry had an image problem: the "wrong" people played guitar. Mass-produced fretted instruments like the mandolin, guitar, and banjo had filtered down to the lower classes through mail-order catalogs, traveling salesmen, and music stores. Stringed instruments, despite their classical roots, had become folk instruments, tools for unschooled musicians playing simplistic music. The same Americans who embraced Up with People in the 1970s had cringed at poor blacks and rural whites playing guitars in the 1930s and 1940s. It was feared that jungle boogie-woogie rhythms and the nasal whine of hillbillies might incite a Bolshevik conspiracy and the fall of civilization. Robert Johnson (who was poisoned with a glass of strychnine-laced whiskey after a three-day fling with a married woman) and Hank Williams (who would be found overdosed in the back seat of his Cadillac in 1953) made lousy poster boys for a clean-cut, strait-laced America.

Music-industry insiders realized that business would improve even more if the guitar acquired the same air of respectability that surrounded pianos, violins, and band instruments. Guitar makers hoped people would believe that dedicated, classically trained musicians played guitars. A propaganda effort ensued that promoted guitar, mandolin, and banjo playing as art forms. While promoting high art seemed like a lofty pursuit, the motive was profit. Smart guitar dealers tried to do what band instrument salesmen had done for years: place instruments into public schools. Guitar dealers had targeted school children since the days traveling salesmen sold Hawaiian guitars door-to-door. Convincing the public that real musicians

Vivi-Tone made a solidbody standard guitar in the mid-1930s, but it failed in the marketplace.

Hank Karch's seemingly noble fight against the "hillbilly monopoly" promoted his own self interest—selling more sheet music.

played guitar made teaching guitar in public schools more acceptable. Dealers envisioned every child taking guitar lessons and every school district buying guitars. Schools already bought Oscar Schmidt autoharps for teaching music theory. If the guitar industry could improve its image, it too could feed at the public trough.

The American Guild of Banjoists, Mandolinists, and Guitarists presented the establishment's mythical ideal, thus bolstering the guitar as a classical instrument with lasting, squeaky-clean cultural worth. The Guild's official publication, *The Fretted Instrument News*, created the image of "real music . . . [and] properly taught performers." It sponsored annual conventions and contests for young players. According to the Guild, fretted instruments promoted "fellowship mixed with musicianship." In 1947 Hank Karch, Secretary-Treasurer of the Guild, articulated lofty goals for manufacturers, publishers, retailers, and music schools that included placing fretted instruments into the public schools, publishing "proper music" for the public-school fretted-instrument orchestrations, and encouraging "good" music on the radio in competition to the "hillbilly monopoly."

From reading Hank Karch's articles in *The Music Trades*, one gathers that he loved fretted instruments in his own limited way. But his worst nightmare was a world where children with no clue about music theory played instruments just for fun—for instance, a world where every child played electric guitar in a garage band. His vision of an ideal world included America's youth joining groups like Ontario, Canada's Waddington School of Music Plectro-Symphony. Wrote Karch, "The American people do not know what fret music is until they have heard these players." Proper music played on the frets was something to rave about, and Karch had his heroes, such as Segovia, master of the guitar; Bernardo De Pace, wizard of the mandolin; and Eddie Peabody, "king of the banjo." One has to wonder if Hank Karch, who probably spoke for the majority of old-timer guitar manufacturers, dealers, and teachers, had ever heard Les Paul, Charlie Christian, Earl Scruggs, or Leon McAuliffe. Eddie Peabody epitomized banjo playing like Slim Whitman epitomized country singing.

Just as the old-timers had limited notions of musicianship and music, their ideas about guitars went back to the 1800s when many people thought guitars were as much art objects as musical instruments. The best guitars made in the 1930s and 1940s, many claimed, were hand-crafted in this European tradition. Stromberg and D'Angelico made fine guitars. Gibson, Epiphone, and Martin did, too. Bona fide builders spent years learning how to fashion and fit internal bracing, carve tops, and shape necks. For companies in the purist tradition, the process

Early-1930s promotional photo for John Dopyera's Dobro company, which made pre-electric guitars with resonators.

was just as important as the product. Logically, the most expensive guitars took the longest to make, but did not necessarily sound or perform better than cheaper models. For example, a Martin D-28 had the same construction as a D-45. However, a D-45 cost twice as much because of its decorative inlays, pretty embellishments that added nothing to the instrument's tone quality or volume.

John Dopyera, who began as a violin maker and repairman, knew that guitarists playing popular music in the 1920s demanded brisker guitars. When traditional guitar-building technology and the old companies failed to produce them, he decided to fill the void. He revolutionized the guitar industry by inventing the National and Dobro guitars. Dopyera's instruments, precursors to electric guitars, used internal metal diaphragms that looked like pie tins but nevertheless amplified sound. Combining Old and New World techniques, workers assembled National guitars with the care of Old World craftsmen. The New World part of the process was predictably less sensitive: metal bodies were stamped out on a press originally designed to make automobile fenders. The National and Dobro companies still made many expensive, highly engraved models—art objects in their own right. Yet Dopyera's focus was on improving guitar technology and production methods. His overall concern was making guitars with consistent tone and volume; handmade guitars all sounded different to him.

With metal-bodied guitars, Dopyera unofficially founded the new, anything-that-works school of guitar making. His profitable approach inspired a host of characters unburdened by the traditional means of making instruments. The new makers brought skills from other fields to the guitar industry. Few either wanted or pretended to learn traditional crafts, so the guitars they produced broke most of the rules. These new makers lived in the real world, designed guitars for working musicians, and embraced any manufacturing means that cut production time and costs and made guitars louder.

Early Electric Guitars

The biggest breakthrough with this approach came in late 1931 when Dopyera's former partner, Kauffman's friend George Beauchamp, hatched the idea for a fully electric guitar with a solid, non-resonant body. Employing a solid body, or near-solid body, was an important key to cutting manufacturing costs. Traditional bodies often had three dozen pieces of wood carefully cut, shaped, and glued together. They took weeks or even months to assemble. Fabricating a solid body was easy, predictable, and quick. For his first steel guitars, Beauchamp selected cast aluminum; in 1935 he introduced Bakelite steels and standards. Whatever the material, Electro String was more

61

successful making steel guitars than standard guitars. Bakelite standard guitars went out of tune, were awkward to hold, and weighed too much. Furthermore, the poorly placed pickup interfered with the player's right hand. Still, these guitars represented a breakthrough.

In 1933 maverick musician/inventor Lloyd Loar formed a company called Vivi-Tone that produced at least two types of electric guitars, one with a solid wood body. (Loar is most famous for inventing Gibson's famous F-5 mandolin and L-5 guitar in the 1920s.) Vivi-Tones failed in the marketplace because they performed poorly; they sounded lousy. Yet they also chipped away at the guitar establishment's notion that a real guitar had a handcrafted, hollow body. As that notion slowly changed, a window of opportunity opened after World War II.

Enter Leo Fender

In 1949, players still bought traditional acoustic guitars with pickups like Epiphone's Zephyr De Luxe Regent, which was a great guitar for some styles. But the need for a more durable, cheaper electric guitar that fit new playing styles—what early solidbodies promised but could not deliver—still existed. Leo Fender saw his opportunity and started where others had left off. In this regard, he was like Robert Fulton. Many people believe that Fulton invented the steamboat, but he had simply created an improved steamboat. Thirty-five steamboats had sailed prior to his. Luckily, he did his work at the dawn of the industrial revolution, making the small but crucial technical advances that led to a commercial bonanza. Likewise, Leo invented an improved electric guitar and capitalized on a turning point in music history, the decline of the Big Band era at the end of World War II.

Leo Fender's upstart, anything-goes attitude made capitalizing on events and taking risks easy. He too came to guitar manufacturing unburdened by traditions and inhibitions. He cavalierly pushed machines beyond their limits, violating a taboo among trained machinists—people who knew better. He had never visited a guitar factory except his own. His manual skills were self-taught, and he designed and made many of his own tools. The musical instrument manufacturing centers were in Chicago, New York, and Europe. In his formative early years, Leo never shared ideas or met with music people from the East, waited until the late 1950s before attending trade shows, and did not go regularly until the 1980s. Like Angelenos Dopyera, Rickenbacher, and Beauchamp, Fender was an outsider, a California rebel with a cause.

While Fender was an outsider to other makers, he made himself an insider to musicians and music. He lived close to the burgeoning and ever-changing entertainment capital of the world, Hollywood, where regional music styles mixed in the name of commercialism. He heard and enjoyed all the popular styles, including a heavy dose of guitar music, more than he would have heard living in Chicago or New York. The West Coast attracted many Hawaiian musicians and their popular guitar sounds. California, once part of Mexico, always had Mexican music which revolved around the guitar. The music of migrant workers from Oklahoma, Arkansas, and Texas quickly flooded the state in the 1930s and assimilated into Orange County's mainstream. Leo, who had grown up on a farm, had no airs. He was open to all styles and especially liked the guitars he heard in country, folk, and western swing. After World War II, Leo heard much western swing on both records and radio.

Catering to California's new citizens, western swing and hillbilly bands filled local radio airways with live broadcasts and disc jockey shows featuring records, transcriptions, and interviews with musicians. Spade Cooley and his Western Dance Gang aired live on KFVD radio from the Santa Monica Ballroom every Friday, Saturday, and Sunday. With a healthy dose of hillbilly music, Buck Nation's weekly show on KFI radio pitched Sunny Vitamins. Cliffie Stone's Western Stars played on KFWB, and KXLA had two western shows, the *Harmony Homestead* and *Dinnerbell Roundup*. Bandleader Red Murrell's radio show on KGER featured the Three Shifless Skonks. Mexico's super station XERB in Rosarito Beach—which later made Wolfman Jack a star—could be heard over much of the Southwest. XERB went 100 percent western in 1946 with shows hosted by Spade Cooley, T. Texas Tyler, and Snuffy Smith. *Roundup Time* on the ABC network, heard in the Los Angeles area on Saturdays, showcased western music.

Since 1944, Leo had wanted to make a better guitar for working musicians, especially those he heard playing western music. In the November 8, 1949, *Daily News Tribune*, he said that his original idea came to him while

A 000-18 Martin converted to electric by Leo at the Fender Radio Service during or shortly after World War II. This guitar was originally owned by Fred Clay, who performed with Bob Stacks and the Nighthawks in southern California.

(Opposite) Leo in a self portrait, circa 1949.

repairing a guitar at his radio shop. He dismantled and studied the instrument, discovering several ways to better the tone, increase the volume, and otherwise improve its performance. Fender said with an inventor's insight, "It isn't a radically different thing that becomes a success; it is the thing that offers an improvement on an already proven item." Sometime after this experience, he and Doc made the radio shop standard guitar pictured in their patent. A letter Leo wrote to Don Randall in 1950 indicates that Fender had made another electric Spanish guitar in 1945 for entertainer Bob Stack. (By the 1980s Leo had forgotten all its details.) He also converted an acoustic 000-18 Martin guitar into an acoustic-electric for Fred Clay, who performed with Stack's band, the Nighthawks. Leo made at least one or two other long-lost primordial elec-

tric standards and conversions in the late 1940s. However, he was too busy with steel guitars and amplifiers to concentrate on other worthwhile ideas. But as Fender steels and amplifiers became well known and respected, especially on the West Coast and in the Southwest, the market became saturated. Randall's salesmen needed something new. Leo once said that he started working seriously on his standard guitar after Charlie Hayes requested a Fender Spanish model.

Hayes, out in the field daily, knew that players and dealers would welcome an improved standard guitar that better fit the budget of the average player. They needed louder guitars with no feedback. At dance-hall volume, the feedback from a typical acoustic-electric guitar—even an esteemed, expensive Gibson or Epiphone, for example—

Leo Fender met Les Paul in 1948 when Paul was playing one of the so-called log guitars, homemade contraptions with no commercial pretensions or potential. The idea for a solidbody like this went back to George Beauchamp's 1930s Rickenbackers.

rolled like a big rig with no brakes down a mountain. Once one of the old hollowbody guitars started its roll, it was hard to stop. Some tricks allowed louder volumes. Players stuffed rags, pillows, and sand into their guitars, while others made long guitar cords and placed their amps at the far end of the bandstand. Some of these guitars may have been elegant and crafted in the revered Old World tradition, but if players had to stuff them full of rags to get them to perform, something was obviously wrong.

Leo recognized another problem besides feedback. Without compensated bridges, the first electric guitars sounded woefully out of tune. Unlike a violin's perfect tuning, guitars use a tempered tuning like a piano's. Fretted instruments have set musical intervals between notes. These intervals, the distances between frets, are mathematical compromises. Furthermore, a string's gauge (thickness) affects intonation. As a result, all guitars play slightly out of tune compared with, say, violins. The rich overtones of an acoustic guitar mask the dissonance just as make-up covers freckles. But string-driven electric guitar pickups eliminate most masking overtones, removing the make-up and highlighting the dissonance. So, an electric guitar demands more accurate intonation, the means for making all notes on the fingerboard sound in tune. Some companies compensated the bridge at the factory to improve intonation. However, the best solution was providing a way for the player to adjust the length of each string. In the late 1940s, few guitars had adjustable bridges.

Leo took Hayes' suggestion and started to design a Fender standard guitar. The project promised to fix problems with bridges, feedback, pickups, and construction; it gathered steam in the summer of 1949. Leo could not compete with the old school of guitar makers at their game. He and his workers lacked the necessary skills to handcraft guitars even if they wanted to. In any case, Leo preferred to develop a standard guitar more like his own steel guitars than hollowbody electrics. He marshaled the resources at his disposal, including a wood shop that resembled a furniture factory, and he used his prodding insight to keep procedures simple. This approach shaped the final product: a high-quality, economical, factory-made guitar, a superior instrument that working musicians and average players could afford. But most important, Leo's new guitar would have a new tone for the electric guitar, something that even top-of-the-line acoustic-electrics could not produce.

By 1949, Leo knew the tone he wanted. Like a red-blooded American rebel in George Beauchamp's tradition, Leo held this truth to be self-evident: an electric guitar should faithfully reproduce the pure sound of vibrating strings. Leo designed a test to demonstrate this sound to visitors at his lab. (He continued doing the test into the 1980s.) He put one end of a 12-inch-long dowel up to the listener's ear and the other end against the headstock of a guitar. Then he strummed the strings. The dowel conducted the sound via the headstock to the ear. According to Leo, the ideal electric guitar had that tone content, a clear, bell-like quality with distinct highs and deep lows. Leo's perfect tone lacked muddled midrange, which he called fluff. He said in the mid-1980s: "When you make lemonade, you want to taste the tangy lemon flavor *and* the sweet sugar. All the other flavors in between are fluff."

A tone without fluff, the Leo Fender tone, cut through the noise in a bar like a sabre cut through gelatin. Fender steels possessed this piercing tone, and Leo wanted his standard guitars to sound like his steel guitars. This notion explained why his instruments came to represent a musical rebellion. Charlie Christian's playing defined jazz tone in the late 1930s with a hollowbody Gibson ES-150. It had a pickup placed in the rhythm position, close to the fingerboard. The guitar produced a woody, throaty sound lacking those stinging, ear-splitting highs Fenders later introduced. Most standard players wanted the mellow Charlie Christian guitar tone with a plunky midrange honk. Few of them sought steel players' or Leo's ideal. Some people have said that Leo got his ideas about tone from country players. But most of the prominent non-steel country players from the 1940s and 1950s such as Hank Garland and Chet Atkins played as well as the best jazz artists and emulated their tone. So while Leo took advice from many players, he listened to steel guitars and concluded that standard guitars should sound so good.

As Leo developed his clear concept of tone, he also planned a well-defined, practical overall guitar design: an improved Rickenbacker. He never admitted using it as a starting point, but the evidence is overwhelming. He boasted in the 1940s that he could improve any existing product as he had done with Philco turntables at the radio shop. During the war years, he must have had an earful of Doc Kauffman's Rickenbacker. Leo noticed its strong points: with a detachable neck, it was easy to make and service. And in the 1980s he talked in detail about its shortcomings. The Rickenbacker had good tone, but not as bright as Leo preferred. It had an uneven pickup response, an awkward shape, and tuning problems. Electro String, he felt, had not planned a guitar with musicians in mind.

One of Gibson's most popular prewar models was the ES-150. Charlie Christian, who pioneered the electric guitar in jazz, played an early version.

Planning for musicians was Leo's strong suit. His guitar would be easy to tune, easy to hold, and easy to play. Here he borrowed from Paul Bigsby and Merle Travis (this part of the story is in the next chapter). As Fender would later say, "I wanted to make the best tools possible for musicians." He would make his guitar from wood rather than Bakelite. Under Leo's guidance, George Fullerton—who later won awards for his oil paintings—drew freehand the body's profile on paper.

George and Lucille Fullerton with their daughter Diane outside the factory in 1950.

George Fullerton

After military service during World War II, Fullerton had no idea that he would devote a lifetime to manufacturing guitars. Since he and his wife Lucille lived in Fullerton, people often asked if he had any connection with the town's founder, railroad man George Fullerton. They were unrelated. George of future guitar fame drove a delivery truck for a Los Angeles furniture store, repaired radios, attended night school, and played guitar in a group called the Gold Coast Rangers. Exactly when and how he met Leo is unclear. In the early 1980s, he said that he first saw Fender's name ". . . on the side of one of those sound trucks that drove through town making announcements." As this story goes, he then happened into Fender's radio shop to buy records and met Leo, the way many musicians did at the time. However, Fullerton's book, *Guitar Legends: The Evolution of the Guitar from Fender to G&L* (Centerstream 1993), states that he met Fender in 1947 at the Fourth of July Arkansas picnic then held annually at Amerige Park in Fullerton. In any case, Fender was particularly interested to know that Fullerton played guitar. Starting that day, whenever they saw each other in town, Leo's greeting usually included, "Come on over, I've got something new to show you." Soon Leo offered him a job at the factory.

Aside from converting his acoustic guitar into an electric as many players did in the 1940s, Fullerton had no experience with guitars or manufacturing. Feeling unqualified, he hesitated accepting the offer until he realized the opportunity it represented. George's first day on the job, joining four or five other employees, was February 2, 1948. As the company grew, Leo hired George's sister, brother, and father. George repaired returned steel guitars and amplifiers. Soon he did woodworking and helped Leo fashion tools for the factory. The flurry of intense work and creativity quickly swept everyone nearby into the most remarkable period of Fender's history. Fullerton remem-

bers Leo expressing his desire to produce standard guitars and designing the instrument. George says, "Gradually, acceptable ideas started coming together." Today he marvels at his unique experience: "I feel like I was part of a happening. I'm still amazed that the Broadcaster, Strat, and P-Bass were so good and that no one has made much improvement since then. That's something you only see once in a lifetime."

Prototypes

Contrary to conventional readings of Leo's philosophy, the first requirement of his design was an easy-to-make body, not necessarily a solid one. The first prototype had a laminated two-piece pine body, which Fullerton remembers cutting. The painters put a heavy coat of white enamel on it. The laminated ash body for the second prototype had hollow chambers like a Rickenbacker. Leo discarded the idea because it took too long to manufacture. Solid bodies were heavy, but almost effortless to cut and rout. The second requirement was a detachable neck. In the 1930s, National, Dobro, and Rickenbacker all used this construction, the simplest and most efficient way to make a guitar. The removable neck appealed to Leo because it took less time and skill to make and would be easier to service after leaving the factory. Gluing a neck into a guitar body—the method employed by Gibson and other traditional manufacturers—was an unforgiving procedure. If the neck's angle changed over time, the factory had to scrap the whole guitar or extract the neck by cutting or breaking the neck joint. Only skilled repairmen could fix a bad neck joint after the instrument left the factory.

The removable neck solved the standard guitar's biggest servicing problem. Leo imagined a player wearing out the frets and replacing the whole neck rather than refretting the old one. This idea came from Rickenbacker as well. By the late 1940s Doc Kauffman had replaced the neck on his Rickenbacker several times. Leo never fully realized the flaw in this plan because he did not play guitar; he had the right idea for the wrong reason. His concept made the neck easy to throw away, yet most players would rather lose their right leg than their favorite old Fender neck.

For these necks, Leo chose strong and even-textured hard rock maple, which had long been used to fashion bowling pins and dance floors. Heat from the sun or stage lights which had little effect on wooden necks put guitars with Bakelite necks out of tune; by the late 1940s Rickenbacker supplied wooden replacements for its 1930s Bakelite guitars. Leo once explained that the World War II aircraft industry used wooden sticks for precise measuring because of their stability. Leo thought his neck would resist warping, twisting, and bending even without the benefit of steel reinforcement.

The first prototype of the Fender Esquire, Broadcaster, and Telecaster models (which was completed in 1949) incorporated a pine body and a steel guitar-like headstock. Its distinctive detachable neck and combination pickup/bridge assembly make it the first *Fender* guitar.

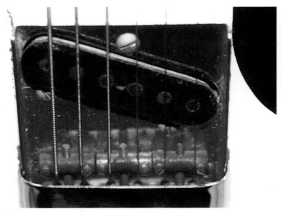

(Above) **Leo was confident his original neck would never warp, even without a truss rod. Employee Hugh Garriott tried to prove the point.**

(Left top to bottom) **All components of the prototype's bridge/pickup assembly were rough-hewn compared with later production versions made with Race & Olmsted dies. The pots date from the 31st week of 1949.**

The first Fender neck, made by George Fullerton, had a headstock shaped like a snake head similar to Leo's steels. As on the steels, the strings pulled straight across the nut instead of turning obliquely towards the tuning keys. Straight string pull, an idea well adapted from the steels, made the guitar easier to tune and stay in tune.

Another steel guitar adaptation was the lead pickup, a unit similar to the Champion lap steel's pickup developed in early 1949. An ad described the steel's tone as "sensitive and powerful across the entire audio spectrum," another way of saying the sound had no fluff. There was nothing revolutionary about the pickup design for Leo's standard guitar. To boost the bass, he slanted the pickup under the strings as Gibson had done on the ES-300 in 1942. With fixed pole pieces, it was not even state of the art. DeArmond for one already offered a pickup with six adjustable magnet pole pieces. But when Leo worked the bugs out of his design, including keeping it from shorting out on itself, it soon became known for its famous Fender tone. Arguably, Leo never improved on this pickup during the pre-CBS years.

While Fender worked on the guitar design, Don Randall pushed Radio-Tel's sales effort, attending the 1949 NAMM (National Association of Music Merchants) show at the Hotel New Yorker accompanied by recently hired salesmen Robert C. Morris and Don Patton. The first NAMM summer show held outside of Chicago had a smaller attendance than the 1948 show. For Randall, spoiled by the splendid weather in Santa Ana, the hot, humid New York July was unbearable. Still, he reacquainted himself with colleagues in the close-knit industry including Al Frost, Valco Manufacturing; Harry Stanley, Oahu Publishing; and Jay L. Kraus, Harmony, to mention a few.

Although Don omitted references to the Fender Spanish guitar in the company's 1949, literature, he hoped to have a sample on hand at the summer trade shows. On July 25, 1949 he wrote to his boss, F.C. Hall: "Try to get Leo to have the samples ready for Chicago [for the International Guitar League, or IGL, Festival]. The Champ set, new Deluxe guitar, and new Spanish guitar. It's really important!!" Hall replied on July 30 that Leo had made deliveries, but not the merchandise that Randall wanted for the Chicago festival.

Randall traveled the East visiting dealers in the interim between July's New York NAMM show and August's Chicago IGL festival. His thinking on the Spanish guitar matured as he became more aware of the Eastern competition. On August 6, he wrote back to Santa Ana: "Tell Leo not to go overboard on the new Spanish guitar until I return. You can tell him, however, that one pickup will not be enough on it. Gibson is making one with three pickups and several other mfgs. are using two. Be sure we get samples to Chicago."

Hall wrote back on August 8: "I don't believe that Leo will have a sample of the Deluxe Guitar or the Spanish Guitar for the Chicago Show . . . I have done everything I know to convince Leo of the importance of having this material for the show and still he states that it is impossible to deliver these items in time." Delivery was impossible. Leo was just completing the prototype.

48TH ANNUAL

MUSIC INDUSTRY TRADE SHOW & CONVENTION

July 25, 26, 27, 28, 1949

HOTEL NEW YORKER MANHATTAN CENTER NEW YORK CITY

VISIT US AT

The records Leo kept at the factory show that Race & Olmsted, a nearby tool and die company, made many tools for Fender over the years. In August 1949 he purchased the first of many special tools needed to make the Spanish guitar: two dies bought between August 6 and August 13, used for forming the bridge plate and fabricating the fiber baseplate on the lead pickup. (A blank die made the initial cuts that readied a piece to be stamped with a form die or machined into a finished object.) That was how the matter stood in the summer of 1949. Leo had left Don high and dry without a suitable single-pickup standard guitar prototype for the all-important summer shows. Without it, Randall could neither promote the guitar nor get reactions from players and dealers.

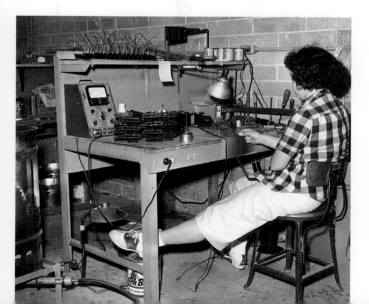

One of Leo's "girls" winding steel guitar pickups in 1950 by guiding wire onto a spinning bobbin attached to a small motor by pulleys and rubber bands. Leo's workers used the same primitive process to wind pickups throughout Leo's career. He said that properly trained people wound the units tighter—a key to Fender tone—than the machines later used in most modern factories.

After the 1949 shows, Leo presumably continued working on improvements in the basic design and started thinking about a dual-pickup model. However, there is little documentation of his work and only vague memories today of the guitar's development at this stage. The second prototype, still a single-pickup model, had some improvements including the now familiar six-on-a-side tuner arrangement. This unique head shape, with its Kluson SafeTiString posts, would become a major Fender trademark. A car salesman at the Ford dealership in Fullerton had shown Leo a picture of Croatian musicians playing traditional instruments with this design.

Dale Hyatt remembers spending time at the factory in 1949 showing Charlie Hayes how to set up Leo's first standard guitar and how to adjust it. Hayes was the first offi-

(Above) The highly modified second prototype (stripped of the finish and neck it had in the picture shown on page 58) was the first to sport the familiar Fender-style headstock. This guitar was made in late 1949.

(Right) Rear view of a non-truss rod neck from 1950 shows a cracked finish, which many early Fenders suffered.

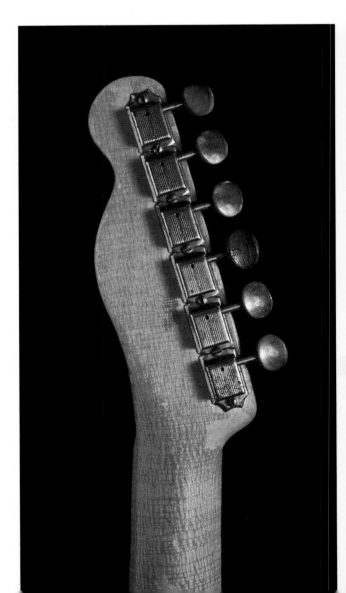

The Eddie Miller Band, circa 1949. Bob Hines (steel guitar) and Eddie Miller (singing) both worked at Fender and probably helped Leo with his first standard guitars. The guitarist in the white shirt is playing an instrument with one of Leo's Direct String Pickups.

Fullerton's *Daily News Tribune*, November 8, 1949. The article stated, "It is very often the case that an industry can be well known throughout the country and yet remain almost anonymous in its own home town."

On the way to a Chicago trade show, J. Fred McCord deals a hand to Charlie Hayes (with cigar). These guys had fun selling guitars and making a ton of money in the process. Hayes hated to drive, so they took the train.

cial Radio-Tel salesman to work with the Spanish electric and took orders for it that fall. No one knows if he carried a sample on the road or if he took orders based on the strength of a photograph. Fender said that Hayes often had the first samples of new products and did what Leo called "dealer testing." Since Hayes was the only 1940s salesman with a southern California home base, he maintained a close working relationship with Leo.

Regardless of the salesmen's relationship with Leo and the factory, Hall's Radio-Tel provided and accounted for all sample instruments used on the road. Hall held salesmen

liable for them. Hayes' 1949–50 samples inventory exists, but lists no standard guitars until 1950. He possibly took an experimental guitar from the factory, the loan going unrecorded. Leo felt trapped by his distribution contract and did go behind Hall's back on other occasions. In any event, a letter from Randall states that guitar orders Charlie Hayes made in 1949 went unfilled until the fall of 1950 or later. Even if samples other than prototypes—with one or two pickups—existed in the fall of 1949, Randall and Radio-Tel shipped none.

Randall and Radio-Tel shipped steel guitars and amplifiers to the Southwest, to the Northwest, and increasingly to the East Coast. Western swing and Hawaiian playing were at their peak, and Fender satisfied a healthy demand with state-of-the-art equipment. But regardless of what Leo would claim in the early 1980s, he had yet to sell a Fender electric standard guitar. He spent most of 1949's summer designing and building a prototype, and sometime in the fall or winter he started an improved second prototype. Randall and his salesmen wanted to add the guitar to the line as soon as possible. However, because of what Leo called "manufacturing problems," he failed to deliver a single one before turning his calendar to 1950.

Fender's 1940s letterhead.

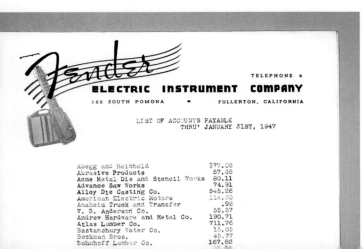

A visitor to Leo's factory test drives the new Esquire, summer 1950.

Hang tag from the early 1950s.

Chapter

Guitars for Everyman

The Esquire

By early 1950, Don Randall's job included shaking sense into Leo Fender, keeping him on task, and making him consider the music world beyond Fullerton. And as Leo's plans for a new solidbody guitar unfolded with little urgency, Randall and the rest of the music world waited. Fender gradually acquired new tooling, buying a bending fixture for fret wire on January 18, 1950. In March he bought dies for the lead pickup cover and elevator plate. The prototype guitar had no elevator plate to adjust the height of its pickup, and Leo failed to describe the plate in the patent application for the pickup assembly. This important feature not only improved the way the pickup went up and down, but also shaped the guitar's soon-to-be-classic tone. Race & Olmsted constructed a special saw and shaper for necks and billed Fender for these tools on March 10. Ten days later the tool makers also billed Leo for the die used to make the fiber fingerboard markers.

Randall made plans to introduce the instrument and considered the competition: National's Aristocrat and Gibson's ES-350 and ES-300 acoustic-electric models already featured two pickups. Gibson had introduced the triple-pickup ES-5 in 1949. Although Leo had yet to purchase dies for making a second pickup, he probably meant to since Don had suggested it the previous summer. But Don concluded that a single-pickup guitar was more affordable and thus had more potential as a student model. That was important to Randall, who felt that the unsophisticated, conservative guitar market would have a hard time at first accepting the solidbody guitar's break with tradition. Street-wise now, he knew that if he established the Fender electric standard in music instruction studios, he would have a hot commodity. If the single-pickup version sold well, it would prime the market for a more expensive double-pickup model. Furthermore, Leo was finally ready—or so he said—to produce the single-pickup guitar.

Steel ace Noel Boggs and Spade Cooley promoted Fender instruments with zeal while Jimmy Wyble was reluctant. A die-hard acoustic-electric jazz player, he held the solidbody long enough for the picture, 1950.

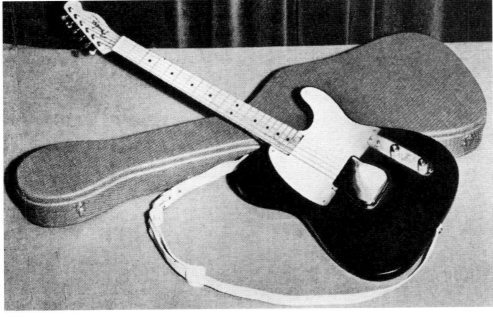

Catalog shot of the single-pickup Esquire in April 1950. The guitar was introduced before the factory could manufacture it in quantity and before the final design was set.

In April 1950 Radio-Tel started promoting the single-pickup Esquire, the first Fender electric standard guitar officially introduced to the public. (*Esquire* came from Randall, the company's namesmith. Leo said in the 1980s that the name sounded regal and implied a certain distinction above other guitars.) The company prepared its Catalog No. 2, picturing a black single-pickup guitar with a tweed form-fit case. Another picture showed Jimmy Wyble, with Spade Cooley's band, holding a blonde Esquire. Both guitars had the utilitarian shape of thousands of Fender guitars to come. "The Esquire guitar features a new style of construction which vastly improves the usability of this type of instrument," wrote Randall in cataloguese. It could be played "at extreme volume"; the neck was a great aid to easy fretting and fast action. He added: "It is also replaceable and can be changed by the owner in approximately ten minutes time. This feature eliminates costly repairs and refretting." Leo still believed the neck was strong enough to resist warping. And if a neck did warp, he planned to mail the customer a new one in a shipping tube.

Dave Driver received his first standard guitar sample, black as he much later remembered, on April 4. (The black finish meant the factory could cut costs by using lower-grade, blemished wood. Later, the more expensive, fancy-grained ash with a blonde finish would prevail.) Charlie Hayes received two Esquires in April 1950, one on the seventh and one on the fifteenth. The charge to the salesmen's accounts was $69.98 per instrument, the original wholesale price for a single-pickup model. The retail price would be $139.95.

Although the salesmen actively took orders for the guitars, the factory did not produce them in quantity. As Hayes' dealers waited for their orders, so did Driver's. He remembered that some remained anxious for over a year before being supplied. The words *prototype*, *sample*, or *pre-production model* describe guitars produced that spring and early summer. *Pre-production* is best because Fender was still acquiring the tools and the room necessary to go into full production.

To add more work space, Leo built a cinder block building adjacent to his two steel buildings in May. It had a heater, a rest room, and another telling feature. Fender had never forgotten that his radio shop's roof sagged and leaked during southern California's heavy winter rains. Water dripping from a ceiling bothers most people, but

Newly completed concrete-block factory building, summer 1950.

(Right) Charlie Aldrich, a well-known performer, holding a single-pickup Esquire in Leo's new building that same summer.

life goes on. To Leo, the roof's failure was an intolerable circumstance, a totally unacceptable lapse in quality. By the time he started manufacturing, he had decided that if possible no product or building with his name on it would fail. When he built the cinder block factory on Pomona Avenue, it had the equivalent of a second roof under the top one. Most contractors would call the design extravagant overkill, but not Leo, who believed in plans that left no preventable mishap to chance. No matter how hard the rain or how strong the wind, the Fender factory stayed dry inside. The double roof also made the building stronger, as a demolition crew would later discover. Leo made things to last, whether they were factory buildings, guitars, or amplifiers.

Later he tied memories of this new building to memories of his first standard guitars. Unfortunately, in the 1980s he mistakenly remembered building them both in 1948. Building permit records on file at Fullerton City Hall proved Leo's mistake. When confronted with this fact in the 1980s, he never really admitted his error and suggested the city's records were wrong. He said, "What I *remember* is that I built that building in 1948, and we started building guitars soon afterwards."

With the building complete—in 1950—Leo bought more equipment. The die used to form the control plate for the 3-position lever switch was purchased on July 26, 1950. Single-pickup Esquires pictured in the 1950 catalog and with musician Charlie Aldrich in the brick factory building appear to lack these switches. The catalog mentions just two tone settings, thus indicating that early models perhaps had 2-position toggle switches. Leo's choice of a lever switch—which allowed three distinct guitar tones—probably coincided with his plans for a rhythm pickup placed close to the end of the fingerboard. His records show that he purchased the dies for cutting the rhythm pickup's top and bottom fiber pieces on June 22, 1950. Race & Olmsted

billed Leo for the rhythm pickup cover form and blank dies on July 26 and August 21, respectively.

Fortunately, the Esquire's body design easily lent itself to both single- and double-pickup configurations. When the bodies went into production, they all had cavities routed for two pickups. It is hard to believe that Leo found the procedure cost-efficient. It involved more time and labor. On single-pickup guitars the empty cavity lay hidden under the pickguard. He wanted players to have the option of adding a pickup in the future. But in the summer of 1950, with a second pickup in the works, Leo put the single-pickup guitar on hold anyway.

The second pickup sat under the strings near the edge of the fingerboard—where the pickup on Charlie Christian's jazz guitar sat—thus sensing harmonic overtones different than the lead pickup. Moreover, Leo intentionally shielded the rhythm pickup with a metal cover meant to cut high harmonics and to emphasize the notes' fundamental tones. The 2-pickup Esquires also had a handy blend control that mixed the signals; in the lead position, turning the tone control knob down blended the rhythm pickup with the lead pickup. In the middle position the switch selected just the rhythm pickup, and in

Fender made both single- and dual-pickup Esquires before introducing a truss rod in late 1950. This black dual-pickup guitar (#0129) has a laminated pine body slightly over 1½ inches thick. Production of non-truss rod Esquires was limited to fewer than two dozen instruments. After showing prototypes at the summer trade shows, Don Randall feared that the un-reinforced necks would bow.

(Below) A view without the pickguard reveals no routing between the front pickup and the neck cavity.

The wiring in 1950 was for a blend control instead of a tone control.

Leo's drying rack in the summer of 1950 held at least six Esquire bodies.

(Below) The alternate finish for 1950 guitars was blonde, which Leo came to favor. These guitars had ash bodies (one measured 1⅝ inches thick; the standard thickness soon became 1¾ inches). Leo took this picture shortly after moving into his new building, and the image graced his company's invoices for several years.

the forward position the switch selected the rhythm pickup with a capacitor that rolled off the highs. (Leo called this "deep rhythm" and reasoned guitarists could play bass lines using the tone.) With a 3-position tone selector switch, two pickups, and a blend control, the player had several options; 2-pickup Fender guitars featured these same electronics until at least 1952. Although the single-pickup guitar used capacitors to mimic the mellow sound of a second pickup, the real thing sounded better. Players like Jimmy Bryant liked the jazzier sound of the dual-pickup guitar better than the sound of the single-pickup one.

Leo liked the 2-pickup guitar, too. Elizabeth Nagel Hayzlett, Leo's secretary at the time, recalled that he immediately set up a darkroom in the new brick building. Taking pictures had become a serious hobby. A week or two later he rushed out and proudly handed her a print of a new double-pickup non-truss-rod Esquire. This photo, plus one plant manager Forrest White found in the old Fender files when he left the company in 1966, came from the same negative. Leo used this image for several years on the company's invoice letterhead. (When shown the picture in the mid-1980s, he claimed that he had never seen it and that the company had used a different-style shoulder strap in the 1950s. Nevertheless, two years later the original long-forgotten negative turned up at G&L with many other photos Leo took in the early 1950s.)

Leo snapped a curious photo in July 1950 that showed the spray booth and drying racks for freshly painted guitar bodies. Close examination revealed six partially painted Esquire bodies, five black and one blonde. Although not filling the orders sent by Radio-Tel, the factory was obviously making a few guitars. McCord's Music in Dallas, where Charlie Hayes spent time, received a couple that summer. But through the early summer of 1950, Don Randall and his salesmen had received no more than a few Esquires, samples used to drum up orders.

Driving from town to town, salesmen could see one or two dealers a day. However, nearly every serious American dealer attended the summer trade shows. The 1950s retail music business revolved around these convention-like affairs where dealers met manufacturers who promoted their hottest new products and took as many orders as possible. Salesmen conducted more business here in three

One of the first magazine ads to feature Leo's new solidbody.

(Below) Al Frost, Randall's friend and co-owner of the Valco guitar company, suggested that Leo add a truss rod to the Esquire's neck. The improvement would be the slim margin between success and failure.

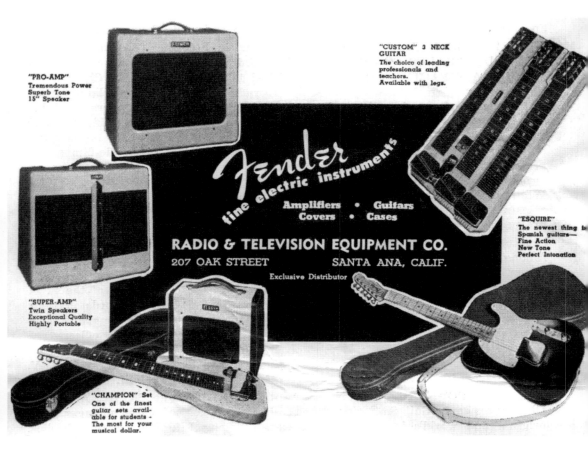

days than in three months on the road. Don Randall had wanted to show a Fender Spanish guitar in 1949, but Leo had let him down. A year had passed, perhaps the most formative one in Fender history. And in that time Leo had created a guitar that Don knew would cause a stir among dealers, players, and rival manufacturers. Now it was time for the Fender standard guitar's coming-out party—its first summer trade show.

Randall carried two sample guitars with him to the July 1950 NAMM show at Palmer House in Chicago. He primed the introduction with advertising designed to arouse curiosity. *Musical Merchandise* magazine announced the guitar in its June issue, and the *Music Dealer—Convention Supplement* publication pictured the single-pickup Esquire in the "Merchandise To See" section. At the show, Don displayed the guitars with other Fender equipment, steel guitars, and amplifiers. Not all reactions to the Esquire were favorable. Salesmen for competing companies derisively labeled it "the canoe paddle" and "the snow shovel." However, the instrument impressed many others, especially competing designers.

Randall carefully listened to comments, but the most important feedback came from one of his friends, Al Frost, co-owner of Valco, makers of Supro and National instruments. His advice supported a notion Randall already entertained: On July 13, in the middle of the show, Don wrote to F. C. Hall: "R: Spanish guitar, I still believe the neck should be reinforced. I talked it over with Al Frost of National and they had a similar experience and it cost them a considerable sum of money." Don added: "He said

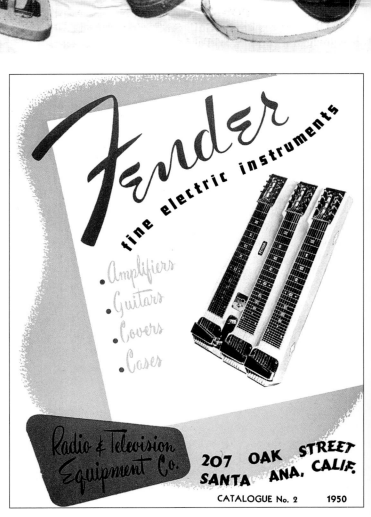

Fender's 1950 Catalog #2 introduced the single-pickup version of the Esquire.

78

they finally overcame most of their trouble by laminating the neck with different types of woods. He suggested Leo build a laminated neck and run a weight test on it and our present neck and see the proof for ourselves." Frost thought that a laminated neck would not warp with a load hanging on it for some time but that Leo's would.

Aside from Frost's suggestions, Randall heard that Gibson's patent on the neck rod had just run out. As he wrote Hall: "Now anyone can use the principle. I really believe that this should be very carefully considered. We could do ourselves a lot of harm by putting out a weak product." With these words, Don tried to influence Leo's basic neck design. Two days later another Randall letter explained that both Esquire samples now had bowed necks. While the defect was minor, it was noticeable to the informed eye. Randall felt that Hall should tell Leo and make clear that players saw the problem and wanted to know Fender's solution. Yet Randall still felt immense pressure to ship guitars: "Get Leo on the ball, we have nothing but complaints about our delivery and I heard at least twenty times today that customers could sell a lot more merchandise if they could get it." Don continued: "The Champion guitars and the two Spanish guitars just must be gotten out immediately and I wouldn't let Leo sleep until this is done. Immediately Immediately Immediately."

With the new Esquire, Randall was stuck between a stack of orders and a pair of bowed necks, a situation salesmen had experienced since April. Either he had to delay the guitar's production to redesign the neck or produce a flawed instrument. He asked himself how customers would perceive the company if it failed to deliver the new guitar. Don's concern was highly justified considering what he believed to be Leo's skewed priorities at the factory (putting the single-pickup guitar on hold while spending time with the dual-pickup guitar) and the large number of unfilled orders stacking up. Randall summed up his feelings towards the end of the show: "I guess I sound like Hayes, but I think if I were on the road I would be worse than him, after talking to all these dealers."

After the NAMM show, Randall hit the road, first to Michigan where he bought a new Buick Model 51. He planned to travel until attending the August 21-25 IGL festival at Cleveland's Hotel Statler. Staying at Detroit's Sheraton Hotel, he reflected on the Palmer House show experience. Again, he wrote expressing his concerns to Hall: "Incidentally, the neck on my Spanish guitar is still warping. The first string is now loose on the nut and buzzes when it is played open." The higher the action, the more the neck looked like Robin Hood's bow. Nevertheless, the delay in the guitar's full production frustrated Radio-Tel's general manager. He suggested to Hall that if Leo further delayed the Spanish guitar and the Student steel guitar, Radio-Tel should take drastic steps. Don presented this scenario: "I know I could take the dies for the Spanish guitar and have it made back here in three weeks time and they wouldn't cost us over $25.00 ea."

FENDER ELECTRIC INSTRUMENT COMPANY
PRICE LIST — August 1, 1950

AMPLIFIERS	WEIGHT	LIST PRICE
Pro Amp 15" Speaker, Linen Covered	45#	$ 199.50
Super Amp, 2 - 10" Speakers, Linen Covered	42#	169.50
Deluxe Amp, 12" Speaker, Linen Covered	27#	89.50
Princeton Amp, 8" Speaker, Linen Covered	17#	64.50
Champion "600" Amp, Two-Tone Leatherette Covered	13#	49.95

CHAMPION SET		
Champion Guitar and Amp Set	24#	98.50

AMPLIFIER COVERS		
Pro Amp, Gray-Brown Water-Repellent Covert Cloth	3#	5.95
Super Amp, " " " " " " "	3#	5.95
Deluxe Amp, " " " " " " "	2#	4.95
Princeton Amp, " " " " " " "	2#	3.95

GUITARS		
Custom 3 Neck Guitar (blond)	36#	259.50
Custom 3 Neck Guitar (walnut)	36#	249.50
Dual Eight Professional Guitar (blond)	30#	184.50
Dual Eight Professional Guitar (walnut)	30#	174.50
Dual Six Professional Guitar (blond)	30#	159.50
Dual Six Professional Guitar (walnut)	30#	149.50
Deluxe 8-string Guitar (blond)	8#	109.50
Deluxe 8-string Guitar (walnut)	8#	104.50
Deluxe 6-string Guitar (blond)	8#	89.50
Deluxe 6-string Guitar (walnut)	8#	84.50
Champion Guitar (mother o'pearl plastic)	8#	39.50
Esquire Spanish Guitar	11#	139.95

GUITAR STANDS		
Set Telescoping Legs for Custom 3 Neck Guitar	6#	39.95
Set Telescoping Legs for Dual Eight Guitar	6#	39.95
Dual Eight Guitar Stand	7#	17.95
Single Neck Stand	7#	13.95

GUITAR CASES		
Custom 3 Neck Case	14#	48.50
Dual Eight Case	11#	32.50
Esquire, Spanish Guitar Case	11#	39.95
Deluxe Case	6#	21.00
Champion Case	4#	8.95

PATENT HEADS		
Double Neck Patent Heads, per pair, 8 string		32.50
Double Neck Patent Heads, per pair, 6 string		30.00
Single Neck Patent Heads, per pair		2.50
Safety String Patent Heads, per pair		2.75
8-String Pick Up Unit		42.00
6-String Pick Up Unit		40.00

MICROPHONES		
556 Shure, Cardioid		92.50
55 Shure, Cardioid		67.50
51 Shure, "Sonodyne"		39.75
520 Shure, "Green Bullet"		16.50
950 Electro-Voice		39.50

SHIPMENTS OF 100 POUNDS OR MORE WILL BE PREPAID

MERCHANDISE MAY BE ASSORTED TO MEET REQUIREMENTS

Radio-Tel's Fender price sheet, August 1950.

Randall drove on to New York. Stopping at music stores, he garnered more orders for merchandise, and his wife Jean flew to meet him in early August. For the rest of the summer the couple traveled together, soon meeting up with salesman Don Patton, pilot of his own single-engine airplane. They covered his territory by air, landing at Lynchburg, Virginia; Richmond, Virginia; and Washington, D. C. Randall developed a taste for flying when Patton let him take over the controls in flight, a precursor of the good times to come.

The week before Randall arrived at the IGL festival, he pointed out another problem to Hall. "We have been letting a great many guitar players play our new Spanish and it really looks hot but it still isn't a very good instrument for rhythm. As a lead guitar it is terrific. I have to apologize for the warped neck and it is quite embarrassing but after we get past that part of it the instrument is well received. Don't let Leo raise the prices!"

Fender prices remained steady in August 1950, but Don continued having problems. He and his wife arrived the weekend before the IGL festival and encountered snags checking into their display room. This snafu set the stage for the most revealing letter Randall wrote to Hall during that summer. It read in part: "Francis, I don't believe you realize the gravity of this Spanish guitar situation. If

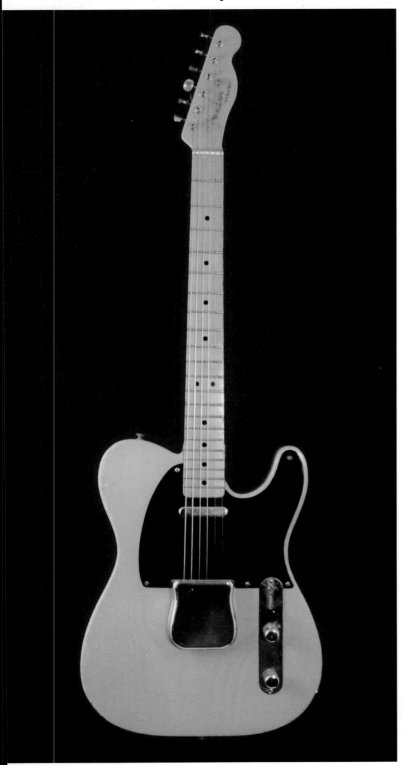

Dual-pickup Esquire #0013, bought at McCord's in Dallas, was one of just a few sold at music stores.

something isn't done soon we will have a very bad name." He added, "The complaints are terrific already and if you could talk to some of these people who have been made so many promises you would understand better what I mean." Don could see the guitar's vast potential and had complete faith in Leo's visionary idea.

Randall continued: "We have the beginning of a very fine product in our Spanish guitar. Nothing has been produced, in the past, by anyone that has created the excitement and speculation among dealers, players and even our competitors as has this instrument." He felt a sense of urgency. "Now if we don't flood the market with our product you can bet your life our competitors will be right behind us with the same instrument only better and much fancier. The idea in our guitar has made a hit and believe me we better get on the ball— every day is precious."

Leo, in Don's opinion, had created a potential bonanza with the Esquire. "It is bigger than any other item we produce and it is also an entree into places where we otherwise would never get in," he wrote. Randall also had some words about Fender. "If Leo misses the boat now I will never forgive him. It is probably the biggest opportunity he or we will ever have to gain wide popular acceptance in one great sweep." Don added: "Don't think for a minute our large competitors will let us get all the glory if they can help it. Not by a long way. Get Leo On The Ball."

Towards the end of the letter Don sounded exhausted, as if he had lost all patience with Leo. "Now—Don't pay him, get a gun, or a goon squad or something. Make him put it out immediately and right—no duds." Don reiterated the guitar's potential: "If we could get that guitar out— right—ballyhoo it to the skies and really drive on it, I know we could sell five or ten thousand the first year. The initial interest in it is terrific." But he also worried that other companies would soon produce their own solidbody guitars. He wrote: "If we wait we will have to share the business with our competitors. And that will be costly because they will put out a fancy instrument that by Leo's standards will have to sell for five hundred dollars."

The salesmen worried little about fancy instruments from competing companies, but certainly felt a growing wrath from dealers. From the Northwest Driver wrote to Hall on August 15 telling of problems: "I hope they start shipping the Spanish guitar soon. I had built quite a lot of interest in it, many places they had fellows come in to see it and I also went out to show it at their request. Now when I call they ride me." On August 18 Don Patton wrote to Hall from the eastern seaboard: "It looks as if

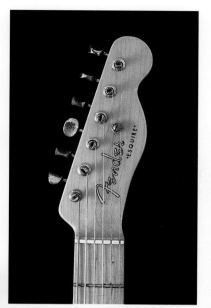

Esquire #0013's owner had Fred McCord add a string retainer to hold the high E and B strings in the nut. There is neither a rout between the front pickup and the neck nor one between the front pickup and the control cavity. Leo's earliest bridge/pickup assemblies used steel bridge pieces.

(Above) Rear view of #0013 shows no skunk stripe, the contrasting walnut piece that would conceal the truss rod on later guitars.

(Bottom) Dale Hyatt bought Leo's radio shop in the late 1940s and started selling guitars and amps directly to musicians. Notice the record displays to the left.

this territory is at last beginning to produce for which I am very thankful. I feel as though it is going to continue to grow especially since we have the new Esquire Guitar added to our line. P.S. Please rush production on the Esquire Guitar."

Meanwhile, Dale Hyatt, who had bought Leo's radio shop, offered Fender amps, steels, and a trickle of Esquires directly to musicians. Since Leo still had an exclusive agreement with Radio-Tel, he slyly maintained that Dale sold factory seconds, flawed merchandise. Don Randall, F. C. Hall, and Dave Driver suspected otherwise. They became convinced that the factory created Dale's so-called seconds as bootleg to provide Leo extra cash. They believed Hyatt's store was in fact the unofficial Fender factory outlet.

Besides selling instruments in Fullerton, Hyatt frequented out of town honky-tonks and dance halls, selling guitars and amps on the stage or out of a truck in the parking lot. Like a Fuller Brush Man for bar musicians, he

surreptitiously took a truckload of Fender equipment, including at least three Esquires, through Bakersfield into California's Central Valley during the summer of 1950. Stopping at a bar in Manteca, just north of Modesto, he showed a musician a guitar, but its lead pickup refused to work. Dale went out to his truck for a second instrument, and to his dismay it also proved dead. On the third trip to the parking lot, he found the one good guitar and sold it. Back in Fullerton, he returned the two bad guitars and told Leo what had happened. Reacting to the experience, Leo quickly modified his pickup with better insulation between the magnets and the coil. He also reversed the hot and ground leads so that a short circuit simply cut the pickup's output rather than stop the show.

The Manteca incident made a lasting impression on Dale and Leo, who both remembered the experience years later. It also illustrated the growing split between Fender and Randall. The two had similar goals for the new guitar, although much later Leo portrayed Don as disinterested. In reality, as shown by the letters he wrote in 1950, Randall desperately wanted it delivered. Leo Fender had no reason to delay the project purposely, except that by now he wanted a new distributor—one reason he sent Hyatt out on his travels. From all accounts, everyone at the factory worked hard, long hours in 1950 making steel guitars and amplifiers by the hundreds. But Leo wanted a perfect standard guitar, and he granted himself the time to make it that way. Ironically, while he quickly fixed flaws in the pickups, he refused to accept that the guitar had another major weakness—a warping, potentially unplayable neck. Randall, first to recognize the problem, agonized about it. Leo, the prideful inventor, resented Randall, Hall, and competitor Al Frost meddling in the guitar's design; Leo needed to discover the problem for himself in his sometimes slow, methodical way.

While Don traveled in the East, the neck on Leo's test guitar slowly started to bow as it sat unplayed at the factory. Leo noticed, and in the middle of August he reluctantly expressed concern to Hall. Leo hated to admit his unreinforced neck posed a serious problem; he still endorsed his earlier, nifty idea—just mail new necks out when the old ones fail. Putting truss rods or any rein-

forcement into the necks made them more expensive and less disposable. But then Hall let Fender read Don's letter describing widespread interest in the Esquires among players and dealers and reiterated Don's opinion that Fender should design a decent, reliable neck and start production immediately. After the meeting, Hall felt that he had successfully conveyed the message and wrote to Don: "Therefore I believe he will come out with a new neck which will be satisfactory. The time when it will be delivered, however, is very indefinite."

In late August, Hall again reminded Fender of Randall's desire for full production of the Esquire, but with an improved neck. Leo defensively said that he had been anxious to produce the guitar in 1949, but that manufacturing problems stood in his way. Some of Leo's problems stemmed from shortages of materials created by the Korean War, which began in June 1950. On September 1, Congress passed the Defense Production Act which gave President Truman authority to allocate and ration goods. For Leo, the future availability of electronic parts and components made from strategic metals such as chrome and cobalt became especially questionable. The magnets used in pickups contained cobalt. All the hardware on his guitars had chrome plating; shipments of chrome-plated Kluson tuners were already delayed. However, Leo had also created his own manufacturing problems by tinkering. Understandably, many of the experiments were necessary, but others seemed inessential. He had first used laminated pine for bodies, then ash with internal chambers, and then pine again. He finally settled on solid ash. He had changed finishes—first white, then black, then blonde. Perhaps his budget had delayed the guitar. Instead of buying all the tools he needed at one time, he spaced these purchases over a year.

Upon the introduction of the truss rod, the dual-pickup guitar went into full production as the Broadcaster and the single-pickup model became the Esquire. This Broadcaster guitar, #0005, has brass bridges, compared with Esquire #0013 on page 80 which has steel bridges. Note that Fender serial numbers were out of sequence from the beginning.

The Broadcaster

When Don returned to southern California in early September, he told Leo once and for all that the new standard guitars had to have reinforced necks. Leo, who had considered the problem since August, probably made plans for a truss rod at this time. On September 21, Hall informed Dave Driver: "We are doing our best to get Leo to produce the Spanish Guitar as soon as possible. I know that it is very important to get it into the field before our competitors get the jump on us." Leo bought the truss rod routing plate from Race & Olmsted on October 3 and finally went into full production in late October or early

Doc Kauffman visiting Leo's place and picking a Broadcaster, winter 1950–51.
(Below) Left to right, Dub Williams, Eddie Miller, Lilly Sanchez, and Leo Fender, winter 1950–51. Williams and Miller wrote the classic "Please Release Me."

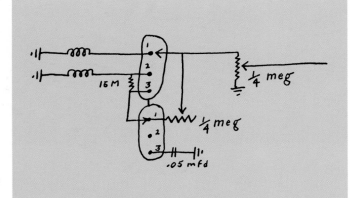

November. The version he produced in quantity had two pickups, as he liked it better than the single-pickup guitar and always wanted the world to know what he was capable of. Caring little about Radio-Tel's earlier marketing strategy (starting with the single-pickup guitar in music instruction studios), he also vainly wanted his best guitar in the hands of professionals as soon as possible. That was his marketing plan.

However, Don's salesmen had taken orders for the single-pickup version. Not only had the catalog and price list featured it, but the catalog pictured a guitar with a black finish. Despite the extra expense, Leo had decided to use a blonde finish instead of black. Thus the guitars he prepared to ship neither fit the catalog description nor matched the original retail price. He rarely let such details bother him or slow him down once he made up his mind (and demonstrated this trait again several times in the 1980s).

Good at working around Leo, Don Randall continued calling the single-pickup guitar the Esquire, but held orders for it. He chose a new name for the 2-pickup guitar: the Broadcaster. No one is sure of the exact day he coined the name, but it coincided with the introduction of the truss rod, as no authentic non-truss-rod Broadcasters exist. Dealers who insisted on single-pickup guitars rather than more expensive dual-pickup Broadcasters waited until single-pickup Esquires went into full production in January 1951 and were delivered in February.

As Randall predicted, the new guitar was an entree into new markets, especially the East Coast. Because of the distance from California, Fender salesmen in the Eastern states had faced some special problems, both cultural and geographical. Randall knew he needed an Eastern way station to compete effectively with companies like Gibson, Epiphone, and Valco. Radio-Tel tried as early as 1947 to set up a warehouse and service center with Charles Jamason in New England, but failed. In 1950, Randall wrote F. C. Hall in a letter from Detroit: "[New York] is a vast market but until we can increase production, get a good reliable Eastern warehouse and become competitive with these boys back here, we will never be too big a factor in this area." Randall added, "There is no complaint about the mdse. and in fact most of the big accounts would like to sell it but not from the West Coast and not at 40 percent." He had heard a New York dealer say, "Why should we risk losing the sale on a Gibson or Epiphone amp and a 50 percent discount to try to sell a Fender amp at a 40 percent discount, and take a chance on having trouble with it to boot." Even before the days of Federal Express, New

Leo drew this wiring diagram for the dual-pickup blend control in 1951.

84

York dealers had overnight or two-day service from Chicago or Michigan.

Endorsements from western swing bands carried little weight on the East Coast. Mike Cole was the salesman for New York Randall hired in 1950 after the Jack Douglas affair (chapter 4). Jody Carver, a steel guitarist and Fender artist who would eventually work for the company, remembers the first time he saw Cole: "About eight months after meeting Don Randall, I get a glimpse of a lot of commotion in the back of the Village Barn [a New York nightclub]. Actually it was the front; I was in the back on the bandstand." Carver saw this man running down the aisle yelling, "Have you seen Jody Carver? Are you Jody Carver?"

Carver remembers asking, "Who are you?"

The short man in the rumpled suit replied, "My name is Mike Cole. Don Randall said to see you. I'm a Fender salesman, and I know you play a Fender steel guitar." Jody was about the only person in New York playing one in 1950.

Cole's real last name was Koladish, and he was the son of impoverished Russian Orthodox immigrants. He had worked as a salesman for Sorkin, an East Coast wholesale distributor, before Randall hired him. Single at the time, Cole was endowed with a frantic, untamed but very likeable and ambitious personality. Carver notes: "He had three brothers—John, Steve, and Frank. These guys were a comedy act in themselves, typical New York guys." They were happy over their brother's success. After landing a job with Fender, Mike was the famous brother.

On the road, Cole drove and slept in his brother's 1950 Chevrolet sedan because he could not yet afford a hotel room. He also latched onto Jody. Mike stopped at the Carvers' house every day he was in Brooklyn, and Jody's mother made him meatball sandwiches packed in brown bags. Always a gung-ho, 100 percent go-getter, Cole traveled from Maine to Florida, a "raging bull" according to Carver. Cole knew nothing about music, so he memorized brochures before seeing dealers. Once he asked Carver how a sales pitch about "case-hardened hardware and genuine luggage linen" sounded. Jody replied that it sounded like a record.

Cole explained, "Well, I memorized the catalog."

Jody asked, "When you're talking to these dealers, what do you do when they ask you something else?"

"I go back outside the store and reread the catalog," Cole said.

After several hard weeks on the road hoping for success, Cole wrote to Randall, "The people here in New York don't know who [steel guitarist-bandleader] Leon

Jody Carver's earliest promo shot for Fender.

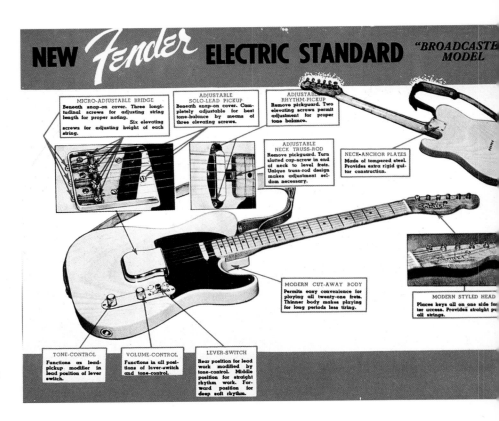

NEW *Fender* ELECTRIC STANDARD "*BROADCASTER* MODEL"

MICRO-ADJUSTABLE BRIDGE
Beneath snap-on cover. Three longitudinal screws for adjusting string length for proper noting. Six elevating screws for adjusting height of each string.

ADJUSTABLE SOLO-LEAD PICKUP
Beneath snap-on cover. Completely adjustable for best tone-balance by means of three elevating screws.

ADJUSTABLE RHYTHM-PICKUP
Remove pickguard. Two elevating screws permit adjustment for proper tone balance.

ADJUSTABLE NECK TRUSS-ROD
Remove pickguard. Turn slotted cap-screw in end of neck to level frets. Unique truss-rod design makes adjustment seldom necessary.

NECK-ANCHOR PLATES
Made of tempered steel. Provides extra rigid guitar construction.

MODERN CUT-AWAY BODY
Permits easy convenience for playing all twenty-one frets. Thinner body makes playing for long periods less tiring.

MODERN STYLED HEAD
Places keys all on one side for easier access. Provides straight pull on all strings.

TONE-CONTROL
Functions as lead-pickup modifier in lead position of lever switch.

VOLUME-CONTROL
Functions in all positions of lever-switch and tone-control.

LEVER-SWITCH
Rear position for lead work modified by tone-control. Middle position for straight rhythm work. Forward position for deep soft rhythm.

(Right) Advertising insert in industry magazines that alerted the Gretsch company to Leo's new guitar, February 1951.
(Below) Gretsch's telegram to Radio-Tel and the letter on the opposite page tell the story.

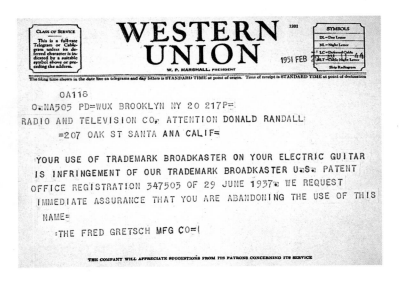

describing it in detail. Arrows pointed to a close-up of the bridge. The copy read: "Beneath snap-on cover. Three longitudinal screws for adjusting string length for proper noting. Six elevating screws for adjusting height of each string." The guitar had what Randall called a "Modern cut-away body" and "Modern styled head." What player could resist the "Adjustable solo-lead pickup"? After all, it was "completely adjustable for tone-balance by means of three elevating screws."

Finally the industry had a production model solidbody readily available to the public. What happened to the two dozen or so made without truss rods? According to Dale Hyatt, most pre-truss-rod necks went bad, and owners replaced them with truss rod necks. Fred McCord remembered that the owner of the first Fender Spanish guitar sold at his Dallas store later replaced the neck. Since the first guitars lacked a channel routed between the neck's slot and the front pickup cavity—the channel that allowed truss rod adjustments—Leo undoubtedly replaced both bodies and necks on some original Esquires. In this case, the guitar retained its original older hardware and low serial number. Some customers may even have exchanged old guitars for new ones.

Fender sold 87 Broadcasters in January 1951 and as many as 65 in February. Many people took note, including managers at the Fred Gretsch Manufacturing Company in Brooklyn, New York.

In Radio-Tel's haste to name the new guitar, the company blindly walked into a bad dream. The February 20, 1951, telegram read: "Your use of trademark Broadkaster [sic] on your electric guitar is infringement of our trademark Broadkaster U. S. Patent Registration 347503 of 29

McAuliffe is." In Tulsa, Oklahoma, he was a major star playing a Fender thousands of fans saw weekly. Still, Leo's steel guitars had few advocates with nationwide stature, except perhaps Alvino Rey. Cole welcomed the new standard guitar when Radio-Tel shipped him a Broadcaster on November 16, 1950. Presumably he never had a non-truss-rod Esquire sample. A Broadcaster also went to Kreigh Music Company in Bartlesville, Oklahoma, in November. Radio-Tel sent the guitar against order No. 51497 taken by Hayes on October 10, 1949.

Musical Merchandise magazine carried the first announcement for the Broadcaster in February 1951. Page 10A of the same issue was a full-page insert

Ad from 1948 shows an earlier Telecaster than Fender's.

JIMMY BRYANT
prefers a
Fender GUITAR

Bryant, who played western-flavored jazz, was Fender's most admired promoter in the early 1950s.

June 1937. We request immediate assurance that you are abandoning the use of this name = The Fred Gretsch Mfg. Co." Gretsch produced drum sets and a line of banjos called Broadkasters.

Don Randall's response was immediate. On February 21, 1951, he wrote a special letter to all salesmen advising them that Radio-Tel was abandoning the Broadcaster name and requesting that anyone with another good name should contact him. Dave Driver suggested that the company sponsor a name contest with the winning dealer receiving a new guitar. Mike Cole suggested that Fender rename the Broadcaster the Dualelectra. Said he, "It's got two pickups, and it's electric."

On February 23, 1951, F. C. Hall wrote to Gretsch that Radio-Tel would drop *Broadcaster* and stop shipping instruments labeled with the name. Hall assured Gretsch that he had been unaware of the trademark and product in the field. Had he been aware, he would never have chosen the name. He added: "We wish to thank you for calling this matter to our attention before these instruments were produced in quantity. At the present time there are only a few samples that have been manufac-

tured." Hall also pointed out that while Gretsch used a *k* in Broadkaster, Radio-Tel used a *c*.

One day later, Randall informed Mike Cole by letter that the Broadcaster was renamed the Telecaster, another classic moniker from Radio-Tel's manager. Don added Radio-Tel's on-the-record public relations reasoning: "This has been done because of some engineering changes which we believe has [sic] improved the instrument but which it would be hard to point out to your customer. In any event, refer to it as the Telecaster Model and it will replace the former dual pickup job. The appearance and price remain the same." Mike Cole wrote back that dropping the Broadcaster name was in fact helpful to him. In his Eastern territory people had confused the Fender with Gretsch's trademark.

At all costs Radio-Tel would avoid infringing on another company's trademark with *Telecaster*. F. C. Hall hired Robert D. Pearson, a registered patent attorney from Los Angeles, to do a thorough trademark search. The closest reference the attorney found was the Thomas A. Edison, Inc., trademark for *Telediphone*, used for phonographs. In the late 1940s, Packard-Bell had produced a television set

Classic Telecasters

Since that first year, Fender has made thousands of original-style Telecasters and variations. But collectors and players usually agree that 1951 to mid-1955, a time when the Telecaster first rooted itself into the foundation of modern music, was the instrument's golden era.

In 1952 Leo replaced the blend control circuit with a conventional tone control circuit. The 3-position switch worked in this manner: the rear position selected the lead pickup; the middle position selected the rhythm pickup; the front position selected the rhythm pickup with a capacitor that rolled off the highs (Leo's bass-like deep rhythm). The blend control knob became the tone control knob. Telecasters came equipped with this wiring until the mid-1960s when the modern switch setup was introduced (middle position selected both pickups and the front selected the rhythm).

One drawback of the 1952 to mid-1960s wiring seems obvious today: it made the 2-pickup combination impossible without delicately placing the spring-loaded switch between settings. When players learned this trick, they got a surprise. Different Telecasters had different sounds using this unintended setting, depending on the rhythm pickup's magnetic polarity, which changed if the magnets were inadvertently installed upside down. Some Telecasters produced a snarly tone similar to the Stratocaster's half-switch sound (a topic covered in chapter 9). James Burton, playing his 1953 Telecaster, exploited this unique old Telecaster tone on the Ricky Nelson recording "Travelin' Man." Other Telecasters offered the robust sound of two pickups heard when Leo's blend control was turned up full.

Why did Leo change the wiring on the first dual-pickup guitars? When asked this question in 1982, he did not remember the original setup, much less why he changed it. Don Randall pointed out that the tone control made a more dramatic change than the blend control's subtle shading. Most buyers in the unsophisticated 1950s guitar world were oblivious to musical nuance and wanted a knob that made a noticeable difference regardless of quality. The new tone control cut the treble quite noticeably.

Another feature on pre-1955 Telecasters was the one-piece maple neck. The earliest Fenders had a pronounced V-shaped neck profile, good for wrapping a thumb around to make barre chords. By early 1951 the neck displayed a more rounded profile. Leo attributed the change to requests from violin teachers teaching guitar: the more

called the Tele Caster, but apparently the name went unregistered. Pearson concluded on March 29 that Fender could legally use the new name. In addition, Fender continued to use the name *Esquire* for the single-pickup model despite complaints from the popular men's magazine of the same name.

The Broadcaster-to-Telecaster name change cost Radio-Tel hundreds of dollars, besides derailing the marketing effort. Hall promised Gretsch that he would have brochures and envelope inserts destroyed. To control damage further, Randall ran a revised full-page insert for the Telecaster and Esquire in the June *Musical Merchandise* magazine. In the July issue he announced, "Now It's 'the Telecaster.'" For Leo or some unlucky worker, the name change meant clipping the word *Broadcaster* off hundreds of decals with a pair of scissors. For several months, the new twin-pickup guitars sported nothing but the word *Fender*. Years later, collectors would coin the name *No-caster* for these early and mid-1951 guitars.

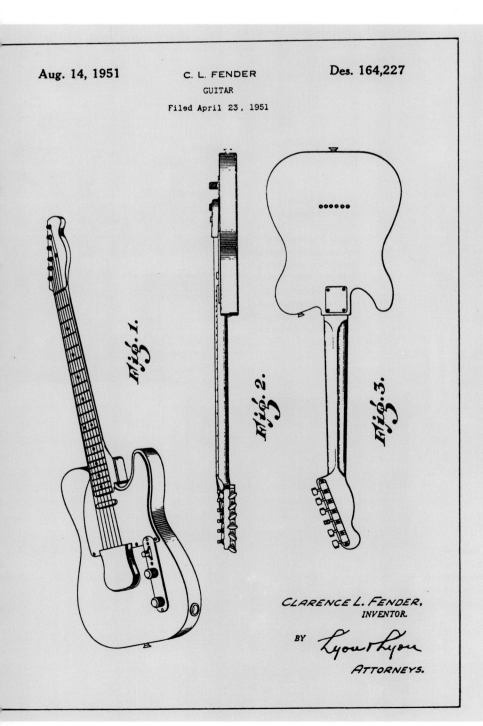

Aug. 14, 1951

C. L. FENDER

GUITAR

Filed April 23, 1951

Des. 164,227

Fig. 1.

Fig. 2.

Fig. 3.

CLARENCE L. FENDER,
INVENTOR.

BY *Lyon & Lyon*

ATTORNEYS.

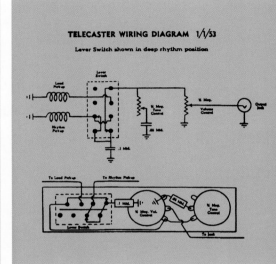

TELECASTER WIRING DIAGRAM 1/1/53

Lever Switch shown in deep rhythm position

The Telecaster's official wiring diagram from 1953 through the mid-1960s.

Design patent for the Telecaster. Until August 5, 1940, inventors could wait up to two years after an invention's first public use or sale to file a valid patent application for it. After that date, the period of first public use or sale was shortened to one year. Leo applied for this patent on April 23, 1951, one year after showing the Esquire in the 1950 catalog.

Worker shaping a head-
stock with a router, 1952.

Leo was always
cryptic describing
his improved tech-
nique for fretting
necks. Here a worker
used the setup Fender
devised, which pulled
each fret into a slot
on the fingerboard.
Most other companies
hammered frets into
the slots.

John Staunch dishing out the front of a
headstock, the area behind the nut, 1950.

Drilling holes for the tuners.
California's mild climate permitted working outside between
the factory buildings almost all
year. Leo's dog Pudgy secured
the area.

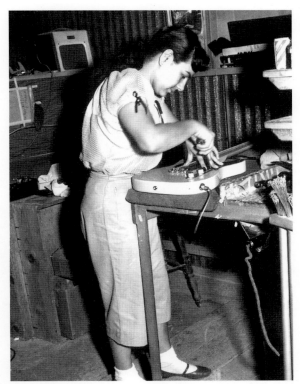

Tightening screws on a pickguard or cranking a string up to pitch in final assembly were routine jobs.

By mid-1951 the Fender factory was in full swing producing standard guitars. The wood shop had solid-bodies stacked almost to the ceiling.

rounded neck better suited their classical technique. Still, the factory's sanding methods made every early Telecaster neck feel slightly different. Because Fender made several thousand guitars in these early years, one hesitates to make sweeping generalizations about necks made after 1951, but usually the ones made in 1952 and 1953 were more round than V-shaped. Those necks made after late 1953 regained a hint of their former V shape. By 1955 necks were both V-shaped and round. Obviously, no one put a high priority on consistency during these early years.

Jeff Beck's highly modified Esquire propelled the Yardbirds in the 1960s. English guitar heroes Beck, Eric Clapton, and Jimmy Page played Fenders in many of their early recordings, defining the sound of a generation.

(Opposite) **A 1953 Telecaster with a Deluxe Amp.**

(Below) **Roy Buchanan revived widespread interest in early Telecasters in the 1970s. In his hands the 1953 guitar shown here produced every imaginable combination of string bend, harmonic squawk, and volume swell. He proved that Leo's original electric was perhaps the most versatile non-vibrato electric guitar ever made.**

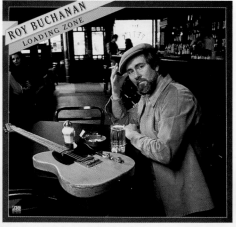

Solidbody Fenders carried several cosmetic changes from 1950 to 1955. The knurling on knobs varied from smooth to rough. Generally, the older knobs were tall and rough. Esquires and Broadcasters from 1950 used the tallest ones. No-caster knobs were usually smoother and shorter than the previous year's. The shortest dome-shaped knobs, used on 1951–54 Telecasters, usually had a rough knurling. Adding grief to the collector's task, some guitars had mismatched knobs, short with tall, rough with smooth. All original knobs were brass.

In 1951 Leo decided to replace single-slot screws on Telecasters with Phillips head screws, which he thought looked better. Never known to waste parts in stock, however, Leo exhausted the existing screws before reordering. With a little practice, one can date early Telecasters to within a few months using the screw changes as a guide. Broadcasters and early 1951 Telecasters used single-slot neck mounting screws while later Telecasters usually employed Phillips head. Pickguard screws had single slots until late 1952 or early 1953. Subsequently, the Phillips heads appeared here, too. The pickup height adjustment screws on early 1953 Telecasters still had single slots, but after 1953 were Phillips. The saddle height adjustment screws always had single slots which Leo hid under the snap-on bridge cover.

ARTHUR SMITH
prefers
Fender
Fine Electric Instruments

(Most 1950s catalogs still showed black pickguards because Randall believed they photographed better in black and white.) These cosmetic changes portended another modification in the electronics that marked the end of the Telecaster's classic era.

The classic Telecasters used level-pole lead pickups that produced an outstanding tone with significant bass content and few offensive highs. However, due to inconsistencies in the manufacturing process, a small number had a bass-heavy low E string that sounded out of balance. So in mid-1955 Leo staggered the pole pieces in height to balance the volume of each string, as he did on the Stratocaster's pickups (chapter 9). The results were mixed: the strings had better volume balance, but the overall sound of the pickup was harsher. Other factors designed to cut production costs soon hurt the tone. By 1958 the bridge pieces changed to a threaded stock with less mass, and the factory stopped putting the strings through the body (from 1958 through 1960). From a player's point of view, these late-1950s guitars represent the shrillest-sounding, least desirable Telecasters made during the pre-CBS era.

In the early 1950s, Telecaster buffs quickly established themselves in bands and guitar combos across the nation. The Fender became Everyman's guitar because of its versatile sound, ease of playing, and reasonable cost. Embraced by a broad spectrum of players, it quickly became the guitar played by artists from blues legend B. B. King to country flatpicker Arthur "Guitar Boogie" Smith. Most serious students could afford the $189.50 price, ensuring a new guitar generation would grow up on Fenders. The Telecaster was a hot commodity that sold itself despite setbacks like the truss rod delay and confusing name change.

While Driver and Hayes barely eked out an existence in the early years, by 1951 they earned good money, due in part to the Telecaster's appeal. Hayes made $45,396.36 in 1952, equal today to several hundred thousand dollars. Cole overcame the obstacles and realized a substantial return, too. Soon he would buy race horses and name one Telecaster. The fledgling Fender company had the momentum of an emerging giant that could do no wrong. Newly empowered in 1951, Leo set his sights on other bold projects, and went to work designing the Fender electric bass guitar.

The earliest guitars used steel bridges ground flat on the bottom. By the end of 1950, Broadcasters boasted brass bridges with the same tooling marks as the earlier steel ones. In 1953 the factory started notching the two outer brass bridge pieces under the low E and high E, thus allowing a lower adjustment for these strings. By 1954 Telecasters employed steel bridges again, but rounded and made from a smaller-diameter stock than the ones from 1950.

Broadcaster, early Esquire, and the earliest No-caster black pickguards showed no bevel. Most had a ring of lacquer on the bottom side left by the lip of the can they dried on. Soon black pickguards had a bevel, a feature that prevailed until the early summer of 1954. Then the pickguards changed to white in time for the summer trade shows; the ash body's see-through butterscotch-like finish was also lightened to a truer blonde with the grain still visible.

Paul A. Bigsby made this guitar for country-picking legend Merle Travis in 1948. It was one of the first guitars to demonstrate the solidbody guitar's potential, as Leo Fender noticed when he first examined it at dances held in Fullerton's neighboring town of Placentia.

Merle Travis was one of the great guitarists of his generation. His playing inspired, guided, and motivated many others, including the best folk, country, and western guitarists of his day. Widely copied, his right-hand style gained the name "Travis picking." Few 1940s guitar fans missed Merle and the guitars he played. He recorded for Capitol Records and entertained a national audience on both radio and television. Full of wit and rhyme, he wrote songs like "Smoke, Smoke, Smoke That Cigarette" and Tennessee Ernie Ford's huge hit "Sixteen Tons." In 1954, Travis appeared with Frank Sinatra in the Oscar-winning movie From Here to Eternity.

An October 1949 fan magazine, National Jamboree, featured a story about Travis and the unique solidbody guitar he played at the time. The instrument's history was simple. As a boy Merle had drawn pictures of an imaginary guitar (he would later become an accomplished cartoonist). Its headstock had all the tuners on the same side, like many older European instruments. According to the article, he always remembered those early drawings and dreamed of someday owning such a guitar. He just needed someone to make it for him.

By the summer of 1948, Merle met Paul Bigsby, a fellow motorcycle enthusiast, an expert machinist and

Paul Bigsby (smoking) and Merle Travis in the summer of 1948 at Bigsby's house.

mechanic, and designer of the Crocker motorcycle. (In later interviews, Merle claimed that he had met Bigsby several years earlier than 1948.) Bigsby had already built custom steel guitars for Joaquin Murphey and Speedy West. After seeing Speedy's steel, Travis approached Bigsby about making a standard solidbody electric. Using Merle's ideas and drawings as a guide, Bigsby made the instrument that summer at his home. National Jamboree writer Glen Claussen stated that by 1949 Bigsby had sold several guitars like Travis' for more than $500 each. Although Leo Fender had made his radio shop guitar by 1944 — as well as modifying several Spanish guitars — there is no doubt that the 1948 Bigsby/Travis guitar, and a few other Bigsbys, predated Fender's first production models by nearly two years.

In the November 1980 Guitar Player magazine, Travis said that he regularly played the Bigsby all over southern California in the late 1940s. Bandleader/promoter Cliffie Stone organized regular Saturday night dances at the Placentia American Legion Hall, only three miles from Leo's Fullerton factory. In the mid-1980s Cliffie said that Leo had supplied amplifiers and a public address system for those dances and visited regularly. Equipped with his usual assortment of screwdrivers, tubes, and fuses, the para-

medic for performers' gear could handle most equipment problems. He also talked with the musicians. Merle Travis remembered meeting Leo there and showing him the Bigsby guitar.

Fender asked to borrow the instrument and promised to bring it back to the next week's dance. Since Leo looked like a trustworthy fellow, Travis, who played acoustic guitar on his weekday radio shows, agreed. According to the Travis account, Leo walked out with the Bigsby. When he returned it the following Saturday, he brought along one of his own for Travis to try — an instrument Merle assumed Fender had just finished. Leo's guitar lacked the Bigsby's attractive bird's-eye maple, fancy inlays, and arm rest, but Merle agreed that from a purely practical standpoint, the Fender pickup sounded better than his and the neck was easier to play. From this simple, friendly exchange of information, a controversy grew.

Merle Travis claimed many time over the following years that Le had copied the Bigsby guitar. Bot Bigsby and Travis often took credi for inspiring Fender's work. Leo, wh considered himself a guitar-makin veteran by 1949, always dismisse such talk as sour grapes, implyin the others, new to guitar making were simply jealous of his success Aware of the implications — an insecure enough to forget the detail — he flatly denied ever borrowin the Bigsby, claiming that he firs saw the instrument at a nightclul several years after those dances in Placentia. Out of loyalty, George Fullerton, who does not remembe seeing Leo with a Bigsby, support Leo's story. Fullerton suggests tha considering Merle's celebrity status having his Bigsby guitar at the fac tory would have been a memorable event. Still, even if Leo did no borrow the guitar, he saw it up close several times. Don Randall also sau the Bigsby.

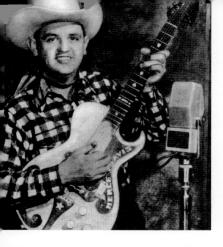

In the summer of 1950, Randall and Don Patton—carting a new Fender Esquire and a Pro amp—met Travis at the WRVA radio station in Richmond, Virginia, where the Old Dominion Barn Dance originated. In a 1950 letter to F. C. Hall, Randall described the scene: "They took us right into the studio where they were broadcasting, hooked up our amp and Spanish guitar and gave us a plug on the air." Randall further explained to non-guitar-fan Hall: "Merle Travis is on the program and he is one of the country's foremost guitar stylists. He is playing the granddaddy of our Spanish guitar, built by Paul Bigsby—the one Leo copied. Merle liked our guitar very well and our Pro-Amp very much." In 1950 Randall knew Leo had seen the Bigsby and its impact on the Fender design.

The Bigsby and the Fender Esquire had only vague, yet significant similarities: the headstock, the solid body, and the single bridge pickup. (Leo's Stratocaster and Jazzmaster headstocks would look more like the Bigsby's than the Esquire's did.) Made the old-fashioned way, one at a time, the Travis guitar had a neck that ran all the way from the headstock to the end pin. This design began with banjo makers, although that fact probably never occurred to Bigsby. He simply made his standard guitars like his steel guitars. Leo's radio shop test guitar had a neck-through-body design as well. However, by the time Leo saw the Bigsby, he favored a more economical, detachable neck like Rickenbacker's. This feature—the key to mass production—soon became the hallmark of all Leo's fretted instruments.

To Leo, the Travis/Bigsby guitar reaffirmed the feasibility and obvious utility of a solidbody guitar. While he saw merit in the Bigsby concept, he saw little merit in the design. Leo had already spent months designing his own guitar before seeing Merle's, and if he did borrow the Bigsby, it was for one of his notorious side-by-side comparisons on the test bench, not for a frantic, weeklong binge of copying. Besides, the guitar that Leo brought to show Travis was not Leo's first solidbody Spanish guitar anyway.

Forgetting the incident was Leo's way of saying without words that the Bigsby guitar failed to impress him. Nevertheless, the milestone Bigsby design, which portended finely crafted solidbody instruments, had a significant legacy. The post-1956 Rickenbacker solidbody guitars and basses, for example, and the Gibson Firebird guitars and Thunderbird basses had neck-through-bodies. Several manufacturers still use the design in high-quality electric instruments. Also, Bigsby's 1948 headstock design unmistakably foreshadowed that of the Stratocaster, still nearly six years away.

Speedy West (on steel) and Merle Travis, 1948.

As dance bands downsized in the late 1940s, some guitar players lost work because they could not double on stand-up bass. According to Leo, they came complaining to him because they did not want to take the time to learn upright technique. They needed a bass they could play like a guitar — a fretted bass.

Don Randall gives credit to Monk Montgomery for making the Fender bass the new playing sensation it was in the early 1950s.

MONK MONTGOMERY
with
LIONEL HAMPTON
says
Fender BASS IS BEST

A 1953 Precision Bass. Leo combined several diverse notions to create the ultimate bass.

7

Chapter

Leo Goes Uptown

In July 1952, music critic Leonard Feather described a new instrument in *Down Beat*. Several months earlier he had seen Lionel Hampton's band play in New York City. Master of the vibraphone, a xylophone-like instrument equipped with soundmodifying electric fans, Hampton led one of the most popular jazz groups in the country. When the music started at this gig, something seemed amiss: Feather heard a bass, but saw no bass player. Almost inaudible in a loud band, a bass player at least was easy to see. Feather wrote, "On a second glance we noticed something even odder. There were two guitars—but we only heard one."

Feather had stepped into the future, not the Twilight Zone. And in a few moments what he saw and heard made sense. One of the guitars had a longer, fretted neck, a peculiar-looking body, electric controls, and a cord running to a speaker. After the first set, the critic asked Hampton to explain. "Sure, man," Hampton was quoted as saying in *Down Beat*, "that's our electric bass. We've had it for months." He introduced Feather to Roy Johnson, the Kansas City bassist who had trudged around the country all year, unheralded, playing what Hampton thought was a sensational innovation.

Johnson told Feather: "It's no trouble at all. I learned to play it right away. In fact, I used it on the job the same day I got it. Tunes the same as a regular bass."

"But," interjected Hampton, "it sounds two octaves deeper!" *It* was Leo Fender's Precision Bass.

During the next set, Feather carefully listened to the Fender bass and its deep, booming tone. Johnson had its volume turned up "a little above normal," and Feather felt the tone surging like an undertow through the bottom of the band. He was undoubtedly the first music critic on the national scene to recognize the Fender bass' implications

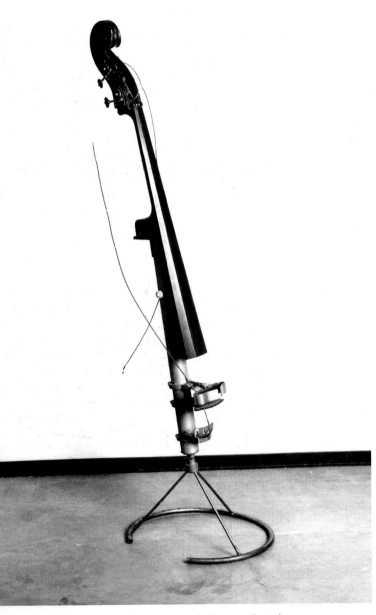

The Rickenbacker bass proved that an electric instrument paired with an amplifier could improve the bassist's lot in life. This example from the late 1930s needs a new set of strings.

for the future of music. In his article, he called Leo's creation a "bass-ic revolution."

Indeed, the Precision Bass was a milestone in musical instrument design, more than just a new model or a new brand. Leo's creation embodied a new class of musical instrument: a fully electric, fretted bass held and played like a guitar. The term *Fender bass* was to become generic whether Gibson, Gretsch, or any other manufacturer made the instrument. Although others would seize Leo's idea, Fender basses—the three pre-CBS incarnations of the Precision and the later Jazz Bass—would be the most popular electric basses ever made. Leo's designs set the standard for judging all others.

Pre-Precision Basses

Surrounded by musicians and steeped in the late-1940s music world, Leo Fender did not produce his bass in a musical or cultural vacuum. The acoustic stand-up bass, which Leo often called the doghouse, suffered several severe limitations. Foremost, it had nineteenth-century volume in the twentieth-century world of trap kits and electric guitars. Before the electric, the bass sound was easily lost on a bandstand because the tone had little projection. Orchestras made up the deficit by using up to six double basses at once. Aside from the acoustic's lack of volume, it was an awkward handful and difficult to move between one-night stands. Acoustic versions came in different sizes, big and not so big. Even a 3/4-size bass was too long for most car trunks; it barely fit into a back seat. Traveling bands often tied the bass fiddle to the top of a car or bus, and probably prayed for dry weather.

By the 1920s, the seemingly obvious solution to these problems was a compact, amplified instrument. Lloyd Loar, who worked for Gibson in the 1920s, reportedly developed a purely electric bass viol. Roger Siminoff wrote in the July 1979 *Guitar Player*, "Loar's approach to designing double basses and violins was to do away with just about everything but the pickup and strings." The bass, as pictured in Julius Bellson's *The Gibson Story*, played like an acoustic with a conventional peghead, neck, and fingerboard. With a small oval body, it used a pickup device that sensed vibrations in the bridge. Such pickups usually produced a weak signal because wood in and around the bridge absorbed the string's energy. At any rate, Gibson never sold Loar's instrument to the public.

Following Gibson's efforts, the 1930s brought further attempts to amplify bass viols. In 1935 George Beauchamp's Electro String produced the first fully electric basses sold commercially, the Rickenbacker stand-up

ELECTRIFIED DOUBLE BASS!
NEW – STARTLING – LONG-NEEDED!

Here is the answer to the Bass player's dream. It is light—It is quickly portable—Full size bass scale; may be bowed, plucked or slapped. Special speaker reproduces true bass tone. It is novel — It is unique — It is very practical. Be the first to show this startling new instrument in your locality.

Specially designed electric pick-up with volume control. Special amplifier to be used only with this instrument.

Every bass player a potential buyer. Fine for all fretted groups as well as orchestras. Operates on 110 volt 60 cycle alternating current.

Complete outfit consisting of instrument, carrying case for instrument and amplifier
Complete $180.00

[25]

An electric upright featured in Regal's 1939 catalog.

The fretted bass that caught Leo's attention, Gibson's Mando-bass in the 1920s.

fretless models which looked similar to Loar's design. The Rickenbacker, however, employed a string-driven pickup, a more efficient design than Loar's bridge pickup. String-driven pickups sense a string's vibration and translate it directly to the amplifier. The Rickenbacker bass pickup—excited by metal wrapped on the bass' gut strings—lost little energy in this translation, producing a strong, pure signal. The first version of the bass featured a cast metal body, sometimes using its amplifier as a support stand. The instrument was 58 inches long and 6 inches at its widest point, sporting an ebony fingerboard, an adjustable end pin, and a rheostatic volume control. In one photo it had a black crinkle-paint finish; in another, it had a polished metal-and-lacquer finish.

The second version of the Rickenbacker appeared in 1938 with a traditional bass peghead, maple neck, ebony fingerboard, and tubular aluminum body standing free or supported by a small tripod. A catalog photo of a 1938 Electro showed narrower pickup magnets than those on earlier basses. However, the tubular bass in Bert Lynn's all-electric orchestra, a group that actively played and promoted Electro instruments, had the wide magnets, suggesting that Beauchamp experimented with magnet sizes. The later Electro bass also used both volume and tone controls. Although the Electro instruments were rare, Don Randall remembers professional musicians using them on stage; if Randall saw them, then so did Leo Fender.

Perhaps Leo noticed 1930s electric basses other than Rickenbackers. Regal advertised a fully electric upright in its 1939 catalog. It followed Rickenbacker's, had virtually

no body, and came paired with an amplifier. The 1941 Oahu catalog showed a Vega electric bass viol with the caption: "Modern science together with modern streamlining has created a new, slim bass." The Regals, Vegas, and Rickenbackers apparently failed to meet most bassists' requirements. Leo Fender recognized one problem: bandleaders often used stand-up bassists for choreographed numbers, and the stick-like electric bass viols made ugly dance partners.

Leo attempted to electrify an upright before 1950; a newspaper ad he ran in 1945 said that his Direct String Pickup adapted to the string bass. But beyond that dubious claim, Leo neither directly addressed the upright players' dilemma nor attempted to make an upright electric bass like Rickenbacker's. He attacked the problem from another angle, pursuing a fretted bass guitar.

The idea for a fretted electric bass came to Leo from guitarists. As dance bands downsized in the late 1940s, some players lost work because they could not double on stand-up bass. According to Leo, they came complaining to him because they did not want to take the time to learn upright technique. They needed a bass they could play like a guitar—a fretted bass. Several acoustic varieties like the well-known Gibson Mando-bass already existed. Gibson produced this instrument for mandolin ensembles and orchestras in the 1910s and 1920s. The Gallion Brothers, Leo's friends and local entertainers, still used one in the 1940s. The company had hailed the Mando-bass as lighter, smaller, and more portable than a double bass; learning the new playing technique was easy,

101

Dobro's family of resonator instruments included at least one bass. Here John Dopyera's brothers Rudolph and Robert (shaking hands with pilot) pose with the Rancho Revelers in 1931 for an incredibly weird publicity event (European-born entrepreneurs meeting women aviators to the sounds of cowboy musicians playing newly invented Dobros). By creating a bass that closely followed the Telecaster's technology and design, Leo made a family, too.

especially for guitarists. However, the Mando-bass had an end pin and stood on the stage like an upright. Played with either a leather pick or a felt-covered hammer, the teardrop-shaped body looked ungainly, reaching as high as a man's waist and producing meager musical returns. Gibson's catalog admitted the serious limitation, the Mando-bass' quickly decaying notes: "Long tones are best sustained by a slow tremolo."

The Patent Office would cite the Mando-bass as "prior art" to Leo's bass because the Gibson had frets. Other manufacturers also produced fretted acoustic basses. Dobro made at least one with an enormous amplifying resonator. Still, none of these clumsy, fragile, powder-puff-toned creations found widespread acceptance. They all lacked sustain and volume.

But the fretted bass guitar fit neatly into Leo's (not too original) idea of a family of distinctive instruments, all designed around the capabilities of his workers and factory. (Gibson had produced a family of mandolin-like instruments that included the Mando-bass. Rickenbacker

Leo leaned on several guitarists for ideas. Oscar Moore, shown here playing a Telecaster with the Nat King Cole Trio in 1951, was one who helped evaluate the Fender bass, according to Leo. *(Below)* This catalog page from 1939 reflected once again the demand for a better bass, one that looked and played more like a guitar.

had made guitars, violins, and basses equipped with its unique horseshoe pickup. Leo saw Mexican mariachi bands in Orange County playing their guitar-like instruments, including the bass guitarron, as well as pictures of European stringed instrument families.) He envisioned an electric fretted bass as big brother in the Fender family. As a stopgap for guitarists looking for a fretted electric bass, Leo produced the Broadcaster's otherwise useless "deep rhythm" setting.

After the Broadcaster went into full production in late 1950, Fender launched his bass guitar design. A wide spectrum of bassists helped him. John M. (Jack) Kelleher worked with Spade Cooley's and Jimmy Wakely's western swing bands and knew Leo's friend, cowboy guitarist Bill Carson. According to Leo, Oscar Moore, who played guitar with the Nat King Cole Trio, field-tested the prototype. Don Randall challenged Leo's memory and said that Moore had tried Telecasters, not the bass. Nevertheless, Moore, one of pop and jazz music's most acclaimed guitarists, gave suggestions in the early 1950s that Leo remembered using on the bass. Roy Johnson in Lionel Hampton's group also helped, as did Hampton himself (who later had his own Fender bass and appeared promoting it in the 1955 Fender catalog).

The prototype was a crude beast. Acceptable tuning keys did not exist, so Fender bought acoustic bass keys and custom-made string posts to fit his peghead design. Both Leo and George Fullerton remembered using steel-wrapped gut strings as George Beauchamp had done with the 1930s Rickenbacker bass. Randall doubts Fender used those strings very long and suggests that he soon turned to piano strings. To go into full production, Fender ordered custom strings and tuning pegs from V. C. Squier and Kluson, respectively. The electric basses required new tooling from Race & Olmsted for the bodies, necks, and hardware.

The Biggest Guitar In The World!
The
REGAL BASSOGUITAR

The BASSOGUITAR is just what the dance orchestra man or string band bass player is looking for. This beautiful instrument combines the vast depth and resonance of the double bass with the brilliant tonal quality of the finest guitar! Strings and tuning are the same as the double bass.

Novelty value of the BASSOGUITAR is very important. It is bound to be the talk of any night club, tavern or stringed group . . . because it is the biggest guitar in the world! It is a "Natural" for small guitar groups using the double bass!

The BASSOGUITAR is played to best advantage by slapping, plucking or picking (leather pick).

The BASSOGUITAR is a perfect instrument — perfect in volume — in tone — and in attention value!

BASSOGUITAR STRONGLY BUILT.
The BASSOGUITAR is strongly built, so that it can stand up under the strain of constant travel.

Each	$75.00
Mackintosh Cover—Snap Buttons	9.00
Covert Cover—Leather trimmed Slide Fastener	15.00

[38]

Although Leo designed it in the image of the Telecaster, only a few parts for the two instruments were compatible, including the neck plate, strap hanger, and jack ferrule.

The bass used a removable neck cut from a 4″ X 33″ maple board. The 34-inch scale length, derived from a physics textbook borrowed from secretary Elizabeth Nagel Hayzlett, a student at UCLA, proved to be perfect. According to Fullerton, Leo tried different scales on his test bench, choosing the longest scale players could easily fret. He saw no use making an instrument some players could not manage. In the 1960s he would develop shorter-scale models that played easier but never sounded quite as good as the originals. Leo's long scale length provided the string tension that created a more euphonic resonance.

103

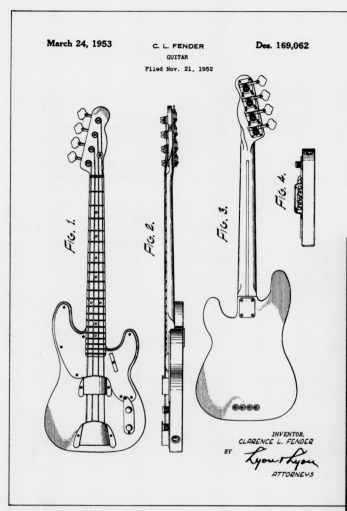

March 24, 1953

C. L. FENDER
GUITAR
Filed Nov. 21, 1952

Des. 169,062

Fig. 1.
Fig. 2.
Fig. 3.
Fig. 4.

INVENTOR.
CLARENCE L. FENDER
BY
Lyon & Lyon
ATTORNEYS

Design patent for the Precision.

One of the first Fender basses, 1951.

The Precision Bass necessarily had a bigger body than the Telecaster. The bass body started as a 14″ X 21″ X 2″ ash board; cut to size and finished, it cost $7.47 to make. To accommodate playing high notes and to cut weight, Leo put deep cutaways in it. The bass' flowing curves followed the function of the cutaways just as swept wings resulted from the aerodynamics of a jet fighter. Since the idea worked well on the Precision, Leo would recycle it to the Stratocaster in 1953. This interplay between guitar and bass designs would continue throughout his career, such as when he contoured the bass body like the Strato-caster's in 1954. But the first Precision Basses had no edge contours, only squared-off cutaways. Additional features included a black pickguard cut from a 4′ X 8′ sheet of 1/16″-thick Phenolite plastic. The single-coil pickup had four poles flush with the top fiber, one pole directly under each string. Each instrument had a tone and volume control. The bridge had two pressed-fiber saddles, sometimes mistaken for Bakelite, and the bridge cover came with a

accuracy of scalpels; it suggested a precise product made in a precise manner. The pickup and solid body made a precise bass tone unpolluted by the harsh, dissonant overtones Leo heard in acoustic basses. The Fender produced even harmonic overtones which sounded the way Leo thought a bass should.

Introducing the Precision Bass and Bassman Amp

Letters and Leo's notes show that the bass lingered in the testing stages during the summer of 1951 while Randall and the Radio-Tel salesmen prepared for its introduction. But no one took a Fender bass to the 1951 trade shows. Leo's records show that the factory produced the first commercial unit in October. In the 1980s, Fender and Fullerton remembered taking it to nightclubs in Los Angeles, driving through night fog to get there. Fog in inland Los Angeles and Orange Counties was rare until October, thus reconciling memories with the written record.

rubber mute on the inside. Early Fenders had a fine musical tone, but modern players rarely hear them the way Leo intended since they came factory-equipped with the mute and lifeless flatwound strings. Even played through Leo's treble-heavy amps, the effect was a big bellow, more like that of a string bass. Modern players, making no pretense of sounding like string bassists, rarely play Fenders with the cover mutes attached or with flatwound strings. Likewise, they rarely choose old Fender bass amps (which have, ironically, the makings of the perfect rock and roll guitar amp—treble and distortion).

Don and Leo coined the name *Precision Bass* for several reasons. The fretted neck offered precise intonation, the exact notes of the piano's tempered scale. Conventional basses, members of the violin family, had fretless fingerboards. Careless, inexact fingering on a fretless fingerboard caused off-pitch notes. (Later Fender would make a fretless Precision Bass, a concept that belied the name.) *Precision Bass* also paid homage to Leo's expensive machines that cut fretboards with the meticulous surgical

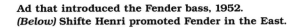
**Ad that introduced the Fender bass, 1952.
(Below)** Shifte Henri promoted Fender in the East.

Still, the perpetual fog of delay at the Fender factory slowed the first deliveries. Randall's salesmen, the last to see the finished product, received their sample instruments in November 1951. Charlie Hayes undoubtedly placed the first Precision Bass orders. One came from the J. R. Reed Music Company in Austin, Texas, on November 8, 1951. Because of the lag time between orders and actual delivery, the first few Fender basses—which were paired with Pro Amps—appeared in stores in late November and early December.

Leo knew that before an electric bass would be practical, it would have to have a good amplifier; the poor quality of amplifiers before World War II had thwarted Gibson, Rickenbacker, Vega, and Regal. Vega's bass amp, for example, developed a mere 18 watts of power. Although the company claimed the amp had "perfect response and clarity of tone," the output was pathetically inadequate for a professional. (Today small professional bass amps usually produce at least 100 watts.) Even in the 1930s a rumbling electric bass needed a heavy-duty speaker, a rugged cabinet without rattles, and loud volume.

Leo created the Fender Bassman Amp in early 1952 to accompany his new bass. It featured a TV front, a 15-inch speaker, and a ported back. Unlike all other Fender amps, part of the original Bassman chassis mounted on the bottom of the cabinet rather than on the top. Still, Leo placed the controls at the top for convenience.

Music Trades first mentioned the "new playing sensation" in an April 1952 ad that showed the Precision and the Bassman. The July issue quoted Randall as saying that a musician played the new instrument in much the same way as a guitar and with considerably less effort than a stand-up bass. At the 1952 trade shows, the Fender bass elicited the same mocking comments the Telecaster had endured. Yet creative and talented musicians started redefining modern music as soon as they picked up the Precision. Two that pioneered it in these early years were Monk Montgomery and Shifte Henri.

According to Randall, Shifte Henri was just that, a little shifty as he played night-clubs in New York City. Randall provided him with one of the first Fender basses and a Bassman Amp. Henri played the Fenders for a couple of months, then called Don to say that someone had stolen them. Randall shipped him a new bass and amp. About two months later, Shifte called again with the same story. Randall, now suspicious, suggested that Henri keep a better eye on the new replacements. They were the last the company could provide free of charge.

The bass helped Fender further shed its regional, cowboy image on the East Coast. Leo had always catered to a variety of musicians, although the 1950 catalog had pictured over thirty grown men wearing Western shirts.

(Spade Cooley's shirt, adorned with large musical notes floating around some hillbilly tailor's idea of a treble clef, made Leon McAuliffe's fringed one look almost urbane.) Virtually no jazz or pop musicians appeared in Fender advertising before the Fender bass. With Lionel Hampton's endorsement, especially, Fender took a major step towards recognition by the national market.

Musicians of almost all persuasions came to the same conclusion: the Fender bass provided the bottom end and compact design that modern music needed. (Traditional jazz and bluegrass players who refuse to play electric bass guitars remain among the last holdouts.) It was to music what the diesel locomotive was to transportation: a streamlined powerhouse built for change and progress. Electric bassists could play melody, chords, and percussion. They made new, stronger alliances with drummers to form rhythm sections with unexplored potential. The electric bass rounded out and balanced the volume of small combos with electric guitars; electric guitar, bass guitar, and drums became the core of most rock bands. The Fender would not share the Telecaster's widespread, instant success, but it eventually would become so commonplace that most musicians, young and old, could not imagine a music world without it. Bass players like Paul McCartney, Jaco Pastorius, and Stanley Clarke would emerge as three of this century's most popular and respected musicians. They succeeded not by playing the violin, piano, or even the guitar, but by mastering the electric bass guitar, a nonexistent instrument before Leo Fender invented it.

In 1951, Don Randall and Leo Fender were on the offensive with a group of eager salesmen penetrating every corner of America. When the established music industry, lulled to sleep by complacency, awoke to the sounds of their ideas, much of the battle was already over. Fender controlled the solidbody market before managers at other companies had put their shoes on. With the bass in production, Leo's family of Fenders started creating a good cash flow. On the brink of financial ruin in 1947, virtually debt-free in 1951, he continued reinvesting his new wealth in real estate, machinery, and tools as fast as he could deposit the checks. Sometimes he was short at the end of the month, but he never again faced financial disaster. On the way to the Jazz Bass, Stratocaster, and famous Fender amps, the problems of success rather than failure brewed trouble in the paradise called Orange County. The creation of Fender Sales and the final confrontation between F. C. Hall, Leo Fender, and Don Randall threatened to turn the efforts of the early years into an epic, acrimonious misadventure.

Singers from Wade Ray's band demo Fender basses in 1953.

Fender ran several ads in the early 1950s that showed the complete line. This one appeared in 1952.

107

Leo believed that continued
success in manufacturing
meant making the Telecaster
obsolete before someone else
did. It meant creating a new
super model that completely
replaced the Telecaster.

The Fender factory, 1952.

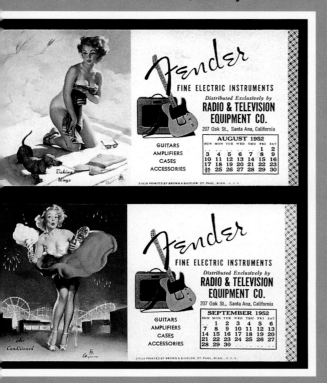

Chapter

Often Copied but Never Equalled

By the 1951 introduction of the Precision Bass, the strained relationship between the Fender factory and Radio-Tel shaded nearly every aspect of the business. But Leo produced better during times of adversity. His creativity, fueled by fury, thrived in a contentious atmosphere as he sought shelter in his lab, escaping the world outside. As a musician friend once said: "World War III could have come and gone and Leo wouldn't have known it. He was too wrapped up in his latest invention." He only came out when he had to come out.

So in spite of the personal problems, the Fender company grew along with the rest of the guitar industry. In the July 1951 *Musical Merchandise* magazine, NAMM reported guitar sales up by 1/3. Many factors played into this historic rise, some mentioned in earlier chapters. But in this article the music association attributed the boom to thousands of people taking up the ukulele in 1949 and

1950. Morning radio show host Arthur Godfrey, king of the airwaves, only advanced the craze. Immensely popular with average Americans, he played uke and endorsed a line of instruments and accessories. The push-button Arthur Godfrey automatic chord maker, which strapped onto the uke's neck, made music fun and easy to play. NAMM stated, "Once a person finds he can have fun making music, he wants to advance and play more satisfying music."

More satisfying music often came with the guitar. The twentieth century's first growth spurt in the 6-string followed the mid-1920s rage for ukuleles, bearskin coats, and bootleg whiskey. Increasing demand for louder, more economical guitars then led to National, Dobro, and Electro String's technical advances. Fourteen-fret necks and D-sized bodies soon appeared on Martin guitars. Gibson's L-5 and Epiphone jazz guitars came to fruition. One can

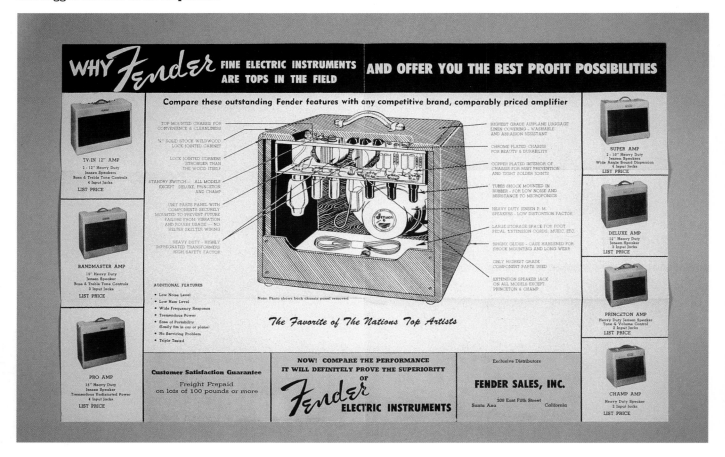

seriously argue that the ukulele helped change American music forever in the 1920s and early 1930s by spurring interest in the guitar as a recreational instrument.

The ukulele—and other Hawaiiana—struck again in the late 1940s. Just as hemlines went up during times of economic prosperity, so, it seems, did interest in ukuleles. As happened in the 1920s, many young 1940s musicians moved up to guitar after mastering the uke or growing frustrated with its limitations. Of course, other factors figured, but this simple explanation was good enough for the guitar industry, which went into high gear. NAMM predicted that total production of guitars in 1951 would exceed 250,000. Playing guitar became an even bigger social phenomenon, especially with the arrival of better electrics and the Precision Bass. Small combos with electric standard guitars flourished, portending the future of popular music and redefining the word *band*. Before the 1950s, *band* meant a group with a bunch of horn players. Now guitars played a dominant role.

Don Randall points out factors that made a direct impact on the sale of Fender guitars in the early 1950s. Music instruction studios started teaching standard

guitar in addition to steel, increasing standard guitar and amp sales as Don had predicted in 1950. Furthermore, novices learned the rudiments from each other. To the chagrin of Hank Karch, the writer who wanted to end the hillbilly monopoly on guitar music, many players found that they could have fun playing just three chords. The word was out, and Americans came up with the money to buy musical instruments.

Wide-Panel Amplifiers

Leo worked to update the Fender amplifier line. Sometime in 1952, he started phasing out TV-front designs in favor of wide-panel cabinets. Wide-panel Fender amps, built from mid-1952 to early 1955, looked angular and strong rather than soft and puffy like their predecessors. *Wide-panel*—another collector term—refers again to the front of the amplifier and the panels that frame the monk's-cloth grille. The first amp with this design was Speedy West's prototype Twin Amp with two 12-inch Lansing speakers. When Speedy started using the new amp, Fender was not ready to manufacture it. That caused another rift with Don Randall, who could not fill the

This classic early-1950s instrumental album featured Fender amps and Bryant's Telecaster recorded live with virtually no trickery—just the pure sound and unequalled talent of the players. On stage at a local bar in 1952, the team used Speedy's prototype Twin and a wooden Professional. West would play the Bigsby steel for several more years and then switch to a Fender.

many requests from those who had seen and heard the amp. From then on, Randall insisted that Fender not provide high-profile professionals with prototypes the factory could not produce in quantity. Leo's approach caused too much ill will. (Prototypes still went out for testing.) During the summer of 1952, Fender finally introduced the wide-panel Twin Amp, but dealer Fred McCord recalled that electronic problems forced a considerable delay in production until 1953. The delay was just another example of Leo's disorganization.

The Twin presented another first for Fender amplifiers: separate treble and bass controls. Although National amplifiers already featured the innovation, Fender made it his own, as he would later do with pulsating tremolo circuits. He followed the Twin with the similarly equipped wide-panel, single-15-inch-speaker Bandmaster, which marked the beginning of Fender amps designed for instruments such as harmonica, violin, and accordion. To sell more amps, Leo wanted all

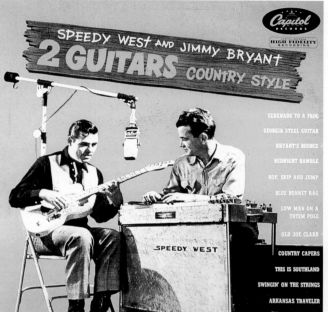

The Harmonicats, circa 1953.

Two views of workers wiring amp chassis at the original factory in the early 1950s.

instruments to go electric. Randall even enlisted the Harmonicats, who used special harmonica microphones, to endorse Fender. Randall could hardly have guessed that 1990s blues harmonica players such as James Harman and Darrell Mansfield would later strongly advocate early Fender amps, too.

Fender Sales, Inc.

Leo had introduced some widely popular instruments but increasingly believed that his distribution deal with Radio-Tel worked against his interests. He claimed that Hall, who had a reputation as a conservative but thoroughly honest businessman, dragged his feet paying bills. (On the contrary, Don Randall says that the bills were paid on time.) When F. C. had loaned Leo money to keep the factory open back in 1947, Fender saw the gesture as a poorly disguised effort to gain control of manufacturing. Indeed, Leo regretted his debt to Hall and felt trapped by it. After hearing more than a few stories from dealers who tried and failed to establish credit with Hall, Leo became even more resentful. On a personal level, he had a difficult time just talking with F. C. Driving home after one meeting with him in Santa Ana, Leo became so emotionally upset that he pulled his car to the roadside, got out, and threw up.

But Hall also had his list of grievances. By the early 1950s Randall's salesmen had established themselves, and Radio-Tel held thousands of dollars in unfilled orders. Hall thought that Leo's factory produced too few instruments. For example, Leo promised to deliver $31,000.00 worth of merchandise in January 1952 but sent only $29,760.10 worth, a 4 percent shortfall. Hall wanted more guitars and amps, as he told Leo in a letter dated February 25, 1952: "One of our salesmen has left the territory and is heading for our office due to this circumstance which is not our fault. It is imperative that we can depend upon promises from your company to back up promises we in turn make to our customers."

Hall also had trouble obtaining replacement parts and repairs from the factory, but the bootlegged instruments caused his biggest concern. He insisted that Leo stop selling instruments through the factory's back door and through Dale Hyatt. To help keep Leo in check, F. C. required that serial numbers be placed on all factory products. Radio-Tel, which sold parts to the factory, counted the speakers sent to Fender, comparing that number with the number sold back to Radio-Tel in finished cabinets. Randall recalls that the whole process humiliated Leo. For several years Fender believed that his first agreement with Hall, signed in 1946, became void when Hall turned down orders and let Fender

A 1953 wide-panel Deluxe.

Factory scenes, 1950–51.

(Left) **Wiring chassis.**

(Below left) **George Fullerton cutting tweed fabric.**

(Below) **Sitting worker knocks a lock-jointed cabinet together while standing worker applies glue to another.**

113

Christmas, 1952.

Dual Eight Professional, 1953

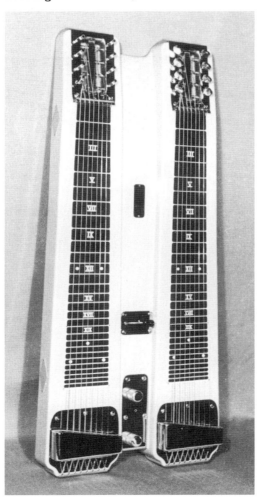

amps sit in storage. (Again, Randall says that never happened.) But Leo hesitated getting a new distributor while he still owed Hall money. As early as 1949 F. C. approached Leo hoping to sign an unambiguous ten-year distribution deal, a contract that, unlike the first agreement, clearly spelled out each party's responsibilities. Since Radio-Tel paid for advertising and in Hall's eyes created the demand for Fender instruments, he wanted assurance that the factory would base prices on a set formula.

F. C. worried that Leo would find another distributor. By 1948 several wholesalers, including the U.S. Musical Merchandise Corporation, sought to carry the Fender line. In 1951, others seeking Fender instruments included Coast Wholesale Music Company; Lipsky Music Company of New York; Peate Musical Supplies, LTD., of Montreal, Canada; David Wexler and Company; St. Louis Music Supply Company, Inc.; Targ & Dinner, Inc.; and J. M. Sahlein Music Company of San Francisco. An increasing demand for guitars existed, especially high-quality instruments. As Fender's reputation grew, more people lined up to cash in on his success.

Caught in the middle of the Hall-Fender feud, Randall shared Hall's concern that Leo might seek another distributor and leave Radio-Tel out on a limb. Randall felt somewhat obligated to Hall, but he also yearned for more freedom to run the sales operation. When Leo paid off his debt to Hall in late 1951, Randall pressed Leo to form a new sales organization that would still include Hall but also give Fender a hand in distribution and Randall the autonomy he needed. The idea for Fender Sales, Incorporated was born. Planning for the new organization started in January 1953.

Fender Sales had four owners and officers in the beginning: Don Randall, president; Charlie Hayes, vice-president; Leo Fender, treasurer; and F. C. Hall, secretary. (Everybody except Hall won, and he did not lose

114

Condensed catalog foldouts, left to right, 1952, 1953, and 1954. No full-size catalogs appeared between 1950 and 1954, but sales boomed anyway.

A wide-panel Pro with a Custom Triple-Neck steel, 1953 promo shot.

everything; he still owned 25 percent of the distribution business.) They filed the articles of incorporation with the State of California on February 5, 1953. Showing where the real power lay, the corporate bylaws gave Leo and Don the power to sign checks. The plan put Hall completely out of Fender Sales' day-to-day operations, duties Randall handled. The newly formed corporation held its first meeting at 10 A.M., April 1, 1953. (The Fender Electric Instrument Company had become a corporation on December 1, 1951.)

Fender Sales established its office at 308 East Fifth Street, Santa Ana, in a building leased for five years from the Orange County Refrigeration and Fixture Company. Radio-Tel's inventory, salesmen, and accounts transferred to Fender Sales on June 1. (The inventory of transferred Fender instruments included two black Esquire samples left over from 1950. Today, if they still exist, they would make the ultimate Fender collectibles.) Still interested in the music business, Hall started negotiating with Adolph Rickenbacher, who wanted to sell his small guitar operation in Los Angeles.

In late 1953, F. C. Hall made a fatal misstep for his future with Fender—he bought the Electro String factory, which made Rickenbacker guitars. Hall had hoped to integrate its operation with Radio-Tel and Fender Sales, thus producing a potentially colossal West Coast musical consortium. But Leo became livid when he heard rumors that Hall told dealers the Fender factory would soon make Rickenbacker instruments, essentially the same guitars George Beauchamp produced in the 1930s. Leo thought that Rickenbacker instruments were dated and inferior compared with his own and wanted no connection with them. Seeking to look modern in every way, he showed unrelenting vanity in matters of inventions.

Leo's reaction to the Rickenbacker purchase mystified Hall, who either misjudged or underestimated Leo's contempt for him. Fender, Randall, and Hayes thought Hall

was now a competitor with a huge conflict of interest and began treating him like a pariah. In addition to Rickenbacker guitars, Hall started selling Nova band instruments through Radio-Tel. Randall and Hayes, also looking to sell band instruments, bought the plant that made Novas, changed their name to Hayes instruments, and raised the wholesale price Hall paid for them. (The 1955 Fender catalog would feature Hayes band instruments.) Paradoxically, the two were still F. C.'s partners in Fender Sales. Perhaps Hall had earlier suspicions; now he had good cause to believe that his associates had formed an uneasy alliance against him. Leo started a move to push him completely out. Charlie Hayes looked for someone to buy Hall's part of Fender Sales and approached both dealer J. Fred McCord in Dallas and salesman David K. Driver to put up cash. Both men refused.

Single-neck steel gets a rub down.

Hank Thompson's Brasos Valley Boys, late 1953. Second from right, Bill Carson on guitar.

Randall, Fender, and Hayes had little in common other than business, but business for them was definitely good. Leo, the introvert with his nose in his work, rarely saw anything outside the walls of his lab except bands in local nightclubs. His idea of fun was pinochle on Saturday night. He also learned to love boats, taking fishing trips along California's scenic coast. Of course, Don flew around the country on business for Fender Sales. In the 1950s he bought and refurbished a P-39 Airacobra, one of the hottest fighters to fly during World War II. He parked it at the Orange County Airport. At one time he planned to break the speed record for propeller-driven planes but gave up the pursuit, finally selling the plane. In addition to business and flying, Randall raised a family. Years later he took hunting trips in the Northwest and enjoyed fishing.

Bill Carson and Freddie Tavares

But Randall and Hayes needed Leo and the factory, and Fender needed their effective distribution network—the salesmen could sell instruments faster than Leo could make them. Fender spread himself thin working long hours, handling problems he did not want to handle. Faced with this reality, he decided to hire an all-around assistant, preferably a musician, to work in the lab and to handle the odd tasks he did not have time for. Fender recognized his weak background in music as a liability and had leaned on musicians for advice since meeting Doc Kauffman. After Doc left, volunteers like Noel Boggs helped but were not always available. George Fullerton suggests that Leo Fender listened to both amateur and professional musicians because he felt that the average player offered something the professional could not and vice versa. But for the lab assistant post, Fender wanted a top player.

Apparently, no one already working for him fit the bill, but he met musicians all the time and had many to consider.

Western swing player Bill Carson traveled from Texas to California in 1951, landing his first music job with Capitol Records artist Eddie Kirk. At the time, the Kirk band played at Anaheim's Harmony Park Ballroom, one of Leo's nighttime stops. As Carson said, Leo's "God-given sense" led him to working musicians to promote his products and to get new ideas. Soon Leo sold Bill a Telecaster and a Pro amplifier on installment for monthly $18 payments. Carson settled in Downey, about 12 miles from Fullerton, and started hanging out at Fender during the days. "The guys that guinea pigged [tested] the product or promoted it would meet at the factory," Bill recalled. Some of the finest players visited the plant on a regular basis, as did the hacks. Carson fell into the first category. He played well, but that was not always enough. To help pay for his Fenders, he started sweeping floors for Leo at the end of the day. Carson learned in the early days how important musicians were to Leo. Fender still struggled tuning a guitar by himself, according to Carson. The musicians helped evaluate products and gave the inventor ideas. When Carson finished pushing the broom or doing other odd jobs, he helped with new projects. Although Leo did not offer him a full-time job at this point, Carson would go on to a distinguished career with the Fender organization, eventually becoming a district sales representative.

In 1953, Freddie Tavares came to Leo highly recommended by their mutual friend Noel Boggs. Born in Hawaii, Tavares was an articulate, well-read individual. When given a manuscript for a Fender book by another author in the early 1980s, he returned it edited for grammar. He was an excellent guitarist, both steel and standard, having played with Harry Owens' Royal Hawaiian

Left to right, Noel Boggs, Leon McAuliffe, unidentified man, and Freddie Tavares discuss a prototype Telecaster and its unique tone control circuit, early 1953.

(Below) Noel Boggs with his long-scale 1953 Stringmaster. Fender eventually dropped this version because the top string broke too often in the popular A tuning. Note the metal pickup covers.

Orchestra, mainstay at Honolulu's Royal Hawaiian Hotel, Los Angeles' Beverly Wilshire Hotel, and San Francisco's St. Francis Hotel. (Harry Owens earned the respect in Hawaiian music that Bob Wills rated in western music. Both of their bands stood at the top of their respective styles.) By 1953 Freddie had settled in southern California; he played steel in Wade Ray's western swing band six shifts a week at a nightclub called Cowtown.

One night Noel, who worked the off nights at Cowtown, told Freddie that Leo wanted a musician/assistant at the plant and hoped to take Freddie out to lunch to talk about the job. The meeting later that week went well, so well that after lunch Leo offered Tavares the job and he stayed at the factory all afternoon. Leo had Freddie work for a trial period to see how compatible they were. The affable Hawaiian complemented Leo; they made a good team. Being a fine musician, Tavares brought skills Fender needed. But Freddie was also an intelligent problem solver like his new boss. They possessed similar dispositions, interests, and analytical ways of thinking. Both loved words. Leo kept a dictionary handy at his lab and frequently used it. Another link in their active, creative minds was that both men used vivid metaphors instead of technical explanations. Tavares often called Fender guitars "machines," for example.

When they first met, Freddie showed Leo a Heathkit voltage meter and offered to sell it to him for the cost of the kit. Later, after Leo took the meter apart and examined it, he told Freddie, "Boy, that's neat." Both the Heathkit design and Freddie's soldering job impressed him; he knew he had found a laboratory soul mate cut from the same bolt of Fender tweed. Freddie filled a unique role at Fender and became the ultimate design insider, another lobe in Leo's brain and an indispensable part of his inner sanctum. Yet Freddie saw limits to the friendship that grew

out of their years together. He was deeply hurt visiting G&L one day in the 1980s when Leo, absorbed in his work, had little time to visit. So while they became good partners and colleagues, Leo still put his work first.

Tavares described his capacity at Fender: "You might say we didn't have an R&D department that was called such. But Leo Fender and myself were the two people in the design end of it." Freddie was not boasting when he said, "I did things like making up the original prototypes of all our well-known amps and putting a shipping tag on them with my name on it authorizing that it be built like that." He added, "When it came to actually building any guitars, I never had anything to do with production. It was never one of my areas of responsibility." In contrast to other musicians close to Leo, Freddie's under-inflated ego boosted his credibility with historians. He never made claims for things he did not do. While sometimes credited as a virtual co-designer of many Fender products, Freddie always said that all the designs were Leo's.

In the early years, Tavares worked part-time at Fender while maintaining his music career—a concession Leo was happy to make. Freddie quit the smoke-filled bars, but played on movie soundtracks, including ukulele on Elvis' *Blue Hawaii*, and on many records. He picked the opening steel guitar glissando on the Looney Tunes cartoon theme song; Freddie's musical passage made Saturday morning complete for millions of kids—young and old—over the years. His daily routine at Fender varied because he did odd jobs, like putting air hoses on the walls of the factory and installing safety guards on the punch presses to

(Right) Buddie (later "Buddy") Emmons, shown here with a Stringmaster, would go on to become a top pedal steel player.

Left to right, Don Randall, Freddie Tavares, and Alvino Rey give Leo's prototype Stringmaster a listen in 1953.

placate an industrial safety inspector who threatened to close the factory. In addition, Freddie drove the delivery truck to the Santa Ana Fender Sales facility on occasion.

With Freddie on board, Leo started his new projects. He scouted locations for a new factory needed to handle the growing demand and bought a tract of land in East Fullerton at 500 S. Raymond Avenue. There contractor Grady Neal built three industrial buildings in the spring of 1953. While still at the old location on Pomona Avenue, Fender started designing a new line of steel guitars and a new standard guitar.

The Stringmasters

Following the Triple-Neck Custom introduced in the 1940s, Leo's new line of Stringmaster steels represented the non-pedal guitar's highest evolution. They had two pickups for each 8-string neck and a novel blend-tone control, which put the two pickups into humbucking mode when both were in use. Fender made 2-neck, 3-neck, and 4-neck Stringmasters. The 4-neck model, with a 48-pound shipping weight not including a case or legs, usually had a bank of bass octave strings and offered the player an amazing range of tunings. A single-neck 8-string steel with Stringmaster features

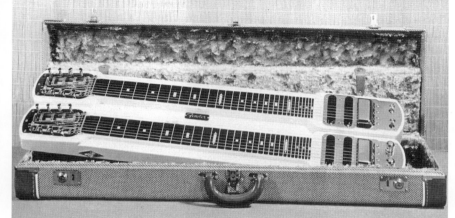

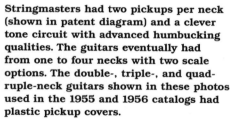

Stringmasters had two pickups per neck (shown in patent diagram) and a clever tone circuit with advanced humbucking qualities. The guitars eventually had from one to four necks with two scale options. The double-, triple-, and quadruple-neck guitars shown in these photos used in the 1955 and 1956 catalogs had plastic pickup covers.

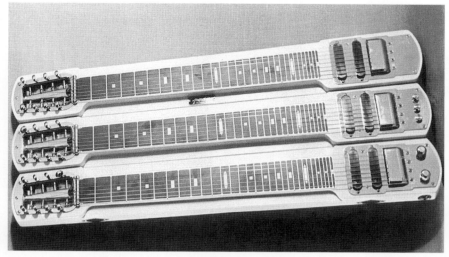

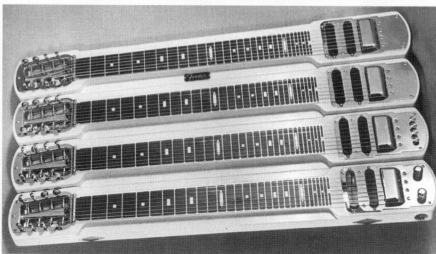

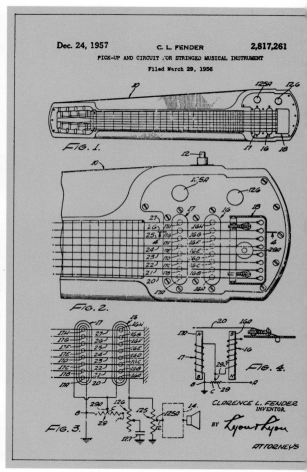

went into production by September 1955. Eventually the company also offered a 6-string model. (Fender Sales called the single-neck Stringmasters the Deluxe 6 and the Deluxe 8, respectively.)

The original Stringmasters had 26-inch scales. Leo used this relatively long scale because it sounded better to him on the test bench and also provided greater space between the frets in the higher ranges. Consequently, these guitars played more easily in tune above the twelfth fret. However, the long scale complicated bar slants, the technique of angling the bar across the strings for a wider

range of intervals, and players sometimes broke the first string when tuning it to a high G# or A.

Starting in July 1955, the Fender company offered two scale lengths for Stringmasters: 22 1/2 inches and 24 1/2 inches. Clearly the shorter scales made bar slants and high tunings easier. The biggest demand for shorter-scale Stringmasters came from Fender salesmen and professional players in the field. These instruments were more affordable, an important plus in a sagging market. The Fender Dual Six Professional, built like a Stringmaster, had two 6-string necks, each with the short 22 1/2-inch

Taken the same day as the factory photo on page 117, this pose shows Leon McAuliffe playing a very crude multi-neck Stringmaster prototype sitting on boxes.

Jimmy Bryant and Speedy West tearing things up in the mid-1950s. Bryant thought that a new guitar Leo started to design in 1953 would be called the Jimmy Bryant Model. When Don Randall picked another name, Bryant refused to endorse the new instrument and stuck with his faithful Telecaster.

scale. The company introduced it in mid-1956, producing it into the 1970s.

The Stringmasters came with single-piece steel bridges that allowed for length adjustment. Although steel guitars had fewer intonation problems than fretted instruments, the adjustable bridge compensated for different string gauges. In an effort to eliminate string rattles, Leo also designed the bridge so that the strings always rested on a level plane. Fender offered three different Stringmaster nuts, each machined for different string-spacing widths.

The first Stringmasters used slider switches to activate the individual necks. Jody Carver complained in a 1954 letter to Randall that the sliders made noise. The solution was a lever switch, but the one Fender used had only three positions. In 1955 lever switches found their way into these 2- and 3-neck guitars, yet the 4-neck Stringmasters still had four push-button switches to turn the individual necks on and off. Leo changed the Stringmaster's pickup covers soon after introducing the guitar; the first had chrome-plated covers while subsequent pickups had plastic covers. Fender made Stringmasters until the 1970s, although very few after the mid-1950s.

Leo had introduced the Stringmasters just as the pedal steel first penetrated popular music with the recordings of Bud Isaacs, Speedy West, and others. For most steel men, the pedal steel's advantages made the older models obsolete. Nevertheless, Noel Boggs and Leon McAuliffe played them long after most players turned to the new technology. Preservationists and purists demand the original sound of a non-pedal Fender, but playing them is almost a lost art today.

Outdoing the Telecaster

While Leo designed the Stringmasters in 1953, he also started planning a new standard guitar. Although the Telecaster was a hit, Fender and Randall knew they had to protect their newly privileged place in the market. To Randall, that meant adding a new, improved model to the line. Jimmy Bryant told his friend Richard C. Allen that Leo originally intended to call it the Jimmy Bryant Model, but Fender said he never had that intention. Don Randall came up with the name *Stratocaster* in 1953. Remarkably similar to the name Harmony chose for its first solidbody, the earlier Stratotone, *Stratocaster* evoked images of the 1950s aviation and rocket programs—the B-52 was called the Stratofortress—which appealed to the pilot in Randall. He realized the Telecaster's enduring commercial appeal and saw the new guitar as a more advanced companion he needed to compete with Gibson and Epiphone profes-

Ad from a summer issue of *The Music Trades*, 1953.

sional models. "In the Stratocaster's case, necessity was the mother of invention," says Don.

Leo accepted Don's reasoning, but also believed that continued success in manufacturing meant making the Telecaster obsolete before someone else did. It meant creating a new super model that completely replaced the Telecaster. As Leo divulged in the 1980s, "We [George Fullerton, Freddie Tavares, and I] thought we'd obsolesce the Telecaster." So the Stratocaster was more than just a new model. It was a reflection of the process at the core of Leo's being: the Stratocaster represented progress, renewal, and vanity.

Leo still believed in the essence of his guitar-making formula: the screw-on neck and solid body. But Telecaster details like the bridge, body shape, and pickups needed refinement. Always thinking up new ideas faster than he could implement them, Fender could have spent another year improving the Esquire and Broadcaster before going into full production. However, by late 1950 Randall and Hall had forced him to stop designing and begin produc-

ing; Leo's business reality separated him from dreamers who seldom turned their schemes into commercial products. Now when he planned to introduce a new model, he had plenty of unused ideas. On top of the list was a vibrato system. (Vibrato is a vibrating or pulsating effect caused by a change of pitch. Tremolo is a similar effect, but usually caused by pulsating changes in volume. The Fender company often interchanged these terms in a confusing manner.)

Fender dismissed Doc Kauffman's Vibrola guitar, with its impractical, built-in mechanical vibrato, and Doc's manual vibrato. Tuning a guitar outfitted with one was almost impossible. Leo's attitude towards the Bigsby vibrato tailpiece was another matter. By the early 1950s, it was fast becoming the industry's standard and a popular item. Merle Travis and many other professionals used Bigsbys on their acoustic-electrics. Soon after the Telecaster's introduction, Paul Bigsby developed a vibrato for it, outfitting some local players' guitars. He had thrown down the gauntlet in Leo's mind. Randall says that Fender

Valco introduced a solidbody National and this Supro Ozark on the heels of the Telecaster.

(Below) Gibson's Les Paul Model proved to be Leo's biggest competition over the years.

was not to be outdone, especially by crosstown rival Bigsby. Leo set out to top Bigsby by developing a built-in manual vibrato for the new Fender. Leo knew Paul Bigsby was surely incapable of creating and manufacturing such a guitar. Thus Fender would also outclass guitars made by Gibson and the other competitors.

Despite opposing views on the Telecaster's eventual fate, both Don and Leo wanted the new model *pronto*: By 1953 National (Valco), Gibson, Kay, and Harmony had all begun producing solidbody guitars that threatened Fender's hegemony in the new field.

Chicago's Valco produced its first National solidbody in 1951. But in trying to undercut Fender's price, it aimed for the student rather than the professional market. The guitar lacked a cutaway, a feature that soon attracted advanced players to the Fender. The National cost less than the Fender, but its single pickup, mounted in the rhythm position, produced the fat, mid-range tone of a jazz guitar. It sounded similar to its acoustic-electric contemporaries, lacking Fender's sparkle—the sharp, crisp tone that defined Leo's solidbody. National's inferior acoustic guitar-like bridge lacked adjustable saddles and contributed little to the instrument's sustain, in marked contrast to Fender's enhanced and improved steel guitar-like ring. National quickly added two cutaway models, a single-pickup version and a double-pickup version. Still, these guitars paled in comparison to the Telecaster and added little to the craft of guitar making. Today, early National solidbody guitars are nearly forgotten, along with the first Harmony and Kay solidbodies. Only one of Fender's early competitors, Gibson, produced a worthy challenge to Leo.

The Gibson solidbody Les Paul Model appeared in 1952. Rather than try to undercut Fender with a student guitar, Gibson attacked by producing a fancier, higher-priced

Jimmy Bryant and an admirer visit the site of Leo's new factory on Raymond Avenue. In mid-1953 the soon-to-be world headquarters of electric guitars stood in the middle of orange groves.

instrument. Still devoted to the old notions of what comprised a real guitar, Gibson made what amounted to an archtop with a solid body. It had a set neck and a carved top, both expensive Old World features with little bearing on an electric guitar's utility. The company sold many of the finely made Les Paul Models, some on the strength of Les Paul's reputation—although most writers say that the consummate player contributed little to the actual design—and many more on the strength of the company's good standing. Most players respected the craftsmanship seen in Gibson instruments, and the company dominated the electric guitar market during the early 1950s when rival Epiphone suffered a crippling labor strike at its New York factory. (Gibson would soon buy the company.)

The Gibson Les Paul possessed strong sustain and melodious tone, but also had a flawed trapeze-style tailpiece and a bridge that lacked individual adjustments. Even Les Paul rejected the bridge design when Gibson's chief, Ted McCarty, first showed him the guitar. The Les Paul cost more than the Telecaster, selling for $210.00 retail in 1953 versus $189.50 for the Fender. Because of the Les Paul's inferior bridge and tailpiece, many players believed the Fender was a better instrument. Eventually, Gibson engineers created a new stop tailpiece and adjustable Tune-O-Matic bridge with six saddles.

Gibson had the advantages of an industry leader and much staying power because of its established line of acoustic-electric guitars; the company initially treated solidbody guitars as IBM would first treat home computers, more as a required sideline than a passion. In contrast to Gibson, by 1953 Leo Fender based much of his business on solidbody guitars. He began designing the Stratocaster with the same passion that Apple brought to the revolutionary Macintosh.

Freddie Tavares and Noel Boggs watch one of Leo's punch presses, which came in different configurations and sizes, being loaded onto a trailer for the move to the new site.

Amp-assembly area at the new factory in late 1953.

Leo, the proud, hands-on owner, posed with his new Multi-Max punch press in 1954. He worked hard in the shop, as his soiled khakis reveal, but never in a production capacity

Drying racks for freshly sprayed bodies.

Amplifiers near completion.

Punch presses.

From this vantage point, two buildings are in view.

The center building's overhang provided working space outside.

Another view of the drying racks.

(Above) Storage bins for parts; boxes of tubes. Large coils of wire sit on top.

By November 1959 Leo had eight buildings at the site, seen here in a rare color picture.

125

Fullerton, Tavares, and Fender all claimed that Rex Gallion first suggested contours for the Stratocaster's body. According to them, the first Stratocaster lacked these contours. Tavares remembered Rex saying to Leo that a solidbody did not require an acoustic sound chamber and therefore did not require a squared-off body.

Rex Gallion playing an early Stratocaster in Leo's lab at the Raymond factory, January or February 1954.

The first Stratocaster with Leo's improved vibrato system.

Chapter

Contours and Cutaways

The Stratocaster

While the Stratocaster's history is less well documented than other Fender sagas, much still remains—catalogs, price sheets, magazine ads, and factory inventories—to bring together a picture of what happened and what did not. Although Bill Carson has said, "The Stratocaster was just a guitar that I hammered out of Leo because I did not like all the other points on the Telecaster," Fender neither designed the Stratocaster for a single player nor relied on one person for advice. As Don Randall says, "The Stratocaster's introduction was market driven. And without minimizing Leo's invention, it was a composite of ideas from many players." These included Bill Carson, Jimmy Bryant, Freddie Tavares, Rex Gallion, and others.

When a visitor tried to coax Leo into talking about the Stratocaster, he usually became uncomfortable, changed the subject, or just ignored the questions. He never made his history an easy subject, as if the inquisitive student

gained something by playing a shell game with the facts. Getting the answer to the simplest question became a research project-cum-archaeological dig into Leo's peculiar thought processes. Taking all his cryptic, erroneous, and sometimes contradictory replies literally was a big mistake; thus, because of Leo's crotchets concerning his own work, he was seldom the best source of information. For example, he once said that he started designing the Stratocaster in 1943. On other occasions he said 1948 or 1950. Had he envisioned the Stratocaster before the radio shop guitar and the Broadcaster? No. Was his mind that careless with dates and facts? Yes and no.

Leo had little use for historical accuracy unless it met his immediate needs. He could never recall long-lost facts that seemed trivial to him. But something more fundamental than disinterest influenced his memory. He saw the present through the eyes of an unorthodox,

Left to right, George Fullerton, unidentified man, Freddie Tavares, and unidentified man. The Stratocaster's design started on this drafting table in Fender's lab at the Pomona and Santa Fe Avenue factory. A drawing of a Stringmaster-style prototype was taped to the wall on this day.

forward-looking genius, putting the world together in combinations others could not imagine. He did the same with his memories. Leo rarely sequenced and categorized the evolution of Fender guitars as others did. He saw his body of work as one continuous stream of ideas, trials, and experiments. In his recollections, the specific guitar models usually blurred together into the generic "Fender guitar," a dynamic, unfolding concept and process—a child growing up. He considered the Esquire, Broadcaster, and Telecaster the same model, despite their small differences. Moreover, Leo often talked as if the radio shop guitar, the Telecaster, and the Stratocaster were simply different evolutionary levels of the same "Fender guitar." Pushing his thinking into the realm of mystics, Leo sometimes included his steel guitars, Jazzmaster (introduced in 1958), and Jaguar (introduced in 1962) in his catch-all category. At Music Man and G&L, Leo continued improving this generic Fender guitar, or so he said.

So in Leo's mind at least, his claim made perfect sense: the Stratocaster started in 1943 when the tinkering process leading to it started. His thinking resembled that of a mountain climber who said he began his ascent of Mt. Everest the first day he tried on hiking boots. But to be accurate, Leo started his highest climb on the day he hired Freddie Tavares in 1953.

Freddie remembered his first assignment for Leo as drawing different renditions of the Stratocaster on the drafting table in the Santa Fe/Pomona Avenue factory. Leo sat next to Freddie as he drew a crisp vertical line. He asked Leo what scale length to use. With that information, Freddie drew a nut, a bridge, and strings. Then they both sketched lines for the body using the Precision Bass as a model, making many false starts and erasure corrections. (Leo had arrived at the bass' profile through much trial and error, achieving the right balance by creating the body horns, a classic case of form following function. Deep cutaways made the upper frets more accessible and reduced an instrument's weight.) Bill Carson, who was at the factory regularly during these weeks and tested the first prototype when it was ready, remembered Leo making several different versions of cutaways for the Stratocaster body. Yet Freddie always maintained that the guitar's outline came from the first drawings he and Leo made, not from experiments on wood. By the time Leo built the first prototype, he had decided on the degree of cutaway.

In addition to deep cutaways, the Stratocaster had what Leo called contours, a scooped-out cut on the back and a smooth bevel on the front under the player's arm. These sculptured areas allowed a snug fit to the player's body.

With the Stratocaster at the height of its popularity in the 1980s, Carson said many times that he thought of its contoured body first. But these accounts differed from the story he told in a 1965 interview with Bob Perine for Fender Sales to use in advertising: the plank-like Telecaster, noted Carson, "mashed my right breast." He said that based on his suggestions Leo came up with the "contoured and offset waist body." A description of this body, used on the Jazzmaster and Jaguar models, follows in chapter 11. Suffice to say here that while Carson claimed credit for the Stratocaster's body in the 1980s, earlier he had claimed credit for the offset body, a different design developed about three years after the Stratocaster's.

(Opposite and left) Leo often found himself standing in a crowd taking pictures. On this night in late 1953 his lens caught one of his "guinea pigs" playing a prototype of the new Fender guitar, the Stratocaster. Freddie Tavares was on steel guitar.

Country ace Billy Byrd playing his custom-built Bigsby. The Bigsby vibrato tailpiece was eventually adapted to all styles of guitars, including Telecasters.

Fullerton, Tavares, and Fender all claimed that Rex Gallion first suggested contours for the Stratocaster's body. According to them, the first Stratocaster lacked these contours. Tavares remembered Rex saying to Leo that a solid-body did not require an acoustic sound chamber and therefore did not require a squared-off body. He implored Leo, "Why not get away from a body that is always digging into your ribs?" Leo probably made bodies with different contours to test (perhaps in part explaining Carson's memory of different Stratocaster bodies). Furthermore, over the years, the contours found on Stratocasters varied from deep to shallow.

The Stratocaster's contoured and deep cutaway body, regardless of origin, gave the guitar its streamlined, modern appearance. It was the first body designed with both the player's comfort and playing ease in mind. Another feature designed for the player but also adding to the guitar's visual impact was the one-piece hard rock maple neck (with added truss rod). From the player's view, the earliest 1954 necks usually had rounded back profiles; by 1955 they were usually V-shaped. Carson remembered that the prototype headstock had a narrower profile than the later, familiar Stratocaster headstock. It was larger than a Telecaster's, and the new curves balanced the guitar and defined its user-friendly attributes.

But the hallmark of Leo's Stratocaster was the built-in vibrato—which Leo insisted on calling a tremolo. It was his first attempt at topping Kauffman's and Bigsby's efforts. Carson says he urged Leo to develop a transposing vibrato system, one that would maintain the integrity of the chord as the player raised or lowered it. With such a system, the guitarist could play an E chord, raise it to an F or lower it to an E flat with the vibrato lever as a steel guitarist did with his steel bar. Leo knew he could build a transposing vibrato, but believed it would cost too much money. His vibrato system added shimmering effects rather than more complicated, precise pitch changes for each string. Moreover, the Fender vibrato aimed at minimizing tuning

Bill Carson in the mid-1950s. In a 1979 *Guitar Player* article Leo said: "We respected Bill's playing and leaned on him for advice. He was kind of our favorite guinea pig for the Strat, because we needed somebody who was dedicated to getting the job done."

problems associated with the old vibratos. Leo's system did what Bigsby and Kauffman vibratos did, and seemingly what most players wanted: it built a little bit of the steel guitar into the standard guitar, the ability to waver the notes in a musical manner.

Still, Tavares and Fullerton remembered that Leo's first attempt was a disaster. He tooled up his factory to produce the system before fully testing it. From most accounts, it functioned much like the later Jazzmaster unit. On both designs the strings rode over the bridge and attached to a tailpiece anchor on the guitar body's face; the bridge and the tailpiece anchor were separate pieces. Fullerton noted that each string on the first Stratocaster was shorter between the bridge and the tailpiece anchor than each string on the Jazzmaster. Unlike later Jazzmaster units, the first Stratocaster vibrato used individual roller bridges which helped the strings return to pitch. Several modern vibrato systems use roller bridges. However, Fender's bridges vibrated laterally, thus dampening the sustain of the strings by absorbing their energy.

George Fullerton remembers Carson passing the first vibrato system in the prototype's field tests, and it apparently sounded fine to Leo at the factory. So he prepared to produce the Stratocaster with a roller-bridge vibrato. However, George claims that the first production version sounded terrible. When Carson took it to work, he thought it sounded like an amplified banjo with no sustain; instead of ringing, the notes plunked. Leo desperately spent at least six months in 1953 trying to perfect the original vibrato system. He lost several thousand dollars on useless equipment and tooling. The most telling evidence of the failed effort surfaced in Leo's stockroom inventory dated December 1953. It listed 400 Stratocaster bridges, 5,240 Stratocaster bridge rollers, and 1,080 "tremolo lever sockets."

After manufacturing all these parts, Leo finally gave up trying to fix the original design and began a new one despite pressure from Fender Sales to deliver a vibrato guitar. If the first one had worked just a little bit better, he might have settled with it. Instead, he quickly re-thought the problem. At this time Rex Gallion replaced Carson—who left southern California playing on the road with Hank Thompson's band—as Leo's primary musician consultant outside the factory. Tavares often worked on stage with Gallion and remained Fender's main advisor at the factory.

Leo did his best work, such as designing the second Stratocaster vibrato system, under pressure. He finished what he called the new "hurry-up design" by the end of 1953. With the new setup, the strings no longer moved across the bridge. Rather, they loaded through an inertia block and moved with the whole bridge, pivoting on a knife-edge fulcrum point like a good gram scale. Leo accomplished this action by placing a hardened screw in front of each bridge section. These screws held the bridge plate against the guitar's body. He countersunk the screw holes in the bridge plate from both sides, thus making their edges comparable to knife blades. He anchored the bridge assembly and mounting block to the back of the instrument with springs; at first he used three, but soon settled on five. The assembly floated like a perfectly balanced seesaw between the tension of the springs and the tension of the guitar strings. The Fender headstock's design let the strings pull straight over the guitar's nut, minimizing the only real source of friction.

Fender believed that the revised Stratocaster vibrato had several significant benefits, some intended and some realized after the fact. It sustained the notes well because it eliminated the length of string behind the bridge by adding the so-called inertia block, a solid anchor for the strings. When a player pressed the vibrato arm, the bridge moved forward and up, putting the slackened strings slightly higher above the pickup's pole pieces. Leo also deduced, after the fact, that the springs mounted on the back of the body provided some shielding for the pickups and electronics. Fender's novel guitar vibrato proved better than any on the market. He applied for a patent on August 30, 1954.

The potential of Leo's Stratocaster vibrato went far beyond anything he imagined. Earlier vibratos like Kauffman's and Bigsby's produced their effects with slight pitch changes. Consequently, Leo thought musicians would use his vibrato in the same limited manner. Nevertheless, the

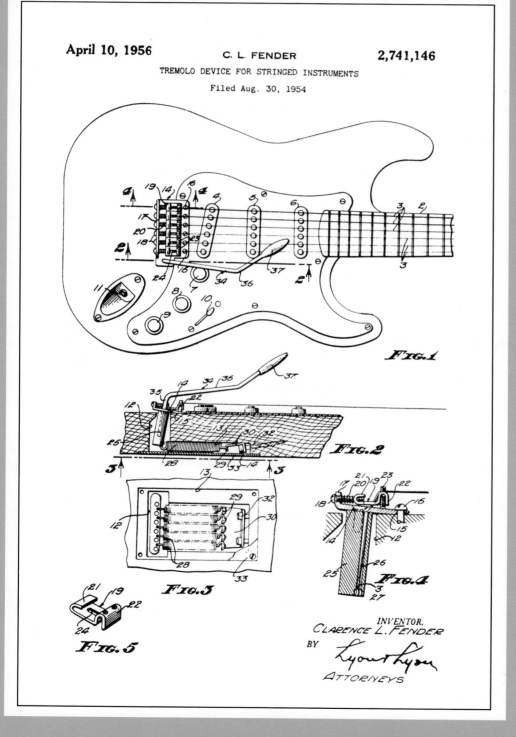

April 10, 1956   C. L. FENDER   2,741,146

TREMOLO DEVICE FOR STRINGED INSTRUMENTS

Filed Aug. 30, 1954

FIG. 1

FIG. 2

FIG. 3

FIG. 4

FIG. 5

INVENTOR.

CLARENCE L. FENDER

BY

Lyon & Lyon

ATTORNEYS

The Stratocaster's patent diagram. Fender's revolutionary vibrato system let a player raise and lower the strings' pitch to produce sound effects. It was not perfect, but worked better than anything else on the market for decades.

Stratocaster design allowed players freedom to lower the pitch at least one-and-a-half tones and return without completely detuning. Few players used this capability until the 1960s, when it became apparent that Leo had built much more than a little bit of the steel guitar into the Stratocaster. With the vibrato in hand, players could make their Stratocasters sound like a dive-bombing Phantom jet or a roaring freight train. Leo did not envision those sounds in 1954, but his Stratocaster's ingenious overdesign made them possible. As luck factored into much of Leo's early success, an industrial-strength vibrato eventually made the Stratocaster an overwhelming commercial success.

No known drawings or photos of the first roller-bridge Stratocaster remain, but Leo saved snapshots of the prototype guitar with the inertia-block tremolo. They show a black plastic Phenolite pickguard, chrome dome knobs, and a Telecaster-type top-hat switch tip. The 3-spring tremolo unit had a thicker handle than production models, and the pickups bore no covers. The neck showed a deep lacquer finish, but the highly figured ash body had none, typical of Leo's test guitars throughout his

career. One early vibrato unit shown in a close-up photo used single-slot screws in the baseplate rather than Phillips head screws. Always pragmatic, Fender was more concerned with the way his test guitars worked than the way they looked.

More Advanced Features

Randall's sales force knew in 1950 that the original three-piece Telecaster bridge was inadequate for precise intonation. Most musicians lived with the problem, but others sought solutions. Spokane, Washington, guitarist Aaron Spere modified his Broadcaster with a six-piece bridge in December 1950. Salesman Dave Driver, who examined Spere's guitar that month, soon suggested in a letter to Don Randall that Leo use a six-piece bridge. Don relayed Dave's ideas to Leo. Two or three years later Bill Carson would make the same suggestion, by then an obvious one. The guitar industry already had companies making six-piece bridges. Before the Stratocaster, Valco Manufacturing in 1946, Sebastiano Melita in 1949, and Gibson in 1952 filed patents in the United States for bridges with length adjustments for each string. Leo

A rear view of Leo's prototype shows only three springs.

One of the first
Stratocasters as
seen on Leo's bench
in early 1954. The
photo clearly shows
the short-skirt
knobs used on the
first examples.

The bridge's six saddles adjusted for
height and length. Notice the staggered height of the pole pieces.

(Below) Leo removed the plastic cover-
plate and a spring to photograph the
ground wire soldered to the vibrato's
anchor plate.

undoubtedly knew about these advances; surely his
lawyer did patent searches. Fender, again seeking to outdo
the other designers, decided to make each Stratocaster
bridge section adjustable for length and height. The prototype tested by Carson had intonation screws that adjusted
from the pickup side—opposite that of later production
models. While the fully adjustable six-piece Stratocaster
bridge came more as a result of the Telecaster bridge's
inadequacies, Leo's new bridge was also a response to the
Melita bridge used on Gretsch guitars, the Valco design
licensed for use on Gibson guitars (but rarely seen), and
Gibson's own Tune-O-Matic bridge.

Leo also wanted to put better pickups on the Stratocaster. In his evaluation, the Telecaster's worst problems
started with the pickups' uneven response between
strings. (As mentioned in chapter 6, the low E string often
sounded louder than the others.) Indeed, incredulous customers returned early Telecasters to the factory because of
the inequity. Some Telecasters had another pickup problem—screeching microphonic feedback when a player
inadvertently held the instrument too close to the amp at
high volume. Fender tested a wide variety of pickup
designs, including coils of varying heights, widths, and
impedances. He also tested pole pieces with different
lengths and diameters, both critical variables in the way a
pickup sounded.

Stratocaster #0100. With the date 4/54 written on the body, this guitar was perhaps the first in a small production run of Stratocasters. Forrest White insisted it was either a sample or an artist's guitar. Regardless, it was sold as new by a music store in El Monte, California in July 1954. Although Fender had made a small quantity of Stratocasters, including this one, by the summer of 1954, an order for the first full production run was not filled until October 1954. *(Below)* Details of the guitar's peghead.

bending easier. The lighter-gauge B string is quieter relative to the other strings and needs a longer pole; modern unwound G strings produce a louder output than the old-style wound ones. Core diameters (which determine the output) of wound D, A, and E strings vary from their 1950s counterparts.

Leo's puttering with pickups resembled art, not science. Still, in the 1950s he accomplished a great deal with his imprecise means. The Stratocaster's three pickups retained a clear, biting, yet musical tone similar to the Telecaster's. The oddball way Leo Fender explained his decision to use three had little to do with music: he had plenty of 3-position switches in stock for steel guitars and Telecasters, so he used three pickups. Whether he acknowledged his competitors or not, he must have noted with Randall that Gibson had introduced the triple-pickup

No one remembers all these trial-and-error combinations. Unfortunately, Leo made only mental notes of his efforts. However, Fender's 1953 inventory sheets list 117 Stratocaster elevator plates—hints of a discarded pickup design. Apparently, he discovered that elevator plates and metal covers contributed to the Telecaster's feedback, so he did not use them on production Stratocaster pickups.

Unlike the earlier Telecaster pickups, the Stratocaster pickups used staggered pole pieces, varying in height to accommodate differing string gauge outputs. Leo trusted his ears to test the volume of each string and to judge the guitar's total balance. With the old-style heavy-gauge sets, the plain B string had a strong signal, so Leo made its pole the shortest. Depending on the year of manufacture, either the D or G string on 1950s Stratocasters had the tallest pole. He would have had different results using today's light-gauge string sets, favored by most modern guitarists because lighter strings make string

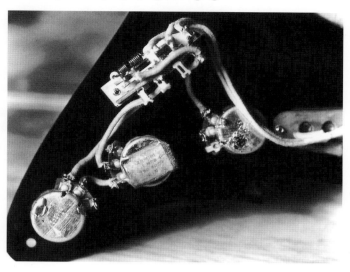

Leo removed the black Bakelite pickguard to take this picture of his prototype's switch and controls. *(Below)* A closer view of Stratocaster #0100 shows the poor quality of early knobs and pickup covers. They wore out with just simple playing and aging.

ES-5 in 1949. Obviously, Leo also found that three pickups worked quite well, but he could not foresee which tones players would like so much today.

By design, the stock Stratocaster switch circuit allowed only three of at least seven possible pickup combinations.Leo liked the pure sound of individual pickups; the middle pickup and the rhythm pickup each had a tone control while the treble-strong lead pickup had none. Remember, Leo found inspiration in the paradise of the Pacific, especially the Hawaiian steel guitar sounds so popular during his early life. In the 1950s, he pinned a Dole Pineapple Company map of the Hawaiian Islands to a wall in the Fender factory. Perhaps by no coincidence, his close collaborator Freddie Tavares hailed from Hawaii and played steel guitar. Inspired by the sound of the Islands, Fender wanted to put the steel guitar's tone and sustain into his

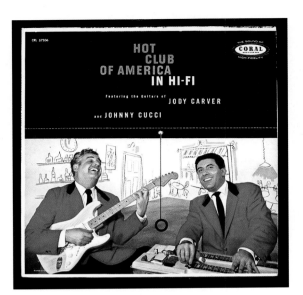

Johnny Cucci and Jody Carver's 1950s album. Cucci called the Stratocaster's half-switch tone "the lisp." Leo never understood why this infectious sound, made famous by Mark Knopfler and Eric Clapton, appealed to guitarists.

(Opposite) A few of the players Leo had in mind when he developed the Stratocaster. The term *rock and rollers* did not apply.

Buddy Merrill was perhaps the most widely seen Fender patron on television until James Burton made the scene as Ricky Nelson's guitarist on the *The Adventures of Ozzie and Harriet*. Both guitarists reinforced the connection between youth and Fender.

solidbody standard guitars. The zing and zip of the Stratocaster's lead pickup was inspired by steel guitars.

Musicians with other ideas quickly discovered quirks inadvertently built into the Stratocaster's switch that opened even more sonic possibilities. By carefully positioning the switch lever between settings, signals from two pickups mixed, producing snarling nasal tones that literally redefined electric guitar sound. The tones were reminiscent of a muted trumpet or trombone, but with the snap and sting of downed power lines. Two so-called half-switch combinations existed: the front with the middle pickup, and the lead with the middle pickup. Over the years some players believed the pickups were electronically out of phase, but it was their unique positioning under the strings that caused the chaos of overtones in the half-switch position. Fortuitously, that chaos blended to become something splendidly euphonic. Leo never intended the Stratocaster to produce its most popular tones. (For a taste, listen to Eric Clapton's "Lay Down Sally" or Dire Straits' "Sultans of Swing.") It happened by pure chance.

Players everywhere figured out the half-switch trick. John Cucci, Jody Carver's 1950s Stratocaster-playing partner, called this sound "the lisp." Lawrence Welk's guitarist Buddy Merrill had no name for the sound, but used it extensively as early as 1955. He thought it cut through on rhythm better than the intended sounds. Today's 5-position switches make these settings easy, but pre-CBS Stratocasters always used 3-position ones. Dick Dale, "King of the Surf Guitar," added a switch to his guitar to get the in-between sounds. He says that Leo, who did not like the half-switch snarl, considered anything extra on Stratocasters a gadget. Leo put 5-position switches into later G&L Stratocaster-style guitars, but then played with the pickup designs to change the characteristic in-between tones produced.

Fender liked the way the Stratocaster went together at the factory. The pickups and controls were mounted onto the pickguard and attached as one unit to the guitar's face. This idea followed the example of Leo's earlier steel guitars

with the Direct String Pickup, tone control, and volume control mounted on a modular plate. The design simplified manufacture since workers made the assemblies as separate units. When the time came to join the Stratocaster body to its electronics, the workers simply attached the pickguard assembly to the body with screws, grounded it to the vibrato, and connected the jack. The modular concept continued with the Jazzmaster and other later Fenders. In the 1970s the idea led to an after-market Stratocaster parts industry that sold custom pickguards, pickups, and knobs.

But Leo quickly learned a major lesson about guitar design: fixing one problem often created another. Although the factory could easily manufacture the Stratocaster pickup assemblies, players found the guitars difficult to service without loosening the strings. In addition, the vibrato made loosening, changing, and re-tuning strings difficult. The pickguard interfered with truss rod adjustments; on early Stratocasters the truss rod nut would not turn without removing the pickguard. On the plus side, the pickguard echoed the shape of the guitar's body, thus enhancing the Stratocaster's visual impact.

The Stratocaster's curves, cutaways, headstock, slanted pickups, and sleek tremolo arm all had flair. Amazingly, Leo squeezed a little more practicality and style into the design with the jack plate—a mundane feature on most guitars. He had placed the Telecaster's jack plate on the bottom side, out of the player's view. As a result, players sometimes fumbled with it and tripped on the cord which hung straight down. Of course, this placement worked, but Leo sought to improve everything. George Fullerton suggested slanting the jack and mounting it on the guitar's face. Most players found the position convenient.

George and Leo reported that the factory intentionally used at least two pieces of wood glued together side by side to make all Fender bodies in the 1950s. Inexplicably, many one-piece Fenders from that era exist, begging the question of when a standard practice started. In any case, most Stratocaster bodies consisted of two or more pieces, which created a problem matching the grain on the tops, backs, and edges. Glued in the sturdiest manner, the grains went in different directions, making an attractive, seamless match difficult. With the blonde finishes, the glue joints showed unless the grain lined up especially well. Factory workers shot Telecasters and Esquires with extra paint coats around the edges to camouflage the joints, but they showed nonetheless.

As the factory increased production, added new models, and used more wood, matching grain became an even bigger problem. Leo lessened his predicament by using dark-bordered sunburst finishes on Stratocasters— the first time he had tried the industry's traditional paint job on large numbers of instruments. It covered mismatched grains on the body edges while leaving the grain

The first ad for the Stratocaster appeared
in several magazines in 1954.

Considered among the most collectible items
in Fender advertising, the 1954 full-size
catalog featured the Stratocaster.

on the face of the guitar exposed. Initially in 1954, Fender
used a two-color sunburst finish that varied in hue from
later batches, suggesting that the painters used a different
mix. (The factory changed to a three-color sunburst with
added red in 1958 and then seemingly back to the two-
color finish in 1959. On some 1959–60 instruments the red
actually faded, leaving the appearance of a two-color sunburst. After 1960, the three-color sunburst became the regular Stratocaster finish.)

In 1954 Leo experimented with different woods for
bodies on Stratocasters. The factory made at least one
1954 Stratocaster either from flamed maple or a flamed
ash. Yet nearly all Stratocaster bodies through late 1956
would be normal-grain ash, a hardwood also used to make
baseball bats and long oars. After 1956, sunburst Stratocasters would be alder, a cheaper, plainer wood used in
cabinetmaking. Leo never liked alder. He said it was
"waxy," hence hard to finish. Also, the glue seams invariably showed on it. Because of the more stunning results
with ash, Fender continued making see-through blonde
Stratocasters from this beautiful, figured-grain wood.

Introducing the Stratocaster

Timing often marks genius, as it did for Leo Fender
and Don Randall. Their success mirrored a shift in musical tastes towards guitar-based music and rock and roll.
After 1954, the guitar's growing popularity and the world's
image of Leo were inexorably tied to rock's rise. Elvis, Bill
Haley, and later the Beatles fueled the country's growing
fascination with guitars. Dale Hyatt says: "It wasn't Leo
that made the guitar popular. It was Elvis and the groups
from England."

In 1954 the ingredients that produced rock and roll were
coming to a boil, ready to bubble out of the pot. Television,
radio, and long-playing records had arrived. On January 4,
1954, Elvis Presley made an acetate recording at Sun Studios in Memphis, Tennessee. In April Bill Haley & His
Comets released "Rock Around the Clock," the first widely
popular rock record. Alan Freed, one of the first to popu-
larize the term *rock and roll*, held packed-to-the-rafters
East Coast dance concerts that proved the new style's commercial potential—a lesson not lost on guitar makers.

The earliest known ad for the Stratocaster, with a vague
rendition of the Atoms for Peace symbol in the corner,

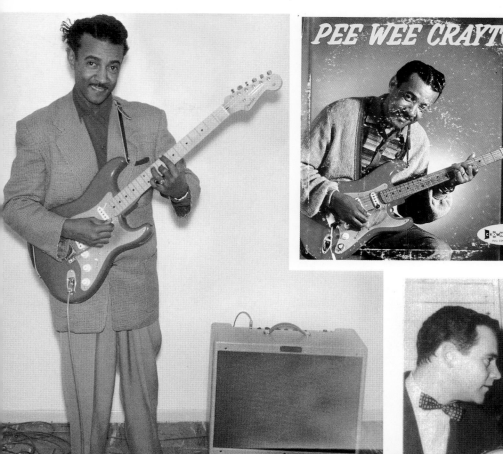

Pee Wee Crayton, a Los Angeles-based bluesman, visited the factory in 1954 and to his surprise went home with a new red Stratocaster and Bandmaster Amp compliments of Leo. *(Right)* Charlie Aldrich, with actors Jack Lemmon and Kim Novak, holds a guitar very similar to Crayton's. Notice the anodized pickguards on both instruments.

appeared in the April 1954 issue of *International Musician*. Other ads in various music publications followed. The 1954 Fender catalog and foldout brochure featured the model for the first time. Here Randall wrote: "The new three pickup Stratocaster guitar represents an entirely new approach to basic guitar design. This instrument is engineered to give the player every possible playing advantage." He lauded the guitar's "big professional tone so long sought by critical players." The vibrato was simple and foolproof. The catalog listed twenty-one Stratocaster features, including "Heavy top grain leather strap and pad."

Several times Leo insisted that he had the guitar ready to manufacture in mid-1953—implying that all the necessary parts were ready to go. However, detailed inventory sheets from December 1953 do not even show Stratocaster decals, much less bodies, necks, or pickguards. The factory made the first few Stratocasters in early 1954 as samples for promotion and testing, some with gold-anodized aluminum pickguards. Since artists usually played them, these examples were probably promotional instruments. Soon Leo realized that the anodized guards made players'

hands turn black, so he switched to single-ply plastic. He still preferred the aluminum because it shielded the pickups. He tried it again on later Stratocasters, student guitars, the electric mandolin, and the Precision Bass. At least one, perhaps three, 1954 Stratocasters came with clear Lucite pickguards backed with gold paint.

In a letter to dealers, Randall promised the first delivery of Stratocasters on May 15, and an early pre-production run—albeit a small one—started in April. Stratocaster #0100 was undoubtedly the first in this series and bore a 4/54 date handwritten on the body. While guitars made at this time probably served as display models and salesmen's samples, most were eventually sold (leading to confusion about what constituted the Stratocaster's first commercial production run). Certain aspects of these early 1954 Stratocasters looked primitive, almost handmade compared with later versions. In addition to machine routing under the pickguards, factory workers used crude wood chisels to finish jobs. The factory stamped serial numbers on the plastic vibrato spring cover rather than on the heel plate.

Immensely practical for all musicians,
Fender guitars leaped racial and economic barriers in a single bound.
(Below) A custom-color Stratocaster is
featured here on the stage at the
upscale Coconut Grove in Los Angeles
and *(right)* at a hillbilly dance at the
Harmony Park Ballroom in Anaheim.
Still, in the 1950s most musicians
thought that Gibson guitars outclassed
Fenders in prestige: traditions were
hard to break completely.

George Fullerton testing the final product.

140

A 1955 Stratocaster without vibrato (left) and a 1954 with vibrato. Both have the usual two-color sunburst finish.

Down Beat insert, 1955. From 1955 through 1965 Fender produced a new advertising insert found in a summer issue of the popular magazine.

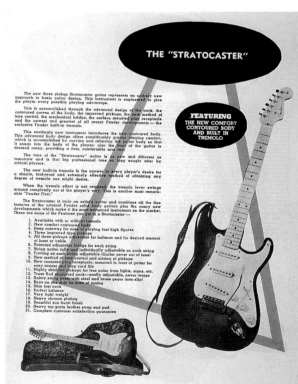

The Stratocaster's 1954 catalog description. Complete customer satisfaction was guaranteed.

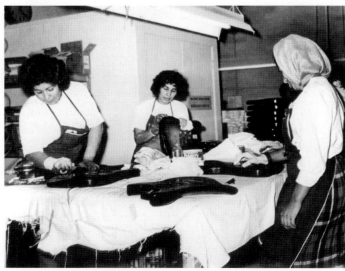

Women workers doing their thing with rubbing compound, 1954.

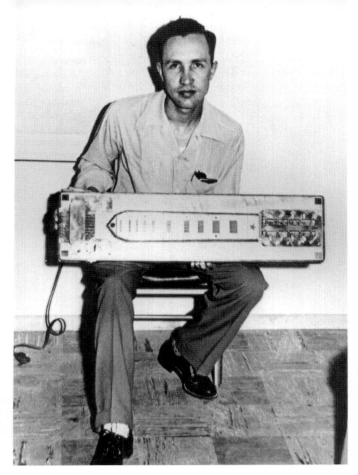

Forrest White in 1951 visiting Fender. Leo gleaned ideas from others, and White's homemade steel impressed him.

White at his desk shortly after becoming Leo's plant manager in 1954. Forrest died of cancer in 1994.

Forrest White

But before Leo delivered too many Stratocasters, he added an important person to his payroll, a new plant manager named Forrest White. (White wrote an account—*Fender, The Inside Story*, Miller Freeman Books, 1994.) Freddie Tavares had suggested to Leo that the factory needed a manager, a job Leo had reluctantly taken himself. As the operation grew, George Fullerton had taken on more responsibilities as the production foreman. Still, the company had reached a critical stage and could not meet the tremendous demand for instruments.

Throughout the early years, the output was agonizingly slow. Dealers always waited for popular items, plaguing the company with cash flow problems and public-relations hassles. Up to this point, manufacturing at Fender was self-taught, ironically a fact Leo pointed to with pride, much like a musician saying that he does not read music well enough to hurt his playing. Fender, Fullerton, and Tavares all lacked formal training in engineering, manufacturing, or management, and running the Fender operation by instinct and intuition created significant problems. As the demand for products grew, Leo needed to increase production levels while maintaining high quality standards. In the mid-1980s, Don Randall remembered the situation well: "Leo was not a production man in the beginning. He was a thinker and a tinkerer, which he still is. It took somebody to go in there and organize things to make it go because it was kind of running by itself." Don

Left to right, Forrest White, Nashville-based guitarist and producer Chet Atkins, and two unidentified guests at the plant in the mid-1950s.

added, "The disorganized factory condition was quite obvious at the time. So that's the way it was." Leo needed someone to streamline his operation and fill the back orders, so he turned to White, a trained analyst and engineer.

Forrest White had grown up in Akron, Ohio, and had prepared for his career at the McKim Technical Institute, Goodyear Industrial University, and Akron University. His curriculum included industrial engineering and business management. During World War II, he worked for the Goodyear Aircraft Company. His first job included nearly every aspect of industrial engineering and plant management: time studies, plant layout, manpower projection, cost analysis, and estimating production times. In 1944 Goodyear sent him to California for six weeks to write the assembly procedures for the P-38 fighter plane tail section and to estimate the man-hours needed for each operation. Later the factory conducted a time study, and White's estimates came within 5 percent of the actual measurements.

White's hobbies included playing guitar and writing gospel, country, and patriotic songs. Some of his song titles included "Put the Muscle Back (In Good Old Uncle Sam)" and "He Should Have Been Fired," an industrial engineer's perspective on the Jesus-Judas affair. Forrest, whose father was a building contractor, made a crude solidbody electric guitar in 1944 with a preset volume and tone control circuit that thirteen years later, he once said, inspired the switching in the Fender Jazzmaster. However, with the homemade guitar's action so high and frets so sharp, he scrapped the instrument for parts in 1946 and built a 10-string steel instead. The lure of the growing music scene in southern California led Forrest and his wife Joan to visit in 1948. He wanted more than anything to meet the people making the new Fender steel guitars. He first met Leo Fender on a June morning at the Fuller-

ton factory. There Ray Massie told White about Paul Bigsby. Being curious, Forrest went up to Bigsby's Downey shop that afternoon, meeting him and Merle Travis.

For the Whites, life in Ohio presented two irritating drawbacks—sleet and snow. Like so many others after the war, they planned a move to California. Forrest knew he wanted to work in guitar manufacturing, so he kept the door open by calling on Leo again in May 1951. On this visit Forrest showed him the handmade 10-string steel guitar. Leo was obviously impressed, because he took Forrest's picture holding the instrument. White worked as an industrial engineer in Riverside until he got a call from Fender in 1954. Forrest remembered him saying: "I've been looking for someone like you for a long time. Someone with your background and someone I can trust to come in and help me run the company." White began work at the Fullerton plant on May 20, 1954.

Leo, in his sometimes oblique manner, told no one why White was there. To become acquainted with procedures, Forrest spent his first two weeks covering amp cabinets. Quietly he assessed the dismal situation. In the mid-1980s White said, "When I started, if I'd tried to make a flow chart of the way the process was for one operation to the other, it would have looked like a spider web." He explained that the guitar and amp assembly areas needlessly overlapped. Workers lost time retrieving parts from out-of-the-way, disorganized bins.

With his experience making airplanes at Goodyear and amphibious tanks at the Food Machinery & Chemical Corporation in Riverside, Forrest realized that Fender needed complete reorganization, an employee incentive system, and quality control programs. He began remodeling the factory in the image of a defense plant. He hoped to make production flow in a more orderly, efficient manner; for instance, he relocated bins for the guitar parts closer to the guitar assembly area, a simple solution to a problem Leo either ignored or overlooked. White asked Fender how he restocked necessary materials. Leo replied, motioning down with his hand, that when the level in a parts bin got low, he ordered more. While that system worked fine in Fender's early years, a major manufacturing concern used thousands of parts a week. The lack of one component could stop production and delay work schedules for a month or more. (For example, the lack of 12-string guitar tailpieces in 1964 delayed the Rickenbacker factory all summer at Beatlemania's peak, when every teenage guitar player wanted to sound like George Harrison.) White quickly established a new materials control system at Fender that re-stocked components long before the bins ran low. It ensured that Fender had capacitors, 6L6 vacuum tubes, and decals at critical times.

When the company did run out of tuners in 1966 due to the supplier Kluson's error, White decided that Fender would make its own.

Two weeks after White started, Leo retreated to his lab and concentrated on what he did best. Forrest ran the factory and handled the day-to-day problems. His first title was assistant plant manager, although by early 1955 it changed to plant manager. Charlie Clark, an engineer who came to the factory in the 1960s, said: "Forrest had a lot to do at Fender. He had to work himself in with Freddie, Leo, and George—the guys who had sat around the shop in the beginning." The company needed an engineer like White to jump-start productivity because, as Clark added, "You can't live on one instrument a year." Forrest probably knew little about making Fender guitars when he started. But the others, including Leo and George, knew little about large-scale manufacturing plants. Forrest did. He brought a new, more professional level of expectations to Fender. Changing the procedures that Fullerton and the old crew

had used necessarily ruffled some feathers and thus created rivalries and resentments that lasted decades. White insisted many times that Fender wanted Fullerton fired then, but Fender would not do it himself. White did not believe a firing was fair or necessary and refused to act. In the 1980s, Dale Hyatt asked Leo to confirm that account, and Fender said that White's story was true.

Charlie Clark said of White, "When you get to know him, you realize that he demands a lot of anyone he associates with because he puts out a lot. . . . But he'd never ask some-

(Opposite) Freddie Tavares (Fender bass), Danny Stewart (steel), and Charlie Opunui (guitar) in the mid-1950s. Freddie played quite often at nightclubs in Hollywood that featured Hawaiian music.

A 1955 Precision bass complete with tag.

one to do something he would not do himself. He was very sharp and very fair." Clark also described Forrest's methods of operation: "Yes, he was very exacting like everything that he was. Why shouldn't it be right? You didn't mind breaking your back for him because he was breaking his."

One of Forrest's first tasks was to put Stratocasters into full production. According to his original records, the factory started listing the Stratocaster with other orders in the summer of 1954 and produced the first recorded full-scale Stratocaster production run in October. (He

George Liberace, bassist Bob Manners, and the flamboyant pianist (left) checking Leo's work. Liberace's popular 1950s television show was another platform for Don Randall's sales effort.

always insisted that all Stratocasters made earlier were pre-production samples or artist models.) The non-tremolo Stratocaster appeared on price sheets in 1954, yet Fender Sales waited until March 29, 1955, to order one. Subsequently, Fender routinely made some Stratocasters without vibrato. They have a more enhanced tone and sustain than the vibrato guitars, according to some players. Indeed, the strings are securely anchored through the rear of the body like those on most Telecasters. (Judgments like this one are still highly subjective, and players argue about whether a heavy body or a light body makes for a better tone. James Burton reportedly always picked the lightest Telecasters, while Freddie Tavares opined that a telephone pole with strings would make the best solidbody guitar.)

Leo once said that he fully expected every player who owned a Telecaster to replace it with a new Stratocaster. He naively thought that all players agreed with his negative assessment of the Telecaster. By 1954 Leo already showed signs of being out of touch with his customers, average guitar players. Only a small percentage of them knew they needed a vibrato, a third pickup, or a contoured cutaway body. Furthermore, the Stratocaster cost $229.50 without vibrato and $249.50 with vibrato. In those days, as Leo said, "A dollar was as big as a manhole cover." Compared with the Telecaster's $189.50, the high price put the Stratocaster out of reach for many players. With the Stratocaster, Leo had conceived a product that would take some time for the average player to appreciate and afford.

In 1954 Fender delivered at least 268 Stratocasters to Fender Sales, all with tremolos. In 1955, the factory shipped 357 tremolo models and 95 non-tremolo versions for a total of 452. Despite a total of 720 Stratocasters in 1954 and 1955, Leo's new guitar failed to equal the Telecaster and Esquire's combined production. From May 1954 to December 1955, the factory made 658 Telecasters and 369 Esquires. The two models together equalled 1,027. To Leo's surprise, the Stratocaster failed to make his earlier guitar obsolete, and Don's idea of an expanded Fender line with different guitar models took hold.

Revising the Precision Bass

Before the end of 1954, partly as a result of the Stratocaster, Leo saw the need to modify the original bass design. He added Stratocaster-like contours to the body. The two-color sunburst instruments with single-layer white plastic pickguards became standard, although the factory also continued to make blonde basses. White pickguards and black pickguards appeared on blonde finishes in 1954 and 1955. Custom-color basses, introduced on a very limited basis in 1954, had white guards. Sometime in early 1955 the pickup began to use staggered-height pole pieces intended to balance the volume between strings. This bass design from 1954 to 1957 led to the more familiar redesigned 1957 version.

(Inset) Custom-color Fender basses at a 1955 trade show.

In Fender's second decade, which started in 1955, each new design represented a building block in an expanding, well-rounded line of instruments. Fender and Randall hoped all of their instruments would hit a target audience.

Christmas-party jam session featuring musician-employees, 1957. Left to right, Gene Galien, Bill Carson, Al Petty, Charlie Davis, and Danny Michaels.

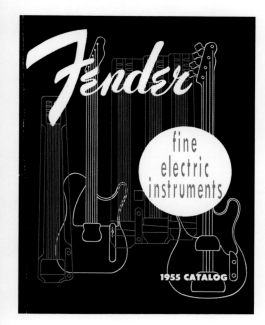

Chapter 10

Fender Fine Electric Instruments

Fender and Randall's working relationship bumped along, Leo often wanting to introduce a new product Randall thought was unneeded. Sometimes the roles reversed. Leo had started an electric violin in 1951 but took until 1958 to complete it. In this case, Don pushed for the violin while Leo resisted. Fender rarely kept his partner fully abreast of his tinkering with old and new creations. Randall would order a thousand Princeton Amp covers, and the latest Princetons would arrive with new dimensions, too large for the covers.

Despite the conflicts that arose because of his miscommunication with Leo, Randall was creating the world's finest organization for selling guitars, with the most recognized brand name in the industry. His salesmen crisscrossed the nation. In 1955 Dale Hyatt had taken Charlie Hayes' former territory in the Southwest. Tom Walker, who first worked for Radio-Tel as a parts salesman, covered

California, Arizona, and Nevada. Art Bates had started in late 1952 and handled the Midwest central states, while David Driver with his son Bud continued in the Northwest. Mike Cole and Don Patton handled the Eastern seaboard; Bob Dayton sold Fenders in the deep South; by the late 1950s Orville Graham worked in the Midwest. Fender Sales brought guitars from Fullerton into the fabric and fiber of American life and experience.

Asked to describe Don's personal qualities, one former associate says, "He was Mr. America: suave, a jock in some ways, personable, good-looking, charming." How did he conduct business? "Very straightforward and honest. He said what he felt and meant what he said. A deal was a deal." Whatever traits Leo lacked, Don made up for. He possessed, and still possesses, a natural combination of organizational, managerial, and intellectual skills. His success was no accident. Given the opportunity, he prospered in

(Right) Left to right, Joe Gillespie (former Fender rep), Don Randall, Nita McCord, J. Fred McCord, and Dale Hyatt.

(Below) Left to right, Leo Fender, Mike Cole, Don Randall, and Bernice Cole. The Coles' visit to Fullerton presented a rare opportunity for Don and Leo to stand together long enough for a picture.

Left to right, Stan Compton, salesmen Don Patton, Bob Dayton, and Dave Driver in 1957.

almost any field, as he later proved with investments in Hobie Cat, a boat company, and the Saddleback Inn hotel.

As an example of Randall's resourceful managerial skills, in 1954 he had formed the National Music Association (NMA) to promote music instruction studios, longtime customers for Fender guitars and amps. NMA held festivals much as the IGL had done earlier. In early 1956 Randall formed the Randall Publishing Company, Inc., and bought the magazine *Music Studio News*, a 12-year-old publication founded by Ray Meany. Under Randall's ownership, *Music Studio News* became *Fretts*. Some unhip subscribers complained about the title's intentional misspelling, yet Fretts was a well-received precursor to magazines like the modern-day *Guitar Player*. With Fender Sales' extensive advertising, music festivals, and publications, Randall promoted guitar sales while strongly pressuring Leo to see the broader music scene.

But Leo was never very grateful. He once said that Don's head was often "lost in a golf bag" during the 1950s. Leo failed to recognize and appreciate the sum of Don's efforts, including his successful negotiations for the sale of Fender to CBS in 1964, which yielded $13 million (chapter 14). Leo's world revolved around his lab. He never openly boasted about his work, but gave himself and his guitars too much credit for the Fender Sales success. When he later founded the G&L company and struggled to make the world appreciate his new guitars, he finally learned the value of an effective sales network. Ideas and good products have a hard time selling themselves in a competitive world. Despite Leo's brilliance, G&L became just one of many small guitar companies.

In Fender's second decade, which started in 1955, each new design represented a building block in an expanding, well-rounded line of instruments. Fender and Randall hoped all of their instruments would hit a target audience, fulfill a need, or fill a niche. Leo improved or expanded other companies' ideas or products. He followed trends, including the growing guitar-playing fad among teenagers.

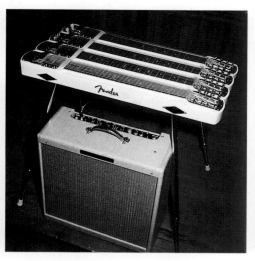

Cleveland, Ohio, trade show, mid-1955.

Narrow-Panel Amps

Many Fender dealers marketed guitars and amps in what was called a step-up program. Students starting with a Champ or Princeton could move up to a Deluxe. After several years of lessons, many students ended up with a Pro or a Twin. After the 1954 summer trade show, Fender amp cabinets started their transition to the narrow-panel tweed style, which would eventually include several mid-sized amps with very small distinctions—the Har-vard, Tremolux, Vibrolux, and Deluxe models. (Within a year the company completed the styling change, used until the shift to Tolex-covered amps in 1959 and 1960. The Champ Amp continued in the narrow-panel style until 1964.) The proliferation of mid-sized amps introduced in the 1950s made the step-up process easier: the stairway reached the same height but had more incremental steps to the top.

Fender's 1956 full-size catalog introduced the mandolin, 3/4-size guitars, and custom colors. It also featured most of the narrow-panel amps shown here.

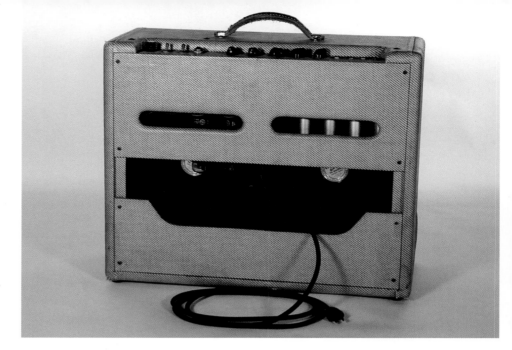

One-of-a-kind 1955 Twin Amp once owned by George Fullerton. This amp came equipped with two 10-inch speakers in a Super-sized cabinet. It shows how Leo experimented with different configurations. Randall decided which ones to sell. The chassis was equipped with two rectifier tubes, typical for both Twins and Bassmans in 1955.

While adding new mid-sized models to the line, Leo also refined the larger professional models during the mid-1950s. Following the development of the Telecaster and Stratocaster, he focused more and more on amplifiers, searching for his idea of the perfect guitar euphony. In the 1980s he said, "I had done just about all I could do with Alnico magnet pickups [the other side of the equation]." Leo's labors with new amp designs paid dividends almost immediately with the most important Fender amp ever made, the narrow-panel 4–10 (four-10-inch-speaker) Bassman.

Bass players blew up Bassmans with single 15-inch speakers quite often. Leo's eventual solution included redesigning the Precision Bass pickup. But the first fix came to the amplifier itself by early 1955; Leo distributed the electric bass' energy over four small speakers rather than one large one. He had noticed this concept in home hi-fi systems. Freddie Tavares, who jumped on Leo's idea, visualized the four 10-inch speakers pushing air in the same manner as a string bass' big top. Both men had also found the Jensen P10R speaker an exceptional design for tone reproduction, a bonus Freddie claimed Jensen discovered by chance.

Fender designed the new Bassman preamp with both guitarists and bassists in mind. He expected players to share one amp on a stage, often with a bass in one channel and a guitar in another. So he sought to fill two uses with one circuit full of crispness. (Again, Fender basses needed presence and treble because of their string mutes and flatwound strings.) Tavares said that Leo thought country-western players, big customers in 1955, would also need a treble-laden sound. Leo made the prototype very quickly. Freddie took it to a music job and played both guitar and bass through it, quickly concluding that Fender had designed his best amp yet.

When Tavares reported the results, Leo hesitated giving his okay to produce the amp because he thought the idea of four speakers in one amp might prove ahead of its time.

Curly Chalker, shown here with an early Stringmaster and Bassman, would later be staff steel player on the long-running *Hee Haw!* show.

Mid-1950s holiday greetings card from the company.

(Right) Christmas present, 1955. Leo gladly accepts a full-size poster of Marilyn Monroe.

Sensing the mistake in Leo's caution, Freddie leaned on him to introduce the new Bassman anyway. Leo listened, but he wanted one more test and had Tavares play both guitar and bass through the prototype at one end of the 120-foot-long factory building. Leo stood at the opposite end of the room. After a careful listen, the master perfectionist finally acquiesced, and one of the best guitar amps ever made came into the music world.

The 4–10 Bassman earned good rock and roll and country credentials from the beginning. Acclaimed steel player Curly Chalker, who later played on the *Hee Haw!* television show, used two Bassmans to create a huge sound in the 1950s. Pictures of Elvis show his original band using one. Country guitarist Buck Owens traveled and recorded with a Bassman before switching to a Twin Reverb. Today Bruce Springsteen frequently has two behind him on stage.

Transitions at Fender Sales

But the Bassman did little to solve the conflicts between Fender Sales in Santa Ana and the factory in Fullerton. When there were flare-ups, traveling salesman Charlie Hayes acted as the peacekeeper. Call his job shuttle diplomacy. On Thursday, June 9, 1955, he spent the day at the Fender plant and went to lunch with Fender, Forrest White, and George Fullerton. George remembered their casual talk of Hayes' newly planted lawn. Forrest

recalled a serious discussion about price changes. In the late afternoon, Hayes started a fateful drive home to Santa Ana; his friends would relive that day many times in the years that followed. On Friday, June 10, 1955, the *Daily News Tribune's* headline read, "Two Die in Traffic Crash," an event described as "an explosion-like head-on collision on Placentia Avenue in Santa Ana." Anaheim youth Raul Garcia Rivera, the perpetrator of the accident, died instantly. Hayes, in the second car, was pronounced dead on arrival at Orange County Hospital. He died at 45, a year after the others had selected him to investigate life insurance policies for Fender Sales board members. His death put the whole Fender organization into a state of contentious shock.

Fender and Randall reached an agreement with Hayes' widow Dorothy based on a 1953 decision to exclude wives from Fender Sales should a stockholder die; she sold her shares back to the corporation. Don and Leo decided they could not continue with Hall; their personal conflicts and differences about the management, control, and operation of the corporation made continuing the agreement that formed Fender Sales in 1953 impossible. However, Hall did not want to sell and resisted. Today Randall says, "We told Francis either you sell to us or we sell to you," knowing that Fender Sales would be of little value without Fender instruments: Leo had the power to change the name of his instruments and choose a new distributor. Finally F.C. sold his stock to them for their take-it-or-leave-it $45,000 offer. They also repaid F.C. $10,000, a loan made in the 1953 pre-incorporation agreement that established Fender Sales, and paid Hall his director's fees up to September 30, 1955. In the 1980s Leo maintained he and Don bought the stock at book value. However, this price did not take into account the company's potential value, which would reach at least $5 million in 1964. Hall had started on the ground floor with Fender and Randall. After 1955, he watched as they rode up to the music industry's penthouse. If Hall felt burned, his attorney was little consola-

tion. Glen Behymer aptly characterized the affairs of late 1955 as the "Fender Sales imbroglio." He accompanied Hall to the stockholders' meetings and billed him $1,000 in fees plus telephone expenses.

New Student Standard and Steel Guitars

Hall went on his way, eventually reviving Rickenbacker with a line of acoustic-electric guitars played and admired worldwide. Leo and Don became fifty-fifty partners in Fender Sales. Besides promoting the new amplifiers, in 1955 Randall and his dealers also pushed for low-priced beginner guitar models to enhance their step-up sales program. Leo wanted to meet music dealers' needs, even if that meant making student guitars with their limited appeal. Dealers already sold children cheap box guitars and a few lessons, but the next step up was a starter electric, a student model designed to keep interest up. After a year or so, if the child stayed in the program, he or she bought a Telecaster or Stratocaster. In September 1955, the factory took the first orders for the 3/4-size, single-pickup Musicmaster, Leo's first student electric. (A 3/4-size guitar was not 25 percent smaller than a full-size one, but had a slightly smaller body and a 22 1/2-inch-scale neck suitable for smaller hands.) The company delivered the first Musicmasters after April 1956. The next addition to the collection was the dual-pickup, 3/4-size Duo-Sonic, appearing the same year. Fender student valedictorian Jimi Hendrix played a Duo-Sonic, among other guitars, before graduating to a Stratocaster.

The Duo-Sonic and Musicmaster used the same double-cutaway body and 21-fret neck. Both were Desert Sand beige, like the first Fender pedal steels; the earliest came with gold anodized aluminum pickguards, although the first ad for the Musicmaster showed a gunmetal blue anodized plate. Both instruments employed one-piece steel

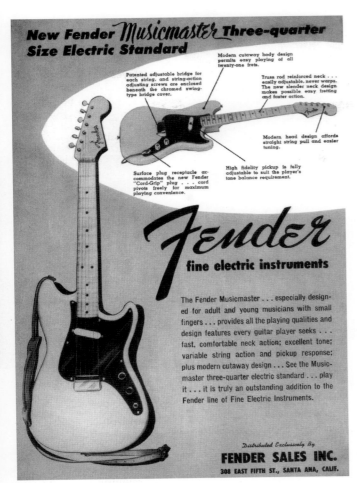

New Fender *Musicmaster* Three-quarter Size Electric Standard

Modern cutaway body design permits easy playing of all twenty-one frets.

Patented adjustable bridge for each string, and string-action adjusting screws are enclosed beneath the chromed swing-type bridge cover.

Truss rod reinforced neck . . . easily adjustable, never warps. The new slender neck design makes possible easy fretting and faster action.

Modern head design affords straight string pull and easier tuning.

Surface plug receptacle accommodates the new Fender "Cord-Grip" plug . . . cord pivots freely for maximum playing convenience.

High fidelity pickup is fully adjustable to suit the player's tone balance requirement.

Fender fine electric instruments

The Fender Musicmaster . . . especially designed for adult and young musicians with small fingers . . . provides all the playing qualities and design features every guitar player seeks . . . fast, comfortable neck action; excellent tone; variable string action and pickup response; plus modern cutaway design . . . See the Musicmaster three-quarter electric standard . . . play it . . . it is truly an outstanding addition to the Fender line of Fine Electric Instruments.

Distributed Exclusively By
FENDER SALES INC.
308 EAST FIFTH ST., SANTA ANA, CALIF.

Magazine ad, June 1956.

Rickenbacker used *Electro*.) The White guitar came as a surprise to Forrest White. One day he was in the wood shop when a stockroom employee asked him where to put the *White* labels. Forrest questioned what he meant and the man said, "You know, the *White* labels."

Forrest replied, "Well, if they're white, send them back." At the time Fender used brown labels with chrome letters.

The employee persisted: "No, you don't understand." He showed White the new tag. Leo had named the new studio steel guitar line without telling him.

Fender Sales first ordered the White lap steel on September 13, 1955, and the plant manufactured it until 1960. The instrument resembled the Fender Champ and Studio steels produced during the period. It had a sculpted body, a single-coil pickup, a plastic pickup cover, and two control knobs. Like all Fender student steels, the White had six strings. The factory also planned a White student standard guitar, but never put it into production.

The White steel and amplifier were made at Fender and usually came as a set sold at music instruction studios.

reinforced maple necks and three-piece bridges, similar to the Telecaster's. The Duo-Sonic's 3-position selector switch operated the pickups, two simple single-coil units with plastic covers. A volume control and a tone control came as standard features, rounding out the design.

Student steel guitars were still a big part of Fender's business as dealers and instruction studios purchased steel guitars and amplifiers to rent or sell to customers. In the fall of 1955, Fender sold two new student steel and amp sets: the Champ Set and the Studio Deluxe Set. The cheaper set featured the Champ Student Steel and the Champ Amp. The Champ steel used a new-style single-coil pickup and a one-piece bridge that adjusted for length and facilitated approximate intonation corrections for more accurate fretting—the first adjustable bridge on a Fender student steel. Still, precise intonation remained elusive because the saddles lacked individual adjustments for each string.

Music instruction studios often found themselves in towns with an authorized Fender dealer. Randall and his salesmen rarely undercut these dealers by selling instruments directly to studios. Rather, a simple solution was to establish another product line, so Leo chose the name White (for Forrest White). In this way, just Fender dealers benefitted from efforts to promote the Fender name. (Other instrument companies did likewise in supplying non-authorized dealers. Gibson used *Epiphone* after 1957 while

153

Aerial view 1954. Citrus groves surrounded the factory until the 1960s.

Leo's lab, 1957 or early 1958. Several experimental instruments leaned against the wall. The sunburst guitar had a Jazzmaster-style body and headstock, a Stratocaster vibrato and jackplate, anodized pickguard, and at least one multi-pole pickup (with seven pole pieces). The Telecaster had a Musicmaster-like bridge and multi-pole pickups as well.

At the Factory in the Late 1950s

Forrest claimed that he did the long-term planning at the factory without sales forecasts or back-order figures from Randall, who kept distribution separate from manufacturing as a way of maintaining control of his domain. Forrest kept a product inventory based on periodic orders; in practice, he guessed what models to manufacture so that Fender Sales did not run out. He was also responsible for the factory's expansion during its fastest growth. In 1958 Fender completed construction of four new buildings, bringing the total number to nine with about 25,000 square feet, real estate then worth a tidy $300,000. The factory leased an additional 6,000 square feet in 1960, and by 1964 the company used twenty-nine buildings. The factory employed between 50 and 75 people in the mid-1950s, 125 by 1961 and 350 by the end of 1964. Astonishingly, decisions to expand work space and to add employees were based on guesswork. One false move would have sunk even a strong company like Fender.

Forrest remembered both Randall and Fender telling him to use his own judgment on nearly every management decision. "Boy, you don't know how tough that job was," Forrest declared, remembering how he walked the fine line between Don and Leo, who in many ways had a marriage of convenience. Randall tried to understand Fender's quirks, like the carrot juice jags that turned his skin yellow from so much beta carotene; Fender never understood why golf was so compelling to Don. Sometimes months passed between meaningful conversations as each did his own job and protected his own bailiwick. Forrest said that, stuck in the middle of this odd couple, he was forced to make decisions involving hundreds of thousands of dollars, in some cases with no clear mandate to do so. Leo avoided the tough calls by staying in his lab.

Leo had a goal during these years: to introduce a new amp or guitar design every three months. Designing products that fit the factory's capabilities contributed to Fender's early successes. In this regard, Forrest, as plant manager, influenced R&D. Still, Leo created all the major innovations while Forrest focused and directed the factory to produce top-quality products at a minimum cost. Despite a rough-and-tumble early start, Fender's factory emerged by the late 1950s as a model for the industry. Randall attributed much of this success to White's skill: "I can tell you straight out that Forrest had a lot of wonderful qualities. He was a super capable guy. And as far as being a loyal, conscientious, hardworking employee, he certainly was that in every respect." Don alluded to the rivalries Bill Carson and George Fullerton had with White: "I had nothing but the highest regard for Forrest. He trampled on a lot of toes because he wanted to get things done, and if somebody didn't perform, why, he would let them know it. He was kind of volatile in that respect. But after Forrest came in, I don't think any factory was ever run as efficiently with as little help as the Fender factory was previous to the CBS takeover."

Leo always spoke highly of White's abilities, but pride stopped him short of admitting that Forrest helped make the factory a success. Mild-mannered, unassuming, and seemingly modest, Leo was nonetheless full of pride. And pride might have been his undoing without a smooth-running, efficient operation backing up what often seemed like indulgence. He pressed to expand into new areas beyond electric guitars, for example. This goal, combined with the challenge of producing something new every three months, showed his lack of business acumen. After a certain point, he produced some items because he could, not because the world demanded that he act. With the factory and sales operations on autopilot, Leo could be Leo, tinkering for hours with Freddie in the lab. But to what end? The chaotic lab scene in the late 1950s resembled the back room of the radio shop, except that the clutter was higher-tech after fifteen years. Against one wall, Leo casually leaned prototype instruments the world would never see. A photo from 1957 captured the first Jazzmaster-style guitar, showing an anodized pickguard and Stratocaster vibrato. Leo's lab also contained a weird Telecaster with experimental 7-pole pickups, and an electric mandolin. Lower production costs, thanks to good factory management, meant higher profit margins on products not particularly popular or profitable, like the electric mandolin.

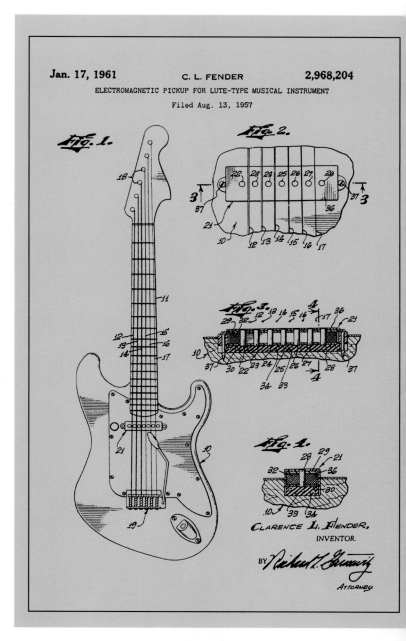

Leo's multi-pole pickup had seven poles on a guitar and five poles on a bass. Leo wanted to cut the harsh percussive attack and rapid decay of some overtones he thought many players disliked on Fender Telecasters and Stratocasters. The patent read, "While the twang or percussive sound may be desirable for some types of music, for example rural music, it is frequently undesirable in that it is unduly harsh instead of sweet." Multi-pole pickups were only used on a few experimental Fender guitars as Leo's confidence in the design wavered. Good thing. A Fender guitar without twang is like a margarita without tequila.

Billy Gray and His W[...]
The Nation's No. 1 Ne[...]

(Right) **An early production-model mandolin, circa 1956.**

(Below) **Prototype mandolin tested on Lawrence Welk's television show. Notice the variation in the body shape compared with the production model.**

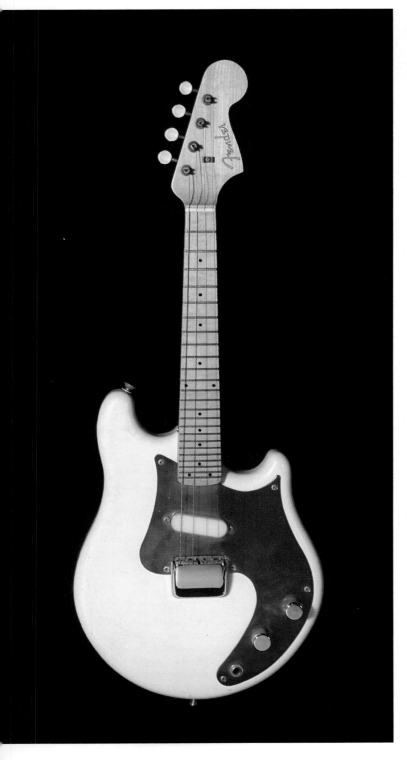

The Electric Mandolin

Fender introduced its solidbody electric mandolin in 1956. With its detachable neck, the instrument was classic post-Stratocaster Fender: interesting, but hardly exciting. Equipped with four strings rather than the conventional eight, it featured the familiar Fender double-cutaway body that the Precision Bass design patent covered. The headstock had all tuners on one side with straight string pull like other Fender instruments, and the fingerboard had twenty-four frets. The mandolin featured a volume control and a tone control for the single-coil pickup; the knobs were knurled like those on the Precision Bass. The two bridge pieces were adjustable for length and height, while the strings mounted through the bridge plate.

Lawrence Welk's Orchestra tested the first three electric mandolins on its nationally televised show in early 1956, and several western swing bands, including Billy Gray's, used the instruments for mandolin ensembles. Jethro Burns, of Homer and Jethro, endorsed the instrument, although he remained a Gibson devotee and played a custom Gibson electric mandolin.

Fender's mandolin was never a big seller as Leo designed it for western swing players and fiddlers who doubled on mandolin. And its introduction followed the western swing craze by several years. But there was still enough interest among musicians to keep the instrument in the Fender line for over fifteen years. When the progressive wing of bluegrass went electric in the 1970s, several prominent mandolin players, including Sam Bush, used Fenders.

The mandolin's features changed in the same pattern as the guitar line's. The first model used an anodized aluminum pickguard: dark blue-gray on the prototype, gold-colored on production models. The most significant design change, as with the guitars and basses, was the addition of a rosewood fingerboard in 1959. Natural blonde and a two-color sunburst were the first standard colors, although by the late 1950s the factory used the three-color sunburst and dropped the metal pickguards for tortoise shell-like plastic. A few mandolins came by special order with custom colors.

use *Fender* Fine Electric Instruments
Exclusively

Left to right, Roy Acuff, Kitty Wells, Shot Jackson, and Decca recording manager Paul Cohen admired Jackson's modified Fender steel, 1955. Many steel players like Jackson encouraged Leo to design a practical pedal steel.

...kwise from top left, Speedy West, Forrest White, machinist ...an Race, and Freddie Tavares with a prototype Fender pedal ...l in Leo's lab. This one had Stringmaster-style pickups.

...ding left to right, Ernest Tubb, Kitty Wells, Johnny Wright, Jack ...lin, Forrest White, and Billy Byrd. Front, Leo Fender and Shot ...kson. Fender presenting the first Fender 1000 to Jackson.

The Pedal Steel

After creating an electric mandolin, Fender turned to advances in the steel guitar—a pedal steel guitar.

The history of the pedal steel goes back to the 1930s and the development of the Gibson Electraharp, a steel guitar with harp-like pedals clustered around its front left leg. The pedals changed the pitch of individual strings. Few known professionals played the Electraharp, probably because it was expensive, revolutionary, or difficult to master. Gibson placed full-page ads for it in several music magazines, but with little impact.

After the war, several companies introduced pitch-changing pedals or levers. National's Electra-Chord, advertised in 1948, featured two pedals mounted at the guitar's base in the center. The Regal Multivox, from the same year, appeared almost identical since the Harlin brothers of Indiana designed both instruments. As with the Electra-harp, few top players used the Harlin design, but the pedal steel idea gained momentum.

According to most written accounts, a Bud Isaacs lick put the pedal guitar in the forefront of steel playing. He played a Bigsby on the Webb Pierce single "Slowly." Paul A. Bigsby had made Joaquin Murphey a non-pedal steel in 1947 and Speedy West a pedal model in 1948. Both were highly respected innovators—West for his manic bar crashes onto the strings and zany sound effects and Murphey for his magnificent jazz phrasing. Many steel players knew these West Coast phenoms played Bigsby steels. By the early 1950s, Bigsby, no stranger to firsts in the instrument world, made custom steel guitars for professionals across the country, including Isaacs. Most had either pedals or a lever changer. At times Bigsby had two to three years of back orders that he leisurely filled by building one

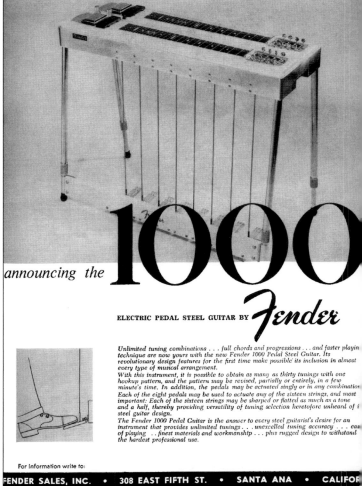

ALVINO REY
an Exclusive
Fender Artist
features his new
1000 Pedal Steel Guitar

announcing the *1000*

ELECTRIC PEDAL STEEL GUITAR BY *Fender*

Unlimited tuning combinations . . . full chords and progressions . . . and faster playing technique are now yours with the new Fender 1000 Pedal Steel Guitar. Its revolutionary design features for the first time make possible its inclusion in almost every type of musical arrangement.

With this instrument, it is possible to obtain as many as thirty tunings with one hookup pattern, and the pattern may be revised, partially or entirely, in a few minute's time. In addition, the pedals may be actuated singly or in any combination. Each of the eight pedals may be used to actuate any of the sixteen strings, and most important: Each of the sixteen strings may be sharped or flatted as much as a tone and a half, thereby providing versatility of tuning selection heretofore unheard of i steel guitar design.

The Fender 1000 Pedal Guitar is the answer to every steel guitarist's desire for an instrument that provides unlimited tunings . . . unexcelled tuning accuracy . . . eas of playing . . finest materials and workmanship . . . plus rugged design to withstand the hardest professional use.

For Information write to:

FENDER SALES, INC. • 308 EAST FIFTH ST. • SANTA ANA • CALIFOR

instrument per month. He built steels for players willing to wait and for serious spenders: Bigsbys started at $500, as much as a 4-neck Stringmaster with no pedals, Fender's top model in 1953.

The lack of high-quality, economical pedal steels made the instrument a do-it-yourself project from the beginning. This fact figured into its evolution, limiting its popularity. Homemade instruments ranged in sophistication from non-pedal steels rigged with coat hangers to custom-built steels made by genuine machinists like Bigsby. Unfortunately, all of these early pedal guitars were custom designs suited to individual players with their own playing and tuning idiosyncrasies.

Then Leo Fender entered the market, using Speedy West to test a single-neck prototype. By 1957 Leo had introduced the double-neck Fender 1000, followed by the single-neck Fender 400. Although West's Bigsby differed significantly from the new Fender, Leo had borrowed the

most practical aspect of Bigsby's design: the board between the two front legs where the pedals mounted. Determined to improve instruments, Leo designed and patented a clever clamp for attaching the pedal board to the guitar's legs. He also patented his own changer system that attached at the bridge end of the steel rather than at the nut.

Many friends besides West offered input into the final design of the new pedal guitars. Noel Boggs, Leon McAuliffe, and Alvino Rey field tested the instruments. (In the 1930s Alvino had helped Gibson develop the Electraharp.) Jody Carver, on the East Coast, had one of the earliest models and also worked closely with Fender. Interestingly, at least one Fender pedal steel prototype had dual pickups and wiring like a Stringmaster steel.

The Fender 1000 and 400 had features that characterized all of Leo's products: rugged construction and case-hardened steel parts with heavy chrome plating. They were easy to disassemble and pack away in their hard-shell cases, the 1000 requiring two cases. Players could easily change the pedal setups and tunings, tailoring them to specific needs; this flexibility was extremely practical. However, the Fenders had a serious design flaw. Instead of rods to pull the changers, they used cables that

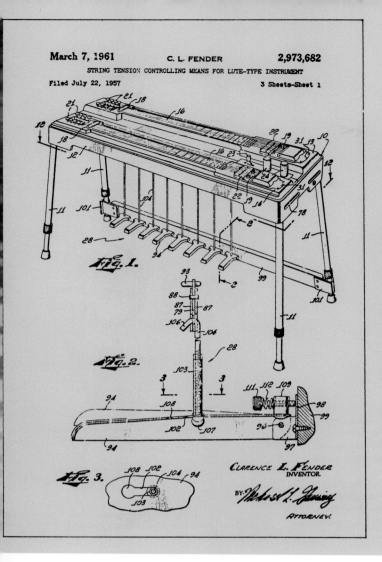

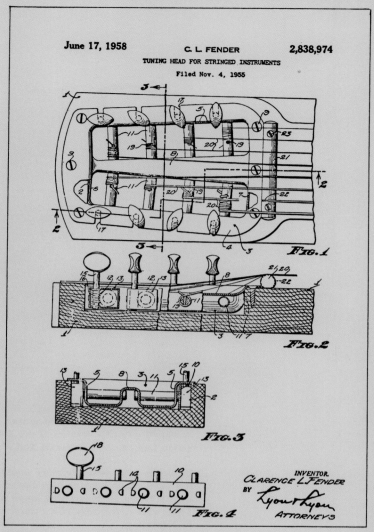

became slack and hard to use without constant tightening. Although the company never rectified this problem, it did fix other flaws. The first significant change appeared in several 1962 Fender ads showing instruments equipped with a roller nut and bridge. By eliminating much of the friction, the rollers improved the strings' return to pitch and reduced string breakage. Fender soon sold a conversion kit with a roller bridge and nut for upgrading older instruments.

Ralph Mooney, premier steel stylist on the West Coast in the 1960s, performed most of his best solos on a Fender 1000 through a Twin amplifier. "You're for Me" recorded in September 1961 with Buck Owens featured bar hammer-ons and footwork unequaled in the decade. Another showcase for the Fender was "Moonshine" on Ralph's collaboration with James Burton, the album *Corn Pickin' and Slick Slidin'*. On all of these Mooney recordings, the 1000 had the unmistakable Fender tone—brisk and punchy.

Classic Late-1950s Amps and Basses

While Leo designed the Fender 1000, he had more projects on his mind, including an updated Bassman. Model 5E6-A from 1955 lacked a mid-range control and had two

James Burton and Ralph Mooney's album from the late 1960s showcased the Fender 1000. Mooney's brisk sound, not to mention Burton's, epitomized the tone Leo sought in electric instruments.

159

(Above) Promotion photograph, 1959. Many guitarists believe that the best guitar amp ever designed was this version of the 4–10 Bassman, which had the 5F6-A circuit and a molded handle.

(Right) In later years Fenders would carry a warning label about hearing loss due to loud noises. In the 1950s, high-powered amps like this 1958 Twin with four power tubes were seldom pushed to distortion.

rectifier tubes. The revisions, model 5F6 from 1956 through 1957 and model 5F6-A from 1958 through 1960, each had a mid-range control and one rectifier tube. The latter was the starting point for Marshall's first amplifiers, the most popular rock amps made after the 1960s.

Conventional thinking says that the Bassman succeeded as a guitar amp because its piercing treble and preamp distortion at modest volumes created a lively sustain. Leo must have realized that roots players liked a little musical distortion; it added life and character to the tone. Even Jimmy Bryant's sound, clean by today's standards, had a faint hint of clipped signal. Most exciting guitar sounds from the 1950s did. After the Rolling Stones' 1965 single "Satisfaction," which popularized fuzztone devices that created distortion, complete sound breakup at full volume became widely accepted. Today 1950s Fender amps are famous for distorting in this fashion, yet another unintended consequence of Leo's genius. (He once noted that the Bassman's output section produced little distortion. Thus the amplifier, despite its preamp distortion, still sounded musical on 12, the highest number on the volume control knob.) He never expected players would turn his amps up all the way, but by overbuilding them with heavy-duty speakers, cabinets, and circuits he made it possible. When asked in the 1980s why the 4–10

Bassman was so popular, Leo reminisced that the positioning of its four speakers created a natural chorus, a pleasing sound to the human ear.

Eventually the Twin and Pro had a preamp with a mid-range control like the Bassman's. The Twin introduced in 1958 used the most thunderous output stage for its time, four power tubes and twice the power of the Bassman. By the late 1950s, bands played loud enough to demand this extra volume; rock and roll had arrived and would forever shape the progression of amplifier equipment and technology. (Today the 4-power-tube Twin amplifier interests collectors and players, including Eric Clapton, Keith Richards, and George Harrison, because of its tone and potential volume.)

The redesigned 4–10 Bassman's companion in 1957 was a completely redesigned Precision Bass. Leo could easily have given the instrument a new name as it employed several new features that set it apart from the two earlier versions. (The 1957 Precision was almost to the 1951 original what the Stratocaster was to the Telecaster.) The entirely new humbucking pickup had two split-coils and two poles for each string. This bi-pole pickup, as Leo Fender called units with two poles per string, held several advantages. Foremost to Leo, it lessened the harsh response, or spike, at the instant of pick

Leo revised the Precision Bass in 1957 with a new headstock, pickguard, and dual-coil humbucking pickup (designed to save speakers from the percussive attack of the earlier bass pickup). This late 1957s example has its covers removed. The patent diagrams show Leo's new pickup and the bass' ornamental design.

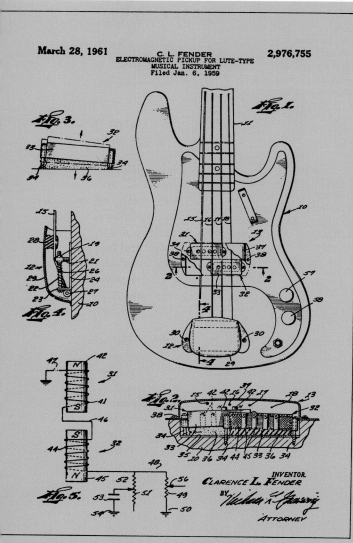

March 28, 1961

C. L. FENDER
ELECTROMAGNETIC PICKUP FOR LUTE-TYPE
MUSICAL INSTRUMENT
Filed Jan. 6, 1959

2,976,755

INVENTOR.
CLARENCE L. FENDER

BY

ATTORNEY

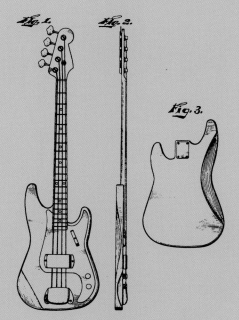

United States Patent Office

Des. 187,001
Patented Jan. 5, 1960

187,001

BASS GUITAR

Clarence L. Fender, Fullerton, Calif.

Application January 6, 1959, Serial No. 54,050

Term of patent 14 years

(Cl. D56—1)

Figure 1 is a front elevational view of a bass guitar showing my new design;

Figure 2 is a left side elevational view thereof; and

Figure 3 is a rear elevational view showing only the the body of the guitar.

I claim:

The ornamental design for a bass guitar, substantially as shown.

References Cited in the file of this patent
UNITED STATES PATENTS

D. 67,190   DiMillo --------------- May 5, 1925
D. 169,062   Fender --------------- Mar. 24, 1953

THE MARY KAYE
TRIO
uses
Fender
fine electric instruments
exclusively

(Left) In Fender marketing a
standard color for one model
was often a custom color for
another. This 1957 sunburst
Telecaster—with a finish like
thousands of regular-issue
Stratocasters and basses—was
either an experiment or a
special order.

ELECTRIC GUITARS AMPLIFIERS STRINGS STANDARD GUITARS

FINE ELECTRIC INSTRUMENTS
1957-58 CATALOG

The 1957–58 full-size catalog featured a centerfold photograph of an entire trade show display. It also introduced the totally redesigned Precision Bass, the 4–10 Bassman with mid-range control, and the Fender 1000 pedal steel.

attack. When players hit a string on a bass with the old pickup, it generated an instant surge of energy that eventually caused speaker fatigue and failure. With its mellowed percussive attack, Leo's bi-pole pickup saved speakers and enhanced sustain.

The new 1957 Precision, while retaining the one-piece maple neck, had a redesigned headstock resembling the Stratocaster's. The feel of the early bass necks varied, as did those on the guitars. Ones from 1954 usually had a chubby feel, while V-shaped necks were apparent in 1957. Some collectors consider the thin, racy necks from late 1957 through mid-1959 Fender heaven. The new bass also sported a gold anodized aluminum pickguard. These features remained constant until 1959, when Fender introduced rosewood fingerboards. Fender did make rosewood-neck basses with the anodized pickguards, but by mid-1960 aluminum pickguards gave way to plastic guards, usually made from a laminated tortoise-shell-like plastic. After 1959, the factory also used laminated white plastic pickguards, usually on the solid-color instruments.

Custom Colors

In the February 1957 issue of *Music Trades* magazine, Fender Sales announced a blonde Stratocaster with gold-plated parts. The factory had made some of these guitars earlier, but with little fanfare. Aside from the cosmetic appointments, these guitars had regular Stratocaster features. Everyone at Fender, including Leo, considered the blonde finish more elegant, and today many collectors consider blonde Stratocasters with gold hardware among the most collectible pre-CBS Fenders. Since the 1980s, they have even rated the nickname *Mary Kaye* after the Fender artist Mary Kaye (as opposed to Mary Kay, the cosmetics tycoon). A black-and-white picture of the Mary Kaye Trio taken in the 1950s and used to promote the Fender company showed her beautiful guitar. In 1957 such Stratocasters retailed for $330.00 compared with $274.50 for the standard vibrato version. A hard-shell tweed case cost $44.50.

In addition to blonde finishes, both the Stratocaster and Telecaster were available in custom colors. The 1950s saw several industrial design trends, including the use of rich colors. Radios came in brightly colored plastic cabinets, and Sears and Roebuck catalogs offered toasters with radiantly tinted plastic handles. Automobile companies offered many colors unseen in earlier years, especially pinks, reds, blues, and greens. Suburban tract homes came fully equipped with turquoise, salmon, yellow, or avocado enameled appliances. Guitar manufacturers like Kay, with its Colorama series, and Gretsch, with its Streamliner guitar in Jaguar tan, experimented with colored finishes.

Fender also experimented with color. In an often repeated account, a downtown Fullerton paint store mixed the first batch of Fiesta Red—a light, almost coral hue—in 1957 for George Fullerton. Highlighting disagreements in the semantics of Fender history, George claimed Fiesta Red was the first "custom color" used exclusively by Fender. Indeed, it was not a standard red, black, or gold. But collectors, as well as Fender Sales, considered earlier solid-color paint jobs custom colors, too. Loosely defined, any color other than the standard finish offered in the catalog was a Fender custom color. To confuse the issue, a standard finish for one model might be a custom color on another. For instance, the Telecaster's late-1950s see-through blonde was a custom finish on Stratocasters. The standard Desert Sand finish on the 1950s Duo-Sonic was a custom color on the Stratocaster. The Stratocaster's standard sunburst finish was a custom color on a mid-1950s Telecaster or Esquire. Fender painted guitars any Duco color available as well as the special mixes like Fiesta Red.

(Right) **Eldon Shamblin, veteran western swing guitarist, and his gold Stratocaster in the 1970s.**

(Below) **Aristocat Art Maryland holds a 1950s custom-color Stratocaster with an anodized pickguard. Leon McAuliffe's red Stringmaster inspired others to ask Fender for solid-color finishes. Yet Don Randall remembers that Gretsch's colored guitars, including a White Falcon demonstrated by Jimmie Webster at the 1954 NAMM show, convinced him to have the factory make Fender's earliest custom-color instruments.**

The custom colors' stylish look conveniently masked the real reasons the factory used solid color. The practice was an attractive and highly practical way of using wood unfit for blonde or sunburst finishes. Using custom colors cut costs. Some custom-color instruments had rejected sunburst finishes hidden underneath. Opaque finishes covered unsightly glue joints, bad grain, and lack of grain. The least attractive woods, still structurally sound, were earmarked for solid custom-color finishes.

When Fender introduced the Stratocaster, the factory made a few special solid-color guitars as trade show samples and artist models. Bill Carson called the color of his first production Stratocaster "Cimarron Red." The inspiration came from Leon McAuliffe, his band the Cimarron Boys, and his red Stringmaster. Blues player Pee Wee Crayton's early Stratocaster was the same shade, which Fender color charts later called Dakota Red. Texas Playboy Eldon Shamblin's 1954 gold-colored Stratocaster,

which followed the Les Paul goldtop, was one of the first Fender instruments using a metallic paint, although later versions like Shoreline Gold usually had a silver undercoat. Shamblin's guitar had a white undercoat. Undoubtedly other custom colors appeared in 1954 and 1955, but no one remembers with certainty what they were. No one at Fender really cared.

The company first officially offered the color option in the 1956 Fender catalog, but with no color listings. Several solid-color instruments played by artists appeared in black-and-white mid-1950s catalogs. The first full-color photograph of a custom-color Stratocaster—red with gold hardware—appeared on the bold cover of the 1958–59 Fender catalog (which set standards for the industry). Other known examples of original custom-color guitars from the 1950s included black and what later color charts and advertising called Desert Sand, Lake Placid Blue, and Shell Pink. The correct names used at the time elude researchers, but this has not stopped collectors from making up their own, like Salmon Pink (a common misnomer for Fiesta Red).

More than names are hard to reconstruct. The original colors were finished with layers of clear lacquer that yellows with age, smoke, and ultraviolet, changing blues to greens in many cases. What may have started as Lake Placid Blue might now look like teal. Sometimes looking under a pickguard reveals a color closer to the painter's original intent.

According to Fender veterans, custom colors won few popularity contests in the mid-1950s, making original examples hard to find today. Even in the 1960s, when the colors began to catch on, the catalogs pictured sunburst guitars in front of the colored guitars because Fender Sales considered sunburst more popular and appealing to the average buyer. Forrest White noted that Fender Sales made the final decision on colors as the orders arrived from dealers. And the orders kept coming.

The exquisite 1958–59 full-size
catalog had the smart, sophisticated
look that reflected Fender Sales and
Don Randall's business acumen. This
catalog introduced the electric violin
and Jazzmaster.

1958-59 CATALOG

America's teenagers knew that the latest trend in guitars was the solidbody, the same way they knew what to wear—they just did. Fenders had a new, streamlined look and a new sound. And young people played them.

Sampling of the earliest Fender ads in the long-running series created by Robert Perine, whose approach was unprecedented in the music industry.

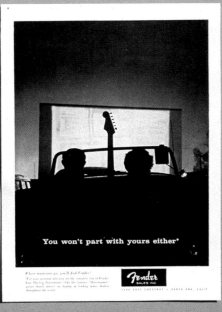

Gene Vincent and the
Bluecaps, featuring
Johnny Meeks on guitar.

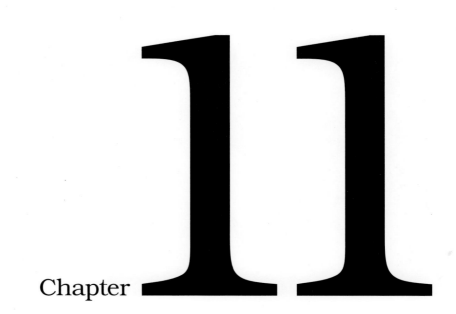

Chapter 11

You Won't Part with Yours Either

In December 1958, *Life* magazine presented a special entertainment issue providing enough information about records, television, and movies to fill nearly two hundred pages. Frank Sinatra's "rat pack" rated an entire article. Other features noted that New Orleans jazz ranked high among popular music styles and that several manufacturers now offered "new stereophonic sound" records and "hi-fi" home stereo systems. The magazine also profiled rock and roll, calling it the "newest music for a new generation."

Life brushed off teenagers' music: "Basically, rock 'n' roll—which has little musical eloquence—is a singer's highly personal way of shouting or moaning lyrics ('The Big Sound'), mostly to a slow, heavily accentuated four-four time ('The Big Beat'), accompanied by guitar or hoarse-honked tenor saxophone." The new style's fans, mostly girls aged 8 to 16, were hardly sophisticated. Further down-

grading the music, the magazine added, "Most adults don't dig it." Rock was hardly a style most Americans took seriously, but its growth was undeniable. Even as early as 1958 it employed at least 3,500 disc jockeys like Dick Clark, host of TV's *American Bandstand*. The American public spent $500 million a year on records, one quarter of that amount on rock records.

Leo Fender never grasped the full impact of his discoveries on rock and roll, or for that matter how the new style would change his life. He never liked rock and surely dismissed the style at first, although he had designed guitars for roots musicians who had laid its foundations in the late 1940s. Fender instruments and amps—born for honky tonks, dance halls, and small recording studios—had already played a hand-in-hand role in rock's short history, but the world would not find that out reading Life's 1958 entertainment issue—it pictured only one Fender guitar.

(Above) **Student competitors with Fenders in the 1950s. At shows he sponsored, Randall made sure all participants left with a ribbon and a feeling of accomplishment.**

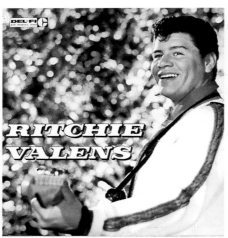

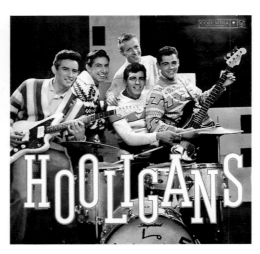

Album covers. Increasingly, Fender guitars became the emblem of young performers like Buddy Holly, Ritchie Valens, and the little-known Hooligans.

Buddy Merrill (with a Jazzmaster in 1958) did not play rock on TV's most conservative bandstand, but he reinforced the idea that a Fender was not your father's guitar.

Still, America's teenagers knew that the latest trend in guitars was the solidbody, the same way they knew what style of shoes to wear—they just did. Fenders had a new streamlined look and a new sound. And young people played them; Fender's rising stars outside of 1950s country music were Buddy Holly, Ritchie Valens, Carl Perkins, and James Burton. Buddy Merrill, Fender's most visible official endorser, played an amazing array of Fenders in the 1950s every week with Lawrence Welk, who often introduced the guitarist as "our youngster." Merrill did not play rock on America's most conservative bandstand, but he reinforced the idea that a Fender was not your father's guitar. A large part of this young, fresh image resulted from Fender's advertising, which despite a halting start had emerged as the most effective in the industry.

Art director and ad designer Robert Perine, 1959.

Stan Compton taking another
order for Fender merchandise
in 1966.

Stan Compton taking another
order for Fender merchandise
in 1966.

Fender Advertising

From 1946 to 1953 Don Randall had either designed Fender ads himself or closely supervised their creation. The results were inconsistent because a reluctant F.C. Hall limited how many ads actually ran. For example, the attractive 1948 ad for the Pro in *Down Beat* had no follow-up. This tentativeness particularly upset Leo, who desperately wanted the Fender name constantly in the public eye. When Fender Sales got rolling in 1953, Randall increased advertising in magazines like *Music Trades*, *International Musician*, *Down Beat*, and *Country and Western Jamboree*, using designers for specific jobs. Still, most of the work fell in his lap. In 1955 he hired Stanley Compton as an assistant to help put ads and catalogs together, among many other duties. Nevertheless, the need for a full-time professional ad agency became more apparent as Fender Sales expanded.

In 1957 Bob Perine, a partner in the Perine/Jacoby agency based in Newport Beach, designed an impressive magazine ad for Rickenbacker. Compton had worked a short time for Rickenbacker, and F. C. Hall gave him Perine's number. Compton called and offered Perine an account with Fender Sales. Today Perine remembers: "I liked Stan immensely. He gave me a simple ad to do, then promptly loved it, and I just kept going. Our relationship just grew and grew." Perine worked with Compton and then with Jim Williams, who came in as Fender Sales' advertising director. When CBS took over in 1965, Perine would continue until 1969 under the direction of Charlie Rosenthal.

Perine had trained in advertising design at Chouinard Art Institute in Los Angeles and was prepared to promote any kind of product, but guitars held a special interest because he had learned to play during World War II. He says: "I thought, what a neat product to get an account for, something I really like to do. That's one of the reasons I kept it. It was pleasurable for me to go up to Fender Sales and see the new instruments, to sit around and play

The Jordanaires, background singers on many of
Elvis' 1950s records, endorsing Fender.

(Below) Fender Sales followed the famous see-through Lucite Stratocaster which appeared at trade shows in the late 1950s with an ad that used an x-ray photo of a Twin Amp.

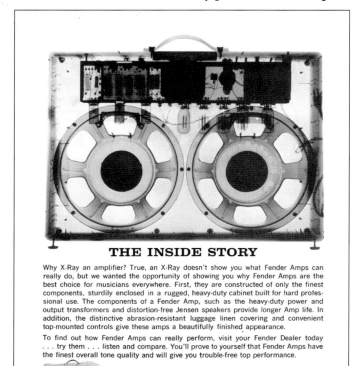

THE INSIDE STORY

Why X-Ray an amplifier? True, an X-Ray doesn't show you what Fender Amps can really do, but we wanted the opportunity of showing you why Fender Amps are the best choice for musicians everywhere. First, they are constructed of only the finest components, sturdily enclosed in a rugged, heavy-duty cabinet built for hard professional use. The components of a Fender Amp, such as the heavy-duty power and output transformers and distortion-free Jensen speakers provide longer Amp life. In addition, the distinctive abrasion-resistant luggage linen covering and convenient top-mounted controls give these amps a beautifully finished appearance.

To find out how Fender Amps can really perform, visit your Fender Dealer today . . . try them . . . listen and compare. You'll prove to yourself that Fender Amps have the finest overall tone quality and will give you trouble-free top performance.

WHEN YOU BUY FENDER, YOU BUY QUALITY FROM THE INSIDE OUT!

Fender
SALES INC.
SANTA ANA, CALIF.

Shown here and above: the Fender Twin-Amp   For complete information write for Fender's 1958-59 Catalog

them. Bob Perine was only one of the many avid guitarists hired by Randall and Fender, who did not play music themselves. The enthusiasm of these employees and associates made their commitment to the company's success that much stronger.

The clean-cut image Fender projected made electric guitars more palatable to middle class parents.

NAPPY LAMARE
with the
Nappy Lamare-Ray Bauduc Sextet
uses
Fender
exclusively

Fender made its biggest inroads into the pop and jazz realms with the Precision Bass.

Perine put a smart, sophisticated spin on the company, a far cry from the perception left over from the 1940s when Leo catered mostly to western swing bands. The choice of artists shown in the 1958–59 catalog, Perine's first for Fender, told the story: only four out of fourteen played country or western music. There was one Hawaiian guitarist, Eddie Bush, and no rock guitarists. The remainder were pop or jazz artists, including Monk Montgomery, the Kings IV, J. P. Morgan, and Nappy LaMare. Fender's clever new magazine ads followed. One showed an x-ray photo of a Twin; another used a trick photo with Perine playing through a Vibrasonic Amp supposedly the size of a garage. The eye-catching and overwhelmingly successful *You Won't Part with Yours Either* series ran in many magazines for nearly ten years. It featured people carrying guitars and amps in outrageous, very unlikely situations: scuba diving, skydiving, and surfing. One showed a man cleverly posed at a funeral home, holding a Fender in his coffin. Randall saw the humor but thought the ad went a little too far, and it never ran (see page 247).

Many of Perine's ads targeted the youth market. The clean-cut, conservatively dressed kids pictured with guitars reflected Fender's and Randall's Orange County politics—Republican. "Both Jim Williams and I realized we wanted to use teenagers in ads," Perine remembers, "because they were basically the market, especially for the 3/4-size guitars and the Champs, the kind of stuff we were trying to push for beginners and students." To find teenage girls that were cute and vivacious and boys that were all-American, most advertisers went to modeling agencies. Bob decided that he would find them himself. "I had three daughters that were going to Laguna Beach High School, so I had sort of built-in helpers. They'd put on searches for me to find the right faces and the right types," he explains. Also, his daughters knew people who played guitar. He points out, "I could usually find a kid that at least could be taught the correct hand position on a guitar neck."

The Jazzmaster was supposed to appeal to Gibson's potential customers, so-called serious players, the music industry's yacht club set.

(Below) A photo used in 1959 brochures.

The Jazzmaster

Despite the Telecaster's and Stratocaster's recognition in the mid-1950s, they missed meeting everyone's requirements or fancy. Most serious, skilled musicians respected jazz even if playing country, rock, or pop tunes paid the bills. Players uninterested in complex chords, intricate improvising, and acoustic-electrics were not considered too serious.

For most young musicians working their way up, the top rung on the ladder after a Telecaster or Stratocaster was a higher-priced, high brow Gibson, Gretsch, Guild, or Epiphone acoustic-electric. A casual look through a mid-1950s Gibson catalog or *Down Beat* shows virtuosos like Herb Ellis, Jim Hall, Barney Kessel, George Barnes, Tal Farlow, and Tony Mottola endorsing Super 400s, L-5s, and ES-350s. (Kessel, Farlow, and Johnny Smith artist models would follow.) These serious men sharply contrasted with Buddy Merrill and his boyish grin. Many teenagers saw these famous players here long before knowing anything else about them; such artist endorsements reinforced the perception that jazz guitars were tops among mature players. Gibsons with large, deep bodies produced "the tonal quality of the acoustic guitar and the advantages of an electric instrument," according to company literature. Orchestra leaders usually demanded them, as did many pop singers. With its expensive materials and craftsmanship, a Gibson S-400CESN cost $790.00 in 1959, nearly triple the most expensive Stratocaster's $274.50 price.

To tap more of the 1950s high-end market and to cut into Gibson's profits, Leo felt obligated to design a guitar for jazz and pop players. He thought it would become the new top rung on the ladder. Soon dubbed the Jazzmaster, the new model would lure more players to solidbodies; both Fender and Randall imagined jazzmen playing Fenders. Going after these players was the logical way to expand before Randall and Fender noticed and appreciated the growing proliferation of rock bands. Leo wanted to convince the guitar world that solidbody guitars were superior to

(Left) The Jazzmaster's feeble bridge doomed it in heavy-handed playing. The strings went flying right out of their grooves.

(Below) A Jazzmaster with an anodized pickguard and tweed case photographed at Fender in 1959.

acoustic-electrics and wanted more professionals to look to Fender for their main guitar, and not just for amplification or for an auxiliary instrument on the occasional rock session. His longing for acceptance probably stemmed from his insecurity, which sometimes amazed those around him. While on vacation in Oregon in the 1950s, he noticed a wonderful Fender display in a music store window. Later he complimented Dave Driver on the fine job he was doing encouraging dealers to promote the product. Surprised to hear that Leo had not gone into the store to introduce himself, Driver asked why. Leo replied, "I was afraid they'd ask questions I didn't know the answers to."

The Jazzmaster offered the advantages—and as it turned out, the disadvantages—of Fender's solidbody design with several changes. The pickups had wide, flat coils that looked much like Leo's first pedal steel pickups. (Curiously, some jazz steel players had complained that the earlier Fender steel pickups could not produce a jazz tone, leading to a new design for the pedal steel.) The wider coil offered broader tonal content but with less bite and a different attack than earlier pickups. The treble pickup positioning, unlike the slanted position on the Telecaster and Stratocaster, added to the Jazzmaster's plunkier tone.

INSTANT SALES!

Not always that fast . . . but
your customers know that
Fender leads the field in
instrument and amplifier design
and quality . . . often copied
but never equalled. They also
know* about Fender's
guarantee of complete customer
satisfaction. These are the
reasons guitarists stay sold on
Fender!

*Fender ads appear
regularly in Downbeat,
Metronome, Country and
Western Jamboree, Fretts
and the two leading music
annuals.

Fender
SALES INC.
Santa Ana, California

SEE THE COMPLETE FENDER AND REGAL DISPLAYS - ROOMS 624, 625 AND 626
NAMM Trade Show   Hotel New Yorker   June 22-25

Another ad aimed at music dealers.

(Below) A 1958 Gibson ad pointed out
the obvious: most top jazz and many
country players endorsed its guitars.

The Fender Sales warehouse, March 1960.

The new lead circuit had a 3-position switch, a tone
control, and a volume control. A second tone circuit, activated by a slider switch above the neck pickup, provided
preset tone and volume controls for mellow and soft
rhythm work usually played acoustically on hollowbody
electrics or straight acoustics. Before the Jazzmaster, Leo
had used a less elaborate preset tone control on the
single-pickup Esquire and toyed with several tone control
circuits in Telecasters. With the 3-pickup Stratocaster, a
player could preset the rhythm tone on the middle and
front pickups, but not the volume. The Jazzmaster was the
first Fender to use two separate tone and volume circuits.

It also incorporated other new features, including the
floating vibrato, floating bridge, and trem-lock. Unlike in
the Stratocaster's design, the strings on the floating
vibrato system went over the bridge and attached to a
separate anchor tailpiece. The length of string behind the
bridge cut the guitar's sustain, a way to enhance jazz
plunk. The floating bridge pivoted on two legs sharpened
like pencils and set into two thimble-like receptacles
sunk into the top, moving with the strings and vibrato
arm and cutting friction. The trem-lock stopped the
vibrato block when locked, permitting strings to be
changed either simultaneously or individually and

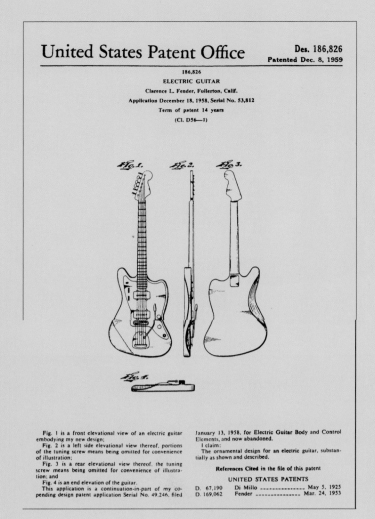

United States Patent Office

Des. 186,826
Patented Dec. 8, 1959

186,826
ELECTRIC GUITAR
Clarence L. Fender, Fullerton, Calif.
Application December 18, 1958, Serial No. 53,812
Term of patent 14 years
(Cl. D56—1)

Fig. 1 is a front elevational view of an electric guitar embodying my new design;

Fig. 2 is a left side elevational view thereof, portions of the tuning screw means being omitted for convenience of illustration;

Fig. 3 is a rear elevational view thereof, the tuning screw means being omitted for convenience of illustration; and

Fig. 4 is an end elevation of the guitar.

This application is a continuation-in-part of my co-pending design patent application Serial No. 49,246, filed January 13, 1958, for Electric Guitar Body and Control Elements, and now abandoned.

I claim:
The ornamental design for an electric guitar, substantially as shown and described.

References Cited in the file of this patent
UNITED STATES PATENTS
D. 67,190   Di Millo ---------------- May 5, 1925
D. 169,062   Fender ---------------- Mar. 24, 1953

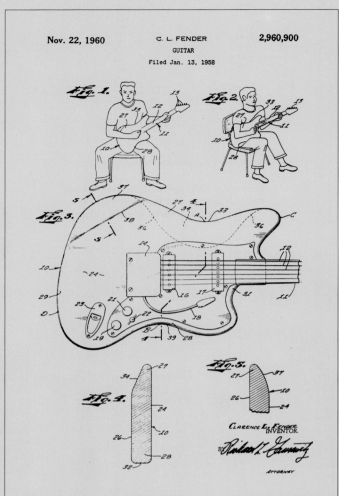

Nov. 22, 1960
C. L. FENDER
GUITAR
Filed Jan. 13, 1958
2,960,900

CLARENCE L. FENDER
INVENTOR.
By
ATTORNEY

preventing de-tuning when one broke in performance. (Since few players locked the vibrato during performances, this feature had little practical value.)

Leo designed the Jazzmaster vibrato for heavy-gauge strings typical of the times, and when equipped as planned, the unit had merits. (The July 30, 1958, Fender price sheet and a 1958 NAMM show announcement listed a non-tremolo version of the Jazzmaster, a rare guitar if it exists.) The unit worked for players with a light touch using light strings, but hitting the strings hard frequently popped them out of the bridge-piece grooves. (In contrast, the Stratocaster's heavy-duty unit provided a much wider pitch range than the Jazzmaster's and adjusted to light strings with ease. Most important, no matter how hard a player attacked the strings—light- or heavy-gauge—they usually remained in place on a Stratocaster.) Leo, with all his attention to design details, still let the faulty bridge slip through. Ironically, some modern players have solved the problem by substituting Fender's original bridge with a Gibson Tune-O-Matic. It works on the Jazzmaster after doweling the two bridge thimbles, redrilling proper holes

in the dowels, and adding a neck shim. There is one drawback: the Gibson is set for the radius of a Les Paul neck.

Another feature first developed for the Jazzmaster was the patented offset-waist body. While players could play the design standing, Leo intended it for players who sat, with their comfortably supported arm in a natural position over the strings. The original catalog description said that playing a Jazzmaster was virtually effortless. Indeed, the offset waist and contoured body, made with a novel combination of asymmetry and recesses and bevels on the body, fit the player even better than the Stratocaster. However, the new body also made the Jazzmaster both heavier and longer than earlier models. With this obvious compromise, Fender must have had good reason to make a guitar for sit-down playing.

In the 1930s, big band guitarists like Charlie Christian sat either in the pit or on a bandstand, as did most guitarists in the 1940s, including those playing western swing, jazz, and pop. When guitarists became stars, they began standing up. Les Paul and Hank Williams usually played standing. (Singing cowboys played guitar riding on

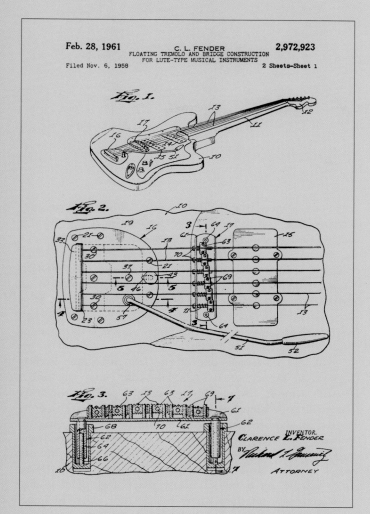

Feb. 28, 1961   C. L. FENDER   2,972,923
FLOATING TREMOLO AND BRIDGE CONSTRUCTION
FOR LUTE-TYPE MUSICAL INSTRUMENTS
Filed Nov. 6, 1958   2 Sheets-Sheet 1

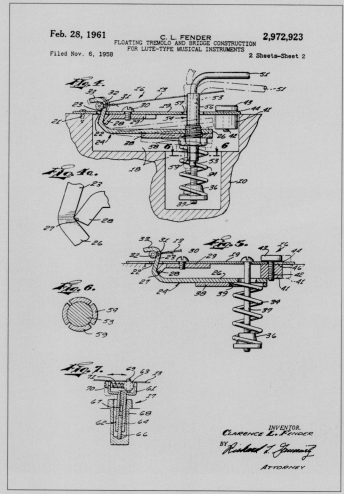

Feb. 28, 1961   C. L. FENDER   2,972,923
FLOATING TREMOLO AND BRIDGE CONSTRUCTION
FOR LUTE-TYPE MUSICAL INSTRUMENTS
Filed Nov. 6, 1958   2 Sheets-Sheet 2

their horses or strolling down a main street.) By the mid-1950s, guitarists in the spotlight like Bill Haley and Elvis Presley not only stood up but danced while they played. Most young guitarists noticed and bought guitar straps. But Leo wanted the Jazzmaster accepted by the notables advertising Gibsons. In the 1950s, to sit or not to sit was a question rarely discussed by these serious players, and yet sitting symbolized the difference between the old and the new, jazz and rock. Leo wrongly concluded that if he built a guitar musicians could easily play seated, they would flock to his instruments. (He persisted with this distorted assumption until the mid-1980s when he finally returned to his original Telecaster and Stratocaster body styles.)

Jazzmaster test guitars went through several incarnations before reaching production. A pre-production example was Freddie Tavares' maple-neck version. George Fullerton's original Fiesta Red guitar, with an ebony fingerboard, also differed from standard models. Still, Leo said that he discarded most test instruments. Fender Sales introduced the Jazzmaster in mid-1958,

Patent diagrams reveal the Jazzmaster's key design features. Diagram second from left shows a multi-pole rhythm pickup with seven poles. Leo believed that the Jazzmaster's vibrato was a big improvement over the Stratocaster's. For the delicate playing he envisioned on the Jazzmaster, he was probably right.

(Below) Guitarist Howard Reed with Gene Vincent's band. While jazz players sat, rockers stood. Teenagers noticed and bought guitar straps.

The Fender plant, 1959.

Players agree that the Jazzmaster sounds mellow, lacking the rock and roll assault of the Telecaster and Stratocaster. Still, it was a highly versatile instrument adaptable to all styles of music. Roy Lanham, a close friend of Leo's, burned country-flavored jazz on his red Jazzmaster. Gospel music's Pops Staples played one. Buddy Merrill, as mentioned, and Neil Le Vang both used Jazzmasters for a time on the Lawrence Welk show. Mickey Baker, of Mickey and Sylvia's "Love Is Strange" fame, played a Jazzmaster after the guitar's introduction.

But Joe Pass was one of the few pure jazz artists known to record with a Jazzmaster. Most wanted a sound almost impossible to create on a solidbody instrument, which Leo would have learned had he consulted more true jazz artists. He did talk to Bill Carson, Alvino Rey, and others while he developed the new model. But Rey said that the inventor was set in his ways by then and less inclined than in the 1940s to take advice. As a result, many players stopped giving him suggestions they knew he did not want to hear. Most people besides Leo believed that he was going to have a hard time topping what he had already accomplished. Rey said in the 1980s, "Everyone thought his first guitar was his best, but no one would tell him that." By the late 1950s, the Telecaster was becoming an integral part of the session player's arsenal. California-based guitarist Howard Roberts endorsed Gibson and Epiphone but also played an old Telecaster on countless rock sessions, as would Tommy Tedesco. These players knew what models recorded best and pleased record producers; Telecasters had the teenage sound. The Jazzmaster quickly flunked this test among the top pros in the studios: its pickups had inadequate shielding and hummed like a box full of killer bees. Leo's trick rhythm circuit sounded toneless and ill-defined, the result of filtering capacitors.

Leo, who in Fullerton was isolated from the Los Angeles jazz and recording scenes just a short drive away, had built what he supposed the top players wanted or needed into the Jazzmaster, with predictable results. After seeing the new model, Bob Perine knew immediately that Fender Sales was on "a hopeless track" selling it to true jazzmen. He talked to Wes Montgomery, Tal Farlow, Jim Hall, and various other well-known jazz players who described the tone they preferred as mellow and funky with less sustain and solidbody rasp. Bob particularly remembers his experience with Jim Hall.

but the Jazzmaster illustrated in the 1958–59 catalog was a prototype rather than a typical 1958 production model. It had a gold anodized aluminum pickguard, chrome knobs for the lead circuit, and black plastic pickup covers. The black-and-white picture appears to show a two-color sunburst rather than the customary three-color commonly used in 1958. The neck had a rosewood fingerboard, but the factory installed the truss rod from the neck's back, as shown by the walnut plug on the headstock.

The factory received orders on August 1, 1958, after the summer trade shows. Nonetheless, its busy schedule delayed production; the Jazzmaster was back-ordered from the summer of 1958 well into 1959. By October 6, 1958, unfilled requests amounted to four hundred. The Jazzmasters pictured in 1959 advertising were production models. The features included three-color sunburst finishes, multi-colored imitation tortoiseshell plastic pickguards, molded white plastic knobs for the lead circuit, and white pickup covers. Solid-color Jazzmasters usually had layered, white plastic pickguards that replaced discontinued aluminum ones. Pickups mounted directly to the pickguard.

(Left to right) Tal Farlow and Jim Hall. These jazz greats would never be lured into playing jazz on Fenders, despite Leo's intentions. However, when record producers asked top session players like Howard Roberts—who was also an accomplished jazz artist—to capture the teenage sound, they often unpacked Telecasters.

"Jim Hall is a real neat guy," Perine recalls. "He was staying with a friend of mine, so I went up to Arcadia one evening and took a Jazzmaster." Perine waited for the right moment. "We were sitting around the living room after dinner and I said, 'Jim, would you mind trying a Fender guitar just for the hell of it? I want to see how it sounds with you playing it.'"

Jim said, "Sure, man." Perine brought in a brand-new guitar and Twin Amp and hooked them up. Hall played for about fifteen minutes.

Perine was not happy with the reaction: "Hall just shook his head and said: 'This is not jazz; this is something else. It's nicely made and everything, it plays nice and it has a nice feel, but God, it's so heavy.'" Perine explains, "You know, a Jazzmaster is a pretty heavy guitar. There again, should a jazz guitar be safely traditional? The jazz guys just liked to play those big Gibson acoustics." Moreover, in 1957 Gibson had introduced its acclaimed dual-coil humbucking pickup, a design that could create the dink-a-dink jazz tone while bucking the hum created by stage lights and room wiring. The company had found just the right combination of traditional construction and technical advances.

But Fender did sell many Jazzmasters as the model found its way into the fabric of the teenage musical subculture, making a big splash with garage bands, especially surf bands in southern California. Instead of the prestigious pros foreseen by Leo, the Jazzmaster attracted kids with limited abilities who hoped a Fender would raise their musical skills to a higher level. (The guitar now seems typecast in that role. In the 1970s, a legion of unknown punks as well as Elvis Costello played Jazzmasters. In the 1990s, grunge bands wear them as often as flannel shirts.) In a sense, Leo's failure illustrated Fender Sales' success—ads with people jumping out of airplanes did not draw Barney Kessel types to Fenders. As planned, Perine's ads attracted teenagers. With the Jazzmaster, he had some help.

Before the Beatles, the Ventures were rock's most emulated combo, their style attracting many beginners. Bob Bogle, who played lead before switching to bass, used a Jazzmaster on the group's original recording of "Walk, Don't Run," which ironically was a rockified jazz tune that showcased the guitar's jazz-less tone and vibrato effect. After flirting with a Stratocaster, rhythm guitarist Don Wilson made the Jazzmaster his main guitar. Although the group would later endorse Mosrite guitars, the Ventures led many teenagers to Fender dealers.

Famous skydiver ad photo from 1964. The guitar landed without a scratch. (Below) The Ventures' second album promoted Fender and forever linked the guitars with the garage-band generation.

177

A comprehensive set
of *You Won't Part with
Yours Either* ads.
Lower right ad is 1995
re-do of 1963 original
on page 166.

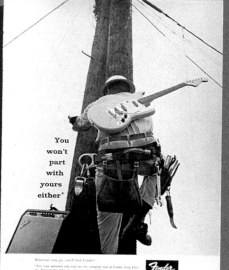

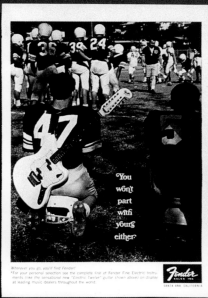

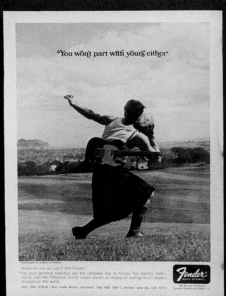

The Electric Violin

Along with the Jazzmaster, the Fender electric violin was another new instrument introduced in the 1958–59 catalog, and another example of the company reaching for a wider audience. According to Stan Compton, Leo initiated the project to round out the family of Fender electric instruments. His records of tool purchases show that he received a template for the violin's neck on September 1, 1951, the same day he received the template for the first Precision Bass neck. On December 28, he acquired what the notes describe as the "saw template for the violin," probably for its body. Whatever the shape of the instrument, F. C. Hall recalled in the early 1980s that Leo started developing it for Bob Wills and his band, but delayed the project for unknown reasons.

The first production model Fender electric violin had a two-color sunburst finish, 1958.

(Right) Other early examples had three-color finishes.

Still, the potential market for electric violins among orchestras and country-western bands was a fertile one. Electric fiddles, first developed in the 1930s, suffered audio feedback problems similar to those of early acoustic-electric guitars. Electro String developed a fully electric Bakelite violin with a radically shaped body that produced little feedback, but the instrument was too heavy for most players. As with guitars, Leo saw a gap in existing technology he could exploit and returned to the violin about 1957.

In addition to the 1958–59 Fender catalog, several magazine ads depicted the pre-CBS version of Leo's emerging violin, which stood somewhere between the radical extreme of the 1930s Rickenbacker and a conventional violin equipped with a bridge microphone or pickup. The Fender used a bolt-on maple neck. The earliest versions had no separate, laminated fingerboards, while the violin illustrated in advertising showed a laminated ebony fingerboard. All pre-CBS versions employed a Fender-style headstock with geared Kluson tuners. The body was hollow, with a top constructed from 1/8-inch plywood. The paint department finished the violins in both two- and three-color sunbursts.

Leo developed an ingenious pickup that mounted on a small steel armature plate. Extending under the bridge and bending down into the interior of the body, it rocked back and forth slightly as the player bowed the strings. An edge of the armature plate hovered over the pickup's two pole pieces. Leo mounted the whole unit under the violin's top with two screws; the distance between the armature plate's edge and the pickup unit was adjusted by two screws on the top. The device had exceptional sensitivity and fidelity, while the bridge armature's slight, imperceptible rocking motion did not change the strings' pitch.

The volume and tone control knobs each had eight settings or stops that clicked into position. Settings were easy to change purposely but hard to change inadvertently with a bow or hand. Leo gave much thought to this feature.

However, he failed to consider the violin's major drawback: its weight balance. Many players thought the whole instrument was too heavy. Others believed that the weighty Kluson-equipped peghead made it difficult to hold under the chin without support, the way fiddlers freed their hands to tighten their bows or to grab a beer. Fender had always endured criticism from traditionalists and forged ahead (the Jazzmaster was a case in point), but he apparently lost confidence in the violin's design. Forrest White's records show two Fender Sales orders for one hundred violins each before the factory dropped the model. (As mentioned in chapter 10, Randall wanted the instrument.) No one knows for certain if Fender filled these orders; only a couple of pre-CBS violins have shown up in collections. (CBS produced a similar electric violin around 1970, but with a conventional scroll peghead. Perhaps some components of these instruments came from the 1950s.)

By late 1958 Leo had apparently lost interest in the electric violin as he turned his attention to projects that interested him—updated Telecasters, Esquires, amplifiers, and a new bass guitar. Meanwhile, Fender Sales further expanded to keep up with Leo's pace at the factory and with the still-growing demand for guitars.

Leo added the violin's design to his patent portfolio, but never cashed in on the instrument's commercial potential, which Randall could taste. He had enlisted George Liberace to play the instrument every week on TV, and a symphony orchestra in San Francisco had expressed interest in going electric with Fenders.

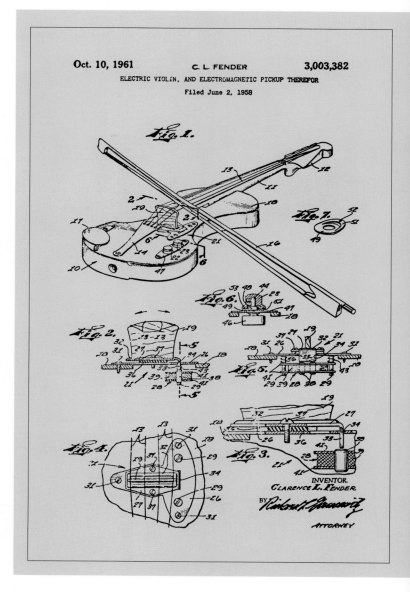

The men's bowling team, 1960. Standing left to right, Forrest White, Bert Stafford, Bud Morgan. Kneeling, Harold Rhodes and Dick Stout.

(Below, clockwise from top left) Seated woman installs magnets in a pickup frame while standing woman puts assemblies into a powerful magnetizer.

Lloyd Chewning shaping a neck.

Woman worker fine sanding a fingerboard.

Ted Ledbetter slotting a bone nut in a Jazzmaster neck, April 1960.

Man sanding headstocks in the wood shop.

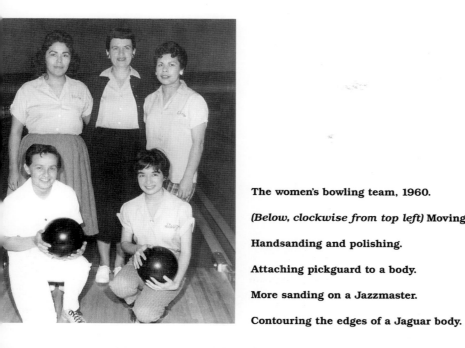

The women's bowling team, 1960.

(Below, clockwise from top left) Moving bodies.

Handsanding and polishing.

Attaching pickguard to a body.

More sanding on a Jazzmaster.

Contouring the edges of a Jaguar body.

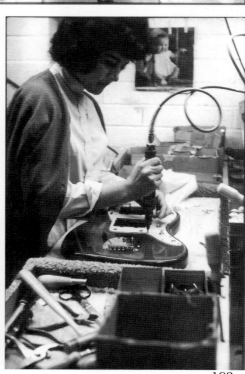

"The Fender people always hope to be close to the feelings of those who buy, sell and play electric instruments because this is the greatest source of information for the continued progress of the company." —1960 FENDER CATALOG

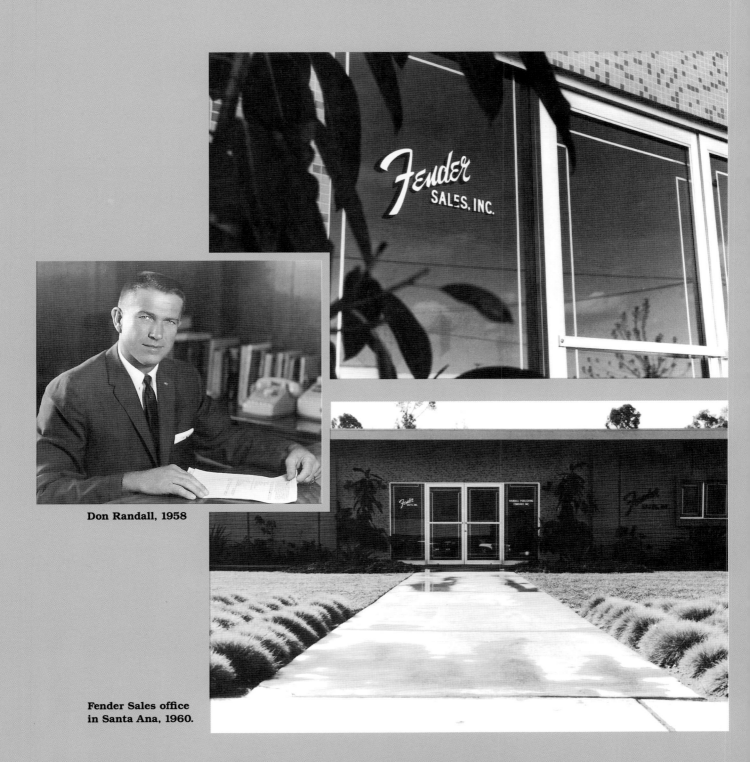

Don Randall, 1958

Fender Sales office in Santa Ana, 1960.

The choice of professionals and students

Fender Fine Electric Instruments

The two-color process, faded-looking 1960 catalog introduced the Jazz Bass. It also showed the Tolex-covered Concert, Vibrasonic, and 3–10 Bandmaster. The smaller amps and the 4–10 Bassman were still tweed. Stratocasters and Telecasters featured rosewood fingerboards.

Chapter

More Firsts from Fender

Service with a Smile

On July 21, 1958, Fender Sales moved to a larger facility at 1546 E. Chestnut in Santa Ana. Randall kept a minimum number of people employed here, about twenty including salesmen, accountants, truckdrivers, and secretaries. But they still provided good service to customers and dealers. Bob Perine says, "I sat in the Fender Sales office many times while Stan Compton talked on the phone to somebody. I just liked the way he treated people. I mean he and Don were really out to help the dealer. When dealers wanted something, boy, they hopped and they got it for them. Especially dealers who had been with them a long time." To improve this service, Fender Sales formed an affiliate company in 1960 called Fender Sales, Inc. of Oklahoma. It had a sales and warehouse facility at 2408 West Skelly Drive in Tulsa managed by steel player Speedy West. In 1964 Fender moved this facility to 912 West Skelly.

With Mike Cole's success in New York and Fender's increasing nationwide popularity, the need for better customer service on the East Coast had become acute in the early 1950s. In 1951 Don Russo had done service work for Fender in the basement of his Long Island home. Russo and Cole were friends, and with Jody Carver they became a trio. In 1953 Mike opened a small service center on his own where Shea Stadium now stands, at 42–15 116th Street, instead of running out to Russo's house. Mike's brother Frank did electronic repairs, brother Steve handled the shipping, and brother John worked on the road as a sub-salesman with Mike.

While the Santa Ana office—piloted by Randall with his neatly trimmed George Gobel flat-top—operated well within the standards of 1950s business decorum, the East Coast service center's hang-loose atmosphere rivaled a Marx Brothers movie. Carver remembers it as a "zoo-like

Left to right, Alex Kroo, interpreter, and Don Randall at a trade show in Frankfurt, West Germany in 1961. Fender's penetration into Europe was problematic in the early 1960s. Randall claims that he helped establish several distributors who then proceeded to produce products that competed with Fender.

Fender's Frankfurt display, 1961.

little hole-in-the-wall office building with a girl at the front desk." Cole aptly tagged it the "Fender Nervous Center." Although Carver's inclination was to play music full time, he went to work there in 1959. Cole told Jody that he was "the manager," so he came to work the first day wearing a sport coat and a tie. When Cole saw him, he said, "You don't have to be dressed up like that. Wear your jeans tomorrow." Carver says today that he didn't know he had to unload trucks. He was the manager, but had four bosses and did the heavy lifting.

Each morning Carver stapled his lunch bag shut and put it into a desk drawer for safekeeping. Jody explained his reason: "The store was filled with cockroaches—pre-CBS Fender cockroaches. They're probably still alive today." One morning he made a delivery, returned, and found his lunch—a meatball sandwich—missing. The UPS driver had picked it up by mistake and sent it to an unsuspecting Fender dealer in South Carolina. As the Eastern highways and warehouses heated up in the summer sun, the seasoned sandwich took on new life. Carver speculates about what happened: "You know what a meatball sandwich smells like at one day old, let alone ten days old in a truck. Whoever got that bag, I don't think he was dealing with Fender anymore."

Jody Carver on steel with his group in the mid-1950s.

Regal guitars made by Harmony and distributed by Fender Sales, 1959.

A May 1960 promo shot featuring the Telecaster Custom.

(Right) Product sheet that introduced Leo's dressed-up solidbodies.

(Below) Buck Owens picks his extra-fancy Telecaster Custom in the mid-1960s.

The Telecaster and Esquire Customs and Rosewood Fingerboards

In 1959 Fender Sales introduced the Telecaster Custom and Esquire Custom, fancy versions of Fender's original guitars. Besides dressing up their plain slab bodies, the added white binding helped protect the edges from wear. Forrest White wrote in his book that the factory made the first Telecasters with binding in 1958 for country guitar pioneers Don Rich and Buck Owens. Yet his own records show that Fender Sales placed the first order for Customs on July 23, 1959. Don Rich, who had not started performing on guitar in bands, first recorded with Owens on December 23, 1959, playing fiddle. Rich then attended college before dropping out and joining Owens full time in December 1960. Don switched from fiddle to lead guitar about 1962; numerous photos show Buck Owens still playing a 1950s Telecaster as late as 1962.

Nevertheless, the Telecaster and Esquire Customs had Jazzmaster-like rosewood fingerboards. These necks looked more traditional and wore better than one-piece maple necks, which picked up dirt and grime where the lacquer wore through and looked used up long before their time. Leo considered the new construction both functional and more attractive, eventually converting the entire Fender line to it.

(Clockwise from top right) Telecaster Custom bodies, 1964.

Necks with rosewood fingerboards, April 1964.

Sanding the original-style one-piece neck, 1957.

From 1959 to 1965, all Fender guitars and basses—including the Customs—came with three distinct versions of the rosewood fingerboard. The first was flat on the bottom surface where it joined the neck base. Collectors call this style the "slab" because of its shape and thickness; these necks usually feel wide and flat. Fender used them until about mid-1962.

In varying heat and humidity, rosewood and maple have different coefficients of expansion that plagued slab fingerboard necks. Soon Leo discovered that he could fashion the shape and thickness of the fingerboard to counteract the difference in the two woods. The second group of rosewood fingerboards, in use for about a year, had an upper and lower surface that corresponded to the curved upper surface on the maple neck base. This fingerboard, although thinner than the slab, was still relatively thick. By mid-1963 Leo determined that a thinner rosewood fingerboard worked better, so the third and final style of fingerboards used a very thin, curved rosewood cap. Despite Leo's experiments with fingerboard thicknesses, all old Fender necks had an inclination to bump up at the fret closest to the body because of the truss rod construction.

Left to right, a 1955 Telecaster, a 1963 Telecaster with a mahogany body, and a 1962 Telecaster Custom.

So the first Telecaster and Esquire Customs came with slab fingerboards. The 1959 *Down Beat* brochure that introduced them also showed standard Telecasters and Esquires with older-style maple necks. For a short period Fender simultaneously produced standard Telecaster and Esquire guitars with maple necks and Customs with rosewood fingerboards. However, at no time during the pre-CBS years did Fender regularly produce Customs with the older style one-piece maple neck. The only exceptions may have been unlikely special orders. However, some pre-CBS Custom Telecasters had maple necks capped with maple fingerboards made in the same manner as the necks capped with rosewood.

While the standard Telecasters and Esquires came with blonde finishes, the Telecaster and Esquire Customs came with sunbursts. A few even had the more expensive custom color finishes. Although most pre-CBS Customs were trimmed with simple white binding, the binding on some custom-color ones was a contrasting dark plastic, an option more common in the mid and late 1960s. A batch of sparkle-finished 1963 Telecasters, probably including the first pair made for Don Rich and Buck Owens, used

thick checkered binding like some Rickenbackers. Forrest White said that he contacted the Martin company to learn the best gluing procedure for this binding. Another guitar made in 1963 for George Fullerton was identical to the pair sent to Bakersfield.

The earliest Customs wore Telecaster or Esquire decals with the standard script collectors call the "spaghetti logo." Soon the decals stated *Telecaster Custom* or *Esquire Custom*. To cut production costs on the first Customs, the strings mounted through the bridge rather than through the body.

By 1960 Fender advertising literature depicted standard Telecaster and Esquire guitars with rosewood fingerboards and the factory returned to strings-through-the-body

Telecaster Custom, 1963. Three Telecasters with crushed-mirror sparkle finishes and checkered binding emerged from the Fender factory in 1963. One went to Buck Owens (page 188). George Fullerton owns this beauty. Notice the laminated maple-cap fingerboard.

Telecaster promo photograph from the early 1960s.

Prototype Stratocaster, 1959. Appearing in the 1959 and early-1960s *Down Beat* inserts, this guitar had a laminated pickguard with only eight screws (instead of the normal eleven) and a walnut plug on the headstock (as seen on earlier one-piece maple necks).

Page 9 of the 1960 catalog.

construction. In the early 1960s the standard versions used a single-layer white pickguard while the bound guitars and custom-color guitars used a 3-layer laminated one—a black layer sandwiched between two white ones—that revealed a contrasting black edge. Eventually all Telecasters had the 8-screw laminated pickguards. Of special note: During the early 1960s, Fender produced a limited number of standard Telecasters with natural-finish mahogany bodies.

In fourteen years the Telecaster had gone from new kid on the block to venerable old guy down the street. Always searching for something new, Leo focused on his pet-of-the-month designs: first the Stratocaster, then the Jazzmaster, Jaguar, and Mustang (introduced in 1964). Many players argue that in the interim Telecasters slipped, hence the higher value put on earlier ones. Nevertheless, since electric guitar collecting started in the late 1960s, most players believe that all pre-CBS Telecasters are worthwhile, especially when paired with a Fender tube amplifier.

Behind the Amplifier Designs

Leo always designed his amps with his guitars in mind; guitars and amps evolved along separate tracks because of inherent differences in the technologies. Pickups were basically coils and pole pieces. The wire and magnets, produced by other manufacturers, came in few sizes that could conceivably perform well under the strings of a guitar. Once Fender found the best combinations—he had his most successful pickup innovations set by 1954—he experimented less until the 1980s, when he began using newly designed ceramic magnets that offered a few additional design alternatives. Amplifiers, however, could contain innumerable combinations of speakers, tubes, circuits, and transformers. Cabinets could be small like a portable radio or large like a refrigerator; seemingly insignificant changes in components made dramatic changes in performance. Even in the 1940s, trying all the possible uncharted combinations could have taken a lifetime, but it was easier and more practical to design amplifiers around the limitations of guitars than vice versa. Fender's work on amplifier advances continued until his company changed hands in 1965.

Coming from the old school of American manufacturers, Leo believed that his customers deserved the best he could offer. His perfectionist compulsion, the engine that powered Fender, pushed him to improve amps by refining and adding features. He used empirical methods designing them, but did not limit himself. Some changes, like the move from a presence control to a bright switch, resulted from tinkering for the sake of tinkering. By the mid-1950s, many players considered Fender amps the best made, the best sounding, and the best value of any on the market. Because of Leo's foresight, all electric guitars sounded good through his amps, especially Gibsons. The added highs made the muffled humbucking pickups from Michigan ring clear.

Fender amplifiers helped promote Leo's entire product line by making the Fender name respectable, even to jazz purists. And Leo spurred other manufacturers to build better amps. Some of them copied Fenders in detail down to the tweed covering, while others came up with their own innovations. After a tour of the Gibson factory in the late 1950s, a music dealer told Rickenbacker salesman Harold Buckner that Gibson engineers had disassembled and analyzed every model of Fender amp. The amps sat in the Gibson lab, opened up like reference books.

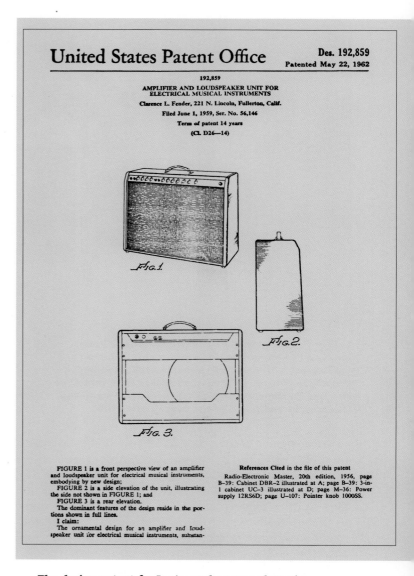

The design patent for Leo's combo amps showed a Vibrasonic. This seemingly obvious design was revolutionary in the 1950s. The controls mounted on an angle in front so that a player could easily see and make adjustments. Incidentally, James Burton used a Vibrasonic on some Ricky Nelson recordings.

Left to right standing, Forrest White, George Fuller-ton, Leo Fender, unidentified guitarist (playing a Jazzmaster with a one-piece maple neck), and Bud Chambers. Sitting, Billy Byrd with Jazz Bass prototype and Buddie Emmons playing a Fender 1000 steel. This jam session was posed at the factory, circa 1959.

With Fender setting the pace and high standards, amplifiers produced by Gibson, Valco, Ampeg, and others in the 1950s and 1960s improved. In the 1980s Leo rightly claimed that tone circuits copied then and still used in most modern amplifiers "should have my name on them." Easily read controls and rugged cabinet construction are other Fender-inspired features. The top-mounted chassis, for which Doc Kauffman claimed credit, predates Fender in National amplifiers; it is nonetheless another outstanding characteristic Fender popularized. Today musicians take advanced features and sound for granted, but in the old days, Leo built his business out of these Fender firsts.

Quality control, a careful check of each amplifier before it left the factory, was the key to Fender's high level of customer satisfaction. And yet Leo could not resist fiddling with his amplifiers. Sometimes two amplifiers made the same day had different characteristics. Dick Dale says: "He

was constantly tweaking the designs, oh God, back and forth, back and forth. Boy, he'd call me up and say, 'Dick, come on down, I got something . . . try this . . . let's see how this works.' So, he always fine-tuned. He never settled. He always wanted to make it better." After tinkering in the lab, Leo would take his new idea to a worker wiring chassis in the plant. Without telling anyone else, he would have her change the value of a component, sometimes in the middle of a production run. Forrest White recalled his confusion one day when a befuddled final inspector noticed units not meeting an important specification. White soon discovered the mystery resulted from Leo's creative tampering upstream. Fed up with such mischief and disruptions, White posted a sign mandating that no one make changes in circuits without his written permission.

Gary Sunda, who designed amplifiers in the 1970s and 1980s for Randall Instruments, the company Don founded after leaving CBS-Fender, says that most of the small changes Leo made in circuits for technical reasons had little effect on the overall product because the human ear could not hear many of the differences. Although amps and speakers from different eras sounded different, they still sounded good to guitar players—the ultimate judges.

(Right, top to bottom) **The 1960 Tolex-covered Bandmaster used three 10-inch speakers and an open-back cabinet. In 1961 Leo introduced the piggy-back Bandmaster with one 12-inch speaker (shown here in tilt-back position). The bottom picture shows the closed-back design, which increased the speaker's performance.**

(Below) **The Vibrasonic featured a JBL 15-inch speaker and circuitry like a Pro. Early versions of the brown combo amps used metal knobs and the control panels read "Bass, Treble, Volume" instead of "Volume, Treble, Bass."**

Tolex-Covered Amplifiers

After the tweed amps, Leo developed Tolex-covered combo-style models. Tolex was a textured, fabric-supported vinyl made by the General Tire and Rubber Company; it came in several colors, but Leo chose brown in the beginning. The 1959 Vibrasonic, the first Fender featuring a factory-equipped JBL speaker, topped his early list. James Burton reportedly used one on many of his early recordings with Ricky Nelson. The Concert soon joined the line and made its name as a stage amp, its four 10-inch speakers capitalizing on interest in 4–10 Bassmans. Leo had a reason—he planned to change the bass amp into a piggy-back model with different speakers.

Piggy-back amps had two components: a speaker box and a separate amp cabinet sitting on top. (These were precursors to so-called amplifier stacks, popular since the late 1960s.) Leo first used the idea on a special 4–10 tweed Bassman. Bob Crooks, owner of the Standel company, who made amps for Speedy West, Merle Travis, and other professionals in the 1950s, claims that Leo saw and copied early Standel piggy-backs. Standel amps, like Bigsby steels, were indeed very popular among the country players in southern California, and as we have seen, Leo often borrowed good ideas from smaller companies. Most early

The first production-model piggy-back amp, the Showman, started as a custom-ordered amp. Speedy West demonstrated one with a Fender 1000 at trade shows.

(Below) Dick Dale was a major regional star in southern California and indispensable to the Showman's development.

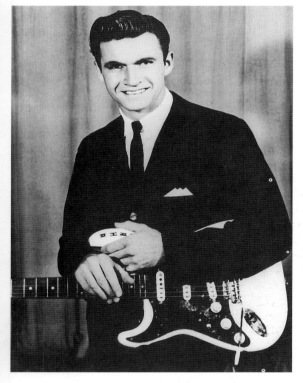

Fender piggy-back amps—custom-built Showman models —went to musicians like Dick Dale. The Champs, best known for their song "Tequila," were pictured with a prototype piggy-back amp at the Fender plant in 1960.

Leo introduced production versions of the Showman amplifiers in late 1960 with the Bassman, Bandmaster, and Tremolux piggy-backs following in 1961. Dick Dale remembered testing a few early Showman amps that were covered in light brown Tolex. Leo had a rolling wall of speakers mounted on casters that he pushed around his lab. When Dale came to the factory, Fender had him plug in a guitar and wail while Leo switched speaker combinations. (Leo attributed his hearing loss to an accident with a Showman during such a test. As he listened to a speaker with his ear against the grille, the amp suddenly blasted his eardrum at full volume, temporarily deafening him.) Dale says: "Everything would sound really good in Leo's cement block building. But then I found it didn't sound as good when I was playing for four thousand people." Leo would change the cabinet or the amp circuit, and Dick would give the new version a test.

Dick Dale and the Deltones, 1963.

196

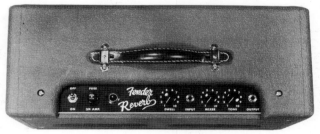

(Left) The Princeton Amp, circa 1962, was somewhere between a Champ and a Deluxe in terms of output.

Surf music relied on the Fender Reverb unit and the crashing, auditorium-like reverberation sound effect it added to the amplified guitar. Fender produced the reverb unit under a license from the Hammond Organ company, which invented the effect for keyboard products.

The feedback from Dale, Fender's most important link to the early-1960s rock generation, proved valuable in other ways. Leo had a cabinet covered in blonde that Dick saw one day at the factory. Wanting one, he said, "Gee, I like this coloring."

Leo explained it was a soon-to-be-discarded experiment, adding: "No, Dick, you can't have that. Everybody's going to want it when they see you playing it." Leo added that the color was impractical: "You spill coffee on it, it'll get dirty."

Dick responded with a fake moan and said, "Gosh, I really want it." Two weeks later he came back to the plant, and the assembly line was producing blonde amps that would soon prove highly successful with young guitarists. Practical or not, they looked as good as a Tijuana tuck-and-roll job. Fifty years old in 1959 and long out of touch with youth culture trends, Fender did not know what looked cool to teenagers until Dale told him. With support from Fender Sales, Dale also encouraged Leo to develop the outboard reverberation unit—an effect that sounded innovative and modern to young people.

Randall and the Fender Sales force had witnessed a variety of portable electronic echo chambers flooding the guitar market in the late 1950s. Fender responded with the Ecco-Fonic in 1959, but it proved unreliable. The Hammond Organ Company had patented a means of electronically mimicking reverberation in a large auditorium. Home organs with this audio ruse sounded almost as good as the Mormon Tabernacle's keyboard. Leo adapted the Hammond design, making it compatible with guitars or microphones, and paid a licensing fee for its use. Once again, Dale tested Leo's first units. Soon a Fender reverb—heard in the thundering sounds of "Surf Beat" on Dick's *Surfers' Choice* album, for example—became a requirement in most teenage bands. The unit led to a whole line of combo amps with built-in reverb.

Young guitarists, especially those emulating Dick Dale or the Ventures, became the ticket to Fender's success after Leo introduced his vinyl-covered amps.

The 1963 Bandmaster had two 12-inch speakers.

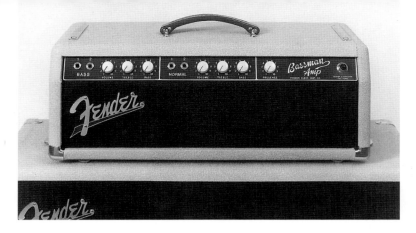

A 1962 Bassman with rough blonde Tolex.

(Below) A model listens to a group of budding musicians at a southern California teenage fair in April 1963.

Bands bought matching sets—all brown or all blonde. (The piggy-back blonde amps were generally more expensive than the combo-style brown amps, but not always. In November 1961 a piggy-back Showman 15 listed at $600.00 while the most expensive brown amp was the Concert with four 10-inch speakers at $359.50. The least expensive piggyback was the Tremolux with one 10 at $249.50.) Fender amps became the ultimate status symbol on stage at a high school sock hop. Fender Sales was soon setting up booths at teenage fairs to promote the latest amps and guitars. Tolex-covered amps ushered in the most colorful period of Leo's amplifier history.

As the company mushroomed in the late 1950s, it became one of the speaker makers' biggest customers. As a result, Leo's power to influence speaker designs grew. Leo usually used Jensen (sometimes called blue cap) speakers in tweed amps and early Tolex amps. However, he dropped Jensen in the early 1960s and turned to Oxford because he wanted speakers with better frequency response and heavier construction. Oxford would make speakers to Leo's specifications when Jensen would not. About 1963 Jensen capitulated and Leo renewed his relationship with the company. (Players generally agree that the Jensen blue caps sound crisper and more resonant than later, more durable Oxfords and

(Clockwise from above) **Final assembly of a blonde piggy-back speaker cabinet in 1964.**

Shipping amps in cartons, 1960.

The procedures used to sand cabinets in 1964 differed little from those used in the early 1950s (page 56).

Jensens made to Leo's specs. Since Leo designed each amp around the speakers' foibles, originals always sound better than replacements.)

Dick Dale remembered an early-1960s drive with Leo to the JBL headquarters on Casitas Avenue in Los Angeles, where Fender laid down the law on specifications for top-of-the-line speakers used in Showmans and Vibrasonics. Dale says, "I kept burning up the JBL voice coil because I was pushing too much with the guitar's volume. So we'd tell them what was going on—we're melting the voice coil, the wires in there were separating. We said we have to get a stronger voice coil." Before Leo intervened, JBL cones pumped so much that Dale's guitar tore them

right out of the speakers. He adds, "We were tearing the ridges on the outside of the cone. So Leo had them rubberize the ridge so that it could flex and last longer and not wear itself out." Fender also recommended that JBL use an aluminum dust cover because it added a little extra sharpness to the treble. "People don't know that, but it does," Dale claims.

Leo's suggestions led to a new line of JBL speakers for musical instruments. The F in JBL's acclaimed 1960s D-Series speakers, including the D-120F and D-130F, stood for *Fender*. Working with speaker manufacturers, Leo probably did more to force improvements in loudspeakers than any person in the music industry.

Fender used a wide variety of logos in the early years.

Corporate Logos

On April 29, 1959, Forrest White became Fender's vice president and general manager while George Fullerton became vice president in charge of production. As the company grew, so did White's stature in the music industry. In 1961 his peers elected him to the National Association of Musical Merchandise Manufacturers' Board of Directors, the first person from west of the Mississippi so honored. Leo, perhaps a bit jealous, said that White's responsibilities at the factory took too much time and forced him to resign from the industry board. Leo wanted to remain isolated on the West Coast; one reason guitar makers joined these associations was to share manufacturing information and production numbers, which Leo resisted. Yet Fender was still quickly becoming part of the music industry establishment.

All established, successful companies—*Time* magazine, Coca-Cola, Nike—have instantly recognizable corporate trademark logos. The shape and design of an effective logo is recognized before the mind verbalizes the words. Advertisers call the phenomenon image power, and the better the logo, the stronger the image. Just catching a glimpse of a trademark is enough to evoke a whole litany of intended feelings and attitudes. The Coke script on a bottle-dispensing machine outside a desert truck stop cools one's thirst before coins can drop through the slot.

Sometime in the late 1950s, Bob Perine began pressuring Stan Compton and Don Randall to update the ever-changing Fender logo and thus create a classic. One day the artist pasted samples of all the old ones in a folder to demonstrate the inconsistencies. Fender, Randall, and the artists they engaged had created almost ten variations. After Perine's presentation, Randall and Compton agreed a change was timely. They wanted to make an effort to coordinate logo use on new instrument decals, on decal reprints for the existing instruments, and in advertising.

One hitch remained: convincing Leo, who apparently believed logo re-styling was a minor issue at best, or that logos could vary with each new instrument. Perine went ahead and designed a good modern trademark and bounced it off Randall and Compton. They decided to proceed with the new design on catalogs and ads. (About this time, 1959, Perine also came up with the *Fretts* masthead design.) Fender Sales used the new logo for several months without input from Leo, so Bob assumed that Randall had neutralized any flak from the factory. The standard way Don and Leo did business was to act, then confront each other and attempt a compromise.

One day Randall called Perine and asked him to go see Leo; certain people were unhappy with the "radical" re-styling of the very personal Fender signature. Randall assured Perine that he and Leo could work it out if Bob took along another design, a kind of compromise version. Unclear as to exactly what that meant, Bob drove to Fullerton with a new sketch. Leo, a bit bothered and feeling put on the spot by the meeting, looked at the rendering a long time. Fender focused on the *F* and gave Bob a mini-lecture on how the Fender *F* was really a German *7*.

Leo said, "It's not a proper *F*, you know."

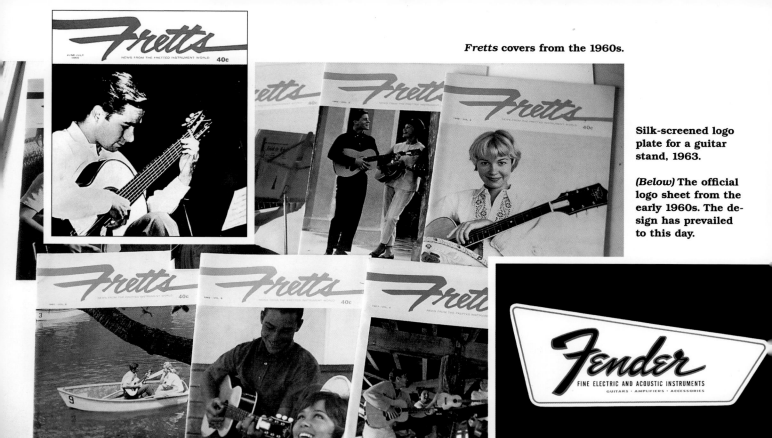

Fretts covers from the 1960s.

"True," Bob replied, adding an appeasement, "but you see them all the time."

Fender smiled and said, "Of course, that's why I like it. But it's having the right curve that counts."

"Beg your pardon?" Bob asked.

Leo ran his finger the length of the letter's contour. "You see, Bob, it should be like the curve of a woman's back; it has to be just right. Higher here, lower there. I don't think you've got it yet."

Having no answer for this subjectivity, Perine laughed, which Fender did not appreciate. Perine could tell that Fender respected his ability, but wanted to stay in the act, to exercise some kind of control over the final outcome. Leo had long dictated the subtle curves of guitar bodies, Bob knew.

"So get that curve right and you're okay," Leo pronounced.

Perine's explanation that he had left untouched the two *e*'s in *Fender* hardly placated Leo. Fender was only concerned about the *F* and summarily dismissed Perine, who had the feeling that he was expected to refine the curve and not come back. Bob recounted his adventure to Randall, who replied simply, "That's Leo." Perine reported to Fender Sales anyway, and does not remember changing the logo to suit Leo's taste in curves. Seeing the guitar builder, as the meeting turned out, was just a formality. Fender Sales quickly made the transition to the new design for promotional materials while the factory took almost four years to apply the new logo to all existing guitar models.

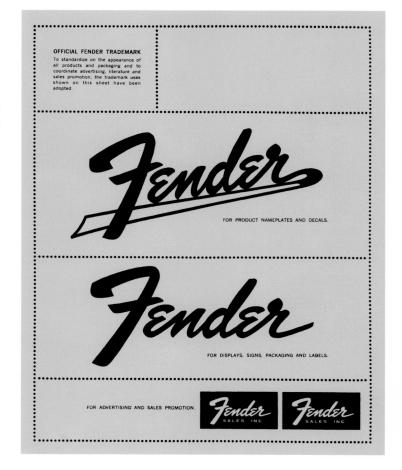

OFFICIAL FENDER TRADEMARK
To standardize on the appearance of all products and packaging and to coordinate advertising, literature and sales promotion, the trademark uses shown on this sheet have been adopted.

FOR PRODUCT NAMEPLATES AND DECALS.

FOR DISPLAYS, SIGNS, PACKAGING AND LABELS.

FOR ADVERTISING AND SALES PROMOTION.

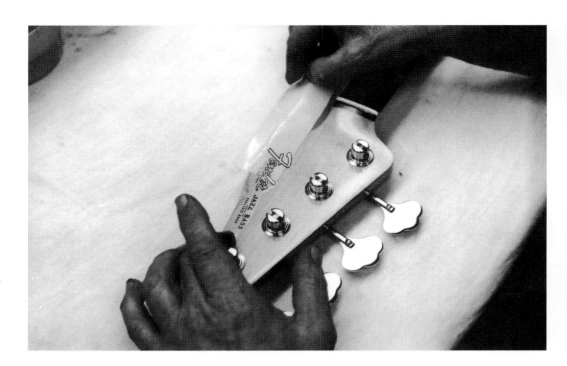

Applying a decal over the finish, 1964.

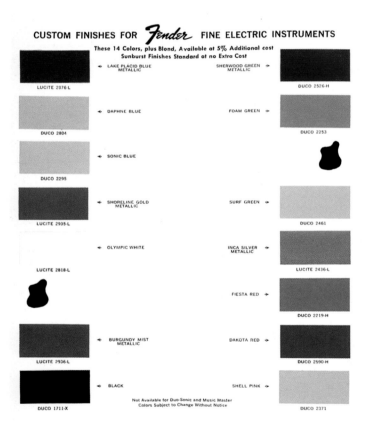

The first color selection chart, 1961.

The original Stratocaster decal had gold letters outlined in black featuring what collectors now call the spaghetti logo, a design that dated to about 1950. Decals on Stratocasters with vibrato read *Fender Stratocaster with Synchronized Tremolo* while non-vibrato Stratocasters read simply, *Fender Stratocaster*. Fender added patent numbers to Stratocaster decals in 1961. Guitars made that year had two numbers while guitars from 1962 through late 1964 had three numbers. In early 1965 the factory finally changed the logo to match the Perine/Fender Sales logo and added a fourth patent number to the decal. (The company still uses Perine's classic logo, but has returned to an older one on vintage-style instruments.)

While logo designs evolved, another cosmetic detail garnered more notice. Recognizing the increasing popularity of custom colors, Fender standardized guitar finish options in 1961 with the first Color Selection Chart. Fender Sales announced it in one of the "Dear Mr. Dealer" letters sent periodically to music stores. A revised chart, although undated, came out in late 1963. Both small folders had fourteen Lucite and Duco paint chips mounted inside; these colors plus blonde were available at 5 percent additional cost. The 1961 chart included Shell Pink while the later chart replaced it with Candy Apple Red, which Fender Sales announced in the November 1963 *Fender Facts #5* newsletter. Such metallic colors were highly popular for hot rods and dragsters of the early 1960s. The side note on page 3 said: "This color is the result of long experimentation to make such a color that would not fade. Now, in cooperation with one of the major paint companies, the correct formula has been set and is now available." Hank Marvin of the Shadows made Fiesta Red extremely popular in England in the 1960s.

The Jazz Bass

Another development came in Fender basses. When Fender redesigned the Precision Bass in 1954 and again in 1957, Fender Sales dropped the old versions. At the time Leo saw little need for more than one model. However, sales office strategies changed in the late 1950s when bassists became more sophisticated and the demand for another model became apparent. Leo soon answered with the Jazz Bass. It differed from the Precision in three important respects: the neck was slimmer and narrower at the nut, thus allowing faster playing; its body had an offset waist reminiscent of the Jazzmaster's; and it used two single-coil bi-pole pickups rather than the split-coil humbucking unit. (Bi-pole pickups had two poles per string—eight poles on a 4-string bass.) Like the post-1957 Precision, the Jazz Bass' individual steel bridges had adjustments for the strings' intonation and height.

Leo went through several revisions of the Jazz Bass. Photos show a prototype with his multi-pole pickup (with five poles for four strings). The original electronics in production models included tandem tone and volume controls, the so-called concentric stacked knobs that permitted mixing pickups while maintaining separate volume and tone settings for each. Fender used the stacked knob controls in 1960 and 1961. Later Jazz Basses featured individual volume controls for each pickup and one master tone control, the 3-control setup. However, a 1959 photo of an early Jazz Bass shows a 3-control setup as found on post-1961 models. Evidently, the design predates the stacked-knob design. In any event, Leo settled on stacked knobs for the first production models, and Fender Sales ordered them on March 3, 1960. Subsequently, Leo returned to the 3-control design, thus proving that tinkerers are never satisfied.

Sometime in early 1963 Fender dropped individual under-string mutes on the Jazz Bass and added a single

(Above) **Page 5 of the 1960 catalog pictured a Jazz Bass, left, with stacked knobs. This instrument had no decal.**

(Left) **This Jazz Bass prototype's decal read** *Fender Bass*. **The front cover hid a multi-pole pickup. Surprising to many bass collectors, the knob setup here predates the so-called stacked knobs used on the first production-model Jazz Basses.**

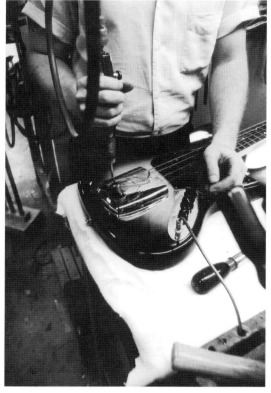

(*Clockwise from top left*) **Close-up view of the bass multi-pole pickup.**

The bridge pickup on a prototype Jazz Bass.

Early ad for the Jazz Bass.

Jazz Bass final assembly.

rubber mute to the chrome bridge cover. Most players removed the cover because it interfered with their right-hand technique, and despite Leo's well-intentioned efforts, mutes never became a popular feature on either the Precision or the Jazz Bass. When players needed the effect, they simply used their right hand to dampen the strings. With or without the mute, the Jazz Bass added a new dimension to modern bass. It had a punchy sound that projected like a guitar, which made it ideal for soloing. The growing reality of the electric bass' potential in popular music led to further innovations.

The 1961 catalog, another two-color printing experiment, introduced the Showman and piggy-back versions of the Tremolux, Bandmaster, and Bassman. Other additions included the Bass VI.

(Below) Bob Perine poses in the Fender Sales recording studio with a bevy of early-1960s Fender gear.

the choice of musicians everywhere

Fender
Fine
Electric
Instruments

Dick Dale always played a Stratocaster, in his words "the only real surf guitar"; yet he influenced thousands of teenagers to buy all Fender models.

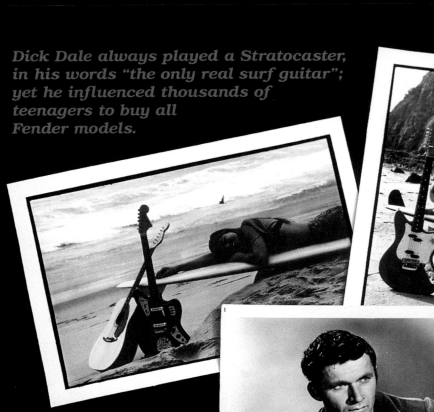

Dick Dale, the Beach Boys, the Surfaris, girls, girls, girls, and, of course, Fender guitars. By the early 1960s Fender had found its place in the sun.

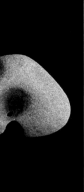

THE SURFARIS
PLAY
DECCA
WIPE OUT
POINT PANIC
WAIKIKI RUN
SURFER JOE *and others*

BEACH BOYS CONCERT

THIS IS THE BEACH BOYS' FIRST "LIVE" ALBUM. HERE ARE THE GREAT SONGS, THE UNBELIEVABLE EXCITEMENT OF AN ACTUAL BEACH BOYS CONCERT — BEFORE THOUSANDS OF SHOUTING, SCREAMING BEACH BOYS FANS! INSIDE: 4 PAGES OF EXCITING ON-STAGE PHOTOS, PLUS NOTES ON THE CONCERT.

The 1962 catalog. Fender's first full-color album-style catalog introduced the Jaguar.

Chapter

The Surf Is Always Up

The Bass VI

Leo's designs always followed his competitors to some degree, and Danelectro produced innovative, high-quality merchandise that posed a real challenge to Fender by the late 1950s. Owner Nat Daniel, whose guitars were a case study in less-is-more, took Leo's ideas about production cost-cutting to the extreme. He used Masonite to make guitar bodies; his pickup covers were surplus lipstick tubes. The results—cheap guitars that sounded expensive—astonished the guitar industry.

Just to irritate Fender sales reps at trade shows, Daniel hung a live Stratocaster in front of a fluorescent light, which made the guitar's amp hum very loudly. Next to the Fender hung a live but silent Danelectro, totally shielded from the light's hum-causing radio waves with about $.02 worth of aluminum foil inside the body. The irony was not lost on Leo, who had wanted to use aluminum pickguards for the same purpose on Stratocast-

ers but stopped when players' fingers started to turn colors. Eventually he did put a shielding plate on Stratocasters, but not before Daniel made his dramatic and telling trade show demonstrations.

In 1958 Forrest White had flown to Nashville, increasingly prominent in the country music recording scene. There he held informative meetings with record producer Owen Bradley and his brother, guitarist Harold. White learned that the simple, unadorned Danelectro 6-string bass had quickly found a place in Nashville studios and on the *Grand Ole Opry*, where it still remains as a key part of the emerging Nashville sound. (The style, popularized by artists like Ray Price, also included lush strings and chorus-like background vocal groups.) The new Danelectro bass sounded rich and full.

Returning to Fullerton from Nashville, White reported his trip and meetings with the Bradleys. As a result, Leo

207

Big Tiny Little (in hat) and his guitarist pose with a Jaguar, Bass VI, and an unheard-of, never-marketed piggy-back Concert Amp.

(Left) Leo's 6-string Bass VI competed with the much simpler and more economical Danelectro.

decided to design a 6-string bass. He believed that he could improve Danelectro's concept by building a more complicated instrument with adjustable bridge saddles, vibrato, and other Fender innovations. Sometime in the 1950s, Fender had lost track of the reasons for his own success. Compared with early-1950s Gibsons and Epiphones, Fenders were a lot more for a lot less. Leo had made a better, dressed-down instrument, and the world had come to him.

In contrast, his 6-string bass made the word "overkill" sound flattering. Introduced by Fender Sales in 1961, the Fender Bass Guitar, or Bass VI, was a 6-string, 3-pickup bass usually tuned one octave below the standard guitar; it had twenty-one frets, a Jazzmaster-style floating tremolo, and a comfort-contoured offset body shaped somewhere between that of the Jazz Bass and the Jazzmaster (the Bass VI had a deeper upper cutaway than the guitar, but shallower than the bass). Guitarists liked the comfortable, close string spacing on the 30-inch-scale, narrow neck. (The Precision's wider, longer-scale one drew complaints from many guitarists with small hands.)

The first version had three pickup selector switches that allowed seven combinations. The 1962 model's pickups had chrome pickup frames and a chrome mounting plate for the selector switches. *Fender Facts #2*, issued in February 1963, announced additional changes in the Bass VI: a mute like the Jaguar's and patented "Jaguar-type" pickup units. Each pickup still had an on-off switch as on the earlier Bass Vis, but in 1963 a fourth tone modification switch was added. Freddie Tavares told *Guitar Player* magazine in August 1978 that Leo called this one the "strangle switch"

A 1963 Bass VI with "Jaguar-type" pickups (see page 212) and another 1963 teenage fair scene.

because it cut out the low frequencies. In 1958 Danelectro sold its bass guitar through Montgomery Ward for $119.95—the right price for an auxiliary instrument used on special songs or projects. In contrast, the Fender retailed at $329.50 in 1962, nearly triple the price of its competitor.

The tone of the Bass VI never matched the deep resonance of other Fender basses or the twangy thump of the Danelectros. (Guitar legend Duane Eddy's 1960s cut "Because They're Young" featured the Danelectro.) Still, some combos used it as their only bass. After all, it was a Fender. George Harrison played a Bass VI on the Beatles' "Hey Jude" promo clip. The Bass VI's most common application was in the recording industry, especially in Nashville and Los Angeles. There, both country and rock musicians usually used a 6-string bass to reinforce a string bass. Some guitarists used it to double standard lead guitar parts. The Bass VI also found its way onto some recordings as a lower-register lead instrument; today this is its most common application. The solo in "The Race Is On" by George Jones is either a Bass VI or a Danelectro.

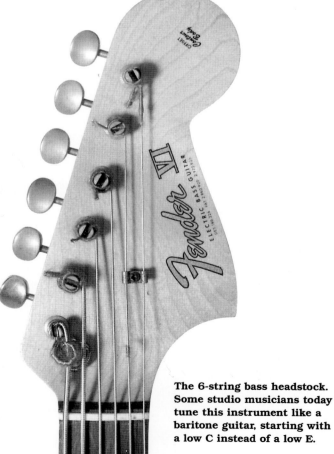

The 6-string bass headstock. Some studio musicians today tune this instrument like a baritone guitar, starting with a low C instead of a low E.

209

The Fender Jaguar on a Jaguar fender, another of Perine's visual puns.

(Below) Burgundy Mist was one of Fender's most striking custom colors.

The Jaguar

By the early 1960s Gibson and the other competitors realized that solidbody guitars were here to stay and filled gaps in their lines with additional models. Competition at the top had become emulation to an extent as Gibson dealers pressured that company to make more Fender-like models. Les Paul series guitars had shorter-scale necks than full-size Fenders until 1961 when Gibson dropped its original design for the longer-scale, lighter-weight SG-style Les Paul model. In 1963 the company also introduced the Firebird series. When considered in the context of the countless designs introduced in recent decades, the differences between SGs, Firebirds, and Fenders may seem more apparent than their similarities. But considering the other designs of the era, particularly Gibson's own models, Leo's influence on the guitars from Kalamazoo was undeniable. It was a two-way street.

In 1962 Fender Sales introduced the Jaguar, fourth in the series of top-of-the-line standards. Offering several new features built around the Jazzmaster body, the Jaguar resembled its predecessor with smaller pickups, different switching, and more chrome. Its most significant departure from earlier full-size Fenders was the short, 24-inch-scale "fast action" neck which Leo thought Gibson players would like. It had an extra fret: twenty-two rather than twenty-one. The new model also used the floating tremolo and bridge, but according to the literature, players no longer needed to remove the bridge cover to dampen strings for special effects. (The first thing most players did with their new Fender was jettison the useless bridge cover.) The guitar had a newly designed built-in mute.

Three slider switches mounted on a chrome plate on the lower half of the pickguard; one was a tone modification switch, and the other two were pickup on/off switches. The preset rhythm circuit resembled the Jazzmaster's and included a separate tone and volume

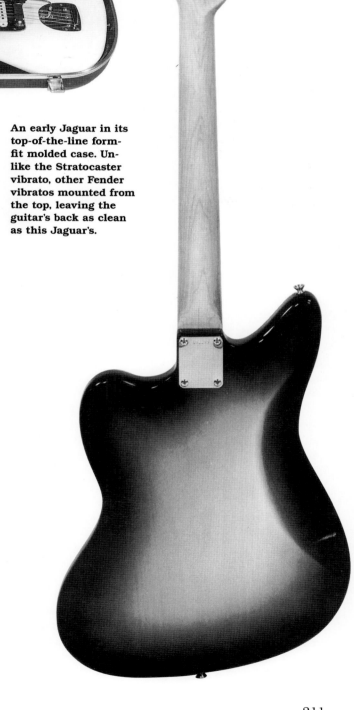

An early Jaguar in its top-of-the-line form-fit molded case. Unlike the Stratocaster vibrato, other Fender vibratos mounted from the top, leaving the guitar's back as clean as this Jaguar's.

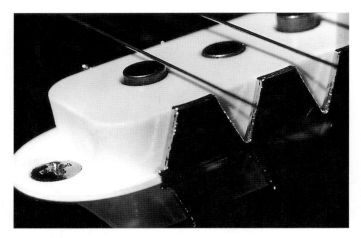

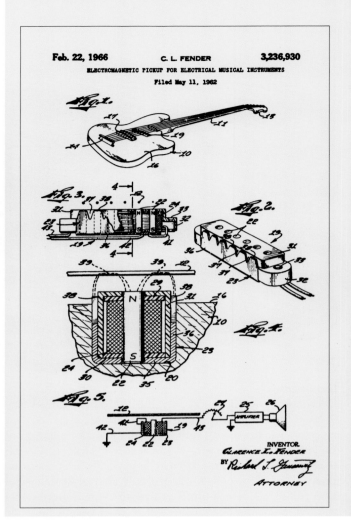

The Jaguar pickup had a notched metal ring (seen in these photos and patent diagram) that concentrated the magnetic field under the strings and reduced hum. The bridge had a built-in mute, which professionals seldom used.

control. The single-coil pickup was narrow and tall, and surrounded by a notched metal ring designed to reduce hum and concentrate the magnetic field under the strings. (Again, Leo thought Gibson players already using humbucking pickups would appreciate this feature.) The unit had a higher impedance and more output than a Stratocaster pickup.

The Jaguar had several drawbacks, including the offset body. The cluttered face of the glitzy guitar sparkled like a Nudie suit—it was not an attractive design compared with earlier Fenders. Leo missed the point about muting and bridge covers. Experienced players muted the strings by second nature, expressing themselves with both dampened notes and ringing notes. Clamped against the strings, a mechanical mute limited experienced players, although it might have attracted inexperienced players who had not mastered the art. A professional racing bike does not need training wheels. Leo's guitar did not need them either.

The short-scale Jaguar would have emerged as a more formidable rock and roll instrument if Fender had equipped it with the Stratocaster vibrato rather than the Jazzmaster's. Instead, like the earlier Jazzmaster, it was lost in 1960s surf music obscurity. Dick Dale always played a Stratocaster, in his words "the only real surf guitar"; yet he influ-

enced thousands of teenagers to buy all Fender models. Eddie Bertrand played a Jaguar with Eddie and the Showmen. Another surf legend, Dave Myers, played one, as did Queen of the Surf Guitar Kathy Marshall. (Robert J. Dalley, surf music historian, wrote that Kathy's technical ability on the guitar in some cases far surpassed that of her male counterparts. She was 13 at the height of her career.)

Several professionals endorsed Jaguars: Paul Guma with Pete Fountain, Roy Lanham, and Mary Kaye. Perhaps the biggest plug for the guitar came in the movie adaptation of the musical *Bye Bye Birdie*. Fender Sales reported in a 1963 press release that producer George Sidney had asked the company to create custom guitars and basses for the movie in which rock and roll star Conrad Birdie was about to be drafted. Jesse Pearson, starring as Birdie, played a solid black Jaguar with gold-plated hardware and a gold-leaf scroll design on the body. Few big rock stars played the Jaguar except the Beach Boys' Carl Wilson in the mid-1960s and the Rolling Stones' Mick Jagger on an early 1980s American tour.

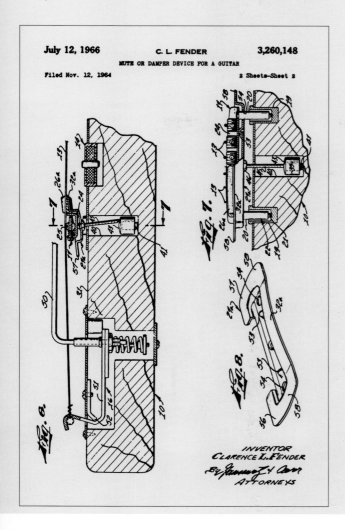

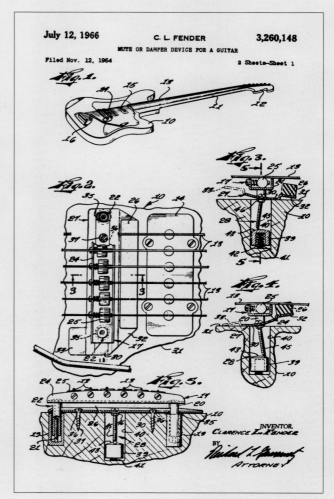

Patent diagrams for Leo's mute.

(Right) Fender Sales' Jim Williams skis for this color ad in 1966.

(Below) Testing a Jaguar through an amp on a rolling cart used to move heavy speakers and amps through the factory and lab, 1964.

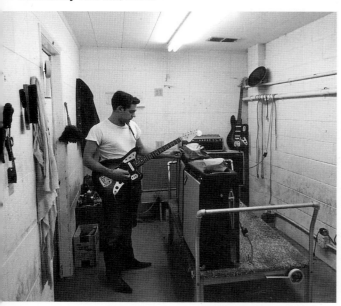

213

Joe and Rose Lee Maphis. Compare the headstock on her guitar, an acoustic modified by Paul Bigsby, to the one on Joe's Jaguar.

(Above) Photos never used in Fender ads.

(Right) This beach scene featured the instruments favored by surf bands: a Jaguar, Jazzmaster, Precision Bass, and Stratocaster.

One of many ads that canonized the Fender head-stock design (which mirrored Bigsby and traditional designs) as a trademark and ironically pointed to the shameless copies that had started to flood the market in the early 1960s.

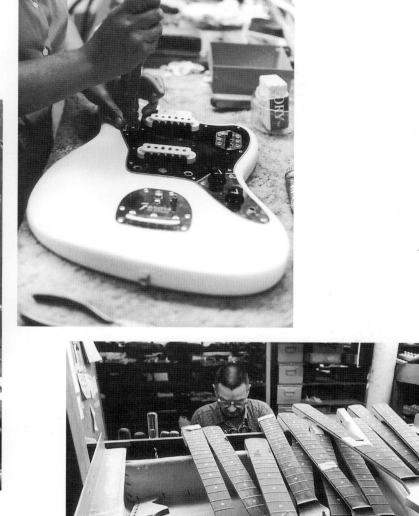

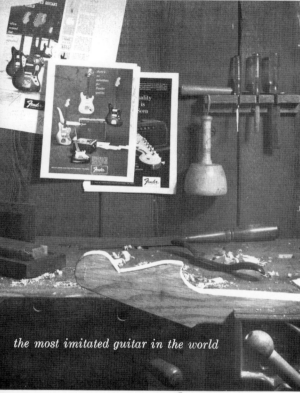

the most imitated guitar in the world

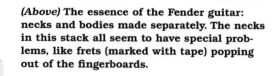

(Above) The essence of the Fender guitar: necks and bodies made separately. The necks in this stack all seem to have special problems, like frets (marked with tape) popping out of the fingerboards.

The short-lived brown Vibroverb has become one of the most collectible Fender amps. It was the first Fender with built-in reverb.

(Opposite) Close-up of the amp's logo.

Leo, always Mr. Curious, examining a tape recorder's insides at the Fender plant in June 1963.

The Vibroverb, Twin Reverb, and Blackface Amps

Leo introduced the Jazzmaster, Jaguar, Bass VI, and Jazz Bass while almost totally submerged in new amp designs. Except for the Jazz Bass, these instruments made meager impressions on music. Yet it is very hard to pick a pre-CBS amp made in the late 1950s through 1964 that is not a classic in its own right. Take the lowly student-model Deluxe as just one example. The 1950s tweed and early 1960s brown versions screamed in the hands of artists like Neil Young and the Eagles, producing countless classic solos. Much the same can be said about Champs, which work extremely well in studios. The Princeton Reverb became one of the most popular recording amps of the 1970s.

The first Fender amp with built-in reverb was the brown Vibroverb introduced in *Fender Facts #2*, February 1963. This model was a tribute to Leo's work ethic and one collectors find irresistible because of its rarity compared with Twins and Bassmans. While the factory built 4–10 Bassmans for six years, it produced just three production runs of original brown Vibroverbs, all in April and May of 1963. Each run had from 50 to 200 units. Like most Fender amps other than student models, the Vibroverb had two channels: Bright, with reverb and tremolo, and Normal, with no effects. Each channel featured separate volume, treble, and bass controls. Powered by two 6L6GCs, the amp produced about 40 watts RMS that drove two 10-inch Oxford speakers designed by Leo. Its cabinet had the so-called smooth Tolex, gold-colored grille cloth, tilt-back legs for better sound distribution, and a brown, flat-spring handle. (The first and only brown Vibroverb pictured in Fender ads had a leather handle.)

The 1963 color catalog introduced the Twin Reverb, other so-called blackface amps, and the Fender-Rhodes pianos. The piggy-back amps featured smooth blonde Tolex.

The brown Vibroverb sounded and performed unlike any Fender amp before or after. Part of the secret was its seemingly unique tone circuit. Matt Wilkens, an engineer at the modern Fender company, has noticed that the original Vibroverb's treble control was tapped, meaning, as he says, "When you set the treble control to the tapped position, about 4, you get a flat treble response." Duplicating that tone with other Fender amps, like the later Vibrolux Reverb, was possible by manipulating the controls. Still, most Vibroverb owners argue that their amps possess a higher gain and more guts, the power to make weak pickups sound stronger.

The built-in reverb added to the amp's unique character. While almost overdriving the springs in the reverb pan, the return signal had a high gain. Reverb in later amps like the Super Reverb or Twin Reverb had a harsher, high mid-range ring. While it had appeal, the full-bodied Vibroverb's had more warmth. The amp's smooth-sounding patented tremolo, although standard fare by 1963, worked with a direct coupled oscillator—half of a phase shifter—rather than a photo cell. (The photo cell was used on later Fender amps and produced a deeper, throbbing, pulsating effect.) Tremolo was highly popular on rock recordings; complete combo amps needed the effect to attract young guitarists.

The brown Vibroverb was a terrific package, but Leo champed at the bit to outdo himself. In the summer of 1963, the factory brought forth the first blackface reverb amps, a growing line that would soon include the Twin Reverb, Super Reverb, Vibrolux Reverb, Deluxe Reverb, Princeton Reverb, and second-generation Vibroverb. Using a black Tolex-covered cabinet and a single 15-inch speaker, the new Vibroverb was totally different from its brown predecessor except for the name—just one illustration of Fender's amazing and confusing lack of continuity with the blackface amps. Super Amps had featured two 10-inch speakers since the 1940s; the Super Reverb had four 10s. The non-reverb 1964 Pro Amp had one 15-inch speaker while the soon-to-be-released Pro Reverb would have two

Front and rear views of one of the earliest (perhaps the first) Twin Reverb, destined to become one of the world's most popular professional-level amplifiers.

(Clockwise from top left) **Bassman, blonde Bandmaster, Princeton Reverb, Deluxe Reverb, and Princeton (without reverb). These 1963–64 photos show early blackface amps.**

12s. The Vibrolux Amp came equipped with a 12-inch speaker for years; the Vibrolux Reverb had two 10s. Still, the blackface amps made their mark almost overnight.

Leo considered the Twin Reverb among his crowning achievements. Certainly, its undistorted power and full-bodied tone reflected his tastes. Dick Dale says: "In his home when I'd go and visit him, he'd listen to Marty Robbins over a single speaker. . . . He wanted sound as pure as you could find it." (That philosophy led Leo to discard ideas like the wireless guitar system Dale tried in the early 1960s at Balboa's Rendezvous Ballroom. The transmitter did not accurately translate the guitar's tone to the amplifier and failed Leo's test of purity.) The Twin Reverb's high fidelity made it the working musician's constant companion during the 1960s and 1970s. The United States Army lugged Twin Reverbs to Vietnam. Disneyland bought them for the Tomorrowland Terrace.

Country bands, jazz bands, and rock bands used them. Guitarists, keyboard players, and steel players all went for this popular amp.

While the Twin Reverb's four 6L6GC power tubes and double 12-inch speakers provided 85 undistorted watts, the Super Reverb, Vibrolux Reverb, Pro Reverb, and blackface Vibroverb used only two 6L6GC tubes, and produced half the power of the Twin Reverb. All four amps used essentially the same circuit, but different cabinets and speaker configurations. The lower-output blackface amps

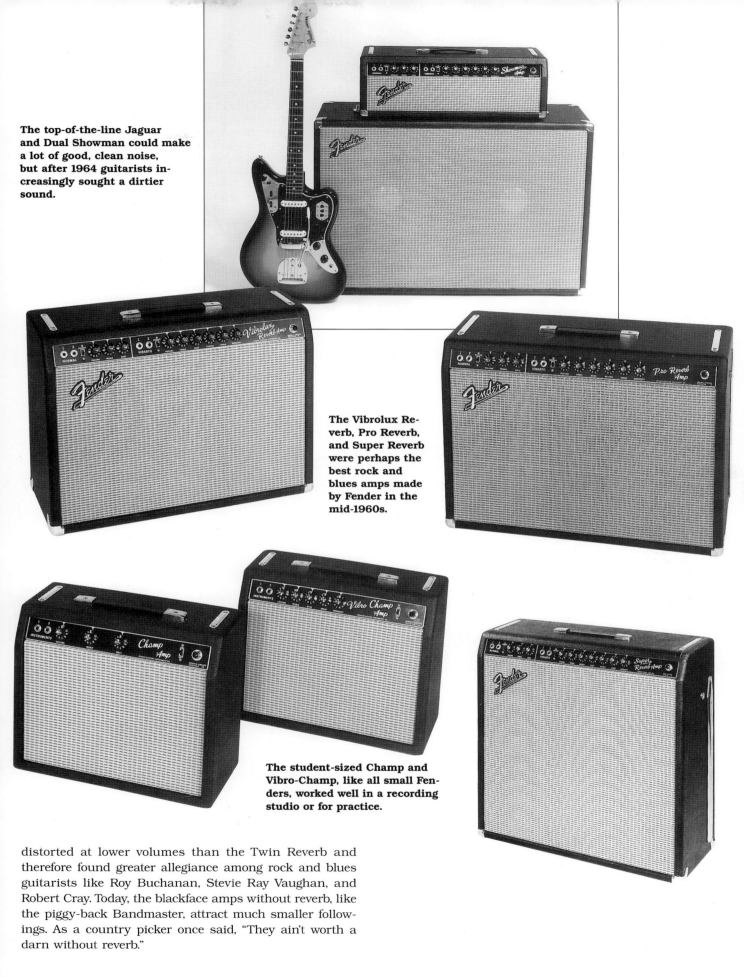

The top-of-the-line Jaguar and Dual Showman could make a lot of good, clean noise, but after 1964 guitarists increasingly sought a dirtier sound.

The Vibrolux Reverb, Pro Reverb, and Super Reverb were perhaps the best rock and blues amps made by Fender in the mid-1960s.

The student-sized Champ and Vibro-Champ, like all small Fenders, worked well in a recording studio or for practice.

distorted at lower volumes than the Twin Reverb and therefore found greater allegiance among rock and blues guitarists like Roy Buchanan, Stevie Ray Vaughan, and Robert Cray. Today, the blackface amps without reverb, like the piggy-back Bandmaster, attract much smaller followings. As a country picker once said, "They ain't worth a darn without reverb."

Building Fender amps was still labor intensive in the early 1960s, and the wood shop still resembled a cabinet shop. The assembly department had no conveyor belts or automation: workers wheeled the unfinished components around on tall carts; they installed components and soldered wires in the chassis by hand. (Today much of the handwork would be done by machines.) Each unit had to pass a thorough inspection by a technician before going to final assembly. Most of the workers in the sanding, covering, and assembly departments did piecework tied to group bonus and quality-control plans instituted by Forrest White in 1956. Each worker acted as an inspector: faulty workmanship had to be fixed, with the costs charged against individual piecework or the group bonus. When first hired, an employee was guaranteed an hourly wage until he could produce enough piece work to exceed the basic pay. The plans worked well. Resisting efforts by outside union organizers to represent them, workers at Fender formed their own union called the United Industrial Employees of California.

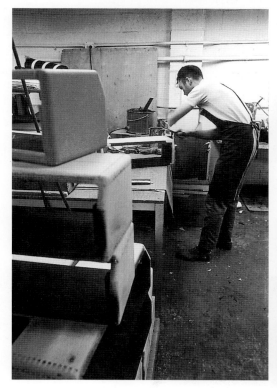

(Opposite) **Fun, fun, fun with Fender acoustics and Bob Perine's even-then-classic '57 T-Bird.**

Fender Acoustics

After introducing the Bass VI and Jaguar and redesigning much of the amp line, Leo turned to another project, a new family of Fender acoustic guitars. Despite the advantages of electric guitars, acoustic guitars were still popular. Flat-top Gibson jumbos and Martin dreadnoughts played a huge role in country music. The early texture of rock borrowed from this tradition: records by Elvis, the Everly Brothers, and Ricky Nelson were filled with acoustics, as were records by the Beatles. Leo and Don had noticed the guitar market's direction in the early 1960s when the folk music revival had created a temporary detour away from electric instruments.

Don had long wanted to distribute acoustic guitars. Radio-Tel, for example, carried a line of cheap acoustics in the late 1940s, probably made by Harmony. On April 19, 1951, Randall received a letter from George Mann, a former executive with Epiphone and founder of the United Guitar Corporation (UGC), that told of plans to manufacture three new acoustic models for Radio-Tel: the 17R student model, the M2 concert-sized dreadnought, and the M3 large-sized dreadnought. Radio-Tel listed the latter two in 1952 as the 300R and 400R. The 17R birch-body babies came packed six to a box (Dave Driver sold a box at every stop along his route). The model had a traditional-looking headstock and a metal tailpiece. The 300R and 400R, retailing for $59.50 and $74.50, respectively, were better guitars. Both had Telecaster-style headstocks and mahogany bodies. No one knows how many UGC made, but they lived a short life. Radio-Tel only mentioned them in 1952 literature. Not too surprisingly, Randall and Fender forgot all about them. Don does remember that Fender Sales bought the Regal trademark in the late 1950s, using it for years on guitars made by Harmony.

One day in the early 1960s, guitar maker Roger Rossmeisl, who had designed some of Rickenbacker's most beautiful acoustic-electric guitars in the late 1950s and early 1960s, showed up at Leo's office. Before the British Invasion put the Rickenbacker company back in the forefront, the company had suffered setbacks, and the German-born craftsman wondered about his future. Confident he could make a job for himself in Leo's expanding universe, Rossmeisl had already moved to Fullerton. He told Leo, in essence, "I'm here, and I'm going to start working for you." Leo liked Roger's cocky self-assured manner, admired his work, and saw the opportunity to put the Fender mark on acoustic guitars. Leo hired him on the spot.

Fender Sales first advertised the Fender acoustic guitar line at the 1963 NAMM show. Production of these

Roger Rossmeisl, January 1967.

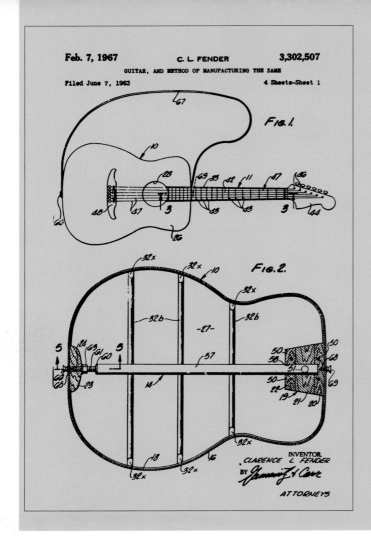

FIG. 1.

FIG. 2.

INVENTOR.
CLARENCE L. FENDER
BY
ATTORNEYS

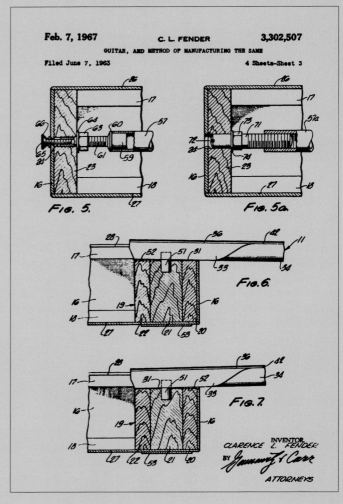

FIG. 5.   FIG. 5a.

FIG. 6.

FIG. 7.

INVENTOR.
CLARENCE L. FENDER
BY
ATTORNEYS

instruments took place at the factory at 500 S. Raymond while Fender and Rossmeisl completed plans for a new acoustic guitar factory on Missile Way in Anaheim. In the February 1964 *Music Trades* magazine, Randall said that production of Fender acoustic guitars at the new plant had begun in January: "Naturally, production will be limited at first; however, each passing month will show an increase." The new acoustic guitar had a natural maple neck with a rosewood fingerboard and an adjustable truss rod. In addition, the neck was detachable like all Fender electric guitar necks. The construction eliminated the heel and the neck joint assembly, the most complicated and time-consuming step in conventional guitar production. Eliminating the heel also allowed the player easier access to the top frets. Rossmeisl attached the pickguard with screws rather than glue so that it appeared to float slightly above the top.

The acoustic body's inside bracing included what Leo called a body-truss, and what others have called a tone bar, running from end to end parallel to the strings. When tuned, guitar strings create more than a hundred pounds of pressure on a guitar top, changing its shape. Leo thought that a distorted top curved up or down by tension

detracted from the guitar's tone. Adjusted at the factory, the body-truss took stress off the guitar's top and back, and it eliminated dishing, warping, and straining of these parts. Fender could make lighter tops with smaller braces than companies like Martin. Supposedly, the Fender's design sounded better and lasted longer.

Initially, Fender and Rossmeisl planned to produce four acoustic models: the King, the Concert, the Classic, and the Folk. A fifth, the Palomino, appeared in late 1964. The 21-fret King and the 20-fret Concert used steel strings and six adjustable bridge saddles. Both sported close-grained spruce tops. The earliest instruments used either Brazilian rosewood or mahogany sides and backs, although in 1964 the company offered new wood options for the backs and sides: vermillion, zebra, or Indian rosewood. The guitars varied in price depending on the wood used. For example, the King Model with Indian rosewood was the most expensive at $375, followed by the King with Brazilian rosewood at $350. Kings with mahogany or zebra wood cost $325. (By comparison, a Brazilian rosewood Martin D-28 was $335 in 1962 and $375 in January 1966. A mahogany Martin D-18 sold for $210 in 1962 and $275 in January 1966.)

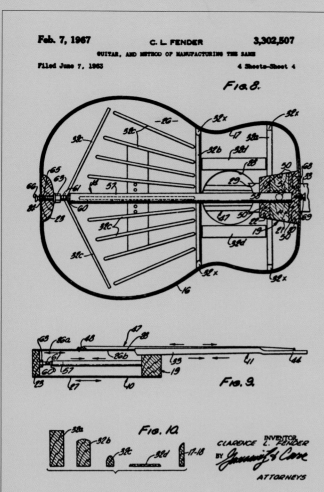

Feb. 7, 1967   C. L. FENDER   3,302,507

GUITAR, AND METHOD OF MANUFACTURING THE SAME

Filed June 7, 1963   4 Sheets-Sheet 4

Fig. 8.

Fig. 9.

Fig. 10.

(Left) Official patent drawings of the Fender acoustic.
(Below) Roger Rossmeisl with Wes Montgomery, October 1966.

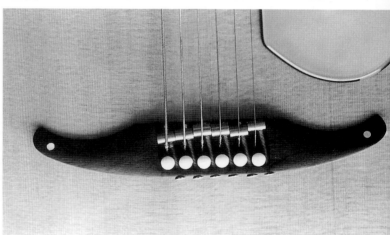

Details of a Fender Concert acoustic: decal, 6-position bridge, and Rickenbackerish checkered binding.

225

Acoustic guitar brochure, 1963.

Left to right, two unidentified visitors, Freddie Tavares, Jerry Byrd, and Leo Fender examining the insides of a Fender acoustic.

After the King's introduction, the Classic followed in early 1964. It was a standard classical guitar with nineteen frets. The top was close-grained spruce, the back and sides available in Indian rosewood, Brazilian rosewood, or maple. A brochure noted that Fender selected the woods for "pattern beauty." The Classic's neck differed from the others because of a slotted headstock.

The last of Fender's original four pre-CBS acoustic models—the Folk Guitar—was an enigma mentioned in ads but never pictured. The copy stated: "The Fender Folk Guitar contains many of the outstanding features of the Classic except that it is made to be used with either steel or gut strings. The Folk model also employs an attractive shell pickguard." Apparently, Fender Sales never listed the Folk model on price sheets during the pre-CBS years. The company introduced the 20-fret Palomino acoustic at the end of 1964. It shared many features with the King and

Concert models, like the removable neck and elevated pickguard. However, it was a lower-budget guitar at $199.50. Its back and sides were mahogany while the headstock had plastic-tipped tuners.

Fender acoustics never measured up in the public's ear to the more traditional Martin, Gibson, or Guild guitars. Unfortunately, making acoustic guitars was still more art than science, a fact Leo learned the hard way. One positive thing can be said: Fender acoustics looked wonderful. Rossmeisl had proved his tasteful sensibilities with earlier Rickenbacker designs, and familiar elements like checkered binding and gold-backed Lucite pickguards, borrowed from his former employer, showed up in the Fender acoustics. When CBS-Fender introduced the acoustic-electric Coronado guitars a few years later, other Rickenbacker-like features surfaced, including a tailpiece with a large F instead of a large R.

(Right) Despite an aggressive ad effort, Fender acoustics never caught on with players. The Wildwoods, introduced after Leo sold the company to CBS, used beechwood colored by injecting dyes into trees during the growth process.

Wherever you go, you'll find Fender!
For your personal selection see the complete line of Fender Fine Electric and Acoustic Instruments on display at leading music dealers throughout the world.

SANTA ANA, CALIFORNIA

The short-lived Fender King, September 1964.

Long-scale Mustang prototype, 1964.

Short-scale Mustang prototype, 1964.

The Mustang

By the mid-1960s, Japanese and European imports with names like St. George, Kent, and Klira, all cheap ringers for Fenders, wedged their way into the low-priced guitar market to challenge the California company. In keeping with the changes made in the top models, Fender had added a rosewood fingerboard to the Musicmaster and Duo-Sonic student models by the end of 1959. The standard finish became a muddy brown/red/yellow sunburst. By 1963 the standard finishes changed to red mahogany and white. The 1964 advertising showed a redesigned offset body and offered a choice between a 22 1/2-inch scale or a 24-inch scale.

At the same time, it became clear that even the student market had become sophisticated enough for vibrato-equipped guitars. The Mustang, introduced in 1964, met this demand with the so-called easy-action

tremolo and floating bridge. Like the redesigned Duo-Sonic and Musicmaster, the new vibrato model also had a choice of neck-scale options, 22 1/2 inch or 24 inch. (Few players chose the short one; noted guitar repairman Steve Soest has never seen one.) Mustangs featured two single-coil pickups with plastic covers; its two 3-position sliding switches (one per pickup) created eight different tone settings. On each switch the middle position turned the pickup off while the two outside positions changed the tone. There was one tone control and one volume control.

Leo's new model also boasted length-adjustable barrel-shaped bridges that varied in size to conform with the crown of the fingerboard. String height was adjusted by raising or lowering the whole bridge channel at either end. According to the 1964 catalog, the instrument was available

A student model with a student model, 1966. This ad sold Mustangs by drawing attention to the guitar's feminine curves.

(Below) Patent diagram for the Mustang vibrato. Another guitar named after a car, this model was by far the most sophisticated student model.

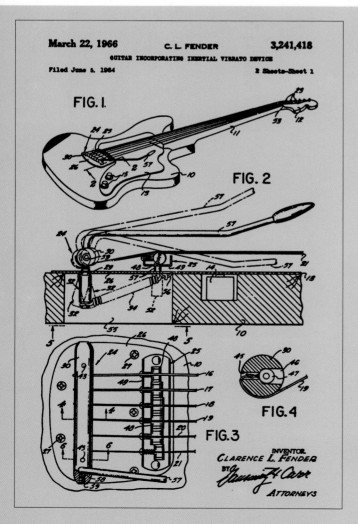

Mustangs went everywhere, too, 1964.

in selected custom colors, usually red, white, or blue—
undoubtedly a subtle way of saying "Made in the U.S.A."

In October 1964, the list price for the Mustang was
$189.50. The Duo-Sonic was $159.50 while the single-
pickup Musicmaster was $129.50. Leo had retailed the
Telecaster in 1951 at $189.50. By 1964, an austere Telecaster
cost $209.50, only $20.00 more than a Mustang. Surely Leo
thought that the student-model Mustang, with its vibrato
and slider switches, was more guitar for the buck than a
Telecaster. His student models filled a need at the low end
of the price schedule. On Christmas morning, many young
musicians must have exclaimed, "Gee, Dad, it's a Fender!"
But predictably, few professionals ever played Leo's student
guitars; Hendrix, Steely Dan's Walter Becker, *Progressive
Blues Experiment*-era Johnny Winter, and Kurt Cobain
were exceptions. (Kurt played a Mustang.)

(Above) The 1964 catalog showed seventeen blackface amp models and the new acoustic guitars.

An early-1960s Musicmaster.

(Left) The Music-
master had an
offset body by the
time Fender Sales
used this photo in
the 1963 *Down
Beat* insert.

(Right) By 1965 the
model had the
appearance of a
dressed-down
Mustang. Notice
the new pickguard
and control plate.

230

**One of the Fender XII proto-
types from early 1965.**

The Electric XII

The 12-string guitar (usually tuned with unison high E
and B strings and octave G, D, A, and low E strings) has
never been as popular as the 6-string. In the 1930s, Leadbelly played one, and the instrument had a respectable following starting in the late 1950s with the folk boom. Glen
Campbell once recorded an album of 12-string instru-
mentals, as did country player Tut Taylor—on a special
12-string slide Dobro. Yet while several companies made
acoustic twelves in the early 1960s, Martin waited until
1964 to introduce one to its line.

Electric 12-string history began in the 1950s when an
obscure company called Stratosphere made versions with
unconventional tunings. Jimmy Bryant played one on his
landmark *Country Cabin Jazz* album. However, the revolutionary Stratospheres—single-necks and doublenecks,
6-strings and 12-strings—promptly disappeared. Undoubtedly, the folk boom prompted Gibson and Danelectro to
make electric 12-strings by the early 1960s, but purist
American folk musicians despised amplified instruments.
Like many home-grown innovations, electric and acoustic
twelves traveled to England and back before most Americans discovered them.

The rousing acoustic 12-string on "Walk Right In" by
the Rooftop Singers, an American folk group, started a
craze in England. So many groups like the Shadows, the
Fourmost, and the Springfields started using amplified
versions in a rock band setting that Britain's April 18, 1964,
Melody Maker newspaper called the 12-string guitar
"Beat's Secret Weapon—The new sound with a 200-year-
old history." According to the article, in early 1964 guitarists played the once obscure instrument on at least one
British recording session every day.

The instrument's popularity hit full stride after George
Harrison played his electric Rickenbacker on "You Can't
Do That" (the flip side of "Can't Buy Me Love"). The sound
shaped a large portion of the Beatles' 1964 catalog—listen
to "I Call Your Name," "Any Time at All," or "A Hard Day's
Night." These cuts inspired musicians around the world,
including the Byrds' Jim (later known as Roger) McGuinn.

Prompted by the Beatles, the Byrds, and Rickenbacker, nearly every major guitar company, including Fender, jumped on the electric 12-string bandwagon. Fender started designing its guitar in late 1964, and working prototypes existed by January 1965. The company unveiled its production model in *Fender Facts #9*, June 1965, claiming the guitar had tone versatility unmatched by any other 12-string. The 4-way rotary tone selector gave the player the option of using each individual pickup, both pickups combined, or both with a "deep-tone" effect.

The Fender XII adhered to Fender's formula. The body, usually made from alder, was similar to the offset-waist Jazzmaster, and the pickups attached to the pickguard. The detachable neck had a rosewood fingerboard. The strings loaded through the body while the twelve barrel-shaped bridge pieces varied in size to conform to the fingerboard's radius. Slightly elevated, sections for the unwound strings made them the same height as the wound strings. Players could adjust string length at the bridge piece and raise or lower the entire bridge channel on both ends.

The neck on one prototype had the so-called clay dot fingerboard markers seen on pre-CBS and early 1965 guitars, although production versions featured pearl-like dots or the later block inlays. The string guide on one prototype was located 1/2 inch farther behind the nut than on the production models. While one prototype had black knobs and a white laminated pickguard, another early 12-string photographed at the factory in January 1965 had white knobs and an imitation-pearl-finished pickguard.

The standard finish was sunburst, but the guitars were widely available in custom colors like Candy Apple Red and Firemist Gold Metallic. Most bore matching painted headstocks. The list price for the 12-string in July 1965 was $339 with a standard finish and $356 with a blonde or custom finish. By July 1968, the last listing, Fender lowered prices to $329.50 and $346.00. Although the guitar appeared in the 1969 catalog, the 12-string fad, like the Jazzmaster and Jaguar's limited popularity, had run its course. The company had played catch-up with the trend since it started in 1964. (The CBS-Fender factory would use leftover 12-string bodies and necks on a new 6-string called the Custom, which made its debut in the 1970 catalog.) The Fender 12-string does have one distinction worth noting. Led Zeppelin's Jimmy Page played one on the original recording of "Stairway to Heaven."

Another prototype, this one had a wider headstock with a slightly different shape than production models. Its incorrect neck length made accurate intonation almost impossible. (The factory made prototypes to work out such bugs.) The pickguard had extra holes that suggest it once held earlier pickups with different dimensions.

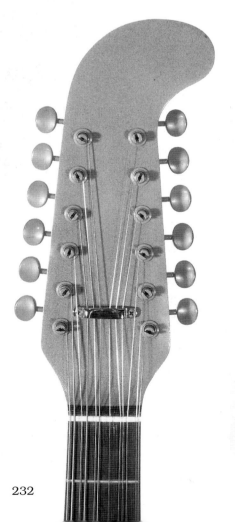

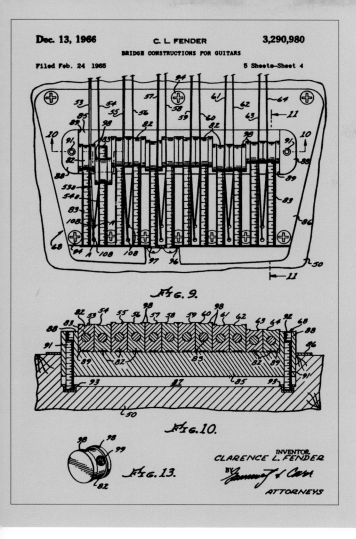

Another unlikely place to find a Fender, but there it is at Laguna Beach High School, October 1965.

(Below) The beautifully-designed 12-string bridge as seen by Bob Perine's camera lens in January 1965. This prototype lacked pickup covers. The headstock required a large string guide (notice how its position here differed from later examples) to keep the strings in the nut.

(Right) Harold Rhodes at the 1967 NAMM show. The Fender-Rhodes pianos put keyboard players in the forefront with a unique sound. Billy Preston's solo on the Beatles' "Get Back" was a great example.

(Below) The Piano Bass, introduced by 1963, was Fender Sales' first keyboard instrument. Later it rocked "Light My Fire" and other hits by the Doors.

The Fender-Rhodes Pianos

Leo Fender's 1960s 6-string bass, acoustic guitar, and 12-string projects followed industry fashion trends. By the time he had entered the fray, other companies had already set standards that needed little improving. Leo had done his best setting the standards himself, exploring relatively uncharted territories in solidbody guitars, amps, and electric basses. Another such area existed. Despite years of effort, in the late 1950s few companies other than Wurlitzer had successfully marketed a portable electric piano. The demand was obvious; musicians needed a piano that fit into a car trunk and stayed in tune on the road. Even moving a spinet-sized piano required a truck or van. Moreover, drums, electric bass, and electric guitars overpowered acoustic pianos. A portable electric piano or organ leveled the playing field for keyboard players. Leo liked this challenge, as did another California inventor named Harold Rhodes.

Born in 1910, Rhodes taught piano in the 1930s at Harold Rhodes School of Popular Piano in Los Angeles; his students included celebrities Harpo Marx, Tyrone Power, and Fred MacMurray. The teacher was also a songwriter, having penned tunes for bandleader Tommy Dorsey. During World War II, Harold taught piano to patients at an Army hospital and designed a portable piano they could play sitting in bed. He fashioned the first ones with materials he found on the base, mostly old airplane parts. Aluminum hydraulic tubing cut like the tubes on a xylophone substituted for strings.

After the war, Rhodes continued designing pianos, soon manufacturing an instrument called the Pre-Piano with $70,000 backing from R. H. Osbrink, who owned a Los Angeles foundry. Like Leo, Harold taught himself the techniques he needed: die-sinking, pattern cutting, and electronics. He designed his own small amplifier for the Pre-Piano and contracted an established manufacturer—whose name is forgotten—to produce his instruments. The venture failed, but Harold's ideas inspired other companies, particularly Wurlitzer, to pursue similar instruments. Rhodes told *Contemporary Keyboard* magazine in 1978, "I had bred a competitor."

Undeterred after the Pre-Piano's untimely death, Harold developed a larger piano housed in a baby-grand-sized cabinet. This instrument caught the attention of Leo Fender. By 1959, Leo had time to think about an electric piano, an on-again off-again interest he had pursued as early as 1948 with Doc Kauffman. Fender had applied for patents, but still no ideas for a commercially sound piano had emerged. He saw promise in the Rhodes design and contacted Harold about a collaborative effort. Forrest White remembered that Rhodes drove "an old Studebaker held together with Scotch tape" to the 1959 meetings in Fullerton. Unlike Harold, Leo had the capital, the space, and the marketing tools to do an electric piano right.

Leo provided Rhodes with work space in the ninth building at the far eastern end of Fender's factory row. The two formed a corporation Leo funded called Fender-Rhodes, Inc., signing an agreement on December 14, 1959. They made a clean start, but Harold became quickly disillusioned as an ego clash crept into the equation. Rather than manufacture the instrument already designed, Harold said that Leo had him work on other projects, including a piano with multiple guitar necks. White disputed that memory; he recalls no instrument that unconventional at Fender. But Leo did start tinkering with Harold's original plan. Don Randall says, "Leo wanted to leave his mark on everything he touched."

The electric piano Rhodes brought to Leo used a principle of the tuning fork. Instead of piano strings, each key had one tuning fork with two prongs of unequal mass, shape, and size. A hammer connected to the key hit the lower, more resilient prong or tine. A player could easily tune each note by sliding a tuning spring along the length of the tine. Harold's original design had a flaw: the .075-inch piano wire tines broke after just forty thousand hammer blows. Leo improved the design by creating a

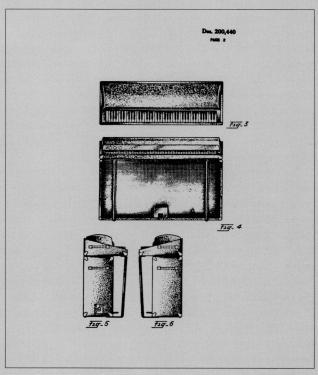

Design diagram for the Fender-Rhodes.

Clockwise from left, the Fender-Rhodes Piano, Piano Bass, Comtempo Organ (designed by CBS-hired engineers), and Celeste. CBS-Fender-Rhodes built all of these keyboard instruments in 1967.

tapered tine with a thicker, stronger base. This tine took up to 1.5 million strikes. Later Fender-Rhodes pianos used tines that survived up to 6 million blows in factory tests. Leo's overriding concern was durability.

According to White, Leo also helped Harold improve the piano's action, the mechanics of the hammer that struck the tine. The patent papers for this improvement, filed September 24, 1962, show Harold's name. But apparently the two Lone Rangers had trouble agreeing on the piano's finer details. White said that Rhodes, a far-out dreamer, always saw a new improvement just ahead and delayed the project by rejecting Leo's suggestions. Randall implies that Fender tried to skirt the Rhodes design because he could add only small improvements. All the while, the world patiently waited for the Fender-Rhodes piano.

Leo had a history of making people wait. Speedy West had waited several hours at the radio shop for his first Fender amplifier. Randall and F.C. Hall had expected Leo's standard guitars to be ready months before they were. On Forrest White's first day at the Fender plant, Leo made him wait in the lobby until noon before putting him to work. Moss would grow on the north side of salesmen waiting for Fender in G&L's lobby. Leo's business ran on his bad-mannered but well-calculated schedule, his way of showing who controlled situations. Things happened when he decided he had time to make them happen. Making people wait was also a way he avoided problems. Sometimes problems just went away, but not the still-unfinished piano.

Sensing another big thing like the Telecaster, Randall urged Fender and Rhodes to tie down one design and manufacture it. Rhodes, whose frustration only grew during the early 1960s, put the delay squarely on Leo's shoulders. "I was with Leo for six long, dry years. . . . For various business reasons, Leo wouldn't let me make a piano," he told *Contemporary Keyboard*. "He wanted to go north and I wanted to go south; it just didn't work." Randall wanted a sound design, but as in earlier years with the solidbody guitars, the factory gave him delays and excuses.

The written record contained in catalogs, price sheets, and advertising reflects the confusion and delays surrounding the introduction of keyboard instruments as Leo and Harold planned several models. Fender Sales did advertise and demonstrate a Fender-Rhodes Piano Bass at the 1962 summer trade show, and Fender did produce this instrument before 1965. (Later the Doors' Ray Manzarek would put the Piano Bass to good use with one of the best-remembered bands of the 1960s.) According to a letter sent to Fender dealers, the factory had developed and field tested a celeste, a 56-key piano, and a 74-key piano by early 1963. Fender Sales prematurely announced on July 18, 1963, that production had started. To further confuse the matter, the 1963 catalog listed 61- and 73-note keyboards, but the one pictured as the Piano 61 had only 56 ivories. The production Fender-Rhodes had 73 keys, which was the standard until CBS later added an 88-key version.

Randall and Rhodes both remembered that Fender-Rhodes, Inc., was sold to CBS before the plant went into full production building keyboards. At that point Randall simply put White in charge, and he got the job done later in 1965. Thus the tale of two inventors ended.

The Fender-Rhodes encouraged new playing styles in much the same way the Telecaster had changed guitar playing. The piano was portable, loud, and, after a few refinements, easy to maintain. Its unique, sparkling tone made a mark on many recordings. Keyboard players readily accepted the new instrument, and as Don Randall has pointed out, "CBS sold them by the truckful."

(Left) Banjo-playing legend Eddie Peabody and Leo inspect one of at least two custom-built instruments made for Peabody in the mid-1960s. The so-called banjoline had no commercial merit, but Leo did not seem to care. He liked the way Peabody played.

(Below) "Thanks for building such a great steel! I just love mine," wrote young Barbara Mandrel about her Fender 2000. The pedal steel thrives today in country-western music, thanks in part to the technology Leo pioneered.

The End of an Era Draws Near

The guitar business kept expanding. In 1964 Fender Sales began constructing a new 36,000-square-foot warehouse and office complex at 1402 East Chestnut on the corner of Grand Avenue, Santa Ana. Work was completed in early 1965, and like the old office, the new facility included a recording studio. For the promotional value, Fender provided free studio time for anyone interested, usually local garage bands.

Although harried by his success, Leo still found time for questionable projects, foreshadowing his next twenty-five years. In 1964, for example, he made an electric banjo-like instrument for Eddie Peabody called the banjoline. Randall realized it had no commercial merit and nipped the idea before it went into production. Eventually Rickenbacker would make a banjoline for Peabody and sell fewer than two dozen units. By even considering such an instrument, Leo showed weaknesses that would plague many of his later efforts: he had no regard for profit or loss. He had noble intentions, but little insight into his own business as it had evolved. In 1964 most of the guitar-buying public listened to the Beatles, not gray-haired banjoists. Fender refused to make custom instruments for most musicians, but continued designing instruments with narrower appeal, like steel guitars.

Although the role of steel guitars in Fender's early years cannot be overstated, by the mid-1960s the market had shrunk considerably. Yet in 1964 Fender introduced two new 10-string pedal models, the single-neck Fender 800 and the double-neck Fender 2000—Leo's last steel guitars. They featured an improved bridge equipped with ten cams, one for each string; the setup did away with the old roller bridge. The new steels also featured narrower pickups than those on older models and built-in mutes. Widening the tuning possibilities, the new cable

mechanism under the steels allowed double sharps and double flats for each string—an amazing capability even for today's steels.

After Leo sold Fender (chapter 14), he abandoned any effort to improve steels, leaving this specialty market to smaller companies like Emmons, Sho-Bud, and MSA. While he had pioneered the designs, others improved and perfected modern pedal steels by making them easier to tune, transport, and play. Few professionals used the original Fenders after the 1960s. The exception, Sneaky Pete Kleinow, played a highly modified Fender with extra pickups, switches, and effects with the Flying Burrito Brothers and others. In the 1980s tradition-minded session players like Steve Fishell, Greg Leisz, and Gary Brandin recorded with stock Fenders to achieve the nostalgic country sounds of the early 1960s.

Despite Leo Fender's eccentricities, by 1964 a very large business had landed in his lap: Fender, Randall, and their employees had built a musical empire—the largest and fastest-growing musical instrument company in the world. In 1953 retail sales of Fender guitars amounted to approximately $1 million. By 1964, the company produced over $40 million in retail sales yearly, and the factory ran double shifts that produced thousands of instruments every week. Young people's all-consuming interest in electric instruments gave Leo the freedom and money to digress.

Fender had become one of rock's first millionaires, although he never played the part. He preferred living quietly in Fullerton and working on his next big breakthrough. (Despite his wealth, he lived in a mobile home during much of the 1970s.) Too wrapped up in his work to appreciate life's changes and the results of his efforts, he told people he was broke, a denial of what he had accomplished and what he owned. Apparently, life at the top produced little happiness or satisfaction for the inventor. Working in his lab—even on projects with no clear future—contented him, but everything else to do with the business was bothersome. The thrill of discoveries in the 1940s and 1950s had evaporated, and very few triumphs lay ahead, as Fender must have sensed. The world around him had changed. Leo seemed confident that he could always improve the guitars he invented in the early 1950s, but he had little control over luck and musicians' tastes, forces that would not always favor his new ideas.

Here a worker dips unwound pickup bobbins in clear lacquer to provide insulation. After winding with many layers of wire, the whole unit was dipped in wax.

Buffing Stratocaster pickguards, April 1964.

All the Stratocaster's electronics attached to the pickguard, which was pre-assembled weeks before coming together with a body and then a neck.

Kathy Marshall with Eddie and the Showmen, circa 1964.
Larry Carlton (with Stratocaster) long before he was Mr. 335.
(From Surfin' Guitars, *Surf Publications, 1988. Reprinted by permission.)*

(Below) Selected items representing the 1960s from the Fullerton Museum Center's exhibit *Five Decades of Fender: The Sound Heard Around the World.*

Eddie and the Showmen featured
Eddie Bertrand, whose blistering
sound rivaled Dick Dale's.

The Challengers, another top surf
band that promoted Fender.

The Chantays. Their hit "Pipeline"
reached #4 in *Billboard* in 1963.

As music's universe changed and
the Fender company mushroomed,
Leo stopped having fun.

With promo photos like
these, Leo must have
thought the world had
turned upside down.

*TRANSLATION: "THE WORLD'S MOST TALENTED GUITARISTS PREFER FENDER."

An ad published in anticipation of a booming market for guitars in Japan.

Chapter 14

The Sound of Success

In 1964 the days of regional stars like Bob Wills and Dick Dale all but disappeared in the time it took Ed Sullivan to say, "Ladies and gentlemen—the Beatles!" The simple pursuit of a better guitar had turned into an international business, and Fender sold products all over the Free World including West Germany, Japan, and South America. The factory offered a full line of 220-volt amplifiers (minus the Princeton and Champ) for export. Fiesta Red Stratocasters winged their way to England in lots of 100. Leo felt as if a tornado had picked up his plant and landed it in an alien world; his corner-store-like operation was gone. He preferred the old days when top western swing bands rolled into town and unloaded road-weary equipment for repair or replacement. He enjoyed taking new guitars to a local country bar where waitresses carried change in their bras and truckers slept off their beers in the parking lot before the final leg

to Carson or some other southern California shipping hub. In dens of din, Fender sipped water while some yokel shrouded in cigarette smoke bluffed his way through "Night Train" or "Guitar Boogie." Leo understood that world and felt at home there.

As music's universe changed and the Fender company mushroomed, Leo stopped having fun. He could not relate to the longhairs from England who replaced western bands and Lawrence Welk. Leo had always been sensitive to his health; now he was becoming a hypochondriac. Thinking he suffered incurable ailments and wondering how long he would live, he took an assortment of medications and spent long hours at a chiropractor's. Both Freddie Tavares and Forrest White said in the 1980s that their boss feared not only for his health, but also for his future in the music business. Being self-taught in electronics, he lacked confidence in his ability to stay on the cutting edge.

243

Leo Fender, left, and Freddie Tavares, right, with
visitors outside the plant in the mid-1960s.

Don Randall at his desk in Santa Ana, October 1966.

Although sometimes portrayed as an engineer in his catalogs, he knew he was not. He was especially afraid that transistor circuitry, which he did not fully grasp at the time, would soon make tube amps obsolete.

To Leo and many of his generation, the transistor and the advances it brought symbolized the eventual demise of the lone inventor and small manufacturer, the end of the good old days when maverick thinkers with little technical training could work in backyard shops or garages and compete. (Much smaller than vacuum tubes, transistors still performed similar functions. They required less current and produced less heat than tubes and consequently revolutionized consumer electronics in the early 1960s. School children carried battery-operated transistorized radios to school. Miniature gadgets with transistor circuits made space exploration possible.) The paranoid believed that well-funded corporate and government teams of scientists and engineers created advances like the transistor to squash the little guys.

Leo always considered himself one of the little guys, one of the mavericks. Paradoxically, despite an enormous penchant for risk taking and a self-assured manner, self-doubt often shadowed his steps. He underestimated the impact of his life's work, never believing that his advances changed the big picture much. (During one conversation about his guitars with this author, he said that his inventions meant little to the world compared with advances in science. He added, "People should be writing about the guys who invented the transistor, not me.") As with many self-doubters, Leo feared that the world would discover his charade, that the little dog Toto would pull down the curtain hiding the Wizard of Guitars and reveal a simple, uneducated man who had made a fortune with smoke and mirrors. Leo believed his success was precarious, one reason he toiled obsessively to make constant progress. In the early 1960s he envisioned a high-technology world of guitars where bona fide scientists—the real wizards—would eventually put him out of business with amazing breakthroughs, robust amps the size of lunchboxes built into the guitar or clipped to a player's belt.

Fender for Sale

Wade E. Tapert, an accountant for the Fender companies who had no experience with music or manufacturing, had suggested in a letter dated April 12, 1957, that Leo sell the Fender Electric Instrument Company and Fender Sales to—of all people—Wade E. Tapert. When shown this proposal in the 1990s, Don Randall was amazed, having never seen it. He believes that Tapert must have ridiculously (and wrongly) assumed that Don would have agreed to it. But as he says, "Tapert was just a hired accountant."

Furthermore, Randall does not believe that Leo wanted to sell anything in 1957. Nevertheless, Tapert must have given Leo something to ponder, perhaps a life without business-induced headaches and ill health.

Although the business did nothing but grow, that growth created its own set of problems. By the early 1960s Randall and Fender's partnership had grown more intertwined and financially complicated: they owned eight corporations between them. Moreover, they both knew that they needed more capital to continue expanding. But the bigger the investment grew, the more Leo (now suffering a lingering strep infection and his transistorphobia) felt uncertain about the risk. He told Don that he did not want to borrow more money to expand and would sell his interest in the Fender companies to Randall for $1 million. Subsequently, Leo must have also mentioned something to Tapert, who made a proposal on February 14, 1962, concerning a purchase by unnamed buyers. Leo turned it down. About six months later, he offered his part of Fender Sales and the factory to Randall for $1.5 million. Soon Leo upped the price to $2 million. For a while Don entertained the idea, and wrote a prospective agreement dated August 6, 1963.

Still, Randall was reluctant for at least two reasons. A savvy businessman, he was not interested in becoming too financially obligated; he saw some risk. He also understood Leo's impulsive nature. Don told him: "If I bought it now, a year from now you would say I robbed you. You'd hate me." Despite disagreements and arguments, Randall's dealings with Fender centered around written contracts rather than loose talk. Prone to loose talk, Leo tended to make oral agreements such as sales offers or job offers that he would later regret or rescind. Today Don says: "I was the only guy that didn't take advantage of Leo. Everyone else took advantage of him." The best situation, Don concluded in early 1964, would be to sell the Fender companies to a third party with cash.

Randall quietly put the word out that Fender was for sale. The Baldwin Piano Company heard the news from the firm Espy & Strauss (Don forgets if they were attorneys or brokers). Established in 1862, Baldwin owned one of the largest keyboard operations in the world. In the early 1960s, its offices were in Cincinnati, its factories in Mississippi and Arkansas. Buying the Fender company was an easy way to jump headfirst into the booming guitar market. Baldwin executives Lucien Wulsin, Jr., and Morley P. Thompson had put their thinking caps on tight, hoping they could pick a bargain and play the profits.

Randall spoke for Fender in all the negotiations, which began in April 1964. Morley, representing Baldwin, offered $5 million minus Fender's liabilities (about $1.5 million including taxes) and 50 percent of the guitar company's profits after taxes until Don and Leo's share reached $5 million or until fifteen years had passed from the sales date. From the outset the piano company balked at including Leo's acoustic guitar and Fender-Rhodes operations, which Leo wanted to sell for his original investment of $470,000. When the talks stalled on this point, Randall and Fender discussed becoming a public corporation through a brokerage house and approached Merrill Lynch's Dean Woodman, who Randall calls a "superior guy." He suggested that the two seek another buyer and introduced the Californians to representatives of the Columbia Broadcasting System—CBS.

CBS's rich history in the entertainment business started in radio, Leo's old field of fancy. CBS had introduced Will Rogers, Bing Crosby, Frank Sinatra, and Kate Smith into American living rooms. After World War II, the CBS television network had created such classics as *I Love Lucy*, *The Ed Sullivan Show*, and Edward R. Murrow's *See It Now*. The premiere of *See It Now* featured a live split-screen view of the Pacific and Atlantic Oceans, a demonstration of the dazzling new technology that brought the U.S. together electronically in the 1950s. In the new medium of television, CBS made history. From 1955 to 1976 it was the top-rated network in popularity.

Buying over forty companies in its brief history, CBS had owned businesses aside from those in broadcasting. The corporation and its president, William S. Paley, had a reputation for paying too much for their acquisitions after the $700,000 purchase in 1938 of the American Record Corporation, owner of the Columbia Phonograph Company, later renamed Columbia Records. Yet Paley proved his critics wrong by making it one of the most successful companies in the business, presenting artists such as Billie Holiday, Count Basie, Bob Dylan, Aretha Franklin, and Bruce Springsteen. In June 1948 CBS Laboratories introduced the Vinylite 33 1/3 rpm long-playing record album, a technological milestone in home entertainment. (RCA announced the 45 rpm disk in January 1949.)

In 1961, CBS's management began to study and devise a long-range policy of business diversification. Its coffers full from the success of its network television, the company could spend millions. A consulting firm, Harbridge House in Boston, recommended that CBS venture into activities associated with or related to communications, entertainment, and education. A corporate buying spree ensued. An empire builder at heart, Paley wanted to buy companies tops in their fields, a rationalization that made the first purchase fly. Ignoring Harbridge House's advice to stay in related businesses, CBS bought the New York Yankees almost on a whim in 1964. No one in the corporation

had much experience in professional sports, but as Paley biographer Sally Bedell Smith notes, the Yankees' aura of quality fit CBS's image as the Cadillac of the TV networks.

Randall started negotiations with CBS's Columbia Records Division in the late summer of 1964, while he was still talking with Baldwin. Clive Davis, who would sign many legendary recording artists and thus become a recording-industry legend in his own right, and John Lorenz led Columbia's acquisition team. The talks were held secretly in at least three different New York hotels on at least six different trips by Randall, who likened the process to reaching a peace agreement in the Middle East. Again, Leo played no role in the process. When Randall or Woodman pressed hard for something in the contract that clearly favored Fender, Davis would say, "I'll have to go back and get a reading." He would then pack his briefcase and return to corporate headquarters. Woodman relished pushing the Columbia team around a bit, according to Randall. Later Don learned why they were able to.

Soon after the negotiations started, CBS had hired another consulting firm, Arthur D. Little, Inc., to study the Fender companies and to make a recommendation about the proposed acquisition. The consultants snooped through the Fender factory; they interviewed Randall, Fender, and many of the managers. In addition, the consultants went out to see the salesmen at work and studied catalogs. The firm's insights were profound (see page 247), its conclusions simple and straightforward: Columbia Records (CBS) should purchase Fender provided two conditions were met. First, an amicable and adequate price agreement was reached. Second, Randall's enthusiastic services were secured. (The report also read, "Without any intention of belittling Mr. Fender's contribution to the company, we visualize that a sharp diminution in his contribution, should Columbia purchase Fender, as a relatively minor risk.") During the early talks, Davis and Lorenz just tested the waters with low-ball offers. After hearing the consulting firm's report, they got serious. Randall finally told Baldwin's executives that he was considering another offer.

Like Baldwin, CBS did not want to buy the acoustic guitar or piano businesses because neither looked promising. But Randall insisted that the corporation pay Leo the cost of his investments. In the meantime, electric guitar sales exploded in response to the Beatles and the British Invasion. Music as a hobby was hitting its historic peak, and thousands of American teenagers wanted to play electric guitar in a band, or so it seemed. Fender made those guitars, and Don turned the salesmen loose, encouraging them to take as many orders as possible. Previously, the salesmen had limited orders to what the

factory could feasibly make. Nothing hurt business more than to let dealers wait too long for products. However, if CBS bought Fender, a new factory in the planning stages would be completed and the orders could be filled. With the back orders mounting, Randall had a strong negotiating position and the momentum to pull off an unprecedented accomplishment in the music industry. With each trip to New York, tension built as the offer from the corporation went higher, until it reached $13 million. Woodman wanted to keep pressing for more. Randall was satisfied with the money, if Harold Rhodes was guaranteed a fair royalty for the electric piano and if Leo was retained as a consultant.

When CBS agreed to include Fender acoustic guitars and Fender-Rhodes in the purchase, the final obstacle was overcome and an agreement was signed on October 16, 1964. The transaction included the Fender electric guitar and amplifier factory, as well as Fender Sales, its warehouses in Santa Ana and Tulsa, the service center in New York City, and the V. C. Squier Company (the maker of Fender strings, which Fender Sales had bought in the early 1960s). The entire Fender operation, employing at least 410 people, would soon become a division of Columbia Records Corporation. Nothing of that magnitude had ever happened in the guitar industry. For Randall, the months leading up to the sale were by far the most exciting period in the company's history. Today he says, "Everything afterward was anticlimactic."

Leo's reaction to the sale stood in sharp contrast. Unfazed by the money and unwilling to travel, he refused to collect a check for $5,735,000 at a deal-closing meeting in New York City. Don picked it up and deposited it for him. Don's check totaled $5,265,000. Another $2 million went into an escrow account to be divided two years later.

Excerpts from the 1964 Arthur D. Little Report prepared for CBS

Randall and Fender

The growth and success of the Fender Companies is almost wholly attributable to the combined efforts of Messrs. Fender and Randall. Mr. Fender has contributed the creation and supply of the products, while Mr. Randall has contributed the over-all business management and marketing. Without any intention of belittling Mr. Fender's contribution to the company, we visualize that a sharp diminution in his contribution, should Columbia purchase Fender, as a relatively minor risk. We believe that if a competent manufacturing executive were placed in charge of the production facilities at Fender, an actual improvement in quality and reduction in cost could be achieved. In our opinion, therefore, the removal of Mr. Fender from the production scene of the company involves no risk. From the engineering standpoint of maintaining present products in a healthy technological state, we believe that a competent chief engineer could accomplish this with little difficulty. From the standpoint of research and development and creation of new products, it would be highly desirable, at least for a period of four or five years, to maintain the active interest and creativity of Mr. Fender.

The case of Mr. Randall we view quite differently. The generation and execution of the marketing activities of the company stem largely from Mr. Randall's continuous efforts. Furthermore, we detected on the part of the sales organization a strong loyalty to Mr. Randall in terms of recognition of his leadership as the factor which has primarily contributed to their economic success. If Mr. Randall chooses to go elsewhere, rather than remain with Fender, it is not clear whether the sales organization would remain with Fender under new management or drift away to Mr. Randall in whatever other activity he undertook. If Mr. Randall can be induced to remain with Fender for a substantial period of time and to devote his enthusiastic and wholehearted support to the organization, we believe that the Fender subsidiary of Columbia would continue to grow and remain profitable. On the other hand, if Mr. Randall does not continue as the chief operating executive of Fender, then we believe that there is a serious risk that Columbia might not be able to maintain the growth and profitability of this subsidiary.

Hence, as noted in our conclusions, we feel that the favorable recommendation to purchase Fender is highly conditioned upon the continuation of Mr. Randall as the chief executive of this subsidiary.

Compensation and Costs at the Factory

The present owners and officers of the companies enjoy rather substantial compensation. By visualizing the management structure required in the Fender organization after acquisition by Columbia and using compensation figures customarily necessary for officers of operations of this size, we believe that a reduction in expense of $650,000 per year could be made immediately.

On the basis of examining material and labor cost content in the products by analogy with similar manufacturing operations, we believe that economies approximating $500,000 per year could be achieved. This would involve actions such as carefully developed "make or buy" procedure, value analysis, and over a period of time a gradual introduction of labor costs more normal than those that presently exist in Fender. As noted, we believe that this cost reduction would be of a long-term nature and might not be achieved until 1970.

New Products and Leo

The research and development philosophy of Fender Electric Instrument Company appears to be almost exclusively the brainchild of Mr. Fender personally. He has the successful, practical inventor's genius for detecting early those relatively small design features in a new product which will be the "right way to do it." He is quite conscious of what constitutes novelty, has retained an apparently competent patent counsel, and is able to secure good claims on these elements. Most of these developments do not involve either highly theoretical or complex concepts. They involve rather simple practical elements; for example, the offsetting of the side depressions in the body of a guitar so that it will fit the contours of the body more comfortably. In our judgement Mr. Fender's contribution to the company can continue to be valuable and significant.

Under any circumstance, should Columbia acquire Fender, we strongly recommend that an aggressive research and development program be instituted so that Fender is not surprised by the introduction of the competition of a light, small, and much more convenient amplifier-speaker combination.

Corporate Structure

The basic corporate structure has been arranged to allow Messrs. Fender and Randall each to apply his own talents to the operation of the Company, yet at the same time to minimize conflicts likely to arise in the close collaboration of two such diverse personalities. The development, engineering, and product manufacturing aspects of the business are concentrated in the Fender Electric Instrument Company. This is essentially the absolute domain of Mr. Fender. As long as Mr. Fender creates and manufactures products which are delivered to the sales organization, within price and on time, Mr. Fender is free to run the Electric Instrument Company as he sees fit. Mr. Randall has as his domain, Fender Sales, Inc., which is responsible for maintaining the Fender image, getting orders, and making shipments. As long as Mr. Randall keeps a continuing flow of orders, there is little necessity for Mr. Fender to pay attention to the sales operation. This arrangement apparently works very well.

The two partners appear to embrace quite different philosophies. Mr. Fender finds it hard to believe that the little business which he started in the late forties has grown to such proportions. He finds that the size of the business is such that he has virtually no time left for doing what he enjoys, namely, engineering. He is clearly not growth-minded. Mr. Randall, on the other hand, immensely enjoys his ever-widening sphere of activity and is clearly growth-minded.

If the guidance of Fender under Columbia is placed in Randall's hand, we believe that a sound policy on growth would be executed skillfully. This presupposes that Mr. Fender concerns himself with new product development.

Columbia should be able to provide Fender with many advantages flowing from the power of the Columbia organization. On the other hand, however, the size and complexity of a large, corporate operation would pose critical problems for the manager of a small company which has been accustomed to flexible and unconventional operation methods. We have seen an excellent small company slowly deteriorate in profitability and vitality as the result of well-meaning "help" by a very large parent. . . . There may be large corporation practices which Columbia takes for granted, but of which Mr. Randall will be unaware.

The Salesmen

Eight salesmen operate under the personal direction of Mr. Randall. All of these men have considerable freedom within their own territories. They operate only on commission — 10 percent (except for acoustic guitars made elsewhere). All domestic sales are handled by these eight men. They operate their own offices, pay their own secretaries, and in some cases engage sales assistants to cover their territories better.

The men we met were presentable, articulate, and possessed of considerable sales enthusiasm and drive. They are a little rough in terms of social polish. Few, if any, have college degrees. They are probably very well suited for the type of trade they call on and are obviously doing a good job. There has been little turnover owing principally to excellent compensation earned.

Conclusion

Columbia Records should purchase the Fender Companies, provided two basic conditions are met. These two conditions . . . are interrelated. The major premise is that Mr. Randall's enthusiastic services as chief executive of the subsidiary be secured. We believe, since Mr. Randall will be a major recipient of the purchase consideration, that to avoid a delayed reaction of injustice or a bad deal, the price and mode of reaching agreement must be adequate and amicable. If this basic foundation for a relation can be established, then we believe that an agreement by Mr. Randall to perform will be on solid ground.

1965 headlines.

(Right, top to bottom) The 1965 catalog showed Fender's ill-fated Marauder, perhaps the first Fender guitar in which Leo had no input. The 1968 catalog featured blackface tube amps and the new transistor line. The promo photos inside showed everyone from Wayne Newton to the Peanut Butter Conspiracy twanging Fenders.

CBS-Fender

The CBS-Fender deal remained a well-guarded secret from everyone until it took effect on January 5, 1965. Newspapers reported that CBS paid $2 million more for Fender than for the Yankees. However, CBS actually bought the Yankees in two installments: $11.2 million in 1964 for 80 percent, and $2 million for the remaining 20 percent two years later. In any event, Fender was now a validated, big-business symbol of American culture owned by a bastion of mainstream entertainment. The electric guitar business entered a new phase. In 1965 *Music Trades* contended that CBS's involvement with radio, television, and records already gave the guitar tremendous exposure. Now, with a $13 million investment in guitar manufacturing, CBS had an incentive to push guitar music even further. Of course, big business had tried such schemes before: RCA created its NBC radio network, in part, to sell the radios it manufactured. As predicted, Fender guitars began appearing on more Columbia record album covers and CBS television shows. Fender pictured Columbia recording artists in catalogs and the *Album of the Stars* series. *The Music Trades* conclusion rang true: "Due to CBS's greater participation in the guitar business, for a long time to come, demand is bound to outrun supply." CBS's success and power would help everyone sell more guitars.

Randall became the vice president and general manager of the Fender Musical Instrument and Fender Sales

(Top to bottom) Leo receives the 1965 Country Music Association President's Award "for his outstanding contribution to the sound of country music" from Tex Ritter.

Jody Carver (with legs crossed) and Charlie Rosenthal at the 1967 trade show.

Forrest White shortly before leaving CBS-Fender. Don Randall has said that Forrest was "hell on wheels" resisting some of the changes CBS brought to the company.

Divisions of CBS. His compensation was $50,000 per year plus performance incentives, which would add about $25,000 each year to the total. He moved into a corner office at CBS headquarters in New York and spent many hours commuting between coasts. Other principal employees such as Forrest White, George Fullerton, and Roger Rossmeisl continued in their positions at the factory, but the sales team soon lost Mike Cole, who died suddenly from a heart attack on January 10, 1965, in Florida. The entire sales force flew to New York for his funeral. A music dealer approached Randall that day and said, "I know this is probably not the right time to ask, but I'd like to take Mike's place." Without missing a beat, a grieving and irritated Randall said he would see if that could be arranged with the undertaker. After reviewing the situation in Cole's territory, Randall sent Jody Carver on the road as a salesman. Carver says the decision made him feel as happy as a New York kid picked to play center field for the Yankees.

Leo took two months off and a new doctor prescribed a stiff dose of antibiotics that cured the persistent throat infection. Always interested in boats, Fender decided to go shopping for a new one. He walked into a Newport Beach dealership one morning to scrutinize a 40-foot power cruiser he had admired on the showroom floor. The salesman noticed Fender's soiled trousers and old leather tool belt and ignored him. Leo had received similar slights in the past at a Cadillac showroom in Fullerton, until the car salesmen discovered their dimwitted mistake. Returning the next day to Newport to look at the boat again, Fender reportedly announced, "I like it; I'll take it." He promptly wrote a check for over $80,000, surprising all those who had casually spotted but ignored him the day before. As soon as Fender started sailing the new yacht, he began designing an improved one he would have custom-built. During this period, he also read a stack of Zane Grey novels and bought an 18-acre tract east of State College Boulevard in Fullerton.

Leo's job as a consultant in research and development would earn him a $25,000 annual salary with a contract

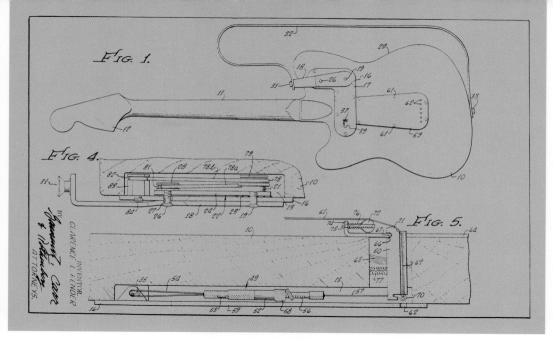

(Below) Unlike his brother Wes, bassist Monk Montgomery, shown here visiting the factory in 1966, embraced Fenders throughout his career. Noel Harrison, bottom, who had a few minor hits in the 1960s, his Cadillac convertible, and a 12-string on loan from Fender, 1966.

lasting five years. He soon gladly moved his lab from the CBS-Fender factory to 1013 East Elm Street in Fullerton, starting his new company, CLF Research. Forrest White let him out of the gate on the last day Leo worked at the plant. The inventor parted by saying, "I don't know what I would have done without you." A month or so later he presented White with a clock and barometer combination for his home. The words engraved on its solid-brass plaque read: "To Forrest White, in appreciation of many things. Leo Fender."

Leo continued work on the Fender-Rhodes piano and developed the Mustang bass, a high-quality, economical instrument for CBS-Fender. He patented his 12-string bridge, an acoustic guitar bridge, and a vibrato tailpiece for acoustic-electrics. Although he stopped designing steel guitars, the historical connection between steel and standard guitars still shaped his ideas. One of his last projects as a consultant for CBS was a B-string bender, a pitch-changing device that enabled the player to make pedal steel effects: pulling down on the guitar strap activated a lever setup in the guitar that attached to the B string. CBS saw little commercial merit in the Fender Bender, despite its clever name. The parent company protected its investment by using ideas that seemed commercially viable. In the old days, Leo would have produced his string bender to benefit the few players who wanted it. Now the inventor had little power and soon felt unappreciated, shut out of decision making. White said that this was the saddest period in Leo's professional life.

Meanwhile, the atmosphere around the factory changed dramatically. Some people believed that corporate purpose and increased profits replaced Leo's original purpose, which was making quality products. White thought that many of the new CBS people had no feel for musicians' needs. New York executives separated R&D and purchasing from manufacturing. (White's title became director, manufacturing operations.) CBS's dismal history in manufacturing presaged Fender's eventual fate in the hands of a corporate bureaucracy. In 1951 the corporation

Mid-1960s Stratocasters with the new larger headstock, similar to the ones Jimi Hendrix usually played, looked visually out of balance but still had the Fender sound.

(Opposite) Models pose with a Fender Coronado acoustic-electric, April 1968. As Fender strayed further and further away from its original solidbody guitars and tube amp designs, the older equipment became more popular with musicians.

had bought Hytron Radio and Electronics, a manufacturer of television sets and tube components. CBS planned to make color television sets, but Paley failed to invest enough in R&D to make Hytron the best possible product. He apparently knew little about long-term planning in manufacturing; he was used to making last-second changes in radio and television scripts. Fortunately for CBS, the government stopped production of color television sets because of the Korean War just before Hytron's inferior sets went onto the market. When the government lifted the ban in March 1953, CBS scuttled its plans to make them. Hytron's black-and-white television set assembly line was shut down in July 1956, and CBS closed what remained in 1961, losing $50 million. Paley later admitted, "We didn't know very much about the manufacturing business, and much more importantly, we didn't care about it, you know, it wasn't our cup of tea." These were the people who had bought Fender.

In June 1966, the corporation formed the CBS/Columbia Group, and Randall became the vice president and general manager of the CBS Musical Instruments Division. (On October 3, 1967, his title changed to president of the division.) Shuttling back and forth to New York and negotiating new acquisitions for CBS, he had almost no time to deal with seemingly minor details at the factory. At first CBS's problems and mistakes at Fender were small but nonetheless consequential. Someone decided to enlarge the headstock on the Stratocaster and unintentionally ruined its visual balance. The rationale was simple: the new design allowed a bigger decal. To save a few pennies on each pickup, purchasing agents ordered a different type of coil wire. Dipping the coils in hot wax, the old method used to prevent microphonic feedback,

melted the new wire's insulation. So, the new CBS-Fender pickups had no wax, sounded different, and squealed at lower volumes than the old pickups had. Soon there were other debacles, such as the one that led to Forrest's resignation.

The new CBS engineers, enamored with the high technology that frightened Leo, designed a portable electric organ and an ill-conceived line of transistor amplifiers. White complained that there was no easy way to service the amps and that they did not have the tone players wanted. The new design contrasted with the old Fender tube amps, the most practical and best-sounding of their day. Fender veterans had watched Leo toy with designs for months, testing them at nightclubs every night. He squeezed every improvement he could into a product before it went into production. Those days were over. Despite obvious problems with the transistor models, the CBS purchasing department ordered enough parts to make one thousand each of the fourteen models. Adhering to principles Leo set in the early days, Forrest refused to sign an authorization to produce them and quit on December 6, 1966. "I was the only former associate that resigned rather than make something that was not worthy of Leo Fender's name," White said with a strong sense of loyalty to Leo and the past. No one knows how Leo, then out of the loop, felt about the issue.

Corporate decision making left little room for common-sense sentimentality like White's. CBS naively believed it had a good thing in the transistor amps; it needed to make profits, regardless of what the veterans believed worthy of Leo's name. With opportune timing, new products meant growth, but the technical challenge of the 1960s was landing on the moon, not

Orange County Teenage Fair, 1968. According to Don Randall, the transistor amplifier series "just didn't do the job."

(Below) **The solid-state Reverb and Model S125 amp from 1966.**

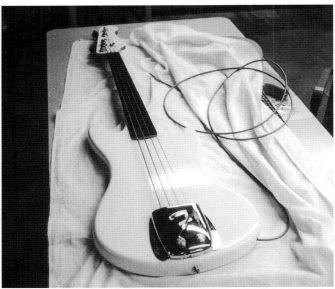

(Above) Prototype bass photographed at Fender in December 1965. The controls were mounted to the metal cover, which presumably went over the pickup and bridge.

(Left) Factory photo of a Marauder with stealth pickups, 1965.

(Right) A CBS-Fender 5-string bass. Showing how quickly he detached himself from the goings-on at CBS in 1965, Leo was surprised to learn in the 1980s that the company had made a 5-string bass.

(Below) The Fender Fantasy, March 1966. Another prototype in which Leo had no input, this guitar predated the Coronado acoustic-electrics.

(Left) **Longtime salesman Art Bates (with glasses) and Charlie Rosenthal.**

(Below) **Freddie Tavares, December 1966. He continued at CBS-Fender in R&D.**

(Bottom) **Don Randall and Bill Carson (seated) at the 1967 NAMM show.**

building a smaller, cooler-running guitar amplifier. Guitarists in the 1960s preferred low-tech tube-powered amps like Leo's Twin Reverb, the Beatles' Vox AC100s, and the Who's Marshall stacks. Large amplifiers made impressive backdrops on stage. Music's theatrical side overruled the practical needs of musicians, many of whom had armies of roadies moving equipment from city to city; many of those large cabinets behind 1960s guitarists were empty anyway.

Moreover, just as CBS introduced transistor amps, guitar players like Jeff Beck, Jimmy Page, and Eric Clapton started turning amps up to create the singing sustain of even-harmonic distortion, the unintended capability built into tube amps. Early transistor amps, including Fenders, did not distort in the same warm musical manner; they sounded shrill and harsh. CBS's cabinet styling also looked more worthy of a hi-fi company's logo than Fender's, the symbol of rugged musical gear. Solid-state Fender amps soon became the laughingstock of serious guitar players and a complete commercial failure. Randall says that approving the new amps was one of his biggest mistakes at Fender. Bins of unused knobs, eventually auctioned off, sat idle in a Fullerton electronics surplus store for decades. Yet CBS had the resources to absorb the tremendous loss, and Fender still made substantial profits in the late 1960s.

But by 1969 Randall had grown weary of his constant travel around the country and of what he calls "the corporate approach." For instance, the new offices at the factory CBS built had to be designed by a well-known architect. The building was much more expensive than something Don or Leo would have had, but it fit the CBS image. Under tremendous pressure from his superiors at CBS, Randall had to lower the salesmen's commissions. By delegating work to a sub-salesman on a salary who traveled and took orders, some of these road warriors had made as much or more than CBS's Paley. Art Bates reportedly earned over $300,000 a year more than once. Dale Hyatt bought airplanes and built a swimming pool shaped like a guitar. Don remembered (and perhaps longed for) the early days in the guitar business when competitors golfed and dined together, when competitors were all close friends. Now he recognized that those days were gone, and he too wanted out. In April 1969 CBS gave him an unconditional release from his contract.

Leo having a dinner discussion with Speedy West, December 1967.

Red, white, and blue. A group of CBS-Fenders including the popular Mustang Bass, 1968.

CBS continued the Fender tradition of using many artists who had made little or no impact on guitar playing to plug its instruments. The exception was Jimi Hendrix. One almost surreal endorsement for the Jazz Bass came from Bob Dylan. He was to jazz what Lionel Hampton was to protest music.

Jimi Hendrix plays

Fender
MUSICAL INSTRUMENTS

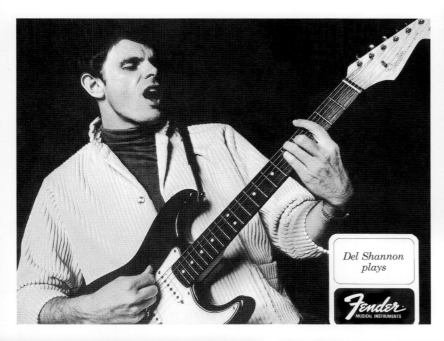

Del Shannon plays

Fender
MUSICAL INSTRUMENTS

Bob Dylan plays

Fender
MUSICAL INSTRUMENTS

The classic test of strength and durability that Leo devised in 1950 still worked in the 1960s. Maple necks were so elastic that they always returned to their original shape.

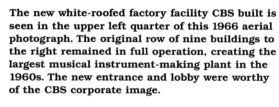

The new white-roofed factory facility CBS built is seen in the upper left quarter of this 1966 aerial photograph. The original row of nine buildings to the right remained in full operation, creating the largest musical instrument-making plant in the 1960s. The new entrance and lobby were worthy of the CBS corporate image.

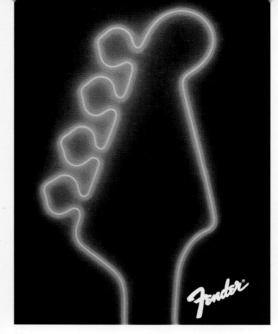

CBS-Fender in the 1970s and 1980s

Despite emerging problems at Fender, CBS's juggernaut had continued swallowing other small musical instrument companies in the 1960s. It purchased Rogers Drums; Electro Music (not to be confused with Rickenbacker Electro String), maker of Leslie speakers; and the Gulbransen electric organ company. In 1972 CBS bought Steinway & Sons, the prestigious piano manufacturer. Later the company acquired Gemeinhardt Corporation of Elkhart, Indiana, a leading maker of flutes and piccolos; Lyon & Healy, manufacturer of concert harps; and Rodgers Organ Company, maker of electronic organs for churches and auditoriums. In 1978, sales for all CBS companies surpassed $3 billion. By 1979, CBS-Fender sold over forty thousand instruments a year, a testimony to the staying power of Leo's name, not to corporate competence or manufacturing skills. (In contrast, Leo had sold about 3,095 steels, guitars, and basses in 1951.)

Quality control slipped markedly, starting in the late 1960s. An older guitar was not necessarily better, but most of the better guitars were old, especially compared with the despoiled assortment of instruments CBS produced throughout most of the 1970s. (By 1970 guitarists and collectors had coined the neologism *pre-CBS* to describe Fender guitars and amps made before 1965. This term—which almost overnight became part of all musicians' vocabulary—denoted sterling-quality workmanship, tone, and playability.) The sloppy neck slots on the so-called 3-bolt Stratocasters allowed necks to slip laterally back and forth, thus changing the guitars' pitch. The design was a good idea poorly implemented. One former employee said that Leo's prized saws became too old and dull to make precision cuts. Throughout the 1970s, CBS failed to reinvest in modern factory equipment. The painters replaced lacquer finishes with durable yet unmusical, almost sticky polyester finishes. Many guitars with flawed finishes found their way to guitar stores. One new 1970s Telecaster hanging in Fullerton Music had a circle drawn in pencil around a knot in the wood. A penciled arrow pointing to the circle and the word "flaw" all showed through the finish. In the early days the factory would have painted that guitar a stunning solid custom color, thus turning lead into gold. But CBS's corporate ladder climbers lacked Leo's skill as an alchemist.

CBS did produce some attractive yet revealing guitar catalogs full of wit and wishfulness. The 1976 edition pictured cartoon scenes inspired by *Alice in Wonderland*, *Jack and the Beanstalk*, *The Three Bears*, and other fantasies. The artwork and clever ad copy unfortunately reflected the corporation's increasingly out-of-touch state of mind as its virtual monopoly with bolt-on-neck guitars slowly eroded. When Leo's early patents ran out, other companies began making generic Fender-style guitars. A few even sold "Fender guitar" kits that players could assemble at home. Some copies, especially the much-improved Japanese imports, were better and less expensive than guitars made by CBS-Fender.

Furthermore, by the end of the 1970s the United States' economy entered a deep recession with double-digit inflation and high interest rates. Compounding CBS's dilemma, interest in guitars started to drop. Teenagers probably bought computer games instead. (This trend continued. *The Los Angeles Times* reported that from 1972 to 1989 total sales of guitars and other fretted instruments dropped by nearly 50 percent to 1.4 million.) Years of corporate neglect, economic reality, and social trends were undoing an American institution. Guitarists watched in disbelief as the original American-made Fender slowly died an ignominious death.

CBS finally saw that Fender needed fixing when the money stopped rolling in. In 1981, the corporation recruited a new management team headed by John McLaren from Yamaha's American musical instrument

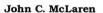

John C. McLaren   **William Schultz**

organization. William Schultz became Fender's president. In retrospect, some employees speculate that CBS hoped new talent could patch Fender's problems—turn back the odometer and put on a coat of wax—before it put the company up for sale. Whatever the motives, the McLaren team set out to remake Fender into a company responsive to its customers and able to compete internationally.

The new managers made some false starts. Their 1982 catalog, supposedly promoting new instruments, depicted nearly every performer playing an instrument made before 1970. It prompted a dealer at Fender's 1982 NAMM show booth to say pointedly, "This is the best *pre-CBS* catalog I've ever seen." The negative image of CBS-Fender instruments, ironically and unwittingly promoted by the corporation's own advertising, was difficult to overcome. However, the new management started making headway with several symbolic gestures that worked. Tipping a hat to the past, they returned to Leo's original headstock shapes and the traditional 4-screw neck construction. Vintage re-creations based on the original specifications included 1952-style Telecasters, 1957-style Stratocasters and Precision Basses, and 1962-style Stratocasters, Precisions, and Jazz Basses. Schultz embarked on a much-needed but belated factory modernization program. Unfortunately, it disrupted and delayed production of the whole Fender line while copies produced by other companies further wore away profits. At this point, guitar making in America looked more than grim to CBS brass.

In contrast, prevailing exchange rates made building instruments in Asia attractive in the early 1980s. The Japanese government helped its guitar industry with generous tax incentives for producing export-bound guitars. In March 1982 CBS decided that if it could not beat its rivals, it would join them by establishing a joint venture called Fender Japan with two Japanese distributors, Kanda Shokai and Yamano Music. Fender Japan made guitars first at the Fuji Gen-Gakki factory in Matsumoto, Japan. They combined the best of Leo's pre-CBS ensemble with the best of early CBS designs: authentic custom colors, stunning two-color sunbursts, black pickguard, and paisley Telecasters (originally from the late 1960s). Inexplicably, Fender Japan also made copies of 1970s-style Fenders, the dreaded instruments that had initiated the CBS downfall.

Americans who saw Fender Japan's catalogs were amazed by the variety and apparent quality of the guitars. Steve Soest, who has repaired thousands of Fender guitars over the years, says, "The early Fender Japan guitars rival anything CBS or Fender ever did." The quality of the necks, fingerboards, finishes, and tone impressed him and many others, so much that a few enterprising American and European dealers resorted to bootlegging products supposedly made just for the Japanese market. The early bootlegs did not carry *Made in Japan* labels and to the unsuspecting eye looked like originals from the Fullerton factory's heyday. The demand for high-quality budget-priced guitars—which the Japanese could easily supply— led to Fender Japan's Squier instruments, first for Europe and then for the United States.

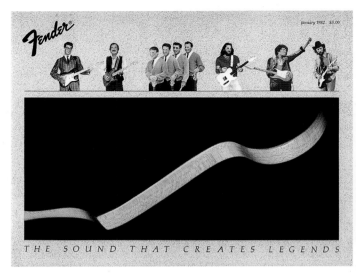

A New Fender Emerges after CBS

Work continued at the Fullerton factory, but eliminating corporate inertia without totally restructuring the business became an impossible task. By 1984 CBS decided to sell everything related to music, wang bars, and maple necks. The entire Fender business went on the block to the highest bidder. Failing to attract anything but low-ball offers, CBS turned to a group of investors headed by Fender executive William Schultz and sold them Fender's name and distribution in a $12.5 million transaction consummated in March 1985. However, the Fullerton factory, located on very costly real estate, was not part of the deal. Until Fender's new management could establish another factory in a less expensive environment, the company sold imports and old stock. In addition to Fuji-made electric models, some guitars came from the Moridaira Musical Instrument Company in Tokyo. By 1985 Fender, which moved its headquarters to Fullerton's neighbor Brea, contracted Korean factories to make Fender-Squier Stratocasters and Telecasters.

Although the Japanese-made Fenders sold well, Fender's new owners still explored ways to re-establish stateside or Canadian production at various competitors' factories. By May 1985, Schultz realized that nothing short of a new American Fender factory would do. For making guitars, the company found space in Corona, California, east on the Riverside Freeway from Orange County. At the new site, the company focused on quality rather than quantity, turning out a meager number of vintage reissue guitars and newly designed, back-to-basics and well-received American Standard models, first a Stratocaster and then a Telecaster. The company so finely tuned its array of new versions of old designs that it eventually used the terms *Vintage*, *Reissue*, and *Classic* for different categories of new guitars. Fender's image, tarnished by

CBS, started to shine again. As the new plant increased its capacity, foreign exchange rates shifted to favor American-made exports. In a remarkable turnaround, the business thrived—what started as a 14,000-square-foot manufacturing area in 1985 became an 80,000-square-foot facility by 1990.

The company eventually moved its corporate offices to Scottsdale, Arizona, to coordinate activities in its satellite facilities: the Lake Oswego plant in Portland, Oregon, home of the Sunn PA systems (which the Schultz group acquired in 1985) and Fender amps; a guitar string factory in Chula Vista, California; and an additional amp and guitar factory in Ensenada, Mexico, to make budget-priced lines. Eventually, the Chula Vista factory also relocated to Mexico, where labor is economical and the plants are close enough to California and Arizona for the Scottsdale office to manage. (Fender also tried to establish a factory in India, but found the location too remote to ensure quality control.) Perhaps even more important than labor costs or proximity, southern California's strict air quality regulatory agency, the AQMD, has no jurisdiction in Mexico. Finishing guitars the old-fashioned way with the old finishes—lacquer or polyester—releases pollutants into the air. California guitar makers battled this problem throughout the 1980s, spending millions to comply with increasingly strict, modern air quality standards. Ultimately, the Corona plant could continue expanding production only by finishing many of its guitars elsewhere. (Any Fender guitar marked *Made in U.S.A.* comes from the Corona plant or Custom Shop, where at least 60 percent of the labor cost was incurred. Many of the components used on *Made in Mexico* Fenders come from the Corona plant, too.)

Today Fender sells a wide range of mass-produced instruments, from the low-end, imported Heartfield and Squier lines to the regular Fender USA line. In 1990 the company offered a comprehensive thirteen-page, single-spaced index listing all its products, including thirty-one different Stratocasters on the first page alone. The 1992 literature pictured forty-four different Stratocasters, twenty-nine Telecasters, and at least twenty-six electric basses modeled after the original Precision and Jazz Basses. But unlike past offerings, the 1990s list of regular production guitars was just a starter. Players failing to find production models fitting their needs could consider a top-of-the-line custom-built guitar from the Fender Custom Shop.

Today's Custom Shop

From the outset, Fender called the Custom Shop its dream factory. Ironically, the idea, a symbol of the company's resurgence, started in the early 1980s. CBS-Fender received several requests from artists for custom guitars, orders filled by the company's R&D model shop. The craftsmen making these guitars, including John Page, envisioned a much larger custom operation serving the

This Custom Shop Stratocaster dubbed the Phoenix symbolized Fender's rise from ashes of the CBS years. Made for the 1993 NAMM show, it had a koa wood set neck and body.

public as well, like Martin's custom shop, founded in 1979. (Page worked closely with Freddie Tavares, who stayed at Fender until retirement at age 73 in March 1985. Tavares died of cancer in 1990.) The concept lay dormant during the CBS years due to corporate foot dragging and transitions in the company. Yet the seed was planted.

After CBS sold Fender, Schultz' team hired George F. Blanda, Jr., as a custom builder. However, he ended up becoming the senior project engineer for guitar R&D, making prototypes and new designs. Then the company tapped John Page and Michael Stevens, a highly respected Texas-based luthier, to create the dream factory.

Management assumed that the Custom Shop would be a prestigious affair: two craftsmen building Rolls-Royces in the building out back. The first space was a paltry 850 square feet next to the new Corona factory. (The Custom Shop and main plant operate as separate entities.) As for numbers, the company expected John and Michael to

The Egyptian Telecaster Custom, brainchild of master builder Fred Stuart, used a synthetic stone called Corian for the top and back to look like the walls of a pharaoh's tomb. George Amicay did the carving, and the figures have eyes made from gemstones.

build five or six guitars a month. The two builders expected about the same, until the first guitars went out to rave reviews in June 1987. Almost six hundred orders came within three months. By the end of 1987, Fender expanded the Custom Shop to 4,500 square feet. By demand, the operation out back became more than just a showcase for Page and Stevens.

While still building guitars, Page—who had management experience with CBS—became the manager for both the Custom Shop and R&D. Combining the units was a brilliant stroke for the company. Ideas, features, and production techniques that worked on custom guitars eventually flowed down to the lower-priced Fender lines. Michael Stevens implored the main factory to change the cutters that shaped Stratocaster contours.

Custom Shop builders also fixed tooling for the Telecaster rhythm pickup cover to make the part look original. They also taught the factory workers how to scallop fretboards on the Yngwie Malmsteen model. Each Custom Shop guitar became an experiment in a guitar-building laboratory, and the Custom Shop made a significant impact on the Fender line from top to bottom. Most Signature Series guitars like the Malmsteen and Eric Clapton models now made in the factory began as Custom Shop guitars.

But the Custom Shop's main purpose was and remains modifying existing models and building completely custom instruments. "We will build as crazy as people want to pay," says Page. Stevens, who left the company in 1990, made a solidbody electric banjo with pedal steel

Master builder John English put together the selectively anodized and engraved aluminum-body "Aloha Stratocaster" for the 1994 NAMM show. Each knob has a Hawaiian scene under a clear top.

tuners for one customer, an 8-string Stratocaster for another. The shop also makes limited-edition instruments in production runs too small or complex for the main factory. Not satisfied with production-model vintage guitars, several customers have ordered Custom Shop versions. To fill these orders, the Custom Shop builders—some of Leo's biggest fans—work like archaeologists poring over old photos, examining old guitars, and re-creating an ancient technology: the tools, techniques, and materials Fender used in the 1950s.

As the Custom Shop expanded, the company hired a diverse collection of master builders including J. W. Black, Larry Brooks, John English, Yasuhiko Iwanade, Fred Stuart, Alan Hamel, Gene Baker, John Suhr, and Stephen Stern. The shop now measures 18,000 square

feet and production exceeds four thousand guitars a year (counting almost five hundred unique ones). The Custom Shop's Signature Series features Clarence White, Albert Collins, Danny Gatton, and Jerry Donahue Telecasters. Stratocasters include the Dick Dale and Robert Cray models. The Set-Neck Series, which uses a set-neck joint developed by Steve Boulanger, includes a Stratocaster with a 22-fret ebony fingerboard and a highly figured book-matched top, a Telecaster with DiMarzio humbuckers, and the Telecoustic Custom with a piezo pickup system, Honduras mahogany back and sides, and a solid spruce top. The Classic Series takes designs kicking and screaming back to their neonatal beginnings with '54 and '60 Stratocasters, the Sparkle Telecaster, and Vintage Precision Custom Bass.

(Above) A buyer can get almost anything from the Fender Custom Shop: the gamut of guitars from pure musical instruments to works of art.

(Right) Icon meets icon. The Custom Shop made 109 "Harley-Davidson Stratocasters." Another joint venture was with Playboy magazine.

Aside from re-creating and reinventing the past, the Custom Shop solved a problem that plagued Fender during the CBS era—staying on the cutting edge for the future. These builders work almost daily with artists, learning their latest needs. Unlike a huge assembly plant, the shop can adapt to changes and suggestions overnight. John Page says: "Trends change and we want to be able to address them. The Custom Shop is trying to lead the way in getting Fender to make any kind of guitar you would want." Some of the new Fenders, especially those from the dream factory, rival those from the past and set new benchmarks for the company. For example, the simplicity of Fred Stuart's Bajo Sexto baritone Telecaster fulfills the promise that eluded Leo's overdesigned Bass VI.

The public pushed Fender to live up to its name, and the company's new owners responded with a do-or-die spirit that combined the best of old and new. The results have been stunning. Fender tripled its sales from the mid-1980s to 1990. Their experience proves that most of their customers want some variation of the Stratocaster or Telecaster. Commercial, cultural, and musical phenomena, these instruments fueled the company's comeback after what Freddie Tavares called the "CBS debacle." In 1987 *Guitar Player* magazine ran a cover story called "Strat Mania." Editor Tom Wheeler called the Stratocaster the "undisputed Guitar of the 1980s." The magazine's cover story for "Gods of the Telecaster" ran in July 1993; Leo's Model T had become the workhorse he intended, fitting into bands as diverse as those led by Tom Petty, Merle Haggard, and Les Brown.

(Above) **John Page at the first Custom Shop facility.**

(Left) **An extra-fancy Telecoustic made for the 1992 NAMM show.**

(Right) **Double f-holes, koa wood, handmade pick-ups, and a set neck make up this Hawaiian-theme Telecaster by John English.**

No electric guitar in history has approached the dominance of the Telecaster and the Stratocaster. Dan Smith, vice president of marketing electric guitars for the new Fender company, estimates that Fender has made 1.4 million Stratocasters since 1954. That number plus the innumerable Stratocaster-style clones from other companies—Smith says that Fender has taken legal action to defend trademark shapes and headstocks at least thirty times since 1981—proves that the Stratocaster is the most commercially successful electric guitar design in history. The Telecaster is undoubtedly a close second.

The new Fender sells proven products and willingly accepts the past as a yardstick for the future. But as John Page says: "Old guitars represent a starting point. Vintage is something you learn from. Then you go on and design something for tomorrow." Having restored an American institution from near collapse, the new owners have created their own place in the history books as keepers of the Fender flame. Meeting the demands of the 1980s and 1990s required a new approach, and, curiously, one Leo would never have taken if he had still owned the company. In many ways Leo mired himself in the 1950s, strange for a man so intent on leaving the past behind. He would have had nothing to do with a custom shop, set necks, or overseas factories. After leaving Fender to CBS, he tried to design guitars for tomorrow. Unfortunately, he stubbornly refused to base his business on proven products or to use his own past, so highly regarded by others, as either a yardstick or a benchmark.

He kept a low profile—many dealers and customers did not know that he was the "music man." He never sought a company as big or as predominant as the old one. What he innocently and naively wanted was a place to tinker and some friends around to have lunch with.

Leo working on a Music Man guitar, July 1977.

Chapter 15

Leo after Fender

Music Man

Leo never said that he felt guilty for selling Fender at the peak of its 1960s success, but he clearly felt responsibility for many former employees left to fend for themselves within CBS's tortuous bureaucracy. With his soiled khakis, Leo had blended right into the blue-collar crowd that had struggled to make the original Fender company a success. In the old days, the plant had a family-like atmosphere with virtually no job descriptions; workers did what needed to be done because of their commitment and loyalty to Leo. It was an honor to work at "Fender's," as many former employees later proudly exclaimed. In contrast, each position at the CBS factory had a notebooksized job description written by systems analysts. If a task was not written down in the book as a responsibility, someone else was supposed to do it. CBS business-suited executives engendered little pride, loyalty, or team spirit.

Forrest White had been the first top person to leave (chapter 14). In April 1969 Don Randall left before completing his five-year contract and founded Randall Instruments, which soon manufactured and sold a line of respected transistorized amplifiers. Fender salesman Tom Walker gave up his position and considered a business deal with Randall that came to nothing. Dale Hyatt dropped his job with CBS and went to work for Randall. Lost in the corporate shuffle, George Fullerton had become a liaison between R&D and manufacturing at the CBS plant; he handled additional responsibilities in public relations. When the corporation tried to lower his salary by pushing him downstairs to R&D, he resigned in March 1970 and soon took a job at Ernie Ball's Earthwood, Inc. in Newport Beach.

As patriarch of the solidbody guitar industry in southern California, Fender had sold his company but not his

Forrest White, who took credit for the Music Man bass headstock design, proudly held the first Sting Ray off the line. Music Man basses were perhaps Leo's best-received post-Fender instruments.

family of former employees. After leaving CBS, several of them competed like sons for his attention: some asked for large personal loans, some for jobs, and some for both. Leo felt no obligation to treat them equally. The only way he could have done so would have been to write a check for everyone, and Fender believed that people should earn their pay (although according to Leo, Roger Rossmeisl returned to Germany without repaying a large personal loan that Leo forgave). Less than two years after selling Fender, Leo entertained the idea of starting another manufacturing company. Forrest White reported in his book that Leo told him in 1966, "What you need is your own company, and if CBS didn't have me tied up in a contract we would start tomorrow."

There is no indication that CBS made Leo an offer to continue as a consultant after 1970, or evidence that he would have accepted. His fears of technological breakthroughs by real scientists had faded when 1960s transistorized guitar amps failed miserably. Moreover, he wanted an outlet for his ideas, often slighted by CBS. In the summer and fall of 1971, Forrest and Leo planned a new company called Tri-Sonics, finally founding it on March 7, 1972. Leo owned 100 percent of the common stock and would design guitars and basses. Tom Walker came on board to handle distribution and to design amps; he owned 50 percent of the preferred stock. White, who would manage manufacturing and help with instrument designs, held the other half of the preferred stock. In early 1973 the owners switched the name to Musitek, but after some confusion with its pronunciation, Leo coined the moniker Music Man.

Although Leo provided major funding for the company, he kept a low profile—many dealers and customers did not know that he was the "music man." He never sought a company as big or as predominant as the old one. What he innocently and naively wanted was a place to tinker and some friends around to have lunch with. With friends like Forrest in tow, he could concentrate on bringing back the good old days without the headaches. So they quickly hired other Fender veterans, including Babe Simoni, Jody Carver, and Bud Driver.

Leo's CLF Research moved to his 18-acre industrial park on Fender Avenue (which as its developer Leo had named after himself) in Fullerton, where as many as 128 tenants leased space. He tooled up to do all the instrument manufacturing and in the process hired George Fullerton, who had left Earthwood. Called a "true southern gentleman" by many, George had been well liked at the pre-CBS Fender organization. Still, his hang-loose managerial style

Sitting in Leo's lab at CLF, Tommy Walker, left, and Leo Fender before going separate ways, July 1977.

Patent drawings showed how seriously Leo took improving bridge designs in his later guitars and basses. In some ways he became so obsessed with the guitar's individual parts that he lost track of the sum of his creations. All the little changes, perhaps improvements in their own right, added up to guitars quite different than his originals, the proven products.

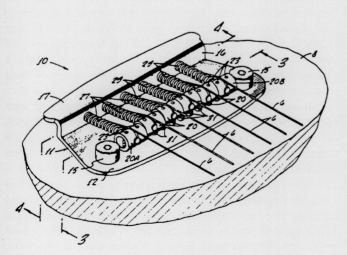

United States Patent [19]

Fender

[11] 4,031,799

[45] June 28, 1977

[54] BRIDGE FOR STRINGED INSTRUMENTS

[76] Inventor: C. Leo Fender, 2851 Rolling Hills Drive Sp. 33, Fullerton, Calif. 92635

[22] Filed: Jan. 26, 1976

[21] Appl. No.: 652,408

[52] U.S. Cl. 84/307; 84/298; 84/299

[51] Int. Cl.² G10D 3/04; G10D 3/00

[58] Field of Search 84/307, 298, 291, 299

[56] References Cited

UNITED STATES PATENTS

2,972,923	2/1961	Fender	84/307
3,174,380	3/1965	Cookerly et al.	84/307
3,178,985	4/1965	Jorsumm	84/307
3,290,980	12/1966	Fender	84/307

3,538,233 11/1970 Compton et al. 84/307
3,399,524 8/1971 Jones 84/298

Primary Examiner—Stephen J. Tomsky
Attorney, Agent, or Firm—Philip M. Hinderstein

[57] ABSTRACT

In a bridge for stringed instruments of the type including a plurality of independently movable drums which permit independent adjustment of the length and height of each string of the instrument, there is disclosed an improved construction wherein all of the drums are urged axially into contact with each other and a fixed post to reduce vibration of the drums and wherein the adjustment holes through the drums are arranged to prevent fraying of the sleeve of a player of the instrument as such sleeve passes over the bridge.

6 Claims, 6 Drawing Figures

U.S. Patent   Sep. 9, 1980   Des. 256,804

FIG. 1

FIG. 2

FIG. 3

FIG. 4

269

Music Man literature. In a guitar world where everything looked Fenderish, the power of the original name and designs prevailed.

(Below) **The Sting Ray I sounded good, but the offset body made it heavier than it needed to be, and the control plate looked like an aftermarket add-on.**

sometimes riled Leo, who wanted problems solved by his managers so he could avoid them. Fullerton's strengths were hands-on in the shop—woodworking, tool making, and drawing. Leo had always needed someone with talents in these areas.

Leo looked forward at CLF and followed two unspoken rules: If it is broken, fix it; if it is not broken, make it better. He had believed since high school that "progress was progress." Now he rejected the notion that there were few improvements left to make in guitars. At Music Man, the Sting Ray and Sabre guitars resulted. He used Gibson's old side-by-side dual-coil humbucking pickup as a starting point for his own humbucker with Alnico pole pieces. He found that it produced more high frequencies than Gibson's earlier design, but still sounded muffled, as he said, "like you'd put a blanket over the amp." While the Sting Ray had an offset-waist body like the Jazzmaster, the Sabre, introduced in 1978, had a contoured body more like the Stratocaster's. The Music Man guitars performed well, but neither carried a vibrato. When Edward Van Halen-style dive bombing became the fad, a guitar without vibrato seemed pretty irrelevant to most young players. The best-received 1970s Music Man designs were the Sting Ray and Sabre basses.

Music Man basses used a trademark peghead with three tuners on one side and one on the other. Designed by Forrest White, it lessened problems inherent in the old Fender basses like the "soft spot" at the fifth and sixth fret on the G string, notes (C and C#) not as loud as the others. The shorter string length behind the nut also helped balance the tone of the first string with the other three. Because the new headstock was shorter, the instrument had a good weight balance. The top-of-the-line Sabre bass used two humbucking pickups, a die-cast bridge, and standard active preamp electronics.

In the 1970s, Leo made clean breaks from the past, especially in these new pickup and preamp designs. However, crippling differences of opinion about business and a soap opera atmosphere often gripped Music Man and overshadowed guitar making. The company lost its competitive edge for lack of a suitable Mesa Boogie-style amp with a click-on distortion channel, the rage of the 1970s. Moreover, it lacked a popular guitar model. According to one former worker, shouting matches among the partners over business decisions became routine. One source close to those events says that Walker maneuvered White out of the decision making. Leo persuaded White to move his office to his home and to sell 1 percent of his stock to Walker. The partners, who had started with great hopes, had failed miserably at re-creating the good old days.

Perhaps everyone would have been happier if Leo had modeled Music Man guitars closer to Stratocasters than to Jazzmasters, mostly forgotten in the 1970s. In failing, he joined other companies and inventors who misread that decade's guitar market. Gretsch, owned by Baldwin at the time, designed the now forgotten Committee Models with input from dealers and player focus groups. These guitars had neck-through-bodies and Japanese-made humbucking pickups. With little success, Gibson introduced the RD Custom, featuring an active electronic preamp with "bright mode," and the RD Standard. CBS-Fender added and soon dropped the Starcaster, a hollowbody with a detachable neck. New models in the 1970s repackaged many old ideas in new combinations— as Leo had done in 1950 with the Broadcaster. But times had changed, and now that once-successful formula had reached its point of diminishing returns.

Most young musicians in the 1970s and 1980s wanted the original packages: Telecasters, Stratocasters, and Gibson Les Pauls. These models had become the icons played by rock's guitar heroes. And the old notion that jazz is tops had slowly eroded; in many cases rock's influence replaced jazz's influence on guitar styles. Studio musicians, led by Larry Carlton, increasingly played thin-bodied acoustic-electrics like Gibson's ES-335. The top rung on the ladder for many guitarists was still an acoustic-electric, but even Carlton would eventually switch to a Stratocaster-style guitar in the 1980s. Most young guitarists who played rock or jazz-rock fusion found the original solidbodies almost tailor-made for the styles.

Amazingly, Leo wanted to expand Music Man's guitar line but refused to build Telecaster- and Stratocaster-style guitars, even in the face of the Fenders' increased popularity. Walker apparently saw little merit in a line expanded with unproven models. In 1980 Leo, who still owned Music Man stock, formed G&L Musical Products and G&L Music Sales with George Fullerton and Dale Hyatt. The CLF factory continued manufacturing Music Man instruments and parts for at least a year while Leo made new G&L models. Hounded by banks, Walker closed Music Man's Anaheim amplifier factory, held an auction to repay loans, and sold the Music Man trademark to Ernie Ball. Leo lost at least $1.5 million. He later regretted not picking up some of the tools in Anaheim he could have used at his factory.

Left to right, George Fullerton, Leo Fender, and Dale Hyatt in an early promo photo for G&L.

G&L Musical Products

G&L Music Sales was Leo's company, despite what the name signified (George and Leo). He contributed the most money, and made the crucial decisions. Hyatt managed G&L Music Sales and pushed Leo's new guitars. Fullerton handled the factory's operations in the early 1980s and did drawings, making contributions to the guitar designs.

Developments at G&L fit a pattern that had started in the old days. Leo conceived a basic plan for a new model while constantly modifying and relentlessly testing and retesting almost every aspect of the guitars, from the tuners and strings to the new vibratos and electronics. He then made a prototype and enlisted musicians to try it on stage or at the factory.

Most of these players, like Buddy Kendrick, Rick "Shorty" Robbins, John Jorgenson, and this author, lived a phone call away in Orange County. Leo also carefully

271

The Cavalier sported Leo's so-called Offset-Humbucker pickups, which had ample highs compared with most earlier humbucking designs. Still, the model failed to intrigue many players.

made comparisons, including the side-by-side run-throughs with vintage Fenders. When he compared a new vibrato guitar with an old Stratocaster, he opined, "Our new guitars burn rubber around the moon." Leo's final judgments led to production, unless Hyatt, who spent hours talking to musicians and dealers about the new guitars, intervened. The whole development process for a new vibrato took months. The 5-string L-5000 bass took several years.

Sometimes Leo modified his designs to suit musicians' concerns, and yet he had problems taking advice if he had already set his mind on some feature or tone. When he tested prototypes of the G&L Cavalier in 1982, several musicians preferred a pickup with less highs. Dale thought he had convinced Leo to forgo his preference, but when the first guitars came off the production line, the quality control inspector noticed the sharp tone of the musician-rejected pickup. Leo had made a switch on the production line (as he had often done in the old days) without telling anyone at the sales office. With G&L guitars, more often than not Leo made the instruments he preferred, and they sounded the way he liked. As he had done in the early 1960s, he made many of his G&L models because he could, not because they were needed. Most had inconsequential commercial appeal.

Leo fashioned a dazzling variety of single- and dual-coil pickups, testing hundreds of different combinations and configurations of pole pieces, windings, and dimensions. (Curiously, some of the units looked more like the old Gibson P-90s than early Fenders.) He based all G&L pickups on his patented Magnetic Field Design with ceramic magnets and fully adjustable soft iron pole pieces. The magnet's bottom surface sat under the coil, away from the strings, and therefore exercised virtually no influence on the magnetic field near the string. The pole pieces, resting on the top surface of the magnet (the opposite magnetic pole), gathered and transferred magnetic pull towards the strings. The entire length of the new pole piece possessed one polarity without the dead spots found in an Alnico pole. The new coils, which Leo extolled whenever given the opportunity, had more output with half as much wire as Fender's older pickups. They produced less capacitance and more highs, as Leo believed players needed even more highs than the Telecaster produced. Still, someone handy with a soldering iron could effectively change the tone content of the new pickups by changing the value of the capacitors in the tone control circuit. The result from a player's perspective was a wide, easily modified tonal spectrum, although few players took advantage of this flexibility.

Leo's research methods at G&L remained imprecise. He failed to maintain a comprehensive, written record of his experiments. Except for the features found in production guitars and some remaining prototypes, the results of these years of toil were lost in the wind. His cluttered lab often looked like organized chaos; piles of notes, mail, and magazines covered his work table. He spent thousands of hours plunking on experimental guitars through a clean-sounding Music Man guitar amp using no reverb, compression, distortion, or phase shifting at a volume that shook his secretary's door two rooms away. His increasingly feeble ears judged tone content years after spectrum analyzers became available. (By the early 1980s he had suffered significant hearing loss. According to Fullerton, Leo's reliance on diminished hearing led to pickups that sounded too shrill. Eventually Leo used hearing aids.) He did his work the old way, which for him seemed to work fine: the patent office granted Leo at least 24 patents after 1975.

In the early G&L years, anyone could visit Leo on Saturday mornings while he puttered around his lab. A brisk tap on the glass door brought him out of the back room with the usual response, "Ah, come on in. Let me show you what I'm working on." He loved putting new visitors through a big show that always included having them stand on a neck (attached to a guitar) to demonstrate its strength and resilience. When Leo wanted to work alone again, he would simply turn around and start working. Sometimes he would stand up and say, "Lots to do." Once he called Doc Kauffman, said hello, handed the phone to

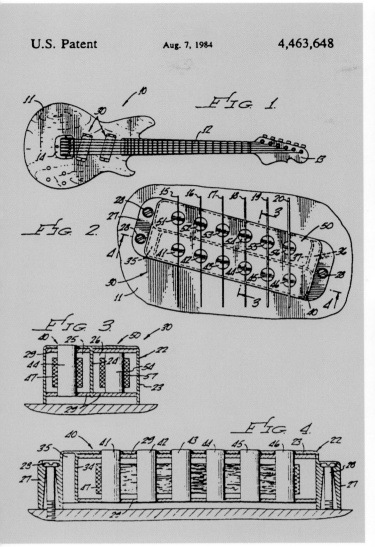

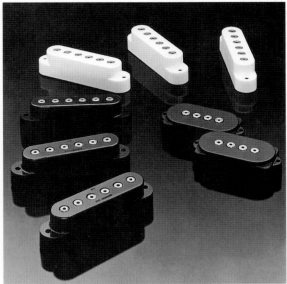

(Above) Patent diagram for the Cavalier pickup.

(Top right) Some G&L pickups (like the ones in this black and white photo) looked similar to the old pickups. However, as this color G&L ad tried to convey, Leo's new design used adjustable polepieces and a ceramic magnet.

(Below) The first G&L brochure, 1980.

a guest, and then disappeared into the factory. Visitors quickly understood when it was time to leave.

Most visitors, especially the younger ones, considered Leo's pre-CBS pickups among the finest ever made. He shunned this opinion, but listened. To purists, any deviation from pre-CBS designs was like changing the formula for Coca-Cola. Part of the Telecaster's signature tone was a quick decay of certain overtones and a percussive attack. Smoothing these—as Leo spent months trying to do on G&L guitars—eliminated the Telecaster-like squawks, whistles, and rings that had hooked thousands of players over the years. Improving the tone meant changing its basic nature and character; what Leo considered progress, many players saw as regression. They asked, why fix something that is not broken? His reply: "I've finally created the sound I've wanted since the 1940s." Leo thought that his new G&L pickups and their small improvements would sell more new guitars. Unfortunately, the music industry had entered a new phase, which Leo should have noticed in the 1970s with the failure of his Music Man guitars. Again, the 1950s recipe for success no longer applied, but he pressed on anyway.

Leo sought more sustain in G&L guitars and designed their non-vibrato guitar bridge following the formula for his well-received bass bridge. The die-cast, heavy metal unit's underside had a boss or protrusion set against the

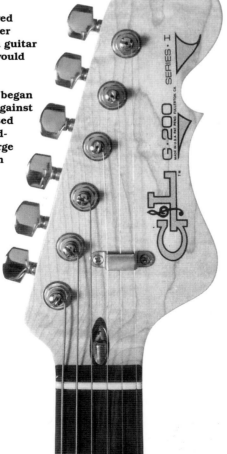

(Top) **The short-lived G-200 was a further attempt to make a guitar Les Paul players would like.**

When CBS-Fender began court challenges against companies that used its trademark headstock shapes, George Fullerton added an extra curve to the G&L headstock.

end grain of the body like an anchor. As a result, the string tension pulled through the bridge and transferred to the body. The strings loaded into the bridge, and the saddles had height and length adjustments. Another adjustment screw compressed the nickel-plated saddles against each other after the player set the action and intonation. In effect the six compressed saddles acted as one, thus eliminating sustain-cutting lateral vibration. Leo believed a guitar should sound like a guitar, not a plunky banjo. The new bridge worked well in this regard, but most players thought an electric guitar should sound like a Telecaster or Stratocaster. Every little technical improvement led Leo further away from the old sound.

Until the 1970s, Leo was always in the forefront with his vibrato designs. Players recognize the Stratocaster's 1954 vibrato as one of the most significant breakthroughs in guitar history. On the earliest G&L F-100 models, Leo used the G&L vibrato, a hybrid improvement that started where the Stratocaster design left off. The new unit had two pivot points instead of six, and the bridge pieces were heavier. Yet as the decade progressed, Floyd Rose locking nuts and vibratos with fine tuners became popular. Anxious to put his stamp on this development, Leo patented the Locktight String Retainer, an improved device for locking the strings at the nut. While Leo perfected his own fine-tuning vibrato and lost sales to other manufacturers, some mid-1980s G&Ls used Kahler vibratos at the insistence of Dale Hyatt. In 1989 Leo produced his unit, called

The G&L bridge gave Leo's new basses good sustain, which many players appreciated. Many bassists readily embraced such technological advances.

The S-500 Stratocaster-style guitar featured Leo's new vibrato and pickups.

The Leo Fender w/Fine Tuners, which did away with roller bridges. It had a smart, compact design.

The early G&L guitars had one-piece maple necks with the truss rod installed through the back, identified by a dark Fender-like "skunk stripe" from behind the nut to the heel. Leo then introduced a neck showing no skunk stripe, made by cutting a single piece of maple into two pieces, installing the truss rod, and then gluing the pieces back together. He claimed its construction ended warping and twisting in the maple. Another advantage was a much higher yield in manufacturing; it produced less waste and lowered costs without compromising quality, one of Leo's lifetime obsessions.

The Precision-Tilt (P-T) neck adjustment was another important feature in G&L necks. The design sprang from 1960s conversations between Forrest White, Leo Fender, and George Fullerton. George held the design's patent, which according to Dale Hyatt Leo always disputed. White believed the idea was his. George Gruhn and Walter Carter state in their book *Acoustic Guitars and Other Fretted Instruments* (GPI Books-Miller Freeman, Inc., 1993) that Johann Georg Staufer created a tilt adjustment for guitars in the early 1800s. Martin used an adjustment mechanism for the better part of that century, and C.F. Hautman patented a detachable neck with a clock-key adjustment mechanism for Martin in 1893. The Fender crew noticed Danelectro's 1960s neck tilt adjustment, and Leo first created his own—the ill-fated 3-bolt neck—in the late 1960s. Fullerton's patent tightened the design, and G&L implemented it, in part, by custom-fitting each neck and body. The P-T neck adjustment allowed very low string action, all easily accomplished without removing the neck or installing shims.

Accolades from the City

The City of Fullerton made Leo Grand Marshal of the Founder's Day Parade held May 11, 1985. With Phyllis by his side and a big smile on his face, he rode in a convertible down Harbor Boulevard that morning. Thousands of

Fullerton Founder's Day Parade

people waved to the man who had put Fullerton's Fender guitars onto every bandstand in the world. Over the years Leo had created hundreds of jobs in Fullerton. He never thought of himself as a local hero. In fact, he had just become one after a considerable uproar in the Fullerton City Council over the fate of his original 1940s factory site on the corner of Santa Fe and Pomona Avenues.

In the late 1970s Fullerton planned a major commuter transportation center that required more parking spaces than the streets allowed. The planners knew nothing about electric guitars or the name Fender. At the time there were more people in Tokyo than in Fullerton who recognized Leo Fender's accomplishments. Astonishingly, Fullerton's downtown area had a historical guide and map with no mention of Leo, his old radio shop, or his original guitar factory. Fullerton Union High School's "Wall of Fame" committee, which honors former FUHS students, also overlooked Fender. When his name was suggested, a spokesperson replied, "Send us his resume, and we will consider him with the others." The bureaucrats' wrecking ball started swinging to tear down Leo's old factory building—occupied in the 1980s by a car-battery business and a ceramics maker—almost before guitar-minded people could react.

A spirited debate at a city council meeting took place in January 1985. One Fullerton bureaucrat argued that the buildings had "no historical significance." One councilman reported that Leo cared little about the factory's fate. No longer owning the property, Leo did live in the present. A Fullerton guitarist claimed that Leo Fender was probably the most important man ever born in Orange County. (Richard M. Nixon, who attended Fullerton Union High School with Leo, was not there to argue that point.) Moreover, the famous guitars that changed the music world began their journey in those blighted downtown buildings. Here Fender developed the Telecaster and Precision Bass and did preliminary planning for the Stratocaster. Someone else pointed out that the pill-box-like cinder block structure had potential as a

guitar museum located just minutes from Disneyland, the unparalleled tourist magnet.

Nevertheless, the city council voted against history, just as it had voted against industrialist Norton Simon's 1964 offer to build a fabulous art museum in Fullerton. In the summer of 1985, a city-hired wrecking crew demolished Leo's original lab and factory buildings. In their place stands a parking structure, part of the transportation center. One good thing emerged as a result of the whole affair: Leo Fender finally received the recognition he deserved. The city commemorated his accomplishments with a brass plaque mounted on the parking structure, and the FUHS "Wall of Fame" committee, after carefully studying Fender's resume, learned about electric guitars.

Leo Fender appreciated the parade, the newspaper articles about his life, and the newfound attention to his mission—the quest for better musical instruments. Still, when the dust settled, he went back to being Leo. He spent Founder's Day afternoon like nearly every Saturday since 1945—alone in his lab comparing guitar pickups. Some weeks his only time off was Sunday mornings, but even in

church thoughts of guitars raced through his mind. During one pious sermon he turned to George Fullerton and blurted loud enough for his fellow worshippers to hear: "I've been thinking about that new bass pickup. Boy, does it sound good!"

Full Circle with the Real Ones—Guitars by Leo

Almost from the beginning Fender, Fullerton, and Hyatt had disagreed over G&L's course. "Leo really didn't want to make it into another Fender," Fullerton says. "He wanted to keep it small, but we could have been much bigger." Fullerton and Hyatt both realized G&L's potential as a top guitar company producing old and new designs, filling the vacuum left by CBS-Fender's rapid disintegration. Yet Leo, who would have nothing to do with the old designs in the early 1980s, set a money-losing course and got a break on taxes. Because G&L made no profits during the decade, Leo often made paychecks good by selling stock from his personal portfolio. When the tax laws changed in the mid-1980s, however, Fender claimed that his tax advantages ended unless he became sole owner of the G&L factory,

which by now resembled a very expensive hobby shop.

Fullerton, who suffered heart disease and underwent bypass surgery in the 1980s, wrote in his book that he left G&L on the advice of his doctor. Hyatt says that this statement is inaccurate or misleading. He claims that Fullerton had no choice but to sell his stock back to Leo, who threatened to close the factory otherwise. After Fullerton acquiesced, he continued a reduced schedule at the factory out of loyalty, and Hyatt quickly changed the company's name to G&L—*Guitars by Leo*—to portray better what had been true since G&L's inception. He also started calling G&Ls "The Real Ones," a stab at the Fender company.

By mid-1985 Hyatt—who worked tirelessly for Leo and suffered his own health setbacks—wanted guitars with more commercial appeal, guitars more like the old Fenders. The 1980 F-100-II used a treble boost that could clear the air in Los Angeles; imagine fingernails against a blackboard amplified. While the active preamps worked well in basses, they came to haunt Leo until he stopped using them in guitars, which did not need extra treble. With the damage to G&L's reputation done, one dealer pointed to an F-100-II control plate and said, "That little red switch killed Leo."

Leo stubbornly heard his critics' suggestions, but had a father-knows-best approach. He privately claimed his old guitars were obsolete. Always the gentleman, he could not say so publicly "out of respect" for his competitors. He incredulously asked: "How could *Guitar Player* possibly call the Stratocaster the guitar of the '80s? . . . We consider our old guitars so inferior that we don't even use them as a starting point for comparisons with our new guitars." The paranoid side of Leo thought that nostalgia for anything pre-CBS amounted to a hoax cleverly designed to sell Fender's new guitars. (After the *Guitar Player* "Strat Mania" cover story, Hyatt pulled all G&L ads from the magazine, and they remained out for years.) Of course, this opinion flew in the face of musicians' perceptions. Leo had the ironic, unenviable job of competing with the reality and legend of his own legacy, which had grown to almost mythical proportions by the 1980s.

(Opposite) **Budget-line SC-1, SC-2, and SC-3s competed directly with imported Stratocasters and Telecasters. Some of Leo's salesmen begged him to change these early versions to look more like the competition.**

(Left) **Early versions of the SB-series basses eventually evolved to look more like the Fender Precision with a split-coil humbucking pickup.**

One growing manifestation of the respect players had for Leo was guitar collecting. Interest in Leo's original designs swelled as the music world realized that a special period in its history had passed when he sold his company to CBS. As fascination in pre-CBS Stratocasters and Telecasters grew, dealers, collectors, writers, and players began analyzing the instruments' finer points and impact on music. Fenders meant different things to different people. To many, a pre-CBS Fender was a piece of Americana, indigenous industrial art representing the best of bygone years. The Japanese, sometimes keen observers of American culture, saw Fender guitars as a symbol of American ingenuity tied to rock and roll and the American cowboy. Through the force of music, Fender guitars (of all vintages) contributed to the globalization of Western democratic values and culture in many parts of the world. Smuggled and bootlegged throughout Eastern Europe and the Soviet Union in the 1970s and 1980s, the instruments symbolized free expression and hope to young people. Dale Hyatt has said that Fender guitars helped win many bar fights. They also helped win the Cold War.

The pure collectors, like museum curators, had a mission: to rescue and preserve the past from the Dumpsters of progress. Players just wanted a wonderful guitar, caring little if someone had turned a screw here or there on it in the last thirty years; most Fender enthusiasts, both players and collectors, considered original pre-CBS Telecasters and Stratocasters the standards for judging solidbody guitars. The comparison was like using George Washington and Abraham Lincoln as a measure of presidents—nobody said these men were perfect, but look at what they accomplished. Leo Fender did not understand most reasons for guitar collecting; collectors and inventors are at opposite ends of personality-trait continuums. Don Randall shared Leo's astonishment: "We thought guitars were like typewriters: people would wear them out and throw them away."

Part of guitar collecting had its basis in objective facts. Old Fender guitars were different, made in a time of affluence and indulgence unlikely to repeat itself. In the 1950s, forests yielded fine woods while electronic parts suppliers produced cloth-insulated wire and wax-coated capacitors. Old paints and lacquer made lasting, natural-feeling finishes but contained hydrocarbons now considered hazardous. Factories in the 1980s, even CBS's or G&L's, could not remake earlier materials and procedures. (Leo did not want to.) Despite years of trying, few manufacturers have equalled the success or lasting power of Leo's guitars. Thousands of old Fenders still appear around the world in nightclubs, studios, and garages. With little maintenance, these guitars get good mileage in today's music. Moreover,

since Leo's originals literally changed the sound of music, the classic tone of those often decrepit, battle-scarred Stratocasters and Telecasters is forever linked to the classic songs and records of an earlier time. The only way to make the authentic, original Fender tones is with original Fender guitars and tube amplifiers.

The universal chord, played on an old Fender, rings through the heavens with brilliance and sustain, the way many players believe electric guitars should sound. Of course, this subjective evaluation of collectible Fenders has large psychological and sociological components. Most baby-boomer musicians remember seeing their first Fender as well as they remember the Beatles on *The Ed Sullivan Show*, and collecting Fender guitars is part of the larger 1950s–1960s nostalgia craze. Any nostalgia-driven craze tends to look back lovingly with little regard for verity; separating facts from fiction sometimes requires a crowbar. For example, a real connoisseur smells an old guitar's finish for originality (this skill is acquired). A veteran also learns to remove the pickguard to check for telltale signs of decades-old rubbing compound. Some claim the formula Fender workers used stained blonde finishes red, but no one knows why. Nevertheless, red stains in the control cavity of a 1950s Telecaster supposedly prove authenticity. And the collectors' belief system says that original guitars sound better. By the early 1980s, the culture and mini-industry of vintage guitars thrived. From there, the trend only grew.

Collectors paid astounding prices for fine examples of stock Broadcasters and custom-color Stratocasters, for example. Prized for being vintage Fenders, some went for over 50 times their original retail price. The value of Fenders previously played by stars went even more stratospheric. A Stratocaster once owned by Buddy Holly was auctioned for $110,000 at Sotheby's in 1991. A *chip* off the old CBS-era Stratocaster Hendrix shattered and torched at the Monterey Pop Festival sold for $8,800. Red Ronnie, an Italian actor, bought the blonde Stratocaster on which Jimi Hendrix played "The Star-Spangled Banner" at Woodstock for $334,620. Yet such value was purely subjective. Long before anyone thought to smell the finish on Jimmy Bryant's original Telecaster, he had discarded it in his children's backyard sandbox for them to play.

Leo was from another generation than most of his ardent admirers and lived a better life after selling Fender to CBS. He never shared the nostalgia players and collectors felt for the old days or the old guitars. He happily moved on to new things. Curiously, there were past designs that Leo remembered with pride and nostalgia— the little boxes he had made and the timbres he had carefully crafted with his soldering iron. He harbored a secret love for amps and felt vindication that his tube designs endured all the high-tech attempts to make them obsolete. At a party for his 80th birthday, he walked up to the musicians and quietly asked: "Ah, what amps are you using? Are you using tube amps?" He smiled, spotting an array of old tweed and brown Tolex models sitting on the carpet. These amps had created a firm foundation for his company in the 1940s; orders for his amps and steels generated the needed cash flow long before the Telecaster brought in a penny. Amp sales had helped build and sustain Fender's pre-CBS dynasty. But more important than making the Fender company profitable, Leo's amplifiers had defined the sound of electric instruments. He had more than a few old amps to smile about.

But what about his old 6-string designs? Were the pre-CBS instruments better than G&Ls? Many factors like the humidity and the voltage of an electrical outlet affect an electric guitar's sound. George Fullerton once speculated that the earth's magnetic poles might somehow figure into the equation. (Avoid facing north, he said with a tongue-in-cheek smile.) Comparing old with new, a musician friend of Leo's once said, "The old guitars sound better because they sound like the old guitars." Pre-CBS Fenders, however, changed so much over the years that sweeping generalizations about their quality or tone made little sense to Leo. The factory made some better than others. Despite his efforts to keep the instruments consistent, Stratocasters and Telecasters produced a range of sound from shrill and penetrating to thick and thuddy. Guitars assembled the same day could sound different. Unlike modern goods made by robots, Fender guitars manifested quirks and irregularities—humanness. Winding pickups by hand yielded variable and sometimes inharmonious results. Each piece of wood in a guitar had different density, causing slightly different resonances.

Time and evolving manufacturing techniques also changed Fenders. A Stratocaster from April 1954 hardly resembled the same model leaving what had become the world's largest guitar factory in 1964. Each carried a Stratocaster decal, but each came from different worlds and sounded different. Small changes, randomly occurring over the years, resulted from improved manufacturing methods or changes in parts suppliers. Leo made notable revisions during the pre-CBS years. Some helped the instruments; some backfired. As an example, with its superior lead pickup and brass bridges, a 1953 Telecaster plays rings around a 1957 Telecaster that Fender thought he had improved. Some players attributed the tone differences in the pre-CBS guitars to fingerboard changes. Yasuhiko Iwanade, a former master builder at Fender's Custom Shop, performed a computer analysis in the 1980s of various Stratocaster neck and body combinations and agrees with the fingerboard theory. For instance, he says the darker sound of early 1960s Stratocasters is definitely tied to the slab fingerboard.

Collectors often confronted Leo Fender with questions he could not or would not answer. By the early 1980s, some vintage guitar experts knew far more about certain details of his first guitars than he remembered. But Leo also had a commercial agenda—selling new guitars with his new designs. (He wanted to stay in business at least.) He said that cobalt levels in Alnico varied significantly in the old days and believed that these inconsistencies altered the tone of the guitars made in different years.

The Nighthawk, another Stratocaster-style guitar, became the Skyhawk after threat of court action from a band using the same name. Thus another G&L rarity was born.

(Above) The trendy, angular Interceptor was in contrast to the more conventional, curved L2000. Both basses here have Kahler vibrato tailpieces.

(Right) The L5000 bass used a headstock reminiscent of Music Man's.

This argument countered the notion that the older Alnico pickups sounded better than his later ceramic ones. By disparaging Alnico and his old pickups, he promoted G&L guitars. Leo also said that electric guitars did not improve over time. But aging that alters tone does take place. Woods dry out, affecting body and neck resonance, even on electric guitars. A guitar stored in Seattle—a cool, wet place—ages differently from one stored in Phoenix's dry desert environment. Some players argue that pickup pole pieces lose magnetism, thus changing a pickup's frequency response.

Leo pointed out rightly that his old company produced few perfect instruments. It usually adhered to strict standards of excellence, but it did not make F-16s. No one died because of a cold solder joint on a guitar, so no one felt too guilty when they slipped through quality control. Leo's workers lapsed on occasion trying to meet deadlines or fighting the boredom of routine factory work. Mistakes happened—painters fumbled neat borders on sunburst finishes; sanding marks showed. Necks fashioned from

green wood bowed, shrank, and exposed fret edges. Despite the company's best intentions and quality controls, guitars with minor flaws landed in music stores. But such imperfections made almost no difference in the guitars' larger performance, and Fenders still outperformed their competitors. Early Fender instruments always had structural and musical integrity, sound basis for the nostalgia they evoke today. Presented with these facts, Leo would list the improvements he had made in manufacturing at G&L. "I would not let some of our old guitars out of the factory today," he claimed several times.

Leo had convinced himself that his old guitars had little significance. Other Fender veterans agreed with him because they had no desire to look back. "I hope I never hear the words *vintage guitar* again," Freddie Tavares said in the mid-1980s. Asked about the Stratocaster, he almost shouted, "Why all this attention to one guitar?" He asked a fair question, and the answer emerged as the 1980s unfolded. Ignoring Fender's heritage and its commercial potential, as CBS began doing in 1965, had consequences. Ignoring what players liked best about his guitars, Leo struggled at G&L. His attitude also complicated Dale Hyatt's job. Sometimes, to get the factory to make the guitars dealers wanted, Dale

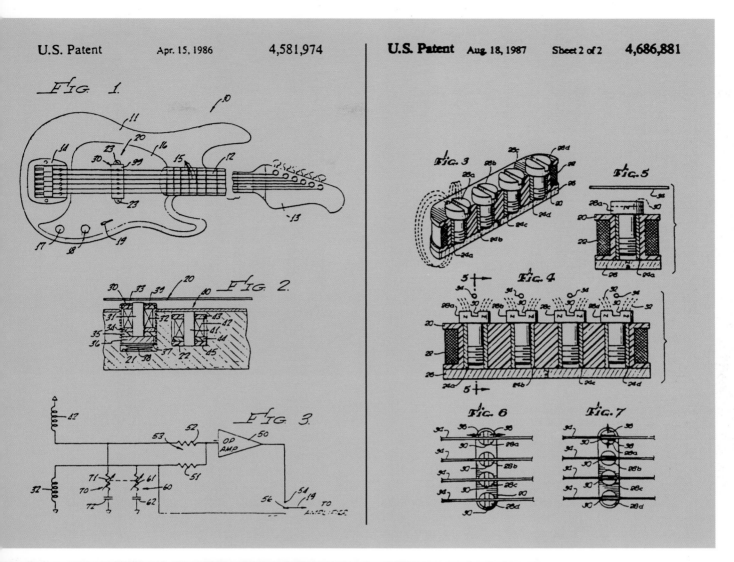

(*Above left*) An experimental G&L pickup with a hidden humbucking coil.

(*Above right*) A design with what Leo called "alterable sound characteristics." The effect was achieved by rotating the large polepieces either parallel to the strings for a single-pole sound like the original Precision Bass or perpendicular for a sound like the Jazz Bass.

(*Left*) G&L was never short of colorful flyers; advertising cost Leo a bundle, which he never seemed to miss.

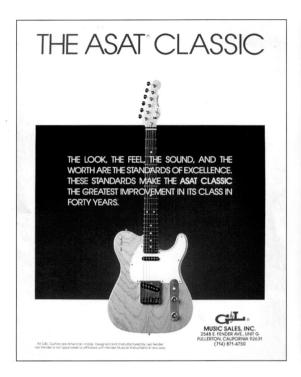

THE ASAT® CLASSIC

THE LOOK, THE FEEL, THE SOUND, AND THE
WORTH ARE THE STANDARDS OF EXCELLENCE.
THESE STANDARDS MAKE THE ASAT CLASSIC
THE GREATEST IMPROVEMENT IN ITS CLASS IN
FORTY YEARS.

G&L®

MUSIC SALES, INC.
2548 E. FENDER AVE., UNIT G
FULLERTON, CALIFORNIA 92631
(714) 871-4750

All G&L Guitars are American made. Designed and manufactured by Leo Fender.
Leo Fender is not associated or affiliated with Fender Musical Instruments in any way.

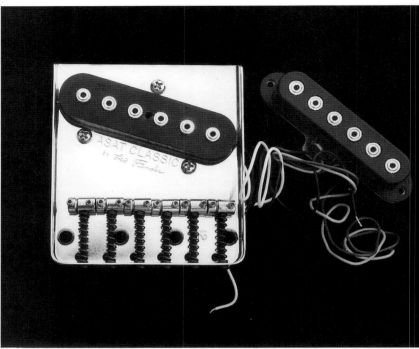

**Leo's biggest success at G&L came when he returned
to more traditional designs like the ASAT Classic,
which had components that were interchangeable
with those on Telecasters.**

simply made crucial decisions without telling Leo. One
month Leo went on a cruise with Phyllis and returned
to find that the G&L Broadcaster—an updated Telecaster-style guitar—had been carefully guided into
development by Hyatt. It had a limited production, only
869 units, due to a continuation of the 35-year-old dis-
pute between the Fender company and Gretsch over
ownership of the name. But Dale had put G&L on the
right path. The highly successful (by G&L standards)
ASAT followed. After reading an article about the Air
Force's anti-satellite missile, this author suggested the
name to Hyatt, who passed it on to Leo. Both liked the
image of a guitar shooting down things in space. Some
believe the acronym stands for "After the Stratocaster,
After the Telecaster."

Although he accepted the Telecaster-style look with
some reluctance, Leo loved the ASAT's full highs, deep
bass, and colorful mid-range tones; he had originally
developed its pickups for G&L's budget line. He wired the
ASAT much like the 2-pickup Stringmaster steels of old;
he omitted the blend control, but the selector switch put
both pickups into humbucking mode. (Without good
examples of old guitars to hear daily, Leo had forgotten
how close some came to his original vision. One Saturday
afternoon he was confronted with a particularly good 1954
Telecaster, and he admitted that its tone came close to his
new guitars. He might have felt like a lost hiker going
around in one big circle for forty years, but his pride would
not let him admit it.) He knew, and many players agreed,
that the ASAT was a fine instrument.

ASAT and Broadcaster maple necks came with and
without ebony fingerboards. Different versions came with
and without vibrato. The ASAT Classic, introduced shortly
before Leo died in March 1991, went even further back
trying to recapture the spirit of early Telecasters. He
designed its pickups, complete with adjustable poles and
ceramic magnets, to fit any Telecaster-style guitar. Except
for the six-piece bridge, the remaining hardware closely
resembled the original Telecaster design. The ASAT
inspired more than a few former Telecaster devotees to
switch to G&L.

While Leo returned to his roots for the ASAT and ASAT
Classic, he also jumped headfirst into the 1990s with a
model called the Comanche. This guitar incorporated the
"Z" single-coil humbucker, a split design similar to the
1957 Precision Bass pickup. With three pickup selector
switches and three switches that split the treble and bass
coils, the Comanche offered over forty different combinations, a plethora of tone variations. Some had more musical potential than others. The guitar also used Leo's new
vibrato with fine tuners.

About the only thing to slow Leo down was his failing
health. By the late 1980s he showed the early signs of
Parkinson's disease, especially impaired speech. Talking to
Leo and understanding his words became difficult and
painful for those who had always delighted in his carefully
crafted observations. Nevertheless, his ideas, still very
much intact, manifested themselves in the work he accomplished. G&L produced an astonishing number of models
and variations for a small firm. In 1989 it offered at least
nine guitars and seven basses, each available with several
options. Leo also made many prototypes and one-of-a-
kind instruments.

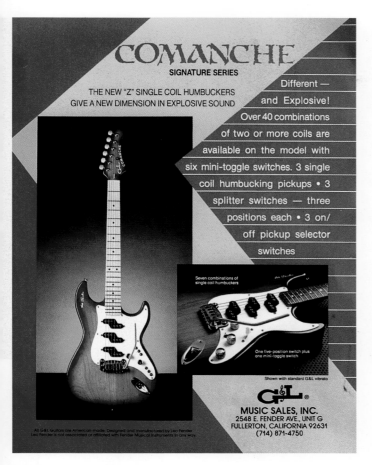
The Comanche was perhaps Leo's
wildest design.

(Below) Left to right, Lloyd Chewning,
Phyllis M. Fender, John Rodriguez,
and John McLaren at the G&L factory. Mrs. Fender receiving the
first commemorative ASAT model,
which came out after Leo's death.

Still, compared with the sales volume of the post-CBS Fender company, G&L made little impact during the 1980s. *People* magazine and *Entertainment Tonight* TV images of Bruce Springsteen, Eric Clapton, Bonnie Raitt, and many others playing old Fenders helped promote new Fenders, thus showing how the new company had regained much of its pre-CBS reputation. The new Fender cultivated artist endorsements by returning to the basics and by creating the Custom Shop. The ever-popular Stratocaster and Tele-caster took on lives far beyond the expectations and experience of their creator. Incredulous, Leo would never quite understand why. According to *Los Angeles Times* writer Carla Lazzareschi, highly successful entrepreneurs often fail to understand the reasons for their initial success, especially luck and the role of early colleagues. She points out that the larger the success, the harder it is to repeat. One might also say that the larger the success, the harder it is to accept a later failure.

Leo believed that history would eventually vindicate his thinking and that his G&L-era designs would prevail. He and Randall had sold the Stratocaster for at least fifteen years before it dominated the field. Overnight success never interested Leo, and in the 1980s he already had money and fame. His motivation, the reason he lost millions in his post-CBS ventures, was much purer and personal. Shortly after Dale Hyatt came to work at K&F in the 1940s, Leo said, "What's the use of living if you don't leave something behind that makes the world better, something people will remember you for?" The more he worked to make guitars better, the more his life had meaning and the more secure he felt about what he would leave behind.

Leo Fender was an American original, the most prolific and successful musical instrument designer of the twentieth century. Time sorts out the meaning and importance of events and inventions, and in time more players may appreciate the full breadth of his contributions, especially the sophisticated guitars he made in his last ten years. Perhaps G&L and Music Man instruments will have their day if a talented young guitarist playing a Sabre, ASAT, or Skyhawk comes along to reinvent music as Jimi Hendrix and Edward Van Halen did for their respective generations. Leo built that capability into all of his guitars, and G&L continues producing many of his designs.

At the very least, Leo's post-CBS guitars represented his insatiable and unselfish quest for perfection, testimony to years of labor and love. Among his last words to his wife Phyllis was a comment about G&L: "I think I've done just about all I can for the company." He had devoted his life to musicians, and for that reason had a clear conscience. Fender's instruments—from his earliest steel guitars to the 6-string bass he left in his lab the night before he died—were engines of musical and social change. They bridged generations, races, cultures, and musical styles, bringing everyone in the world closer through music, one of the great pleasures of life. Few men leave such a legacy.

Leo's first and last guitars. Photomural by Robert Perine of Leo Fender, 1966. The radio shop guitar, 1944. Magnifying glasses, 1980s. G&L 6-string bass prototype, 1991.

Epilogue
Faded Love

Even in old age after suffering several small strokes and progressive degeneration from Parkinson's disease, Leo Fender was dedicated to the point of obsession. He continued working every day he was able, sometimes seven days a week. Both Dale Hyatt and George Fullerton increasingly became more caregivers than business partners in G&L's convalescent home atmosphere. Leo wanted to be in his lab following old routines. Once asked why he did not retire and enjoy the fruits of his success, he replied, "I owe it to musicians to make better instruments." Leo Fender personified the American spirit of invention. He went to work the day before he died.

About 10 A.M. on Thursday March 21, 1991, Phyllis Fender found Leo unconscious in the room where he slept. She quickly called paramedics who arrived in less than five minutes. Two days later she said, "Nothing could have prepared me for those five minutes." She knew he was gone. Indeed, the paramedics' efforts to revive Leo failed. Doctors at St. Jude Medical Center in Fullerton pronounced him dead, reportedly from complications of the Parkinson's disease. He was 81 years old.

Fender's funeral services were held on March 26 at Fairhaven Memorial Park in Santa Ana, California. Family, friends, and close business associates including George Fullerton, Dale Hyatt, and Forrest White attended this observance. Joe Lumusio and Donald Andersen, ministers from the Baptist church Fender attended in the 1980s, conducted the funeral services. The ceremony closed with Leo's favorite song, the ballad "Faded Love" made famous by Bob Wills and the Texas Playboys, played by this author on a 1953 Fender double-neck steel guitar. Leo was buried that day at Fairhaven next to the grave of his first wife, Esther.

On Saturday March 30, during a memorial service at the Temple Baptist church in Fullerton, musical and spoken tributes came from many of Leo's old friends, including electric guitar pioneer Alvino Rey, western swing star Hank Penny, cowboy singer Eddie Dean, and country-rock guitarist John Jorgenson. Leo Fender left many friends.

Appendices

Appendix 1   286
Appendix 2   287
Appendix 3   287
Appendix 4   289
Appendix 5   292

Appendix 1

Tool and Die Purchases, the Broadcaster

The most accurate outline of the Broadcaster's design and evolution, from its beginning as a hand-built single-pickup prototype to the end as the first full-fledged modern solidbody, comes from a long-lost folder Leo made in 1951. Here he listed, among many other production-related details, tools and dies he bought from Race & Olmsted, a company formerly located in Fullerton. The highly specialized tools, like a mandrel for holding a neck in a shaper, were often used in just one guitar-making operation. The dies were the type used for cutting and forming metal and plastic on his punch presses: blanking dies that made the initial cuts (creating a blank to be stamped again or machined into a finished object) and form dies that made final products from the blanks.

Below is a chronology of Leo's purchases. Keep in mind that Fender made much of his own production apparatus in addition to what he purchased. But while he was able to make prototypes and rough-hewed parts before buying many of the items below, he was unable to go into full production. This chronology shows when Leo had the capability to make his guitars in numbers, and sheds light on his thinking and priorities. (For instance, he geared up to made the lead pickup before anything else.) Each tool here marks a point along the trail of his successful effort at making the solidbody a musical fact of life, appreciated and played in every style of music.

July 12, 1949
Blanking die for the top of the pickup bobbin (the same die used on the Champion lap steel's pickup).

August 6, 1949
Blanking die for the lead pickup bobbin's fiber bottom.

August 10, 1949
Form die for what Leo called the lead pickup's baseplate (now commonly called the bridge plate).

August 13, 1949
"P.B. die" for the pickup's baseplate. Karl Olmsted, co-owner of Race & Olmsted, said in 1995 that this note refers to a cheaply-made blanking die, also known in the trade as a pancake die. These dies would wear out much faster than more expensive class A dies. Leo ordered a pancake die when he was not sure how many units he would eventually need to make—that is, when he was unsure how popular the item would be or if he had not settled on a design. If the product proved to be successful, he would have a class A die made.

January 18, 1950
Bending fixture for fret wire. Frets, cut to length from special wire, need to be shaped before insertion.

March 10, 1950 Form die for lead pickup cover plate.
Table and mandrel (which held the neck in place during cutting) for the neck shaper.
Saw for cutting the neck.

March 14, 1950
Die for trimming the tuning keys, one of the few components Fender did not make. Kluson, the manufacturer, would not fabricate them to order, so Leo modified what he received to fit his headstock.

March 20, 1950
Blanking die for the lead pickup's elevator plate (an afterthought not included in the original plan).
Blanking die for the neck's fiber markers. (At this point Leo actually made several pre-production, single-pickup Esquires. On April 7, 1950 salesman Charlie Hayes received the first sample.)

April 26, 1950
Die for the neck plate.

June 22, 1950
Die for cutting the rhythm pickup's top and bottom fiber pieces.

July 26, 1950
Form die for the rhythm pickup cover.
Blanking die for the control plate.
Blanking die for the pickguard.

August 21, 1950
Blanking die for the rhythm pickup's cover.

October 3, 1950
Truss rod routing plate. The truss rod required a channel routed down the back of the neck. (Necks cut earlier than late 1950 without a channel were retrofitted, accounting for neck dates on some Broadcasters that predate truss rods.) Soon after this date, Broadcasters started leaving the factory. On November 16, 1950 Radio-Tel shipped salesman Mike Cole his first standard guitar sample. Others were available to dealers.

December 30, 1950
Router plate for the neck. (Presumably, this plate replaced the one listed above.)

Tool and Die Purchases, the Precision Bass

Leo left a paper trail of the Precision Bass' development. The list below, compiled from his records, shows when he purchased the tools necessary to put the bass into full production. (The first production-model Precision Bass left the factory in October 1951.)

August 14, 1951
Die for trimming bass keys.

August 28, 1951
Saw arbor (mandrel) for the neck.

August 31, 1951
Die for the bridge plate.

September 1, 1951
Template for the neck.

September 7, 1951
Die for the pickup's fiber top and bottom.

September 13, 1951
Template for the body.

September 28, 1951
Template for the pickguard.
Template for routing the neck's truss rod channel.
Template for the body. (Leo needed one template for cutting the body and another for cutting the neck slot, pickup, and control cavities.)

October 25, 1951
Three dies for the pickup and bridge covers.

Appendix 2 *(Source: Leo Fender's notes.)*

Sales by Unit, 1951

Steel Guitars

6-string Deluxe	124
8-string Deluxe	87
6-string double-neck	42
8-string double-neck	323
Triple-neck	235
Student (Champion)	1083

Amplifiers

Pro	616
Deluxe	1539
Super	216
Student (Champion 600)	1090
Princeton	432
Bassman	0

Basses

Precision	83

Standard Guitars—Sales by Unit Each Month, 1951

	Telecaster*	Esquire**
January	87	0
February	65	63
March	63	39
April	39	0
May	118	6
June	34	23
July	50	15
August	120	13
September	66	3
October	69	38
November	62	30
December	95	20
Total	868	250

*The Telecaster was called the Broadcaster until February 21, 1951.
**Single-pickup version.

Proposed Production Schedule for January–June 1952

Steel Guitars

6-string Deluxe	150
8-string Deluxe	80
6-string double-neck	60
8-string double-neck	210
Triple-neck	159
Student(Champion)	1200

Standard Guitars and Basses

Telecaster	700
Esquire	250
Precision	400

Amplifiers

Pro	700
Deluxe	1200

Appendix 3

Patents

Leo Fender's patents covered a large body of work, almost every facet of the electric guitar's design and manufacture. He wanted his ideas protected, especially after a bad experience with a record changer invention (see chapter 2). Here is a partial list of the government grants issued to him and/or his associates (where noted) that pertained to products made by Fender, Music Man, and G&L. For further study, patents can be easily obtained by mail for a nominal fee from the Patent and Trademark Office (U.S Dept. of Commerce, Washington, D.C. 20231).

Utility Patents from the Fender Years (1944-1970)

Utility patents give inventors the right to exclude others from making, using, or selling inventions for seventeen years. They can cover anything useful—a process, a machine, a composition of matter. They can (and usually do) protect new and useful improvements on prior inventions. Utility patents include busy drawings and verbose explanations in small type (you will need reading glasses). Still, they can offer valuable insight into the history and nature of Leo's inventions.

2,455,575 Leo Fender and Doc Kauffman. Radio shop guitar and Direct String Pickup. Filed September 26, 1944. Granted December 7, 1948.

2,573,254 Telecaster bridge (with three saddles) and pickup baseplate. Filed January 13, 1950. Granted October 30, 1951.

2,741,146 Stratocaster floating tremolo. Filed August 30, 1954. Granted April 10, 1956.

2,784,631 Tone control for electric guitar (shown on a Telecaster, but never put into production on any model). Filed July 31, 1953. Granted March 12, 1957.

2,817,261 Stringmaster-type humbucking pickups and circuit. Filed March 29, 1956. Granted December 24, 1957.

2,817,708 Amplifier with tremolo circuit used on tweed amps like the Tremolux. Filed January 16, 1956. Granted December 24, 1957.

2,838,974 Tuning head for steel guitar. Filed November 4, 1955. Granted June 17, 1958.

2,960,900 Offset body design seen on the Jazzmaster, Jaguar, etc. Filed January 13, 1958. Granted November 22, 1960.

2,968,204 Multi-pole pickup (never used in full production). Filed August 13, 1957. Granted January 17, 1961.

2,972,922 Issued to Harold B. Rhodes. Fender-Rhodes electric piano. Filed March 9, 1959. Granted February 28, 1961.

2,972,923 Floating bridge and tremolo used on the Jazzmaster and Jaguar. Filed November 6, 1958. Granted February 28, 1961.

2,973,681 Tremolo circuit used on early Tolex-covered amps. Filed June 8, 1959. Granted March 7, 1961.

2,973,682 Means for controlling string tension on pedal steel guitar. Filed July 22, 1957. Granted March 7, 1961.

2,976,755 Two-coil bass pickup (the humbucking unit seen on the revised Precision Bass in 1957). Filed January 6, 1959. Granted March 28, 1961.

3,003,382 Electric violin and pickup. Filed June 2, 1958. Granted October 10, 1961.

3,009,378 Removable pedal mounting board for pedal steel. Filed January 6, 1959. Granted November 21, 1961.

3,143,028 Adjustable neck with curved rosewood fingerboard. Filed August 26, 1963. Granted August 4, 1964.

3,236,930 Jaguar-type pickup. Filed May 11, 1962. Granted February 22, 1966.

3,241,418 Guitar with inertial vibrato device as used on Mustang. Filed June 5, 1964. Granted March 22, 1966.

3,260,148 Jaguar-type mute for electric guitar. Filed November 12, 1964. Granted July 12, 1966.

3,270,608 Issued to Harold B. Rhodes. Piano action for Fender-Rhodes electric piano. Filed September 24, 1962. Granted September 6, 1966.

3,285,116 Issued to Harold B. Rhodes. Portable Fender-Rhodes electric piano with sustaining pedal. Filed June 15, 1964. Granted November 16, 1966.

3,290,980 Bridge construction with string length adjustments for guitars, including acoustics and 12-strings. Filed February 24, 1965. Granted December 13, 1966.

3,302,507 Acoustic guitar and "tone bar" method of manufacture. Filed June 7, 1963. Granted February 7, 1967.

3,550,496 Ill-fated three-bolt neck with tilt adjustment used by CBS. Filed July 14, 1969. Granted December 29, 1970.

Design Patents from the Fender Years (1944-1970)

Design patents protect—usually for fourteen years—the appearance (but not the structural or utilitarian features) of new, original ornamental designs. They come with little written explanation: order them if you like line drawings.

Des.164,227 Telecaster guitar. Filed April 23, 1951. Granted August 14, 1951.

Des.169,062 Precision bass with slab body. Filed November 21, 1952. Granted March 24, 1953.

Des.186,190 Double-neck pedal steel guitar. Filed August 20, 1958. Granted September 22, 1959.

Des.186,826 Offset body design, Jazzmaster type. Filed December 18, 1958. Granted December 8, 1959.

Des.187,001 Contoured body for electric bass. Filed January 6, 1959. Granted January 5, 1960.

Des.192,859 Amplifier cabinet with front-mounted controls (as used on combo amps like the Vibrasonic). Filed June 1, 1959. Granted May 22, 1962.

Des.200,440 Issued to Harold B. Rhodes. Fender-Rhodes electric piano. Filed June 18, 1964. Granted February 23, 1965.

Des.200,439 Issued Harold B. Rhodes. Fender-Rhodes electric piano. Filed June 18, 1964. Granted February 23, 1965.

Des.204,098 Mustang vibrato. Filed March 17, 1965. Granted March 15, 1966.

Des.214,592 Vibrato tailpiece for acoustic-electric models. Filed July 29, 1968. Granted July 1, 1969.

Utility Patents from the G&L and Music Man Era (1972-1991)

3,678,795 Issued to George W. Fullerton. Neck mounting as used by G&L on guitars and basses. Filed November 15, 1971 (when Fullerton worked at Earthwood, Inc.). Granted July 25, 1972.

4,002,994 Tone control circuit with a low-impedance output. Filed January 26, 1976. Granted January 11, 1977.

4,031,799 Bridge for stringed instruments that reduces lateral vibrations. Filed January 26, 1976. Granted June 28, 1977.

4,046,050 Tapered string post for guitars. Filed February 23, 1976. Granted September 6, 1977.

4,074,606 Truss rod assembly. Filed October 20, 1976. Granted February 21, 1978.

4,220,069 Pickup for guitars. Filed January 20, 1979. Granted September 2, 1980.

4,281,576 Bridge for bass guitars. Filed October 29, 1979. Granted August 4, 1981.

4,319,510 Splitter switch for humbucking pickups. Filed May 5, 1980. Granted March 16, 1982.

4,463,648 Angled humbucking pickup for guitars. Filed May 2, 1983. Granted August 7, 1984.

4,517,874 String lock mechanism. Filed June 19, 1984. Granted May 21, 1985.

4,528,886 Guitar neck and method of construction. Filed January 14, 1983. Granted July 16, 1985.

4,581,974 Humbucking pickup with an unmagnetized, disassociated coil. Filed April 9, 1984. Granted April 15, 1986.

4,581,975 Humbucking pickup with an unmagnetized, disassociated coil (and preamp). Filed April 9, 1984. Granted April 15, 1986.

4,670,955 Method for assembling necks. Filed March 11, 1985. Granted June 9, 1987.

4,671,157 Vibrato assembly. Filed November 25, 1985. Granted June 9, 1987.

4674,389 Tuning system for vibrato guitar with string lock. Filed June 11, 1986. Granted June 23, 1987.

4,686,881 Pickup with slotted pole pieces. Filed September 30, 1985. Granted August 18, 1987.

4,724,737 Tuning system for vibrato guitar with string lock. Filed February 18, 1986. Granted February 16, 1988.

Leo Fender's Design Patents from the G&L and Music Man Era (1972-1991)

Des.256,803 Control panel for electric guitar. Filed March 6, 1978. Granted September 9, 1980.

Des.256,804 Bridge assembly for electric guitars. Filed March 6, 1978. Granted September 9, 1980.

Des.268,272 Saddle for bass guitar bridge. Filed April 18, 1980. Granted March 15, 1983.

Des.268,845 Vibrato bridge for guitars. Filed July 1, 1980. Granted May 3, 1983.

Des.269,440 Guitar bridge. Filed May 26, 1981. Granted June 21, 1983.

Des.270,544 Guitar peghead. Filed June 5, 1981. Granted September 13, 1983.

Des.280,640 Control panel for guitar. Filed May 23, 1983. Granted September 17, 1985.

Appendix 4

Dating Pre-CBS Instruments and Amplifiers

Neck date on an early Telecaster. TG stands for woodworker Tadio Gomez.

Instrument Neck and Body Dates

It is very difficult to fix the exact manufacture/completion date of a Fender instrument made before 1965 because neither the factory nor the sales office maintained records. Furthermore, original shipping invoices from the factory to Fender Sales rarely exist. As a result, collectors bent on pinpointing when certain instruments were made have turned to other clues.

Most Fenders have dates written or stamped on them: on the neck's heel and/or somewhere in the body's neck slot or pickup cavity. (On Stratocasters, another place is underneath the vibrato springs.) Moreover, many pre-1955 guitars also have a date written on masking tape, placed under the controls by the assembler. Why were the guitars dated? Not for future generations and certainly not for collectors. Each worker at Fender acted as an inspector screening mistakes, and the dates were part of the quality control program. Forrest White said that the last worker in the wood shop passed a neck or a body by dating and initialing it. If someone down the line—say, in the finish department—discovered a flaw, he could take the piece back to that person. The practice started early on, suspended only briefly in late 1959 when a customer found an obscene message under a pickguard written by some randy worker. In the 1950s Fender employees wrote in pencil. After the spring of 1962, they used an inked rubber stamp.

The very nature of the company's manufacturing procedures created a drawback for collectors trying to use neck and body dates to determine the age of an old Fender. After finishing with lacquer, the guitar's separate parts often sat on racks for weeks or months before final assembly. Workers made no effort to assemble them in any order—the first neck on a rack might have been the last one put onto a body. As a result, neck and body dates sometimes varied by a year or more. Even if they seem close together, relying on them to determine the time of final assembly could be a mistake. For instance, non-tremolo Stratocasters with

neck dates from 1954, which several collectors have noted, are not necessarily "1954 Stratocasters" (they are Stratocasters with 1954 neck dates). The records kept by Forrest White show that the factory first filled orders for non-tremolo Stratocasters in 1955—undoubtedly with necks and bodies dated earlier. (Factory inventories show that eighty non-tremolo decals were used in the last six months of 1954.) Similarly, a Broadcaster with a May 1950 neck date is not a May 1950 Broadcaster—the name did not exist yet. Still, while neck and body dates do not indicate the actual day a guitar was completed, they are important clues.

Instrument Serial Numbers

Another important clue dating an instrument is the serial number; all Fender standard guitars and basses had serial numbers (some have two—a so-called double-strike plate). The key to understanding Fender serial numbers' limitations as date indicators is that the company made its own serial number plates, with no effort to keep the numbers consecutive during stamping, deburring, and plating. As a result, workers never applied serial numbers to guitars in order—there was no reason to (and no one imagined there ever would be). Serial numbers were simply used to identify instruments. Like neck dates, they were never intended to indicate a date of manufacture.

The pre-CBS Fender company used several numbering schemes from 1946 through 1964. In the early years certain models had their own, often overlapping, sequences (it is possible, for example, to have a Broadcaster, a 1951–52 Precision Bass, and a 1954 Stratocaster with identical numbers). Generally, after mid-1954 the factory lumped all models together, thus making identical numbers very unlikely. Nevertheless, as production increased, the factory's numbering system changed several times, often in midstream. Here is a summary of the systems seen by this author and reported by reliable sources. It is meant to be a guide only, as in all fields of collecting exceptions (see the year 1957 on the chart) are not uncommon.

—Three digits stamped on the bridge. (Reportedly seen on early basses.)
—Four digits under the 6000s stamped on the bridge plate. (Seen only on 1950–54 Esquires, Broadcasters, Telecasters, and Precision Basses.)
—Four digits stamped on the Stratocaster's spring cover. (Used only on the earliest 1954 Stratocasters.)
—Four digits stamped on the heel plate. (1954–1955)
—Five digits stamped on the heel plate. (1954–1964)
—A minus sign (–) followed by five digits stamped on the heel plate. (1957–59)
—Six digits beginning with 0. (1957–58)
—An L followed by five digits (the so-called L series). (1961–65)

Serial Number/Neck Date Correlations

In the 1970s, collectors started sharing lists of serial numbers correlated with neck dates. (They put an emphasis on neck dates, perhaps because nearly all instruments have them.) The process was less than scientific. Forged dates and unintentional errors slipped into the mix, but the collecting community was nonetheless able to see patterns emerge. The lists served an important purpose: making accurate guesses easier. Since sellers rarely let a potential buyer take a guitar apart before money changes hands, buyers welcomed the information. It eliminated the need of taking a neck off in most cases, an inconvenience that could mar and lower the value of an instrument.

James Werner has compiled and circulated his list—which by now has become a collecting-industry standard—for many years. The table below, put together by Greg Gagliano from this list, is based on a January 1995 update. Only serial numbers on guitars and basses that have a complete neck date (month and year) were used. The ranges in the table represent the lowest and highest serial number for a given year. In some cases, more than one range is given per year due to an overlap in systems; see 1961 as an example. Armed with this information, a reader can use a serial number to estimate a guitar's vintage—assuming that the instrument and number are original (an accurate determination that requires years of experience examining guitars and judging facts beyond the scope of this book).

Ranges for Fender Serial Numbers by Year 1950-64

Year	Lowest Serial#	Neck Date	Highest Serial#	Neck Date
1950	0005	May 1950	2547	Nov. 1950
1951	161	Oct. 1951	860	Dec. 1951
	0043	Oct. 1951	4941	Sept. 1951
1952	546	Jan. 1952	738	Aug. 1952
	0003	March 1952	5279	May 1952
1953	0608	Feb. 1953	5097	Nov. 1953
1954	0001	June 1954	10146	Dec. 1954
1955	0585	March 1955	12842	Aug. 1955
1956	08863	April 1956	16957	Dec. 1956
1957	0819 & -17347*	April 1957	43767	April 1957
1958	02749	May 1958	79542	Aug. 1958
1959	7914	April 1959	88209	July 1959
1960	02485	Jan. 1960	91245	Aug. 1960
1961	45408	Feb. 1961	82655	Dec. 1961
	L08931	Oct. 1961	86255	Dec. 1961
1962	30405	July 1962	99817	Dec. 1962
	L00435	June 1962	L76456	Aug. 1962
1963	07489	July 1963	99802	Feb. 1963
	L00201	Feb. 1963	L84306	Nov. 1963
1964	27656	Jan. 1964	80927	Sept. 1964
	L07397	July 1964	L89643	July 1964

Amplifiers, Date Codes on Speakers

Invariably, the first question asked about a vintage Fender amp is, "When was it made?" Dating old Fender amps does not require chasing minutia such as knob type, nameplates, or handles, although mind-numbing details are compelling to most serious amp collectors. The key is learning the simple codes placed on chassis, speakers, and other components for inventory and quality control purposes at the time of manufacture. Nearly all the speakers used in early amps had a date-of-manufacture code applied by the speaker's maker. This clue that can help approximate an amp's date of manufacture. (The information here pertains to original Fender amps with original speakers.) From the late 1940s to the early 1960s most Fenders used Jensen Concert Series Alnico 5s, what collectors call "blue cap" speakers.

Jensen speaker code. The *220* stands for Jensen, while the *122* stands for the 22nd week of either 1951 or 1961.

Beginning in the early 1960s, Fender dropped Jensens and relied on Oxfords for most models (Showmans and Vibrasonics used JBLs). Eventually, Leo returned to Jensen when it started producing improved speakers that better met his expectations. In time Fender's production increased to the point where he called on other companies such as CTS and Utah for additional speakers. Still, most pre-CBS Fender amps came equipped with either Jensens or Oxfords.

Jensen, Oxford, and most other companies placed their codes—which were assigned by the Electronic Industries Association—onto the back of each speaker's frame. Jensen's company code number was 220 while Oxford's was 465. CTS was 137, Utah 328. (JBL used no number.) These codes were followed by a three-digit date code. For example, on a Jensen with the code 220843, the fourth digit *8* stands for 1958, and the fifth and sixth digits *4* and *3* stand for the 43rd week. Similarly, on an Oxford with the code 465–244, the *2* stands for 1962 while the *44* represents the 44th week.

Only one problem arises using these codes: both Jensen and Oxford repeated the numbering schemes every decade. The *1* in our pictured example could have meant either 1951 or 1961. A *2* could mean either 1952 or 1962. Fortunately, cabinet styling almost always suggests the decade in which Fender made an amp. Moreover, Jensen changed the styling of its labels. Carefully examine as many old amps as possible to learn these differences, remembering that speakers were often replaced or updated even in the early years.

Oxford speaker code. The *465* stands for Oxford, the *244* for the 44th week of 1962.

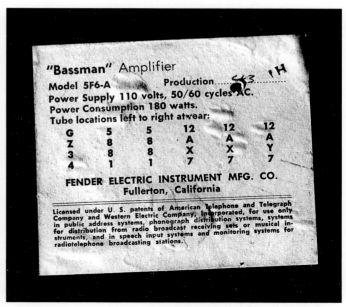

Tube chart with date IH (upper right). The *I* stands for 1959, the *H* for August.

First Letter		Second Letter	
A	1951	A	January
B	1952	B	February
C	1953	C	March
D	1954	D	April
E	1955	E	May
F	1956	F	June
G	1957	G	July
H	1958	H	August
I	1959	I	September
J	1960	J	October
K	1961	K	November
L	1962	L	December
M	1963		
N	1964		
O	1965		

How close are these speaker codes to the actual time Fender completed an amplifier? If a speaker is original, its date will always be earlier than the amp's completion date. Fender bought speakers in large quantities, but since it built so many amps, the speakers had a short stay at the factory. Unless a speaker was hidden away by accident, it sat around unused in the Fullerton plant for several months at the most. So speaker codes should suggest an amp's date of manufacture within a range of four or five months, and probably much closer.

Date Codes on Tube Charts and Chassis

Amps made after mid-1953 usually had a date code stamped onto their chassis and tube charts, which were glued inside the cabinet on self-contained units and inside the head on piggy-back models. Most amps still have the tube chart. Information here also includes the production run number, model number, and serial number. Two small letters in ink, applied with a rubber stamp, comprise the date-of-manufacture code. The first letter of the tube-chart date code stood for the year, the second letter for the month. Fender based the code on January 1951: 1951 was A, 1952 B, 1953 C, etc.; January was A, February B, March C, etc. For example, the date code CJ found on a wide-panel Deluxe shows that Fender finished the unit in October 1953. A tube chart with the code IH hails from August 1959. Here is a complete listing of the date code letter and number correlations up to 1965.

Other Clues

Certain components like capacitors and pots have date codes that resemble those found on speakers. Occasionally, tweed amps still carry a piece of masking tape from the factory signed, dated, and stuck inside the chassis. On Tolex-covered amps the date of manufacture (month and year) was often written on the inner part of the chassis in black ink. But be wary: on units returned to the service center, employees often stamped the date of servicing on the chassis, too. Again, external or cosmetic details can help the collector fix the general period of manufacture.

Appendix 5

Pre-CBS Amplifier Models and Designs

Cabinet and Chassis Style

Model	Wooden	TV Front Tweed	Wide Panel Tweed	Narrow Panel Tweed	Tolex Combo Brown Faceplate	Tolex Piggy-back Brown Faceplate	Tolex Combo Black Faceplate	Tolex Piggy-back[1] Black Faceplate
Princeton	1946–48 aka "The Student." 1–8" Essential early Fender for the collector.	1948–52 Overshadowed by the Deluxe, but looks good next to a hula lamp.	1953–55 For a guitar amp, pay for a Deluxe or a later version. Early Princetons are gutless.	1955–61 Bigger cabinet, but not much better than before.	1961–63 1–10" Tremolo. New and definitely improved: the Princeton you want to play through.		1963 Spring for the reverb model.	
Deluxe	1946–48 aka "Model 26." 1–10" Lots of crunch. The point where serious collections start.	1948–52 1–12" Weak, muddy sound that loses something.	1953–55 Starting to find a new, tighter voice and more sparkle.	1955–61 Deluxe of the stars—Neil Young, etc. You want sustain?	1961–63 Tremolo. Deluxe of Keith Richards.		1963–66 Spring for the reverb model.	
Pro	1946–48 aka "The Professional" 1–15" The sound of Jimmy Bryant.	1948–52 The sound of western swing.	1953–55 Design dated compared with Twin and Bandmaster of the same years.	–1955 / –1956–60 added presence, bass, and treble controls. Overshadowed by Twin and Bassman.	1960–63 Tremolo. Overshadowed by Vibrasonic.		1963–65 Spring for the reverb model.	
Super[2]			1952–55 2–10" Harmonics from on high. ("It's the 3/4-inch voice coils," says Don Randall.)	1955–60 Added bass, treble, and presence controls. Cognoscenti's choice.	1960–63 Tremolo. Another cool combo amp (it's hard to go wrong with a small amp from this period).			

[1] Available in smooth blonde or black. Black became standard in Aug. 1964

[2] The Super, which had a V-front cabinet until 1952, was called the Dual Professional in 1946.

Model						
Champion (Champ)[1]	—1948 Champion 800 1–8" Collectors' Holy Grail in gray tweed. —1949–52 Champion 600 1–6" Two-tone covering.	1953–55 New tweed design more attractive. Limited guitar amp.	1955–64 Rumored to be the 1980s sound of George Harrison. Just add a mike and a Stratocaster.			—1964 (Tolex-covered tweed-style cabinet) —Mid-1964–68 New-style, front-mounted treble and bass controls.
Bassman	1952 1–15" A rare amp suitable for collections, but probably not bass playing—speaker blows.	1953–54 Similar design to earlier version. Still prone to speaker failure.	—1955–56 4–10" Added bass, treble, and presence controls. —1957–60 Added midrange control Fender's ultimate amp.	Late 1960 4–10" (Rare Tolex-covered tweed-style cabinet.) Players' choice. (Sorry, it's too big for most Tokyo apartments.)	—1961 1–12" —Nov. 1961–63 2–12" An excellent guitar amp, still.	—1963–68 Spring for an earlier version. —1968 Larger, vertical speaker cabinet.
Bandmaster		1953–55 1–15" Bass and treble controls.	1955–60 3–10" Added presence control.	1960 3–10" Tremolo	—1961–62 1–12" —July 1962–63 2–12"	—1963–67 Spring for an earlier version. —1968 Larger, vertical speaker cabinet.
Twin		1952–55 2–12" 2 power tubes. Bass and treble controls.	—1955–57 Added presence control. —1958–60 4 power tubes. Added midrange. Highly sought for good reason.	—1960 Brown Tremolo 2 power tubes (as listed in ads). —1961–63 Blonde, 4 power tubes.		
Tremolux			1955–61 1–12" Tremolo. Play an accordion, go to prison.		1961–62 1–10" July 1962–63 2–10" A piggy-back with edge.	1963–66

[1] After mid-1951 in different literature, this amp was called the Champ 600, the Student 600, the Student, or the 600.

Amp				
Harvard	1955–61 1–10" Just another Ivy-League Fender. Where's the Yale?			
Vibrolux	1956–61 1–10" Tremolo.	1961–63 1–12" Now has 6L6GCs, a step above the Deluxe in power.	1963–64 A short-lived amp.	
Concert		1960–63 4–10" Tremolo. Why do these amps make low E strings so loud?	1963–65 Super Reverb is a better choice.	
Vibrasonic		1959–63 1–15" JBL Tremolo. Popular studio amp in the early days—you too can capture the teenage sound!		
Showman 12"		1960–63 1–12" JBL Tremolo. Dick Dale says that the first ones had brown cabinets.	1963–66	
Showman 15"		1961–63 1–15" JBL Tremolo.	1963–68	
Dual Showman		1962–63 by special order: 2–15" JBLs. aka "the Double Showman" (but faceplate still reads Showman). This amp shreds.	–1963–67	–1968 Larger, vertical speaker cabinet. Power-to-the-people styling never fit Fender's image.
Vibroverb		1963 2–10" Tremolo/Reverb Choice of collectors and players.	1963–64 1–15" Tremolo/Reverb The sound of Stevie Ray Vaughan.	

Model	Years	Speakers	Features	Notes
Twin Reverb	1963–68	2–12"	Tremolo/Reverb	Leo's choice.
Super Reverb	1963–68	4–10"	Tremolo/Reverb	Popular, but has same problem as the Concert Amp.
Deluxe Reverb	1963–68	1–12"	Tremolo/Reverb	Late-1960s studio standard.
Vibro Champ	1964–68	1–8"	Tremolo	
Princeton Reverb	1964–68	1–10"	Tremolo/Reverb	Studio standard; prime for mods.
Vibrolux Reverb	1964–68	2–10"	Tremolo/Reverb	Poor man's brown Vibroverb.
Pro Reverb	1965–68	2–12"	Tremolo/Reverb	A best buy, until everyone reads this.

General Notes: This chart is not intended to show all variations in amps. Power ratings vary even in otherwise identical models, so the author has chosen not to include them.

Index

Abbott, Clifton T., 20
Acoustic-electric guitars, 2. *See also*
     Electric guitars
     feedback problems with, 63–64
     tuning on, 64
Acoustic stand-up bass, 100
Acuff, Roy, 18, 157 fig
Acuff Museum, 18
Adams-Camel machine shop, 14
Aldrich, Charlie, 75 fig, 139 fig
Allen, Richard C., 120
American Guild of Banjoists,
     Mandolinists, and Guitarists, 60
American Record Corporation, 246
Amicay, George, 262 cap
Amplifiers, 2, 7 fig. *See also* Fender
     amplifiers
     early, 11
     early K&F, 24
     Leo's test, 35 fig
     music theatrics and, 255
     6-string guitar plus, 14
Anglin, Jack, 157 fig
Arthur D. Little, Inc., 246
     excerpt from report prepared for CBS,
          247–248
Asbestos, use of, 34
Asia, guitar industry in, 260
Atkins, Chet, 143 fig

Bakelite, 15
Bakelite Spanish guitar, 15, 61–62
Bakelite steel guitar, 61–62
Baker, Mickey, 176
Baldwin Piano Company, efforts to
     purchase Fender, 246
Ball, Ernie, 271
Banjoline, 237 fig
Barnard, Junior, 46
Barth, Paul, 14, 15
Bass guitars, pre-Fender, 100–101
Bates, Art, 147, 255 fig
Beach Boys, 206 fig
Beauchamp, George D., 14 fig, 48, 61
Beck, Jeff, 92 fig
Behymer, Glen, 152
Bertrand, Eddie, 212, 241 fig
Big Band era, peak of, 45
Bigsby, Paul A., 157–158, 36, 95–97
Bigsby/Travis guitar, 96–97
Bigsby steels, 157
Bigsby vibrato tailpiece, 121–122,
     129 fig
Blanda, George E., Jr., 261
Body truss, 224
Boggs, Noel, 21–22, 35, 48, 50, 52, 116,
     117, 123 fig, 251 fig
     and pedal steels, 158
Bogle, Bob, 177
Bridges
     Fender patent drawings, 269 fig
     on Fender standards, 94
     floating, 173
     G&L, 275
     Gibson Tune-O-Matic, 123
     on Jazzmaster, 172 fig
     six-piece, 132–133
     on Stratocaster, 132–133
     on Stringmaster, 120

British Invasion, electric guitar sales and,
     246
Broadkaster banjos, 86–87
Bryant, Jimmy, 36
     12-string guitar, 231
     at new factory, 123 fig
     and Stratocaster, 120
Buchanan, Roy, 93 fig
Burton, James, 136 fig, 159, 193 cap, 88
     and Vibrasonic, 195
Buzz Bazzell and his Cowboys, 1
Bye Bye Birdie, 212
Byrd, Billy, 129 fig, 157 fig
Byrd, Jerry, and Fender acoustic, 226 fig

California
     in 1930s and early 1940s, 10
     steel guitar innovations in, 22
Campbell, Glen, 231
Carlton, Larry, 240 fig
     acoustic electrics of, 271
Carson, Bill, 255 fig
     as Fender musical consultant, 116
     and Stratocaster, 127, 128
     and vibrato, 130
Carter, Walter, 275
Carver, Jody, 39, 85, 120, 136 fig, 185–186,
     187 fig
     at CBS-Fender, 250
     and pedal steels, 158
CBS/Columbia Group, 252–253
CBS
     other musical instrument company
          purchases, 259
     purchase of Fender companies, 246–247
     purchase of Fender-Rhodes, Inc., 236
CBS-Fender, 249
     catalogs, 259
          1965, 249 fig
          1982, 260 fig
     corporate reorganization, 259–260
     factory atmosphere, 251
     Fender Bender, 251
     Fender Coronado acoustic-electric,
          252 fig
     Fender Fantasy, 254 fig
     group of guitars, 256 fig
     Leo at, 250–251
     Maurader guitar, 249 fig, 254 fig
     Model S125 amp, 253 fig
     Mustang Bass, 251
     new factory, 258 figs
     production errors, 252–253
     promoting Fender products, 249
     prototype bass, 254 fig
     quality control at, 259
     Reverb amp, 253 fig
     sale of, 260
     salesmen's commissions, 255
     Starcaster, 271
     Stratocaster, 252 fig, 259
     transistor amps, 253–254
     5-string bass, 254 fig
Chalker, Curly, 151
Challengers, 241 fig
Chambers, Bud, 194 fig
Champs, The, 196
Chewning, Lloyd, 182 fig, 283 fig
Chicago Musical Instruments (CMI), 41

Christian, Charlie, 45
Clapton, Eric, 92 fig
Clark, Charlie, 144
CLF Research, 251, 268
Cliffie Stone's Western Stars, 62
CMI. *See* Chicago Musical Instruments
Cohen, Paul, 157 fig
Cole, Bernice, 148 fig
Cole, Mike, 85–86, 148 fig, 185
     Broadcaster trademark problems
          and, 87
     death, 250
     financial success of, 94
Columbia Broadcasting System. *See* CBS
Compton, Stanley, 185
     and Fender advertising, 169
Consolidated Ice and Storage Company, 7
Contours
     on Stratocaster, 126, 128–129
Cooley, Spade, 48, 62
Country Music Association President's
     Award, to Leo in 1965, 250 fig
Crayton, Pee Wee, 139 fig
Crazy Horse Saloon, 5
Crooks, Bob, 195
Cucci, Johnny, 136 fig
Custom Shop, 261–265
     Bajo Sexto baritone Telecaster, 264
     Classic Series, 263
     Egyptian Telecaster Custom, 262 fig
     first, 265 fig
     Harley-Davidson Stratocasters, 264 fig
     Signature Series, 263
     Stratocaster, 261 fig
     Telecaster, Hawaiian theme, 265 fig
     Telecoustic, 265 fig
     Yngwie Malmsteen model, 262

Dale, Dick, 136, 206 fig
     as consultant, 196–197
     and Fender amps, 218–219
     Fender spokesman, 212
Dalley, Robert J., 212
Dallmeir, Paul, 51 fig
Danelectro, 207, 209
Daniel, Nat, 207
Davis, Clive, 246
Dayton, Bob, 147
Defense Production Act, 82
Desert Rose Band, 5
Detachable necks. *See* Necks, Detachable
Dies, 23
DiMarzio humbuckers, 263
Dinnerbell Roundup, 62
Direct String Pickup, 18, 21
     on Deluxe model, 49
     design of, 38–39
     on double-neck guitars, 52
     on early K&F guitars, 24
     on triple-neck guitars, 52
Distortion
     even-harmonic, 255
     popularized, 160
Distributors, musical instrument, 41.
     See also Fender Sales, Inc.; Radio-Tel
Dobro
     fretted acoustic basses, 102
     guitars, 61
Doghouse. *See* Acoustic stand-up bass

Dopyera, John, 22, 61
Dopyera, Robert, 102 fig
Dopyera, Rudolph, 102 fig
Douglas, Jack, 42
Douglas Aircraft, 16
Driver, David K., 43–44, 52, 147
    and Esquire, 80
    Broadcaster trademark problems and,
        87
    financial success of, 94
    first standard guitar sample, 74
Dual-pickup blend control, wiring diagram
    for, 84 fig
Dunn, Bob, 21
Duran, Loana, 238 fig
Dylan, Bob, 257 fig

Eddie and the Showmen, 240 fig, 241 fig
Eddie Miller Band, 71 fig
Eddy, Duane, 209
Electric bass guitar, 1
Electric guitars. See also Acoustic-electric
        guitars
    early, 61–62
    Fender-improved, 62–65
    first, 3
Electric pianos, Harold Rhodes, 1
Electro String Instrument Corporation,
        14–16
    first electric basses, 100–101
    guitar manufacturing, 61–62
    purchase by F. C. Hall, 115
Emmons, Buddie, 118 fig, 194 fig
English, John, 265 cap
Epiphone
    De Luxe Regent, 62
    double-8-string-neck guitar, 50
European market, Fender distribution to,
        186 fig

Farlow, Tal, 177 fig
Feather, Leonard, 99
Feedback, on acoustic-electric guitars,
        63–64
Fender, Clarence Leonidas. See Fender, Leo
Fender, Leo, 148 fig, 194 fig
    age 14, 4 fig
    Arthur D. Little report on, 247
    assistant for, 116–118
    and Bigsby/Travis guitar, 96–97
    boating, 250
    at CBS-Fender, 250–251
    concept of tone, 65
    Country Music Association President's
        Award, 1965, 250 fig
    death and funeral, 284
    disparaging old Fender instruments,
        279–280
    and Don Randall
        working relationship with, 147, 148
    early 1970s, 12 fig
    early life, 5–6
    eccentricities, 238
    electronics as hobby, 7
    and Fender acoustic, 226 fig
    and Fender Sales, Inc., 114–116
    financial problems of, 31–32, 56
    financial success of, 107

first and last guitar, 284 fig
first repair shop, 8
as Fullerton, CA's Grand Marshal of
        Founder's Day Parade, 275–276
full ownership of G&L, 277
G&L promo, 271 fig
G&L research methods, 272
Hall's mortgage to, 112, 32
health concerns, 243, 282
high school years, 7
historical inaccuracy of, 127–128
honored by Fullerton, CA, 276–277
improving electric guitar design, 62–65
influence on musicians, 3
insecurity of, 172, 245
instrument design of, 1
July 1977, 269 fig
laboratory, 154 fig
lack of attention to music changes,
        274
lack of nostalgia, 278–279
loss of eye, 6–7
mid-1960s, 244 fig
musical instrument interest, 11
and musicians, less consultation of,
        176–177
and Music Man guitar, 266 fig
1950, 84 fig
1957, 172 fig
photography hobby, 77
poor business sense, 237
post-CBS-Fender innovations, 251
post-college years, 7–8
pride, 155
radio repair, 7
and rock and roll, 167–168
sale offer to Randall, 245
saxaphone playing, 7
and West, Speedy, 256 fig
Fender, Phyllis M., 283 fig, 284
Fender, post-CBS. See also Custom Shop
    new U.S. factory, 260–261
    promotion of, 283
Fender acoustic guitar, 223
    brochure, 226
    Classic, 226
    Concert, 224, 225 fig
    Folk guitar, 226
    King, 224
    patent drawing of, 225 fig
    production of, 223–224
Fender advertising. See Fender Sales, Inc.,
        advertising
Fender amplifiers
    Bandmaster, 111, 218 fig
        piggy-back, 195 fig, 196, 205 fig
        Tolex-covered, 195 fig
    Bassman, 105 fig, 106, 198 fig, 218 fig
        4–10, 150–151, 160 fig
        Model 5E6-A, 159–160
        piggy-back, 195, 196, 205 fig
    blackface, 217–218
    building, 220–221 figs
    with built-in reverb, 216–219
    Champ Amp, 153, 216, 219 fig
    Champion 600, 49, 55, 57 fig, 105 fig
    Champion 800, 55
    combo amps, design patent, 193 fig
    Concert, 195
        piggy-back, 208 fig

Deluxe, 216
    TV-front, 55, 56 fig
    wide-panel, 113 fig
Deluxe Reverb, 218 fig
development of, 193
Dual Professional, 36–38, 37 fig
Dual Showman, 219 fig
early defects in, 34
early design of, 35–36
early wooden, 33 fig
first, 36
first tweed, 36–38
as industry leaders, 193–194
Model 26, 33 fig, 36
narrow-panel, 149–151
piggy-back, 195–196
popularity with teenagers, 197–198
Princeton, 33 fig, 36, 57 fig, 197 fig
    TV-front, 55
Princeton Reverb, 216, 218 fig
production process, 199 fig
Professional, 160, 217, 36
    TV-front, 55
    wide-panel, 115 fig
Pro Reverb, 217–218, 219 fig
quality control, 194
Showman, 196 fig
    piggy-back, 205 fig
sound of, 35
Super, 38
Super Amps, 217
Super Reverb, 217, 219 fig
termite infestation of, 31
Tolex-covered, 195–199
treble and bass controls, 111–112
Tremolux
    piggy-back, 196, 205 fig
    TV-front, 55–56
Twin Amp, 112, 150 fig, 160
    prototype, 110
Twin Reverb, 217 fig
Vibrasonic, 193 fig, 195, 195 fig
Vibro-Champ, 219 fig
Vibrolux, 218
Vibrolux Reverb, 218, 219 fig
Vibroverb, 216 fig, 216–218
walnut wood for, 30–31
wide-panel, 110–112
wiring chassis, 112 fig
Fender bass, 100
Fender Bass Guitar. See Fender electric
    basses, Bass VI
Fender Bender, 251
Fender Ecco-Fonic, 197
Fender electric basses
    Bass VI, 208 fig, 208–209, 209 fig
        tone of, 209
    Jazz Bass, 185 fig, 203–204
        prototype, 194 fig, 203 fig
    Precision Bass, 99–100, 145 fig,
        170 fig
        body design, 104
        design patent, 104 fig
        promoting, 104–106
        redesigning, 145, 150, 160–163
    prototype, 103
Fender Electric Instrument Company,
        38
    backdoor sales, 81–82, 113
    brochure, 1953, 111 fig

Fender Electric Instrument Company
    (continued)
    catalogs
        1947, 32–33 fig
        1948, 43 fig
        1949, 52 fig
        1950, 78 fig
        1952, 1953, 1954, 115 fig
        1954, 138 fig
        1956, 149 fig
        1957–58, 162 fig
        1958–59, 165 fig
        1960, 185 fig, 192 fig, 203 fig
        1961, 205 fig
        1962, 207 fig
        1963, 217 fig
        1964, 230 fig
    cinderblock factory, 74–75
    distribution for, 41–44. *See also*
        Radio-Tel; Fender Sales, Inc.
        changing, 114
    East Coast image, 106–107
    environment for early success, 44–48
    expansion of, 154
    factory, 108 fig
        1959, 176 fig
    factory scenes, 113 fig
    fretting necks, 90 fig
    guitar production at, 259 figs
    men's bowling team, 182 fig
    new factory, 124–125 figs
    prices, 232
        1950, 79
        1954, 145
        1964, 230
    producing standard guitars, 91 fig
    production of instrument family,
        102–103
    production problems
        on Esquire, 82
        and Forrest White, 142
    relationship with Radio-Tel, 109
    reorganizing, 143–145
    sale of, 245–247
    second decade of, 148
    women's bowling team, 183 fig
Fender electric mandolin, 156, 156 fig
Fender electric violin, 180 fig, 180–181
Fender, Esther, 8 fig
Fender Facts, first six editions of, 238 fig
Fender guitars
    beginning of, 7 fig
    early defects in, 34
    evolution of, 279
    finish, 162 fig
        custom colors, 163–164
    finishes, 137–138, 228
        Burgundy Mist, 210 fig
        Color Selection Chart, 202
        Telecaster and Esquire Customs,
            191
    first, 18–20
        neck-through-body design, 18 fig
    popularity of, 3
    step-up program, 149
    student models, 152–154
Fender Japan, 260
Fender logos
    official sheet, 1960s, 201 fig
    variety of, 200 fig

Fender Manufacturing Company, 30
    early problems of, 31–32
    early production problems, 34
    unsafe working conditions at, 34–35
Fender Musical Instruments
        Corporation, 3
Fender mute, patent diagram for, 213 fig
Fender Nervous Center, 186
Fender Radio Service, 8–9
    Dale Hyatt ownership of, 81–28
    Doc Kauffman and, 16
    newspaper ad from, 1 fig
Fender reverb, 197
Fender-Rhodes, Inc., 235
    purchase of by CBS, 236, 256–247
Fender-Rhodes pianos, 234 fig, 235–236,
        236 fig
    Celeste, 236 fig
    Contempo Organ, 236 fig
    design diagram for, 235 fig
    Piano Bass, 234 fig, 236, 236 fig
Fender Sales, Inc., 114–116
    advertising, 166 fig
        Bob Perine and, 169–170
        and Fender headstock design, 215 fig
        pre-1957, 169
        unused photos from, 214 fig
        You Won't Part with Yours Either
            series, 170, 178–179 figs, 246 fig
    customer service, 185–186
    distribution to European market,
        186 fig
    East Coast office, 185–186
    sale of, 245–247
    salesmen's commissions, 255
    Santa Ana office, 184 fig
    transitions at, 151–152
    warehouse, 173 fig
Fender Sales, Inc. of Oklahoma, 185
Fender Sales imbroglio, 152
Fender solidbody guitars. *See* Fender
        standard guitars
Fender standard guitar, 64
    Broadcaster, 82 fig, 84, 94 fig
        #0005, 83
        promotion of, 86
        prototype, 67 fig
        renaming, 87
        trademark problems of, 86–87
    cosmetic changes to, 1950–1955,
        93–94
    Duo-Sonic, 152–153, 230
    Electric XII
        design, 232
        prototype, 231 fig, 232 fig, 233 figs
    Esquire, 58 fig, 72 fig
        #0013, 81 fig
        and Bigsby/Travis guitar, 97
        dual-pickup, 75–77, 80 fig
        early success of, 84
        later design, 191–192
        neck problems, 82
        non-truss rod, 76 fig
        pickup problems, 82
        production delays, 79–82
        production problems, 82
        promotion of, 78–82
        prototype, 67 fig, 73
        single-pickup, 73–75
    Esquire Custom, 188–191

Jaguar, 207 fig, 208 fig, 210 fig, 211 fig,
        211–212, 219 fig
    testing, 213 fig
Jazzmaster, 171 fig, 171–172
    circuitry on, 173
    design of, 173–174
    patent diagrams, 175 fig
    popularity of, 177
    producing, 182–183 figs
    sound of, 176
    v. Stratocaster vibrato, 130
    test guitars, 175–176
Musicmaster, 152–153, 230, 230 fig
Mustang, 228–229, 229 figs
neck problems, 78–79
No-caster, 88
prototypes, 66–71
    second, 70 fig
Stratocaster, 2, 120–123
    #0100, 134 fig, 135 fig
    bridges on, 132–133
    contours on, 126, 128–129
    design of, 128
    early, 133 fig
    fingerboard analysis of, 279
    first ad for, 138 fig
    full-scale production of, 145
    historical dominance of, 265
    introducing, 138–139
    manufacture of, 136–137
    Mary Kaye, 162 fig, 163
    1954 catalog description, 141 fig
    original decal, 202
    patent diagram, 131 fig
    pickguards on, 139
    pickups on, 133–135
    prototype, 129 fig, 132 fig
    prototype 1959, 192
    prototype switch and controls,
        135
    see-through Lucite, 170 fig
    servicing, 137
    switch, 135–136
    tone of, 135–136
    with vibrato, 141 fig
    without vibrato, 141 fig
    vibrato on, 129–132
student, 152–153
Telecaster, 2, 176
    Bigsby vibrato tailpiece for,
        121–122
    case, 105 fig
    with Deluxe amp, 93 fig
    design patent, 89 fig
    G&L efforts toward, 282
    golden era of, 88–94
    historical dominance of, 265
    introduction of, 87–88
    later design, 191–192
    neck of, 88–92
    obsolescing, 121
    official wiring diagram, 89 fig
    pickups on, 133, 94
    prototype, 67 fig
    wiring of, 88
Telecaster Custom, 188–191
    bodies, 189 fig
tone of, 65
tools to make, 69
truss rods included on, 83–84

Fender steel guitars
    Champion, 49–50
    Champ set, 153
    Custom Triple-Neck, 52, 115 fig
    Deluxe model, 33, 34
        8-string single-neck, 49
        pickup on, 39 fig
    Deluxe set, 153
    double-neck, 50–52
        first, 51 fig
    Dual Eight Professional Steel, 52
    Dual Six Professional, 119–120
    early, 28
    early single-neck, 32–34
    Fender 1000, 158–159, 194 fig
    Fender 2000, 237–238
    Fender 400, 158–159
    Fender 800, 237–238
    Organ Button Model, 32–34, 33 fig
        pickup on, 39
    pedal, 157–159
    Princeton model, 34
    Stringmaster, 117 fig, 118–120
        Leon McAuliffe's, 164 fig
    student, 153
    Student Steel, 49
    White model, 153
Fingerboards
    rosewood, 188–191
    slab, 190
Floyd Rose locking nuts, 274
Fluff, 65
Frances, Kay, 40 fig
Fretted electric bass, concept of, 101–102
Fretted Instrument News, The, 60
Fretts, covers, 201 fig
Frost, Al, 78
Fuji Gen-Gakki, 260
Fullerton, CA
    honoring Leo, 276–277
    Leo as Grand Marshal of Founder's Day
        Parade, 275–276
Fullerton, California, Fender's early life
    in, 5–6
Fullerton, Fred, 53 fig
Fullerton, George, 96, 128 fig, 194 fig, 66,
    113 fig
    at CBS-Fender, 267
    at CLF Research, 268–269
    and G&L Musical Products, 271–275
    G&L promo, 271 fig
    health, 277
    and jack plate, 137
    and P-T neck adjustment
    selling G&L stock, 277
    testing Stratocaster, 140 fig
    and vibrato, 130
Fullerton City Hall, dedication of, 9 fig
Fullerton Museum Center's Fender exhibit,
    240 fig
Fulton, Robert, 62

G&L Musical Products, 271–275
    advertising, 281 fig
    ASAT, 282
        commemorative model, 283 fig
    ASAT Classic, 282
    Broadcaster, 282
    bridge, 275 fig

Cavalier, 272 fig
    patent diagram for pickup, 273 fig
conflict over future of, 277
efforts toward Telecaster, 282
F-100, 273
F-100 II, 277
first brochure, 273 fig
G-200, 274 fig
guitar designs, 274
    early, 275
Interceptor, 280 fig
L-2000, 280 fig
L-5000, 280 fig
L-5000 bass, 272
Nighthawk, 279 fig
pickups, 272, 273 fig, 281 fig
S-500, 275 fig
SB-series basses, 277 fig
SC-1, 277 fig
SC-2, 277 fig
SC-3, 277 fig
vibrato, 274
visitors to, 272–274
Gallion, Rex, 126, 129
    as Fender musical consultant, 130
Gallion Brothers, 101
Garage bands, Jazzmaster and, 177
Garland, Judy. See Gumm, Frances
Garriott, Hugh, 68 fig
Gene Vincent and the Bluecaps, 167 fig, 175
Gibson
    400CESN, 171
    ad, 173 fig
    bass efforts, 100
    Electraharp, 157
    ES-300 acoustic electric model, 73
    ES-335, 271
    ES-350 acoustic-electric model, 73
    F-5 mandolin, 62
    high-end guitars, 171
    L-5 guitar, 62
    Les Paul Model, 122–123
    Les Paul series, 211
    Mando-bass, 101–102
    RD Custom, 271
    RD Standard, 271
    six-piece bridges, 132–133
    triple-pickup ES-5, 134–135, 73
    Tune-O-Matic bridge, 123, 133
Gillespie, Joe, 148 fig
Godfrey, Arthur, 109
Goodyear Aircraft Company, 143
Graham, Orville, 147
Gretsch Manufacturing Company, 86–87
    Committee models, 271
Gruhn, George, 275
Guitar
    image of
        changing, 59–61
        early, 59
    rise in popularity of, 44–48
    traditional manufacturing of, 60–61
    12-string, popularity of, 231–232
Guitar collecting, 278
Guitar industry
    in Asia, 260
    growth of, 109–110
    rock and roll changing, 243
Guitarists, playing sitting v. standing,
    174–175

Guitar straps, 175
Gumm, Frances, 14

Hall, Francis Cary
    early life of, 26
    and Electro String purchase, 115
    as Fender competition, 115
    Fender nationwide sales effort, 38
    and Fender Sales, Inc., 114–116
        ousted from, 152
    grievances with Leo, 112–113
    mortgage to Leo, 32, 112
    at 1956 trade show, 26 fig
    and Radio-Tel, 26–27
Hall, Jim, 177 fig
    and Jazzmaster, 176–177
Hall's Radio Service, Radio and Television
    Equipment Company. See Radio-Tel
Hammond Organ Company, reverberation
    and, 197
Hampton, Lionel, 99, 103
Harbridge House, 246
Harmonicats, 112 fig
Harmony, Regal guitars, 187 fig
Harmony Homestead, 62
Harrison, George, 209, 231
Hawiian guitar. See Steel guitar
Hawiian playing, 2
Hayes, Charles R., 42–43, 71 fig
    death of, 152
    Esquire samples, 74
    and Fender Sales, Inc., 114–116
    and Fender Spanish guitar, 63–64
    financial success of, 94
    and first Fender standard, 70
Hayes band instruments, 115
Hayzlett, Elizabeth Nagel, 77
Heathkit voltage meter, 117
Hendrix, Jimi, 252 cap, 257 fig
Henri, Shifte, 106
Hines, Bob, 71 fig
Hopper, Slim, 14 fig
Hospitality Night, 1
Humbuckers, DiMarzio, 263
Hyatt, Dale, 147, 28, 30, 31, 32, 38
    and double-neck steels, 50
    Esquire promotion, 81–82
    and first Fender standard, 70
    and G&L Musical Products, 271–275,
        277, 280–282
    G&L promo, 271 fig
    ownership of Fender Radio Service,
        81–82
    at Randall Instruments, 267
Hytron Radio and Electronics, 252

IGL. See International Guitar League
    Festival
Independent jobbers, 41
International Guitar League Festival
    1949, 69
    1950, 79
Intonation, 64–65
    of Stratocaster, 135
Isaacs, Bud, 157
Iwanade, Yasuhiko, 279
Jack plate, on Stratocaster and Telecaster,
    137

Jackson, Shot, 157 fig
Jagger, Mick, 212
Japan, guitar industry in, 260
JBL speakers, 195
Jensen speakers, 198–199
　　P10R , 150
Johnson, Laura, 7
Johnson, Robert, 59
Johnson, Roy, 99, 103
Johnson, Waldo, 7
Jordanaires, 169 fig
Jorgenson, John, 5

K&F Manufacturing Corporation
　　amplifiers, 23 fig
　　early amplifiers of, 24
　　formation of, 20–21
　　full production at, 24
　　guitar production, 22–23
　　lap steel and amp sets, 20 fig
　　logo plate, 22 fig
　　punch press operation, 23
　　Radio-Tel distributing for, 28
　　record changers, 20 fig
　　　selling, 22
K&F steel guitars
　　differences in, 25 fig
　　pickups on early, 21
　　pine-bodied crinkle-paint, 24
Kahler vibratos. See Vibratos, Kahler
Kanda Shokai, 260
Karch, Hank, 60
Kauffman, Clayton Orr. See Kauffman,
　　Doc
Kauffman, Doc, 11, 84 fig
　　and double-neck steels, 50
　　early 1970s, 12 fig
　　early life, 13
　　and Fender Radio Service, 16
　　leaving K&F, 28
　　making electric steel guitars, 16
　　Vibratone guitars, 15–16
　　Vibrola, 14–16
Kauffman Fix-It Shop, 16
Kaye, Mary, 163
Kelleher, John M., 103
Kleinow, Sneaky Pete, 238
Klosky, Esther, 8 See also Esther Fender
Kluson SafeTiString posts, 70
Koefer, Bob, 47
Koladish, Mike. See Cole, Mike
Kroo, Alex, 186

Lanham, Roy, 176
Lap steel guitar, 18
Lawrence Welk's Orchestra, 156
Lazzareschi, Carla, 283
Leadbelly, 231
Ledbetter, Ted, 182 fig
Lemmon, Jack, 139 fig
Levy, Jack, 41
Liberace, George, 145 fig
　　and Fender electric violin, 181 fig
Life magazine, entertainment issue, 167
Lisp, 136
Little, Big Tiny, 208 fig
Loar, Lloyd, 62
　　electric bass viol, 100

Lorenz, John, 246
Loudspeakers, redesign of, 36
Lyons, Darrell, 40 fig

Magnetic Field Design, 272
Mandrell, Barbara, 237 fig
Mann, George, 223
Manners, Bob, 145 fig
Manzarek, Ray, 236
Maphis, Joe, 214 fig
Maphis, Rose Lee, 214 fig
Marshall, Kathy, 212, 240 fig
Martin, converted 000–18 model, 63 fig
Mary Kay Trio, 163
Maryland, Art, 164 fig
Massie, Ray, 24, 28 fig, 35
　　and double-neck steels, 50
Massie Electronics, 24
McAuliffe, Leon, 21–22, 35, 51 fig, 52,
　　117 fig, 120 fig
　　and pedal steels, 158
McCarty, Ted, 123
McCord, J. Fred, 148 fig, 43, 50, 71 fig
McCord, Nita, 148 fig
McCord's Music, 43
McLaren, John, 259–260, 283 fig
Meeks, Johnny, 167 fig
Merrill, Buddy, 136 fig, 168 fig, 176
Merrill Lynch, 246
Midrange dip, 36
Miller, Eddie, 71 fig, 84 fig
Montgomery, Monk, 251 fig, 98 fig
Montgomery, Wes, 225 fig
Mooney, Ralph, 159
Moore, Oscar, 103
Moore, Scotty, 46
Moore, Tiny, 48
Morgan, Bud, 182 fig
Morris, Robert C., 69
Murphey, Joaquin, 157
Musical instruments, families of
　　distinctive, 102–103
Musicians. See also Guitarists
　　demonstrations to, 47–48
　　endorsements in post-1957 ads, 170
Music Man
　　basses, 270
　　business problems, 271
　　designs, 270–271
　　guitar, 266 fig
　　literature, 270 fig
　　Sabre guitars, 270
　　Sting Ray I, 270 fig
Myers, Dave, 212

NAMM show. See National Association of
　　Music Merchants show
National Association of Music Merchants
　　show
　　1949, 69
　　1950, 78
　　1963, 223
　　1967, 234 fig
National Music Association (NMA), 148
National String Instrument Corporation,
　　14, 61
　　Aristocrat model, 73
　　Electra-Chord, 157

Nat King Cole Trio, 103 fig
Necks
　　detachable, 66
　　Fender, 215 fig
　　on Fender bass, 103
　　for G&L ASAT and Broadcaster, 282
　　on Jaguar, 211
　　maple, 257 cap
　　on Mustang, 228
　　problems on Esquire, 82
　　problems on Fender standards, 78–79
　　on Stratocaster, 129–132
　　of Telecaster, 88–92
Nelson, Ricky, 88
New York Yankees, 246
Nixon, Richard M., 276
NMA. See National Music Association
Northwest, early Fender sales in, 44
Nova, band instruments, 115
Novak, Kim, 139 fig

Oahu Publishing Company, 43
Offset-Humbucker pickups, 272 fig
Opunui, Charlie, 145 fig
Orange County Teenage Fair, 1968, 253 fig
Osbrink, R. H., 235
Owens, Buck, 151, 188 fig
　　and Telecasters, 188
Owens, Harry, 117
Oxford speakers, 198–199

Pacific Music Supply, 22
Page, Jimmy, 232, 92 fig
Page, John, 261–262, 264, 265, 265 fig
Paley, William S., 246
Pass, Joe, 176
Patton, Don, 147, 69, 79
　　and Esquire, 80–81
Paul, Les, 64 fig
Peabody, Eddie, 237 fig
Pearson, Jesse, 212
Pearson, Robert D., 87
Perine, Robert, 169 fig, 205 fig
　　Fender ads by, 166 fig
　　and Fender advertising, 169–170
　　and Fender logo, 200–201
　　and Jazzmaster, 176–177
Perine/Jacoby agency, 160
Phoenix, 261 fig
Philco Cobra automatic record changer,
　　upgrading, 8
Pianos. See Fender-Rhodes pianos
Pick-click, 18
Pickguards
　　Fender standards, 94
　　Precision Bass, 104
　　Stratocaster, 139
Pickup coils, 15
Pickups. See also Direct String Pickup;
　　Offset Humbucker pickups
　　on Champion guitar, 50
　　coil on, 18
　　for early Fender standards, 68
　　on early Fender steels, 34
　　on early K&F steel guitars, 21
　　on electric basses, 100–101
　　Fender's multi-pole, 155 fig
　　Fender designs, 193

on Fender electric violin, 181
on first Fender, 18–20
G&L, 272, 273 fig, 281 fig
humbucker, 270
on Jaguar, 211
multi-pole
on Jazz Bass, 203, 204 fig
on Precision Bass, redesigning, 150
problems on Esquire, 82
and steel guitar bodies, 22
on Stratocaster, 133–135
on Stringmaster, 119 fig
on Telecaster, 94
problems with, 133
Popular music
historic rise of guitar, 44–45
late World War II, 45–48
Pre-CBS, 259
Precision-Tilt (P-T) neck adjustment, 275
Pre-Piano, 235
P-T neck adjustment. See Precision-Tilt
neck adjustment
Push-button Arthur Godfrey automatic
chord maker, 109

R.T.E.C. See Radio-Tel
Race & Olmsted, 69
Race, Lyman, 157 fig
Radio-Tel, 26
credit department, 43
distribution of cheap acoustic guitars,
223
as distributor
for Fender, 31
for Fender, problems, 112–114
for K&F, 28
Don Randall and, 27
establishing on East Coast, 84–86
Musical Instrument Division, 38
promoting single-pickup Esquire, 74
relationship with Fender Electric
Instrument Company, 109
sales effort in 1949, 69
salesmen for, 41–44
sample instruments, 71
unfilled Fender orders, 78–82, 112
Radiotron Designer's Handbook, 35
Rancho Revelers, 102 fig
Randall, Don, 148 fig
Randall, Donald D., 118 fig, 255 fig
and army, 26–27
Arthur D. Little report on, 247
and Bigsby/Travis guitar, 97
at CBS/Columbia Group, 252
early life, 10
and Esquire, 73
and Fender advertising, 169
Fender nationwide sales effort, 38
and Fender Sales, Inc., 114–116
and Fender sales organization, 147
in Germany, 186 fig
and K&F steels and amps, 27–28
Leo's sale offer to, 245
and Leo Fender, 11, 26
working relationship with, 147, 148
October 1968, 244 fig
personal qualities, 147–148
position at CBS-Fender, 249–250
promoting Esquire, 79–80

Radio-Tel's sales effort, 69
resignation of, 255
and standard guitar neck problems,
78–79
Randall Instruments, 194, 267
Randall Publishing Company, Inc., 148
Ray, Wade, 107 fig
Reed, Howard, 175 fig
Regal
electric bass, 101
Multivox, 157
Remington, Herb, 50, 51 fig
Rey, Alvino, 45, 47, 118 fig
and Jazzmaster, 176
and pedal steels, 158
Rhodes, Harold, 234 fig, 234–235
Rich, Don, and Telecasters, 188
Richards, Keith, 1
Rickenbacher guitars. See Rickenbacker
guitars
Rickenbacher, Adolph, 14
Rickenbacher, Eddie, 14
Rickenbacker guitars
detachable necks on, 66
electric bass, 100 fig, 100–101
F. C. Hall and, 115, 26
Vibrola and, 14–15
Rivera, Raul Garcia, 152
Roberts, Howard, 176
Rock and roll
changing guitar industry, 243
Fender's success and, 138
impact of Fender on, 167–168
Life review, 167
Rodgers, Jimmie, 21
Rodriguez, John, 283 fig
Rooftop Singers, 231
Rosenthal, Charlie, 255 fig
Rosewood fingerboards, 188–191
Rossmeisl, Roger, 223, 225 fig
loan from Leo, 268
Roundup Time, 62
Russo, Don, 185

Salesman. See Radio-Tel, salesmen;
Traveling salesmen
Sanchez, Lilly, 84 fig
Santa Fe Railroad Company, 30
Scales, on Stringmaster, 119
Schultz, William, 259–260
CBS-Fender sale to, 260
Sebastiano Melita, six-piece bridges,
132–133
Shamblin, Eldon, 165 fig, 46
Shannon, Del, 257 fig
Siminoff, Roger, 100
Smith, Dan, 265
Smith, Sally Bedell, 246
Solidbody electric guitars, 2. See also
Fender standard guitars
Spanish guitar, 2. See also Fender
standard guitar
v. steel guitars, 21
Stafford, Bert, 182 fig
"Stairway to Heaven", 232
Standard guitar. See Spanish guitar
Standel Company, 196
Stanley, Harry, 43
Staples, Pops, 176

Staufer, Johan Georg, 275
Staunch, John, 90 fig
Steel guitars, 2. See also Fender steel
guitars
bodies of and pickups, 22
double-neck, 50–52
early popularity of, 21–22
first, 3
mid-1960s market for, 237–238
v. Spanish guitar, 21
Stevens, Michael, 261–262
Stewart, Danny, 145 fig
Stone, Cliffie, 96
Strangle switch, 208–209
"Strat Mania", 264
Stratosphere, 231
Strings
on Jazzmaster, 174
lighter gauge v. old-style, 134
Stuart, Fred, 262 cap, 264
Sunda, Gary, 194
Surfaris, 206 fig
Surf music
Fender guitars and, 212
and Fender reverb, 197

Tapert, Wade E., 245
Tavares, Freddie, 128 fig, 7, 116–118, 123 fig,
145 fig, 157 fig, 255 fig
and 4–10 Bassman, 150
and Fender acoustic, 226 fig
mid-1960s, 244 fig
and Stratocaster, 128
Taylor, Tut, 231
Tedesco, Tommy, 176
Teenagers, Fender amps popularity with,
197–198
Texas, selling in, 42–43
Texas Playboys, 46–47, 47 fig
Tone bar. See Body truss
Transistor, effect on inventors/small
manufacturers, 245
"Travelin' Man", 88
Traveling salesmen, 41
and trade shows, 77
Travis, Merle, 36, 95–97
Trem-lock, 173–174
Tremolo, 121. See also Vibrato
Tri-Sonics, 268
Truss rods, 78 fig
included on Fender standards, 83–84
Tubb, Ernest, 157 fig
TV-front amplifiers. See Fender amplifiers,
TV-front

UGC. See United Guitar Corporation
Ukelele, popularity of, 109–110
United Guitar Corporation (UGC), 223
United Industrial Employees of California,
220 cap

V.M. Corporation. See Voice of Music
Corporation
Valco, 78
National model, 122
six-piece bridges, 132–133
Supro Ozark model, 122 fig

Vega
    bass amp, 106
    electric bass, 101
Ventures, 177
Vibrato, 121
    Bigsby, 129 fig
    floating, 173
    G&L, 274
    Kahler, 274
    Leo Fender w/Fine Tuners, 274–275
    Stratocaster, 129–132
    on student-market guitars, 228–230
    transposing, 129
Vibratone guitars, 15–16
Vibrola, 13–14
Vibrola Spanish Guitar, 16
Vinylite 33 1/3 rpm long-playing record, 246
Vivi-Tone, 62
    solidbody standard guitar, 60 fig
Voice of Music (V.M.) Corporation, 22

Walker, Tom, 147, 267, 269 fig
    at Tri-Sonics, 268
Washburn, Jim, 2
Watkins, Roy, 58 fig

Welder, Phlange, 34
Welk, Lawrence, 168. See also Lawrence Welk Orchestra
Wells, Kitty, 157 fig
West, John, 7
West, Speedy, 34–35, 97 fig, 157 fig
    and Fender Sales, Inc. of Oklahoma, 185
    and Leo, 256 fig
    and pedal steel, 157, 158
    and prototype Twin Amp, 110
Western Dance Gang, 62
Western swing, 46, 62
Wheeler, Tom, 264
White, Forrest, 77, 142–145, 157 fig, 182 fig, 194 fig
    and Danelectro competition, 207–208
    at Fender factory, 154–155
    at Music Man, 268 fig
    and quality control, 194
    resignation from CBS-Fender, 253
    stature in music industry, 200
Wholesale distributor representatives, 41
Wide-panel amplifiers. See Fender amplifiers, wide-panel
Wildwoods, 227 fig

Wilkens, Matt, 217
Williams, Dub, 84 fig
Williams, Hank, 59
Williams, Jim, 169, 213 fig, 246 fig
Wills, Bob, 36, 46–48
Wilson, Carl, 212
Wilson, Don, 177
Wood
    for early Fender steels, 32
    for Esquire, 77 fig
    for Fender acoustics, 224–226
    for Fender necks and fingerboards, 188–191
    for G&L ASAT and Broadcaster, 282
    grain alignment problems, 137–138
    for Precision Bass, 163
    for Stratocaster, 138
    for Telecaster neck, 88
    walnut purchase for amps, 30–31
Woodman, Dean, 246
Wright, Johnny, 157 fig
Wyble, Jimmy, 46
    promoting for Fender, 74 fig

XERB, 62